MACQ

ABORIGINAL WORDS

MACQUARIE

ABORIGINAL WORDS

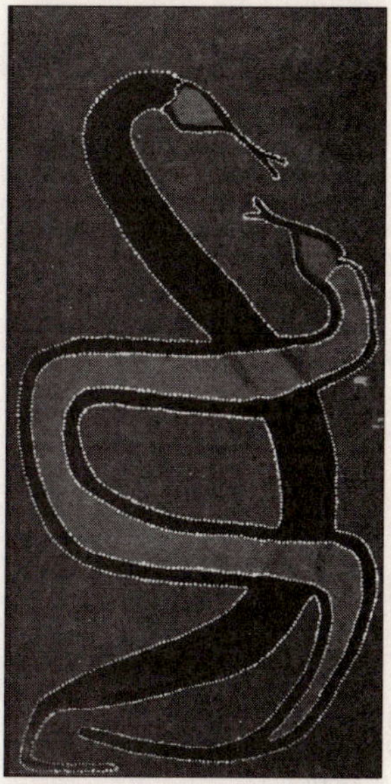

Macquarie Aboriginal Words:
a dictionary of words from
Australian Aboriginal
and Torres Strait Islander
languages

GENERAL EDITORS

NICK THIEBERGER
WILLIAM McGREGOR

MACQUARIE
LIBRARY

MACQUARIE EDITORIAL STAFF
Richard Tardif
Alison Moore
Susan Butler
Ann Atkinson

Cover painting:
Rover Thomas
Kukaja/Wangajungka
Australia, born 1926

Wungurr is the name for that snake. 1983.
natural pigments on plywood
120.0 × 60.0 cm

Collection: National Gallery of Australia, Canberra.
By kind permission of Mary Mácha

Published by The Macquarie Library Pty Ltd
The Macquarie Dictionary, Macquarie University, NSW 2109 Australia

First published 1994

Typeset in Australia by
The Macquarie Library Pty Ltd

Printed in Australia by
McPherson Printing Group

National Library of Australia Cataloguing-in-Publication Data

Macquarie Aboriginal words.

Includes index.
ISBN 0 949757 79 9.

1. Australian languages - Glossaries, vocabularies, etc.
2. Papuan languages - Glossaries, vocabularies, etc.
I. Thieberger, Nicholas. II. Title: Aboriginal words.

499.15

CONTENTS

FOREWORD

When Aboriginal coastal nations discovered Captain James Cook sailing up the east coast of Australia in 1770 he was not to know that Aboriginal Australia was more ethnic then than it is today. We had 500 different nations each with separate languages and dialects. This book receives my blessing because it resurrects languages from that long epoch of Australia's ancientness. It is very pleasing to know that researchers enjoy a duty of care towards our systems and that they faithfully reproduce our material. I wish this publication well.
Burnum Burnum

This book is a White step in the Black direction. I am very proud that such a book has at last been compiled. My mob, the Aboriginal people of Australia, have always been aware of the distinct differences as well as the similarities between ourselves. Now we can work on you white fellas. Thank you Macquarie.
Ernie Dingo AM, Performer

What a good idea! The book looks great to me. It should be very useful to people, and lead to a broader range of understanding of Aboriginal people. It will let people know that these languages are still operating and show the different facets of the languages.
Jeanie Bell, Community linguist, south-east Queensland

Congratulations to the people involved with the book. It's deadly to hear that some of our languages are being published. The preservation of these languages in such forms ensures that our culture will continue to grow.

I am unable to speak the Bundjalung people's traditional language because to my knowledge no-one knows or speaks the lingo of my area any more or there is no extensive documentation to look to. In the tradition of orally passing down the knowledge of our culture, this book will always be there to fall back upon for the clans involved. Educational for all.
Brenda Webb, Performing artist

Languages are the voices of our land. This book is very exciting, and it is good to have it published.
Janama (Robert Mills), Chair, Federation of Aboriginal and Torres Strait Islander Languages (FATSIL)

Foreword

We have needed a book like this for some time. Until now there has been no book that gathers, in one volume, sketches of languages from across the continent and presents, in a non-technical way, the diversity and wealth of their vocabularies, grammars and cultural settings. Everyone interested in Australia's heritage should have a copy of this book on their shelves.
Assoc. Prof. Nicholas Evans, Head, Department of Linguistics, University of Melbourne; Vice-President, Australian Linguistic Society

I think it's great. I'm very pleased to endorse it.
Larry Corowa, MBE, Rugby league player for Australia, NSW and Balmain

The sheer diversity of indigenous languages in Australia must be close to the greatest and richest component of this country's national cultural heritage. I am continually astounded how the Aboriginal languages with which I am familiar disclose an amazingly idiosyncratic concern with identity. Closely neighbouring groups maintain esoteric variations of language or dialect, seemingly more out of pure intellectual delight than reason, and yet also exhibit pan-regional and indeed pan-continental filiations which to scholars betray ancient and common roots.

This book is much-needed, as it gives a sense of the richness of a heritage which is disappearing in many areas of the country, and which will ultimately be lost if its intrinsic value is not soon appreciated by all Australians. I expect that the Sydney Opera House can be rebuilt by future generations and that the Rock will stand for millennia to come. But the original languages of this land may well go for good if we do not value these true voices that speak for the people, the land and the culture.

Macquarie are to be commended for this brilliant production.
Noel Pearson, Executive Director, Cape York Land Council

I am pleased to be able to endorse the publication of a book which reinforces the richness and diversity of Aboriginal culture, manifested in language, and presents it in a form which will add to understanding by the general public of the many identities of Aboriginal peoples in Australia.
Greg McIntyre, Mabo barrister

As Aboriginal elder of Jagera country, which takes in the entire watershed of the Brisbane River, Queensland, I am privileged to endorse this book.
Neville T Bonner, AO

Foreword

Language is the basis of understanding each other. It's about time everybody, black and white, found out about these things. I hope to goodness our children will, through books like this, come together and appreciate one another. I very much support this project — a fantastic book.
Justine Saunders, Actor/producer/director, whose grandmother was of the Durrumbul tribe, and who is of the dugong moiety

Most Australians believe that there is only one Aboriginal language, and previous books of this nature have grouped Aboriginal words together haphazardly without worrying where they came from.

This volume of Aboriginal words put out by The Macquarie Library Pty Ltd breaks new ground in more or less deconstructing the fallacy perpetrated by these other books. The reader will discover how rich the language tapestry of Aboriginal Australia was and is.
Mudrooroo, University lecturer and author

It is with great pleasure that I endorse this Macquarie Dictionary of Aboriginal Australian languages.

I am hoping that readers will find the 17 languages selected for their geographic, cultural and ecological diversity, interesting and exciting to learn Aboriginal culture from.
Mandawuy Yunupingu, Yothu Yindi

This is a valuable contribution to Aboriginal studies throughout Australia and I wish it every success.
Commissioner Charles Perkins, Aboriginal and Torres Strait Islander Commission (ATSIC)

The book is a great idea and I would like to take this opportunity to congratulate all who worked on the Dictionary. I am personally very happy that you have included my language group the Bundjalung. Too many times you have to convince some that there are languages in NSW that have survived.

My father the late pastor Frank Roberts was a respected Bundjalung elder who grew up on Cabbage Tree Island with an understanding of the culture and history of our people. But it was his knowledge of language that gave him a strong sense of identity and belonging. In the light of the fact that not long ago culture and language was discouraged and in some areas declared illegal, this book is a testimony to a new era of understanding. It guarantees the continuance of our language for future generations. And just as Aboriginal children are taught English in school maybe one day all Australians will be taught the rudiments of Aboriginal languages.
Rhoda Roberts, Vox Populi, SBS

Foreword

Congratulations on publishing accurate information about Australian languages. This is a work that should appeal to both academics and to the general public as well as providing all the boat names that anyone could ever want.
Dr William Jonas AM, Principal of the Australian Institute of Aboriginal and Torres Strait Islander Studies

This book of Aboriginal words is a publication that is long overdue. It goes a long way in correcting the anomalies of earlier works such as Endacott or Reed and Reed, which neither provided any systematic way of identifying the means of pronouncing each word nor of providing the grammatical context in which the word or phrase could be comprehended.

I endorse this publication also because it will be available to many Aborigines who now live in urban Australia and who will need a publication both to refresh their memories and to teach their children to incorporate such words into their daily lives.
Gordon Briscoe, BA, MA.

PREFACE

The wordlists in this book are from seventeen Australian languages scattered widely across the continent and on nearby islands, representing a number of different families and types of languages: Pama-Nyungan and non-Pama-Nyungan; traditional and post-contact; Australian and Papuan. Some of the languages are still used every day, while others (such as Sydney, Kaurna and Wembawemba) are no longer spoken.

The book is divided into six parts, one for each mainland state, beginning with New South Wales and working around the continent in a clockwise direction to end with Queensland. (Unfortunately, it was not possible to include a wordlist for any Tasmanian language. For a brief description of Tasmanian languages, see Crowley and Dixon 1981, or Plomley 1976.) For each state, between one and five languages are represented, each being assigned a separate chapter. The wordlists for each language have been compiled by specialists in the various languages.

Each chapter begins with a brief introduction giving some background information on the language: where it is spoken, its present state, some salient features of the culture, and so on. A brief description of the spelling of words in the language is followed by the wordlist itself, which is described more fully in the Introduction. Some points about the grammar follow the wordlist, and a bibliography indicates where further information may be found.

There are two indexes at the end of the book. One is ordered alphabetically by English meaning, and refers the reader to the relevant chapter(s) and section(s) where the particular word can be found. This index does not include many placenames, nor does it include the sometimes lengthy explanations given for certain words in the wordlists. The other index is ordered alphabetically by words of the seventeen languages in the book. This list is provided for readers interested in locating a particular word in the languages.

Acknowledgments
We would like to thank the Australian Linguistic Society, Tamsin Donaldson, Nicholas Evans, Merrin Mason, David Nash, Jane Simpson and Melanie Wilkinson for their advice and assistance.

INTRODUCTION

There were, and still are, hundreds of different Aboriginal languages spoken on the Australian continent. Before the invasion which began in 1788 Aboriginal people did not belong to a single political unit such as Australia now is; they were divided into something like 700 different political groups which have traditionally been called 'tribes'. There were approximately 250 different languages spoken on the Australian continent when Europeans first arrived on the shores. These languages are as rich and complex as any human language.

Widely available wordlists such as Endacott (1924/1990) and Reed and Reed (1965/1974) help perpetuate erroneous beliefs about Australian languages by listing together words from various parts of the continent, and from very different languages. For instance, Endacott gives no information in his list as to which language the words come from, and Reed and Reed provide in places only some very general locational information — whether the word is from Queensland, the Northern Territory, Central Australia, and so on. Such books are of no greater value than would be a European wordlist which included words from all over Europe, but gave no indication of which languages the words came from.

This book provides reliable information about words in various Australian languages, in a form that is accessible to the general public, while avoiding the pitfalls of the wordlists of Endacott and Reed. Words have not been selected (as in the earlier wordlists) on the basis of sounding 'pleasant' or being easy to pronounce for an English speaker, because this would give the false impression that Australian languages have only such euphonious words. Rather, they have been selected more to give some small inkling of the character of the languages.

NUMBER AND TYPES OF AUSTRALIAN INDIGENOUS LANGUAGES

The approximately 250 distinct Australian languages can be divided into around 26 different family-like groups, that is, groups of languages which are related to one another, and can most likely be traced back to a common ancestor language.

One of these families covers about nine-tenths of the continent, the entire land mass except for the Kimberley and Arnhem Land. This group of languages is referred to as the Pama-Nyungan family (named after the words for 'man' or 'person' in many languages of Cape York and the south-west of Western Australia, *pama* and *nyungar*, respectively). The other families are also named, but they are frequently all grouped together and referred to as non-Pama-Nyungan languages. Non-Pama-Nyungan languages are similar to one another in a number of respects, and different from Pama-Nyungan languages. Most of the wordlists in this book are from Pama-Nyungan languages, with Murrinh-Patha (chapter 14) and Gooniyandi (chapter 10) as examples of non-Pama-Nyungan languages.

The languages spoken on various nearby inhabited islands, including Groote Eylandt (Anindilyakwa), Bentinck Island (Kayardild), Mornington Island (Lardil), and Montgomery Island (Yawijibaya) are related to Australian languages[1]. The same may also be true of the languages of Tasmania, but there is too little information on them to be sure; nor is it known for sure whether Tiwi, spoken on Melville Island is related to Australian languages. Many, but not all, of the languages of the Torres Strait islands are related to Australian languages. Kala Lagaw Ya (spoken on Saibai Island) is an Australian language, but Meryam Mir (spoken on Murray Island) is not: it is a Papuan language, related to various languages spoken in Papua New Guinea. (A wordlist for Meryam Mir can be found in chapter 15.)

Since the arrival of Europeans in Australia just over 200 years ago, many significant changes have occurred. Most of the traditional languages are no longer used as the normal medium of communication among descendants of speakers of the languages; for many of these languages all that remains are the memories of a few words, or written or audiotaped recordings (these records are the basis for the wordlists presented in Kaurna, chapter 8, Wembawemba, chapter 6, Wiradjuri, chapter 5, and the Sydney language, chapter 4). Of the remaining languages, most are spoken by just a small (usually less than 100) number of adults, while children are not learning to speak them, but have switched to speaking some variety of English instead. There are around 20 really viable traditional Australian languages which are being used as the normal vehicle of communication within their community and are being passed on to the children. These viable languages are all spoken in northern and central Australia.

There are various reasons for the decline in use of Australian languages. In some cases whole communities of speakers were decimated, either by systematic killing by whites, or by introduced diseases (or both). Where such communities were not completely wiped out, they were reduced to such small sizes that they could not sustain their own identity or language, and were effectively absorbed into nearby groups. This seems to have been the fate of the Unggumi people, who lived around Windjana Gorge inthe West Kimberley. Late last century large numbers of them were massacred during the campaigns against the

[1] Note that the term 'Australian languages' will be used here to indicate all Australian indigenous languages.

guerrilla fighter Jandamarra (also known as Pigeon), who threatened white occupation of the region. When the linguist Arthur Capell travelled through the area in 1939, he could find no more than a few descendants of the Unggumi and speakers of the language. They belonged to communities in which Bunuba and Ungarinyin speakers dominated — the last fluent speaker of Unggumi died in 1993.

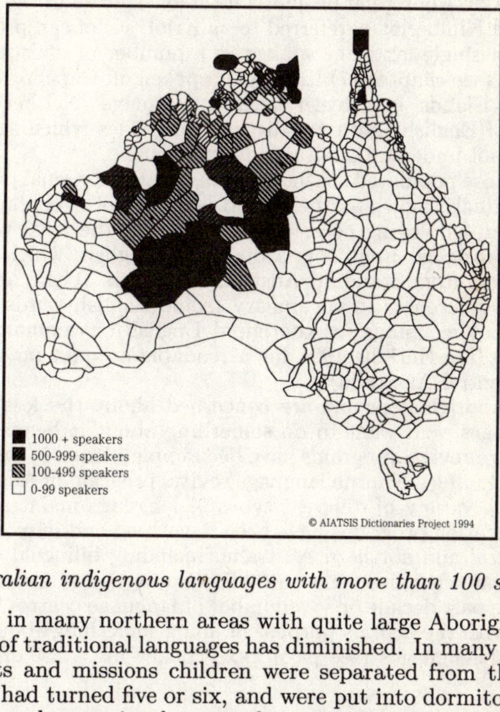

Australian indigenous languages with more than 100 speakers

Even in many northern areas with quite large Aboriginal populations, use of traditional languages has diminished. In many government settlements and missions children were separated from their parents once they had turned five or six, and were put into dormitories — they were often only permitted to see their parents on weekends. The use of traditional languages was usually not permitted in dormitories, and children would be punished if they were heard speaking anything but English. In some places whole groups were forcibly moved from their traditional lands to reserves which may have been located a considerable distance away, sometimes in the country of traditional enemies. The fractured communities that developed on reserves were not ideal places for the continued use and passing on of traditional languages.

Where the use of traditional languages diminished they were normally replaced by some non-traditional, or post-contact language, although occasionally another traditional language acquired the status of a *lingua franca*, and was used as the main language of the community. Over large parts of northern Australia a simplified variety of English developed, initially from contact with whites, and came to be used more and more frequently among Aboriginal people. Such a language is referred to as a pidgin. Sometimes a pidgin language becomes the mother tongue and primary language of the children, in the process becoming a full language called a creole. The pidgin English spoken in northern Australia creolised in many parts of the Northern Territory, Kimberley and Cape York, and the resulting creole is in many areas the main language spoken by Aboriginal people. The creole spoken in the Northern Territory and Kimberley is referred to as Kriol. Kriol can probably be regarded as a single language spoken in a number of dialects. Torres Strait Creole (see chapter 17), the creole spoken on Cape York and the Torres Strait islands, is a rather different language. Neither language is a dialect of English; both are distinct languages which speakers of English can not understand without learning them.

In the more populated southern areas, most Aboriginal people now speak Aboriginal English as their main language of everyday communication, often employing occasional words from the local traditional language. Aboriginal English is a dialect of English, which differs in certain respects from Standard Australian English. There are, for example, some differences in vocabulary (some English words can have rather different meanings in Aboriginal English), grammar, and the norms of use (see Harkins 1994 for a readable account of Aboriginal English in Central Australia).

Many Aboriginal people are concerned about the loss of traditional languages, and want to do something about it before it is too late. Language revival programs have been implemented in some southern areas, including a Kaurna language revival program in Adelaide (see chapter 8). A variety of different types of language maintenance and bilingual education programs have been developed and implemented in parts of central and northern Australia, including bilingual education in Arrernte (at Yipirinya school in Alice Springs) and Yolŋu (at Yirrkala). In the past decade or so a number of language centres have been established with the express purpose of doing something about the loss of traditional languages (see page xxxiv below for a list of language centres).

Aboriginal cultures and societies

Language and culture are closely intertwined and it is necessary to know something about the culture of a group in order to understand how the language is used interactively as a vehicle for making and communicating meaning. Even properly understanding the grammar and semantics (meanings of words) of a language requires some knowledge of the culture, just as knowledge of language is important to a full understanding of a culture.

Introduction

Just as there is considerable linguistic variety in Aboriginal Australia, so also is there considerable cultural and social diversity. Different groups practise different ceremonies, organise their social life in different ways, employ different technologies, and have different mythologies and religious beliefs. However, the differences between neighbouring groups are not normally particularly large, and in many respects the social organisation of Australian Aboriginal groups are reasonably similar across the continent, and quite different to the ways in which European, Asian and African societies were organised. For example, Aboriginal groups do not have chiefs or kings, and social division of labour is not according to class. Aboriginal groups were hunter-gatherers, rather than farmers; all adult members of a group were involved in the day-to-day business of hunting and gathering food, as well as in ceremonial and religious activities.

In all Aboriginal societies kinship plays a prominent role. They may be described as kin-based societies in the sense that the ways in which people interact with one another are to a significant extent dependent on their kin relationships. In Aboriginal societies, as distinct from European societies, everyone is considered to bear some kinship relationship to everyone else. This relationship could not of course be always a tie of 'blood' (genealogy) or marriage. Those not related by such ties are treated as though they are, and related by what anthropologists call 'classificatory' kinship relations. The classificatory kin relationship between two individuals regulates the way they interact with one another, in a similar way to 'real' (from the European perspective) kin ties. A pair related together by a classificatory brother-sister relationship, for instance, behaves in ways appropriate to the brother-sister relationship. The term 'cross-cousin', which appears in the following chapters, simply refers to a person's mother's brother's child, or their father's sister's child.

In virtually all Aboriginal societies a man and his mother-in-law could be expected to behave in a restrained and circumspect way with one another, and in one another's presence. In some cultures they are not permitted to even speak together, while in others they can do so provided that they avert their gaze and use a special style of speaking, which is usually called 'mother-in-law language' or 'mother-in-law style'. These mother-in-law styles differ somewhat from language to language. At one extreme are languages like Dyirbal where the mother-in-law style has no words in common with everyday speech, but is virtually identical in grammar (Dixon 1972, pp 32–33). At another extreme are languages like Jaru, where there is a single word which is peculiar to the mother-in-law style (Tsunoda 1981, pp 215–220). Most languages fall somewhere between these extremes. The restrained nature of social and linguistic interaction between a man and his mother-in-law normally extends to the brothers and sisters of each, albeit usually to a lesser degree. Among some groups avoidance behaviour involves brothers-in-law more than mothers-in-law; this is the case amongst the north Queensland group the Guugu Yimidhirr (Haviland 1979).

By contrast, a man and his mother's mother's brother could, in many Aboriginal societies, engage in quite unconstrained and familiar interaction with one another. In some cultures a man can take the property of his mother's mother's brother, as well as joke obscenely with him, and insult him; this behaviour is normally reciprocated. (Thompson 1935 and Stanner 1982 provide excellent descriptions of this relationship in Cape York and the Northern Territory respectively.)

Aboriginal tribal groups are divided into various social groups on the basis of age, sex, locality, and other characteristics which are too complex to go into here. However, mention must be made of three important types of social division which are found over a large part of the continent, and which are relevant to a number of groups mentioned in this book: moieties, sections and subsections.

Over quite a large area of Australia tribal groups are divided into two halves or moieties, each person belonging to one or the other of them. Usually the moieties include everything in nature, not only people. This is the case amongst the Yolŋu people of north-eastern Arnhem Land, who distinguish the *Yirritja* and *Dhuwa* moieties, and among the Murrinh-Patha people (see chapters 12 and 14). In some groups, moiety membership of a person follows that of the person's father; in other groups, it follows that of their mother.

Many tribal groups are divided not into two, but four or eight subgroups, called sections and subsections respectively by linguists and anthropologists, and 'skins' in Aboriginal English. The Yindjibarndi people are divided into four sections (see chapter 11), while the Gooniyandi distinguish eight subsections (see chapter 10). Everyone in these tribal groups belongs to a section or subsection. Marriage is arranged according to the section or subsection systems. For example, in Gooniyandi a *jawandi* man should ideally marry a *nyawoorroo* woman (while marriage with a *nangala* woman would also be permissible, this would be his second preference). Children are assigned to (sub)sections according to the (sub)section membership of their parents. Thus children of a *jawandi-nyawoorroo* marriage (in Gooniyandi) would be *jawangari* (if male) and *nawangari* (if female). If the marriage were second choice or 'wrong' the subsection of the child is worked out from the mother's, ignoring the father. (This system is described in some detail in McGregor 1990, p. 15.) One of the advantages of section and subsection systems is that knowledge of someone's (sub)section permits you to work out your (classificatory) kinship relation to them, by virtue of the marriage and offspring rules. To give a simple example, a *jawandi* man and a *nyawoorroo* woman would usually call one another *garingi* 'wife' and *ngoombarna* 'husband', irrespective of whether they are actually married — they would be classificatory husband and wife. Similarly, the *jawandi* man would call a *jawangari* man either 'father' or 'son'.

The above remarks provide a very brief and somewhat simplistic discussion of a couple of important aspects of Aboriginal social life. For a readable discussion of Aboriginal social life see Maddock (1972/1974), and for further information on kinship see Elkin (1938/1974, especially chapters IV and VI), Berndt and Berndt (1962/1992, chapters III and IV) and Yallop (1981, chapter 6).

The nature of Australian languages

To speak a language you need to know not just a list of words, but also how to put them together into sentences, as well as the right form of the word to convey the meaning you intend. In English you need to know that the subject goes before the verb, and the object follows it. If you change the order of the words, a different meaning will result. For example, *The man saw the dog* means something very different to *The dog saw the man*; in each case the noun preceding the verb is the subject, the one who does the seeing, while the noun following it is the object, the one who is seen. Notice also that the verb *saw* takes different forms depending on whether the seeing happened before (*saw*), is happening now (*sees*), or will happen later (*will see*).

Grammar deals with the ways in which words of a language go together to form sentences — which is called syntax — and with the structure of words — which is called morphology. The grammars of Australian languages are complex, and different in many respects from the grammars of English and other European languages. In particular, the morphology of most Australian languages is more complicated than the morphology of English. In some respects Australian languages resemble Latin and Greek more than English. There are usually many different forms of the verb depending on the time of the event referred to, and in many languages, who did what, and to whom. There are also, in most Australian languages, different endings for nouns — called case inflections or case suffixes — which indicate whether the noun is subject, object, or has some other role in the sentence.

In many Australian languages the subject of an intransitive sentence (that is, a sentence with a subject but no object) takes no ending at all, just like the object of a transitive sentence. These nouns are in what is called the absolutive case. By contrast, the subject of a transitive sentence takes a special case-ending, called the ergative case. This is illustrated by the following pair of sentences from Nyulnyul, a non-Pama-Nyungan language spoken near Beagle Bay, on the Dampier Land peninsula, north of Broome.

wamb	*injalk*
man	he:fell

'The man fell.'

wamb	*-in*	*barn*	*inaw*	*burruk*
man	-ergative	shoot	he:gave:it	kangaroo

'The man shot the kangaroo.'

The first sentence is intransitive, and its subject *wamb* 'man' occurs without any ending. The second sentence is transitive, again with subject *wamb* 'man'; but in this case it is followed by *-in*, the ergative case suffix. And the object of this sentence, *burruk* 'kangaroo', takes no ending, just like the subject of the intransitive sentence.

Most Pama-Nyungan languages, as well as a number of non-Pama-Nyungan languages, organise their case systems like Nyulnyul. However, the ergative suffix is normally different in different languages and language families. Pama-Nyungan languages often have either *-nggu* or *-lu*. Many have both. For example, many dialects of the Western Desert language have *-nggu* (usually spelt *-ngku* in those languages) on common nouns (that is, nouns like *minyma* 'woman', *marlu* 'kangaroo', etc.) but *-lu* on personal names ending in vowels.

In most Australian languages you can tell which noun is the subject of a transitive sentence and which is the object by the case marking on the nouns. In the second Nyulnyul example above, the subject has the ergative case marker, while the object has no ending. Because of this, there is no need for the subject to go before the verb and the object to follow it, as in English. Thus, the order of words in Nyulnyul — and most Australian languages — is usually free. You can normally switch the words around in almost any order without changing the meaning. The words of the second Nyulnyul example above could occur in any of the following orders while retaining the meaning 'the man shot the kangaroo':

wamb-in burruk barn inaw
burrukwamb-in barn inaw
burruk barn inawwamb-in
barn inaw wamb-in burruk
barn inaw burruk wamb-in

The only restriction is that *barn* 'shoot' must go immediately before *inaw* 'he/she/it gave him/her/it'.

In many languages, the order of words in a sentence has to do with the topic of discourse and emphasis. In Nyulnyul, for instance, the first word of a clause is the topic, the thing that is being spoken about. If you were talking about the man and what he had done, you would put *wamb-in* first in the sentence; if you were talking about the kangaroo, you would put *burruk* first. Thus *burruk barn inaw wamb-in* would be better translated as 'The kangaroo was shot by the man' than as 'The man shot the kangaroo' which is better as a translation of *wamb-in barn inawburruk.*

Various other case suffixes are found which express meanings expressed by prepositions (words like *at*, *in*, *on*, etc.) in English. It is common to find different case suffixes marking meanings such as: 'with, using' (instrumental case), 'in, at, on' (locative case), 'towards' (allative case), 'away from' (ablative case), 'via, through' (perlative case), 'for' (dative case), 'with, in association with' (comitative case), and various other such meanings (see Dixon 1980 for a fuller discussion of these issues).

Many Australian languages have fuller and more complicated systems of pronouns than English. All distinguish between 'you singular' (one addressee) and 'you plural' (more than one addressee); some languages also have a distinct form for 'you two'. Many languages make a distinction between two different types of 'we' or 'us', depending on whether or not the hearer is included. For example, in Warlpiri *ngali* means 'we two including you' ('me and you'), whereas *ngajarra* means 'we two not including you' ('me and someone else'). The first form is referred to technically as the first person inclusive (because the hearer is included), the second, first person exclusive (because the hearer is excluded).

Some languages make even more complicated distinctions in their pronouns. Yindjibarndi, for example, has different forms of the word 'they' depending on whether the people being referred to are of the same generation level or a different generation level.

English has three third person singular pronouns, *he*, *she*, and *it*. These indicate the gender of the thing referred to, whether it is masculine (male), feminine (female) or neuter (non-human or inanimate). Many Australian languages do not make such a distinction in their third person pronouns, and use a single form irrespective of gender. For instance, in Gooniyandi the third person singular pronoun is *niyi*; this pronoun is used when referring to a man, a woman, or an animal. A number of languages — including a few Pama-Nyungan languages and a fair number of non-Pama-Nyungan languages — do make gender distinctions in their pronouns. For example, Diyari (chapter 7) has *nhawu* 'he' and *nhani* 'she'; Kalaw Kawaw Ya has *nuy* 'he' and *an* 'she'. Languages like Ungarinyin and Dyirbal make not only a distinction between 'he' and 'she', but also between different types of 'it'. Exactly how the two types of 'it' differ from one another is not completely clear. Oversimplifying somewhat, one of the 'it' classes in Ungarinyin includes places and plants (particularly edible ones), while the other includes times, trees, wood, and various abstract things such as language, names, and so on. Similarly, in Dyirbal one 'it' includes edible vegetables and fruit, while the other 'it' includes most other inanimate things except a few which are treated as masculine or feminine.

As has already been mentioned, verbs in many Australian languages are morphologically quite complex, although they are usually much more complex in non-Pama-Nyungan languages than in Pama-Nyungan languages. In Pama-Nyungan languages verbs usually take various suffixes to indicate such things as the time of the event; whether it has already happened (past tense), is happening now (present tense), or will happen later (future tense) — whether or not the event happened over a period of time (as in the distinction made in English between *ate* and *was eating*), and whether it is a statement or a command. Most Pama-Nyungan languages have between two and six verb classes or conjugations, which is usually indicated by a conjugation marker which directly follows the verb root. Different forms of the verb suffixes are also used depending on the class of the verb. Pintupi (spoken in the Northern Territory), for example, has four classes, while Yidiny (northern Queensland) has three.

Verbs in non-Pama-Nyungan languages usually contain information not only about the time of the event, but also about what is the subject and what is the object, and much else as well. Murrinh-Patha is such a language (see chapter 14). A single verb form may be used to express what requires a full sentence in English. The single word *kardithurrulkthaydeyidadha*, for example, means 'He/She was foaming at the mouth again'. This word can be divided into component parts as follows:

kardi	*-thurrulk*	*-thay*	*-deyida*	*-dha*
3rd pers. sing. subject	-foam	-mouth	-again	-imperfective

As this example illustrates, verbs in non-Pama-Nyungan languages normally have prefixes which indicate what is the subject and object of the sentence, and various suffixes as well. By contrast, Pama-Nyungan languages normally have suffixes only. (Donaldson in chapter 2 gives an example of a similar kind of sentence in a Pama-Nyungan language). Thus Pama-Nyungan languages are sometimes referred to as suffixing languages (they have only suffixes), while non-Pama-Nyungan languages are sometimes referred to as prefixing languages (they have both prefixes and suffixes).

Vocabularies of Australian languages

Contrary to popular belief, Australian languages have extensive vocabularies, with words for whatever the speakers need to talk about: the physical environment (including the land, flora and fauna), artefacts, people, their cultural practices (including kinship and ceremony), and so on. Unlike English, however, Australian languages were spoken by small groups of people, who lived within fairly small areas, with limited communication and contact with people other than their immediate neighbours. This is reflected in the vocabularies of the languages. For example, languages spoken in the north do not have words for 'snow', since this phenomenon does not occur in their natural environment. Languages spoken hundreds of miles inland often have no term for 'sea', and languages spoken in areas lacking rivers (such as the Dampier Land peninsula) usually have no terms for 'river'.

How many words are there in Australian languages? It seems reasonable to assume that an average Australian language would contain something like 10 000 words — approximately the number of words the average speaker of a European language would be familiar with and actually use themselves. But whereas the latter usually know only a small fraction of the vocabulary of their language partly because of the existence of highly specialised 'registers' of scientific discourse, technology, etc., and partly due to the existence of specialised technologies (writing, in particular) for the storage of words — speakers of an Australian language would usually know most of its words. But the vocabulary of a language is never static: some words go out of fashion or are tabooed (in many Australian languages there is a rule that words sounding like the name of a person who has recently died cannot be spoken), and are replaced by other words. In addition, many Australian languages have borrowed heavily from English.

Introduction

Aboriginal people have an intimate knowledge of their physical environment, and its flora and fauna, and this knowledge is reflected in the elaboration in these parts of the vocabulary. There are normally specific terms in daily use for a large range of different types of flora and fauna which in English would only be distinguished by botanists or biologists. For example, English speakers usually group together many different types of tree as 'gum tree', or 'wattle tree'; these would normally each have their own name in an Australian language. Similarly, most speakers of English distinguish two classes of macropods: wallabies and kangaroos. Speakers of Australian languages normally have many distinct terms referring to various species which they keep rigidly distinct. For example, the Guugu Yimidhirr word *gangurru*, from which the English borrowing 'kangaroo' derives, refers specifically to the large black or grey kangaroo; there are other terms for other species of kangaroo, including *nharrgali* 'large red kangaroo', *wudul* 'whip-tail kangaroo', *bibal* 'small scrub kangaroo', etc., as well as various terms for different species of wallaby (Haviland 1979, p. 173).

Australian languages are also well endowed with words for parts of the body, the average adult speaker distinguishing organs and bones which in mainstream Australian culture are distinguished only by medical practitioners. There are, for example, usually different words for the stomach (the internal organ) and the external surface of the abdomen, and the former would never be used in reference to nearby internal organs such as the intestines. Most Australian languages have distinct terms for body hair and hair of the head, the former usually also referring to the fur of an animal; some have different terms for armpit and pubic hair. On the other hand, there are some distinctions which are made in English that are not made in most Australian languages. For example, one term usually covers both fingernails and toenails, and another both hand and finger.

The landscape associated with each tribal group is richly supplied with placenames. Along large river systems it is common for there to be names for many stretches of the river. In some northern areas these correspond to waterholes which are all that remains at the end of the dry season; there may not be a word for the entire river (since this may span the territory of a number of groups). In desert regions, it is not uncommon for every claypan of reasonable size to be named. In some language areas placenames generally have meanings which may refer to something that happened at that place in the Dreamtime (mythological past); in other languages placenames generally have no meanings. Unlike the situation for European languages, places are usually not named after prominent people. Terms also exist for such geographic or topographic features as exist in the speaker's experience: rivers, creeks, hills, caves, cliffs, or whatever. There are words for various types of rock, sand and ochre, as well as for the sun, moon, sky, stars, clouds and so on.

Australian languages generally have no words for units like seconds, minutes or hours. There are, however, ways of referring to natural units such as days, months and years. For example, in Gooniyandi the term *riwi* 'camp, place' is used to refer to a day (this is presumably based on the association of a camping place with a day); *jaalinyi* 'moon' is used for 'month'; and *gamba* 'water' is used for 'year' (a year is counted from one wet season to the next). The neighbouring Walmajarri people also use their terms for 'camp', 'moon' and 'wet season' for the same stretches of time. Furthermore, each language has terms for the seasons, and for parts of the day, although these need not correspond very closely to European divisions. In Walmajarri, for example, three seasons are distinguished: *parrangka* 'hot season', *yitilal* 'wet season', and *makurra* 'cold season'; and the day is divided into *kumanta* 'morning', *jininyara* 'mid-day', *karuwarra* 'afternoon', *pukanyja* 'night', and *rakarra* 'half light of dawn'. Other Australian languages have similar sets of time words.

Most Australian languages have few number words. There is normally a word for 'one', 'two', and 'three, a few'; in addition, there would be a word for 'many'. This does not, however, mean that Aboriginal people are unable to count beyond two or three. For example, counting may be accomplished by the use of tally marks (Harris 1982, p. 165) or by showing hand signs. But there are exceptions: Gurindji (spoken in the Wave Hill area, Northern Territory) has terms for each of the numbers between one and fifty (Harris 1982, p. 168). Kukatja (Balgo, Western Australia) has recently developed a number system, for school use. The first four numbers follow the traditional system: *kutju* 'one', *kutjarra* 'two', *marnkurrpa* 'three' (also 'few, several'), and *kutjarra-kutjarra* ('two-two') or *murntu* ('many') for 'four'. The number 'five' is *raka* or *marumpu* 'hand', and the remaining terms allude to the shape of the Arabic numeral. A similar system has developed in Warlpiri.

An area of particular elaboration is kinship, where many more distinctions are made than in English. For instance, maternal (mother's side) and paternal (father's side) grandparents are frequently designated by different words. It is not unusual for Australian languages to have thirty or more kin terms. Various stages in a person's life are distinguished and given names. These are normally rather different to the stages distinguished in white culture. For example, in Nyangumarta, spoken in the Pilbara region of Western Australia, the main stages in a woman's life are as follows (from McKelson 1989, p. 59):

mukunya	young girl
wangkurta	teenager
ngama murt	pubescent
pilyurrja purnta	promised in marriage
kalinta	marriageable woman
kurri	married, but without children
mirlkarr	woman
kalapi mulyukurru	woman who has given birth to a child
pirirrijartiny	married woman (literally: with a man)

Artefacts are of course named. Usually there are generic words for spears, boomerangs, coolamons and so on, in addition to terms for their specific types. The generic term sometimes takes its name from one specific type.

Australian languages usually have no separate grammatical class of adjective, although there are words (usually nouns) for colours, shapes, sizes, textures, etc. Usually there is a fairly rich class of adverbs, providing information about the time and place of an event. Australian languages generally have words for the cardinal directions ('north', 'south', 'east' and 'west'), as well as for vertical and horizontal directions ('up' and 'down'), 'this way', 'that way', and so on. In addition, those groups which reside near the large rivers frequently have words for 'upstream' and 'downstream', which are commonly used to indicate spatial location.

Each language contains a large number of verbs embracing: verbs of state ('sit', 'lie', 'stand', etc.), motion ('go', 'run', 'swim', 'fly', etc.), induced motion ('put down', 'drag', 'push', etc.), violence ('hit', 'spear', 'burn', 'burst', etc.), speech and vocalisation ('talk', 'tell', 'name', 'ask', 'answer', etc.), cognition and perception ('see', 'hear', 'think', etc.), and bodily processes ('eat', 'drink', 'shrug shoulders', 'cry', etc.). In addition, each language contains extensive sets of verbs for ceremonial actions ('dance shake a leg', 'circumcise', etc.) and culturally specific activities ('avoid speaking to someone', 'observe food taboo', etc.), for which English often has no simple translation equivalents.

An important general principle of the semantics of Australian languages is that the same word often refers to an item and its source, the material from which it comes. Thus many languages have the same word for both 'fire' and 'firewood', and the same word for both 'milk' and 'breast'. Likewise, verbs may cover both an activity which could have some result, and one which actually does have that result. In most Australian languages the same verb covers both 'hit' and 'kill', both 'sink in the water' and 'drown', both 'hear' and 'listen', and both 'see' and 'look at' (the distinction between these can of course be made. See, for example, Donaldson's discussion in chapter 2).

Although many wordlists are available for Australian languages, some quite extensive, there are only a few reliable and comprehensive dictionaries. This means that many claims about the size and extent of vocabularies of Australian languages must be treated with caution, especially claims about their inadequacies or deficiencies, which may reflect deficiencies in the material gathered rather than in the language. It must also be borne in mind that wordlists normally give only the most basic information about the words, and do not provide information about their full range of meanings.

Metaphor and extension of meaning

Sometimes a word is used for something or some idea that it is not literally applicable to, in order to suggest a resemblance, as for example in *a flood of protests*, and *fire in the belly.* Such usage of a word is called metaphor, and this is a very important phenomenon in all human languages. Most of the published information about metaphor in Australian languages relates to body part metaphor — the use of words for parts of the body to refer to things that are not parts of the body. There are two main types of body part metaphor, orientational or locational, and emotional or mental; other types also exist, but are less common.

In the first type, body part terms are used to denote spatial relationships, similar to the use of head to mean 'top' in the expression the *head of the stairs*. This type of metaphor is common in Murrinh-patha (chapter 14). The word *pangkin* 'back', for example, is used metaphorically to mean 'ridge'; it is also used in the expression *mayern pangkin wangu* 'overland road'. Another form of the word for 'back', *-rdarri-*, is incorporated into verbs and is used in a number of metaphorical expressions for being behind, as in 'hide behind', 'talk behind someone', 'sense someone's presence behind', 'imitate' (follow behind), etc. Similarly, *-marda-* 'belly, chest' is used metaphorically to express the notion of 'frontness'.

In body part metaphor of the emotional or mental type a body part word is used to refer to some emotional or mental state believed to be associated with that part. For example, intelligence is generally believed to be located in the ear. Thus the Walmajarri word *pina* 'ear' is used metaphorically in expressions such as *pina-pina-karri* (ear-ear-stand) 'think', *pina-ngu tarrparta* (ear-subject grab) 'memorise it, listen and absorb it', and *pina-rri* (ear-*rri)* 'knowledgeable'. The Walmajarri consider the stomach (rather than the heart) to be the seat of the emotions, and there are idioms such as *munta kayan* (one stomach) 'to have a fixed purpose', *muntaparrparr* (hot stomach) 'anger', and *muntakirtily* (cool stomach) 'at peace, content'. In the northern Kimberley language Ungarinyin, by contrast, it is the kidney that is considered to be the seat of the emotions, and *ngiyamadju barij wi* (my: kidney rise it: is) 'my kidney rises' is an idiomatic expression for 'I am happy'.

Other ways in which words are used indirectly or figuratively are euphemism and dysphemism. Euphemism refers to the use of a mild or indirect term instead of a blunt or harsh one, while dysphemism denotes the opposite. An example of euphemism in English is *pass away* instead of *die*, and an example of dysphemism would be the affectionate use of *bastard* amongst Australian males when addressing a close friend or associate. Euphemism and dysphemism are both employed in Australian languages, although not much information is published. For example, in Gooniyandi the verb *nyin-* 'forget' is used euphemistically to refer to the death of a close relative; on the other hand, in Nyulnyul the noun *riib* 'bad, rubbish' is used dysphemistically to refer to the most sacred traditional artefacts.

Terms for new items and concepts

Like English, Australian languages have not remained static over the past two centuries, and many changes have occurred. They have acquired terms for introduced items (including artefacts, animals, plants, etc.), concepts and activities (for example, for various cultural practices peculiar to whites, such as work, God, mustering, etc.), just as English has acquired terms for many animals and plants that they encountered on the continent which were new to them.

There are three main ways in which new items, beliefs or concepts can be incorporated into a language: (a) a word may be borrowed from a language which has a word for the item; (b) the meaning of a word already in the language may be extended; and (c) a new word may be coined using the grammatical resources of the language. Below are some examples of these processes.

(a) *Borrowings.* As might be expected, many terms for introduced items and concepts have been borrowed from English. For instance, in Walmajarri we find *kilayij* 'glass', *rijap* '(Aboriginal) reserve', *kuul* 'school', *mutuka* 'car', *tuwa* 'store', etc.; almost exactly the same terms are found in the nearby, but unrelated Gooniyandi. Many Australian languages have terms like *wajbali* 'white person', and *mijiji* 'white woman' (from 'missus').

Borrowings are usually adapted to the sound system of the borrowing language. Sounds that are not found in the borrowing language are changed or omitted, and unfamiliar word structures are adjusted to what is normal for the language. For example, in *rijap* 'reserve', the two sounds *z* and *v* (which do not occur in Walmajarri) have been changed to the closest Walmajarri sounds *j* and *p* respectively; in *kuul* 'school' the *s* has been lost entirely, as it has also been in *tuwa* 'store'. In *pilangkirr* 'blanket' and *kilayij* 'glass' a vowel has been put between the two beginning consonants (since words can't begin with *pl* or *kl* in Walmajarri), and the final *t* has been changed to *rr*.

When a word is borrowed into an Aboriginal language it does not always retain its English meaning. For example, the Kukatja loan word *tjilipinpa*, from *slippers*, means 'thongs', and the Gooniyandi loan *badig* from *paddock* means both 'paddock' and 'fence enclosing a paddock'.

English is not the only source for borrowings. In Arnhem Land there are hundreds of words borrowed from Macassarese traders who visited the north coast over the last few hundred years. Words can also be borrowed from other Australian languages, and such words are sometimes found over very large areas. *Magarda* 'hat' is widespread in Central Australian and Kimberley languages, and comes from *mokarta* 'head' in Kaurna, the traditional language of the Adelaide region (see chapter 8). Other widely distributed words include *dimana* 'horse', which occurs across northern Australia from the Queensland border to the Kimberleys (Walsh 1992 discusses the different terms used for 'horse' across Australia).

(b) *Extension of meaning.* In many Australian languages the word for 'stone, pebble, rock' is used in an extended sense to also cover 'money'.

The word for 'rock, stone' in the Kimberley languages Nyulnyul (*kumbarr*), Nyikina (*wanangarri*), Gooniyandi (*ngaarri*) and Wangkajunga (*purli*), and in Yindjibarndi (*marnda*), Paakantyi (*yarnda*), and many other languages, all show this meaning extension. Some other very common meaning extensions include: the word for 'sand' in reference to sugar, as in Nyikina and Gooniyandi where the word is *walyarra*; and the word for 'water' in reference to beer and other alcoholic beverages, as is the case for Kukatja and Wangkajunga (*kalyu*), Nyulnyul (*wurl*) and Gooniyandi (*gamba*). A particularly interesting meaning extension involves the Gooniyandi word *yoorroo* 'spider's web': it is also used in reference to the telephone, presumably by reason of the apparent web pattern of telephone wires extending out from post offices, and to the airways on which aeroplanes travel.

Some kin terms also show semantic extensions whereby they now designate human classifications which did not exist in traditional times. One very common extension is for the term for 'father' to be used for 'God' and/or a priest, bishop, or religious minister. The Nyulnyul term *ibal* 'father', for instance, is used in this way, as is the Gooniyandi word *ngaboo* 'father'. Gooniyandi also uses *marni* 'sister' in reference to a nursing sister.

(c) *Coining a new word.* Sometimes the grammatical system of a language is employed to construct a new word denoting the introduced concept. This is how the word for 'policeman' is formed in a number of languages. In Wunambal the word is *yirrkalngarri* from *yirrkal* 'rope, chain' plus the suffix *-ngarri* 'with, having': 'the one(s) with ropes or chains', recalling the not too distant past when the police chained up suspects and witnesses alike for transportation to the towns. Compare also the Kukatja and Jaru term *wayin-watji* ('chain-possessor'). The Gooniyandi term *mirnmirdgali* is formed in a similar way from *mird-* 'tie up' and *-gali* 'good at doing, habitually doing', as is the Kalkatungu term *ganimay-nyjirr* 'one who ties up (people)'.

Some terms for items of clothing are also constructed by coining a new word, usually from a term for the part of the body with which the clothing is most closely associated. This happens in Kaurna, where the suffix *-ana* may be added to a body part noun to derive a noun referring to an article of clothing associated with that part of the body. For example: *kanti-ana* 'trousers' (from *kanti* 'thigh'), *mukarti-ana* 'hat, cap' (from *mukarti* 'head'), *tiki-ana* 'waistcoat' (from *tiki* 'ribs'), and *nukke-ana* 'handkerchief' (from *nukke* 'nose mucus'). Another way of forming words for items of clothing in Kaurna is by combining the body part term with *balta* (from *paltendi* 'knock, push, throw, pull'), as in *tidna-balta* 'shoe, boot' (from *tidna* 'foot'), and *yerko-balta* 'stocking' (from *yerko* 'leg') .

Spelling and pronunciation

Traditionally, Aboriginal people did not write their languages. Today, however, many of the languages, particularly the more widely spoken ones, do have written forms which are being used in books, newspapers, and various types of literacy materials. Like English, all of these languages use writing systems with Roman letters. Partly because of its long history of being written, English spelling is notoriously complicated, and the same sound is frequently spelt in two or more different ways — for example, the *f* sound of *from* is also spelt *gh*, as in *enough*, and *ph* as in *photograph*. On the other hand, the same letter is often used to represent different sounds — for example, the *g* sounds in *get* and *ginger* are different). It would be pointless and confusing to carry these complexities into writing Australian languages, and so a general principle has usually been adopted of one spelling for one sound. This means that it is relatively easy to pronounce a word once you know how it is spelled, and to spell a word when you know how it is pronounced. (This ideal has not always been met, and in some cases it has been sacrificed for ease of transfer from English spelling.)

Different language groups have chosen different spelling systems to represent the sounds of their languages. For instance a sound a bit like English *j* in *jar* is written *j* by Warlpiri, *tj* by Pintupi, *ch* by Wik-Mungkan. It does not matter which system a group uses, as long as they find the system convenient and easy to use. To hear examples of sounds in some Australian languages see *Australia's languages* (Thieberger 1994).

The following is a brief guide to the pronunciation of the main consonant sounds found in Australian languages. Not all the sounds are found in every language — most languages make a selection from this set.

b, p	similar to the *p* of *spin*, or to the *b* of *bin*. In some languages the *p* sound is the more common, while in other languages, the *b* predominates
ch/dj/j/tj	similar to the *j* of *jam*, or to the *ch* of *chill*, in some languages this sound is more like the *d* of *dew*
d/t	similar to the *t* of *stick*, or the *d* of *din*; depending on the language, the *t* or the *d* pronunciation predominates
dh/th	to most English speakers this sounds like the ordinary English *t* or *d*, but is pronounced more like the English *th* of *thing*. It is made by putting the tip of your tongue just behind the back of the upper teeth
g/k	similar to the *k* of *skin*, or to the *g* of *girl*
l	similar to the English *l* of *long*
lh	English has no equivalent sound; *lh* is like a thick *l* sound made by putting the tip of your tongue just behind the back of the upper teeth
ly	this sounds a bit like the *lli* of *million*, and is almost identical with the Spanish *ll* of *llave* 'key'
m	similar to English

n	similar to English
ng, ŋ	similar to the *ng* of *sing*, but not like the *ng* of *finger*. The *ng* in Aboriginal languages often comes at the beginning of words, which it does not do in English. With a bit of practice you can pronounce *ng* at the beginning of a word. Repeat *singer* a few times, adding greater emphasis to the second syllable, and finally dropping off the syllable *si*
nh	there is no equivalent sound in English; this sounds to the English speaker just like the *n* of *nothing*. It is made by putting the tip of your tongue just behind the back of the upper teeth
ny	similar to *ni* of *onion*, and the *ny* of *canyon*
r/r̲	this letter is normally pronounced like the *r* of *run*, even at the end of words (as in many Americans' pronunciation of *car*)
rd/d̲/rt/t̲	there is no equivalent sound in English; this sounds like the English *t* or *d*, but is pronounced with the tongue tip bent back in the mouth, much like the final sounds in the American English pronunciation of *lard*
rl/l̲	there is no equivalent in English; this sounds like English *l*, but is pronounced with the tip of the tongue bent further back in the mouth, much like the final sounds in the American English pronunciation of *Carl*.
rn/n	there is no equivalent in English; this sounds like English *n*, but is pronounced with the tongue tip bent further back in the mouth, much like the final sounds in the American English pronunciation of *barn*
rr	similar to the *tt* of *butter* when spoken quickly; this is never pronounced like the *r* of *run*. Sometimes the *rr* is 'rolled' like the *r* sound of Scottish English.
w	similar to English
y	similar to English
yh	there is nothing like this sound in English. It sounds like a *y* said with your tongue between your teeth
'	the glottal stop is similar to the pronunciation of *tt* in 'bo*tt*le' in Cockney speech.

In most Australian languages there is no difference between *b* and *p*, *d* and *t*, *rd* and *rt*, *j* and *ch*, *g* and *k*, and you do not get any meaning difference when using one rather than the other, as happens in English where *bin* and *pin* have very different meanings. In most Australian languages a word written with a *b* (or *p*) could be pronounced with either a *b* or a *p* without affecting the meaning: the Warrwa word *Bangaran* (the name of the area across the mudflats from the town of Derby, where the Leprosarium was located) can be pronounced as either *Bangaran* or *Pangaran*. Only a few languages distinguish these consonant sounds, one of them being Murrinh-Patha (chapter 14).

In writing some Australian languages the letters *b*, *d*, *rd*, *j*, *dh*, and *g* (the letters representing the 'voiced' sounds in English) are sometimes used, while in other languages *p*, *t*, *rt*, *ty*, *th*, and *k* (the letters representing the 'voiceless' sounds in English) are preferred. It does not really matter which choice is made (except in those few languages in which the differences in voicing carry meaning differences). In fact, many languages use some letters from the first set, others from the second.

Most Australian languages have only three distinct vowel sounds. These are usually written with the letters *a*, *i*, and *u*. *a* is sometimes pronounced as in *mat*, and sometimes like the vowel of *but*, *i*, as in *bit* (never like the *i* sound in *bight*); and *u* as in put (never like the *u* sound of *but*). The vowel *u* often sounds like the *oo* vowel in *boot* (except that it is somewhat shorter), and in some languages (e.g. Gooniyandi) this sound is written with *oo* instead of the usual *u*. Some languages distinguish one or two (rarely more) additional vowels, usually *e* (as in *met*) and *o* (as in *nod*).

In a fair number of languages these vowel sounds come in two varieties — short and long. Normally the short one is represented by a single letter, while the long one is represented by doubling the letter. Thus, *ii* represents a long *i* sound, like the *ee* in *steel* (only perhaps slightly longer), and *aa* represents a long *a* sound, like the *ar* in *far*.

One important rule for pronouncing words of most Australian languages is that the first syllable of each word should be given the main stress or accent. For instance, the Ngiyampaa word *kurrukun* 'cattle' is pronounced ***ku**-rru-kun*, with the first syllable loudest and most prominent; it is not pronounced *ku-**rru**-kun* or *ku-rru-**kun***, with emphasis on the second or third syllables.

Structure and content of the wordlists

The wordlists for each language contain approximately 500 words, which, as has already been stressed, represents a tiny fraction of the vocabulary of any language. It was felt that a list of this size would, however, be large enough to provide some notion of the character of each language — it would allow scope for the inclusion of some unusual or interesting words while not becoming too unwieldy. Contributors were requested to include among the 500 words a basic list of 166 common or basic words, which has been used over a long period of time by linguists working on Australian languages. Although no strict guidelines were issued for the remaining words, it turned out that most contributors selected fairly comparable (though certainly not identical) sets of words.

We have tried to make the chapters as consistent with each other as possible, but in some instances we have allowed author's preferences for the style of entry to override this general principle.

There is really no ideal way to organise the wordlists, and the organisation adopted here has been chosen for a number of mainly practical reasons. The wordlists are each divided into sections, which are described more fully below. Each section contains a number of words in the language, together with a brief English equivalent or *gloss* indicating its main meaning(s). The word is given first, in the left-hand column, followed by the gloss, in the right-hand column. Within each section, words are listed alphabetically by the language headword.

We are aware that there are some disadvantages in this style of organisation, and some contributors would have preferred to have the gloss first, and ordered the words alphabetically by gloss. This would have facilitated English speaking users finding words. However, it is believed that having the language word as headword will encourage browsing; it was felt that users would be less likely to want to find the words for specific items such as 'emu', than find words for various different birds. And given that the sections generally contain between five and twenty words, it should not take much longer to locate the word for an item by looking down the second column, rather than the first. Furthermore, words are sometimes not just given single word glosses, but a short explanation of extended meanings or uses; this sort of information is easier to present if the Aboriginal language word comes first. Finally, and perhaps most importantly, we wished to give greater prominence to the language words than to their English glosses.

---

atnerre *n.* brave, confident, game, not scared. ◇ Ayenge atnerre ingwemerntele alhetyeke. *I don't mind going in the dark.* ◇ Ayenge atnerre itne atningkele atwetyeke. *I can take it if a whole lot of them all beat me up.* ◇ Artwe nhenhe atnerrele akwele arle ikwere-arrpe arleke nayepe ante anpelheke iperre re rlkerte anthurre anteme awelheme nayepe iperre re. *This man thought he was so brave when he gave himself the sorry cuts, and now he's really feeling the pain.* ◇ Ampe nhakwe atherrele warle akertne-ntyele kwene-akerle areme. Itnyemele apeke untye ultakelheketye atere-irretye-akenhe, atnerre anthurre akwele. *Those two kids are looking down from the top of the house. They might fall and break their necks but they aren't scared. They think they're so tough.*

⇒ See also **irrpelthe**, **ahe-akngerre**. Opposite of **atere**. Can sound similar to (forms of) **artnerreme**.

atnerre-ileme *-le vb.*

1. give someone confidence, stop them being scared.

2. break in a horse, tame an animal. ◇ Apmere ikngerre-werne atheke apeke-arle alhele-iweme kamule awethe arntirrkwemele atnerre-ilemele arntirrkwerlte-anetyeke. *Maybe they are going east to catch some more camels and tame them.*

Sample entry from an Arrernte dictionary

It must be stressed that this book is not a conventional dictionary. Only very basic information is provided for each word: usually an English gloss, sometimes with a short explanation. No detailed information is consistently given about how the word is or may be used in a sentence, or of the range of its meanings. It is important to realise that words in Australian languages may be used quite differently to their English glosses. A word like *make* in English is used in a wide range of constructions where it has different meanings, and words in Australian languages which are glossed as *make* do not necessarily share these uses. The Gooniyandi word *ngarag-*, for instance, is normally translated as *make*, but only in the sense *construct*; it is not used like *make* in *That makes me sick*, or *Two and two make four*. A good dictionary of a language would provide information about how the word can be used, and give examples of its use in a sentence. On the previous page is a sample entry from the *Eastern and Central Arrernte to English Dictionary* (Henderson and Dobson 1994) which illustrates the type of information that might be included in a dictionary.

The words of the wordlists have been divided into groups which have similar meanings. When the first drafts of the chapters were received it was clear that most contributors were using very similar, even though not identical, groupings. It was obvious that it would not be too difficult to select a standardised grouping which could be adhered to most of the time, and that doing so would facilitate use of the book. The editors were then faced with deciding on this standard grouping. The one decided on was as follows:

1. Body parts and products
2. Kin relationships
3. Human classification
4. Language, mythology and ceremony
5. Human artefacts
6. Food, cooking and fire
7. Topography
8. Elements
9. Mammals
10. Reptiles
11. Birds
12. Aquatic life
13. Insects and spiders
14. Plants
15. Physical qualities
16. Non-physical qualities
17. Motion
18. State
19. Vocalisation and thought
20. Bodily functions
21. Impact and violence
22. Holding and transfer

23. Location, direction and time
24. Interjections and particles
25. Pronouns and demonstratives
26. Placenames

Each chapter employs the above domains in the above order as its backbone. However, it was not considered essential that they be rigidly adhered to, and some variation occurs. In some cases a category does not appear, because the writer has no relevant words for the language, or because they have decided that it is more appropriate to expand on one of the other domains. Sometimes, on the other hand, a chapter may have an additional section or two, where the contributor considered that another domain was of considerable interest. Such sections have been added in at the relevant places in the wordlists, and numbers adjusted accordingly. For the reader's convenience, a list of the categories employed in each wordlist is given at the head of the wordlist.

It cannot be stressed too strongly that these groupings were chosen mainly for reasons of convenience. They are based on groupings which have been previously used by many linguists for Australian languages, including for example Wurm (1967), Sutton and Walsh (1979), and Dixon and Blake (1979, 1981, 1983, 1991). They do not necessarily reflect groupings which would be made by speakers of the languages; nor do they represent the best possible groupings. For example, the grouping adopted confuses criteria of meaning and grammar; and for some languages better groupings can be devised which take into account their grammatical structures. However, for a book such as this, a means of organisation which is usable for each language clearly has advantages over a language-specific organisation, in that it permits greater ease of use by the non-linguist. Furthermore, the organisation adopted does have the advantage that it is similar to most others in use by Australianist linguists up until now, and most wordlists the reader is likely to encounter will be arranged in a similar way (or be alphabetically ordered).

References

Berndt, RM and Berndt, CH 1962/1992, *The world of the first Australians*, Aboriginal Studies Press, Canberra

Crowley, T and Dixon, RMW 1981, 'Tasmanian', in Dixon and Blake (eds), 1981, pp 394–421

Dixon, RMW 1972, *The Dyirbal language of North Queensland*, Cambridge University Press, Cambridge

Dixon, RMW 1980, *The Languages of Australia*, Cambridge University Press, Cambridge

Dixon, RMW and Blake, B (eds) 1979, *Handbook of Australian languages, Volume l*, Australian National University Press, Canberra

Dixon, RMW and Blake, B (eds) 1981, *Handbook of Australian languages, Volume 2*, Australian National University Press, Canberra

Dixon, R M W and Blake, B (eds) 1983, *Handbook of Australian languages, Volume 3*, Australian National University Press, Canberra

Dixon, R M W and Blake, B (eds) 1991, *Handbook of Australian languages, Volume 4*, Oxford University Press, Melbourne

Endacott, S 1924/1990, *Australian Aboriginal words and placenames and their meanings*, Acacia Press, Melbourne

Elkin, A P 1938/1974, *The Australian Aborigines*, Angus and Robertson, Sydney

Harkins, J 1994, *Bridging two worlds: Aboriginal English and crosscultural understanding*, University of Queensland Press, St Lucia

Harris, J 1982, 'Facts and fallacies of Aboriginal number systems', in *Language and Culture*, ed. S Hargrave (*Work Papers of SIL-AAB*, series B, vol. 8), Summer Institute of Linguistics, Darwin, pp 153–181

Haviland, J 1979, 'Guugu Yimidhirr', in Dixon and Blake (eds), 1979, pp 27–180

Henderson, J and Dobson, V 1994, *Eastern and Central Arrernte to English Dictionary*, Institute for Aboriginal Development, Alice Springs

Maddock, K 1972/1974, *The Australian Aborigines: a portrait of their society*, Penguin, Harmondsworth

McGregor, W 1990, *A functional grammar of Gooniyandi*, John Benjamins, Amsterdam

McKelson, K 1989, *Topical vocabulary in Northern Nyangumarta*, Nulungu Catholic College, Broome

Plomley, N G B 1976, *A word-list of the Tasmanian Aboriginal languages*, N G B Plomley, Launceston

Reed, A H and A W 1965/1974, *Aboriginal words of Australia*, A H and A W Reed, Sydney

Stanner, W E H 1982, 'Aboriginal humour', *Aboriginal History*, vol. 6, pp 39–48

Sutton, P and Walsh, M 1979, *Revised linguistic fieldwork manual for Australia*, Australian Institute of Aboriginal Studies, Canberra

Thieberger, N 1994, *Australia's languages*, Australian indigenous languages information stacks (HyperCard interactive multimedia), Australian Institute of Aboriginal and Torres Strait Islander Studies, Canberra

Thompson, D 1935, 'The joking relationship and organised obscenity in North Queensland', *American Anthropologist*, vol. 37, pp 460–490

Tsunoda, T 1981, *The Djaru language of he Kimberley, Western Australia*, Pacific Linguistics, Canberra

Walsh, M 1992, 'A nagging problem in Australian lexical history', in *The language game: papers in memory of Donald C. Laycock*, eds T Dutton, M Ross and D Tryon, Research School of Pacific Studies, Australian National University, Canberra, pp 507–519

Wurm, S 1967, *Linguistic fieldwork methods in Australia*, Australian Institute of Aboriginal Studies, Canberra

Yallop, C 1981, *Australian Aboriginal languages*, Andre Deutsch, London

Language Centres

Address list of Aboriginal and Torres Strait Islander Language Centres, produced by the Yamaji Language Centre (current at May 1994)

NEW SOUTH WALES
Niigarr Lingo Gumbi - NSW Aboriginal Language Management Committee
84 Derribong Street, Trangie, NSW 2823
Phone: (068) 88 7136

Muurbay Aboriginal Language and Culture Co-op Ltd
648 Sherwood Road, Sherwood, via Kempsey, NSW 2440
Phone: (065) 66 9353
Fax: (065) 66 9143

NORTHERN TERRITORY
East Arnhem Language Centre
via Yirrkala School, PO Box 936, Nhulunbuy, NT 0881
Phone: (089) 87 1224
Fax: (089) 87 1725

Institute for Aboriginal Development
PO Box 2531, Alice Springs, NT 0871
Phone: (089) 52 2688
Fax: (089) 53 1884

Kardu Numida Incorporated
OLSH, C/- The Brothers, Port Keats, NT 0822
Phone: (089) 78 2477, (089) 78 2363
Fax: (089) 78 2300

Katherine Regional Aboriginal Language Centre
PO Box 89, Katherine, NT 0851
Phone: (089) 71 1233
Fax: (089) 71 0561

Nauiyu Nanbiya Language Centre
PMB 28, Daly River, NT 0822
Phone: (089) 78 2427
Fax: (089) 78 2590

Papulu Apparr-Kari Language Centre
C/- PO Box 1108, Tennant Creek, NT 0861
Phone: (089) 62 3270
Fax: (089) 62 3280

West Arnhem
Minjilang, Croker Island, via Darwin, NT 0822
Phone: (089) 79 0299
Fax: (089) 79 0297

QUEENSLAND
Djabugay Tribal Aboriginal Co-op
PO Box 34, Kuranda, QLD 4872
Phone: (070) 93 8806, (070) 93 8859
Fax: (070) 93 7629

Guugu Yimidhirr Language Centre
C/- PO, Hopevale, QLD 4871
Phone: (070) 60 9261, (070) 60 9232
Fax: (070) 60 9262

Kombumerri Aboriginal Corporation for Culture
154 Rochedale Road, Rochedale, QLD 4123
Phone: (07) 341 5575
Fax: (07) 341 9385

Thoorgine Education Centre
PO Box 363, Pialba, QLD 4655
Phone/Fax: (071) 24 4100

Language Centres

Torres Strait Islander Art and Craft Corporation
PO Box 5647
Townsville MC, QLD 4810
Phone: (077) 78 6682
Fax: (077) 81 4033

SOUTH AUSTRALIA
Yaitya Warra Wodli
1 Lipson Street, Port Adelaide, SA 5015
Phone: (08) 241 0227
Fax: (08) 241 0228

TASMANIA
Tasmanian Aboriginal Language Program
Head Office:
198 Elizabeth Street, Hobart, TAS 7000
GPO Box 569F, Hobart, TAS 7001
Phone: (002) 34 8311
Fax: (002) 31 1348

North and North-West Region:
163 John Street, Launceston, TAS 7250
PO Box 531, Launceston, TAS 7250
Phone: (003) 31 6966
Fax: (003) 31 4258

VICTORIA
Lordjba Victoria
190 Graham Street, Port Melbourne, VIC 3207
Phone: (03) 646 7255

WESTERN AUSTRALIA
Fitzroy Crossing Annexe of KLRC
PO Box 86, Fitzroy Crossing, WA 6765
Phone: (091) 91 5124

Kimberley Language Resource Centre
PMB 11, Halls Creek, WA 6770
Phone: (091) 68 6005
Fax: (091) 68 6023

Mirima Dawang Woorlab-gerring
PO Box 162, Kununurra, WA 6743
Phone: (091) 69 1029
Fax: (091) 68 2639

Noongar Language and Culture Centre
16 Little Street, Carey Park, Bunbury, WA 6230
Phone: (097) 91 2165

Wangka Maya Pilbara Aboriginal Language Centre
PO Box 693, Port Hedland, WA 6721
Phone: (091) 73 2621
Fax: (091) 73 2973

Wangkanyi Ngurra Tjurta Aboriginal Corporation
PMB 3, Kalgoorlie, WA 6430
Phone: (090) 21 1655
Fax: (090) 21 8128

Yamaji Language Centre
PO Box 433, Geraldton, WA 6530
Phone: (099) 64 3550, (099) 21 4477
Fax: (099) 64 2634

1

Bundjalung

MARGARET SHARPE

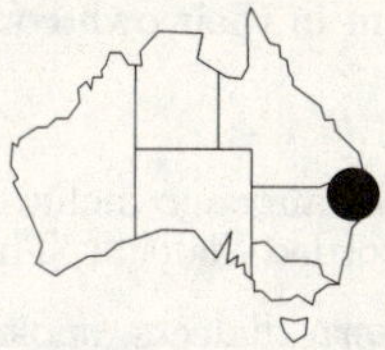

The language now called Bundjalung was spoken in the Northern Rivers area of New South Wales and as far north as the Gold Coast and its hinterland. There are only a few old people still alive who learnt Bundjalung as their first language, although a number of words and expressions are still used by many modern-day Bundjalung people in their everyday English.

The name 'Bundjalung' used to refer to one or two of the dozen or more dialects of this language. The dialects often had different names according to whether the people were talking about themselves, or whether a neighbouring group was talking about them.

Most of the dialect names indicate how that group said certain words. For example, Wiyebal, Wahlubal, Wehlubal and Wudjehbal are the names of dialects that used *wiye*, *wahlu*, *wehlu* or *wudjeh* for 'you'. Yugambeh refers to those who say *yugam* or *yugambeh* for 'no', Galibal to those who use *gali* for 'this' (when indicating something visible), and Ngahnduwal to those who say *ngahndu* for 'who'. Gidhabal (often spelt Gidabal), the name still used for the dialect at Woodenbong, indicates that *gidha* is the word used to mean 'all right'. Currently the Gidhabal and Yugambeh people use these names, not the name Bundjalung, for their language.

The Bundjalung people, unlike their neighbours, did not have a section system (see page xvi in the Introduction), so their kin system is a little different to other groups. Because there was a lot of white settlement and disruption to traditional life in the Bundjalung area, it has been hard to get a really clear picture of how it was decided who would marry whom. It is known that most young men got wives from a different dialect area in the Bundjalung region, and that they often lived in their prospective wife's area for about 18 months before the wife came to live with them in their own country.

About the wordlist

The vocabulary list for this language includes words from a number of the better studied and recorded dialects. These are:

- Y Yugambeh and northern dialects, spoken in the Beaudesert area and across to the Gold Coast hinterland, including Tamborine Mountain
- GC Gold Coast (only a few words quoted — most are similar to Yugambeh words, but there are some significant differences)
- G Gidhabal, from the Woodenbong area
- W Wahlubal, south of Woodenbong to Tabulam
- We Wehlubal, from Baryulgil — very similar to Wahlubal, but a few differences, notably in the pronunciation of 'you' (singular)
- B Birihn, from Rappville, between Casino and Baryulgil
- Wi Wiyebal/Wuhyebal, from the Lismore–Coraki area
- C dialect recorded by W E Smythe, probably from the Casino area, and possibly the dialect Gidhabal people call Galibal

The wordlist illustrates that some words are the same or almost the same throughout the dialects. Some common words (for 'man', 'woman' and 'hand', for example) have two forms, one generally used further north, and the other further south (or perhaps coastal versus inland). On the other hand, some words differ considerably from one dialect to another, and a number of words change meaning subtly as you move from one place to another. It is also possible that some dialects don't have words other dialects do — for example, inland dialects may lack words for some ocean fish, southern dialects may lack words for some more northern trees, and so on. This explains some of the gaps in the following wordlist.

There are also gaps because complete vocabulary lists were not collected when the language was in full use. So this short list may at times include a word as being in general use, when it is not attested in all previously collected lists. It is also possible that some items had a number of names, but through happenstance one form was told to the person writing things down in one area, and another form told to a person writing things down somewhere else. It is not unusual for there to be a number of words for some things, both in Aboriginal languages and in English.

The pressure was strong on many Bundjalung people not to use the language, so it hasn't been learnt or even heard much by most adults middle-aged and younger, although many middle-aged people of today do remember hearing phrases of the language when they were younger, and one non-Aboriginal adult recalls her grandfather (who learnt the language) singing Bundjalung lullabies to her.

The Bundjalung language was nevertheless used long enough after European settlement for there to have been a need to borrow or invent words and expressions for the new things that came in with the *dagays* or *yirilees* ('white people'). Some words were taken from English and changed to fit the sounds and patterns of their language. For some new things they made up words, for example by adding suffixes to their words for 'eye', 'head', 'leg' and 'foot' for things like glasses, hat, trousers and shoes. In other cases, they made verbal nouns — for example, the word for a spade or shovel is *duwalihgu*, which literally means 'for digging'.

Spelling and pronunciation

For writing Bundjalung we use the following letters:

a, ah, b, d, j/dh, e, eh, g, i, ih, l, m, n, ny, ŋ or ng, r, u, w, y

It should be noted that the sound represented by *ny* is written *yn* at the end of a word or syllable, the *l* and *r* are flapped or trilled, and the *h* indicates that the vowel is lengthened.

The Bundjalung people have opted for the use of the symbol ŋ for the *ng* sound as in English 'singer'. If this symbol were not used, it would be necessary to write *ngg* for the *ng* sound in English 'finger', and *n.g* for the sequence of *n* and *g* (*g* is always hard, as in *get*). Except for a very few words ending in *dh*, Bundjalung words do not end in stops (that is, *b*, *d*, *j/dh* and *g*).

The stop consonants in Bundjalung often had very soft (fricative) sounds. The sound written *d* was always hard like English *d*, but the sounds written *b* and *g* could be quite soft. That is, with *b*, the lips were not always completely closed to stop the air prior to the *b* sound. With *g*, a similar thing happened — the back of the mouth, which is completely blocked just before the release which makes the *g* sound in English, was often kept slightly open, making the sound less sharp and hard. Because of this, in some of the early wordlists (from the 1880s on), *g* was written as *h*.

The sound which is written *j* was usually softer than the *j* of English. After a vowel, it is written in this wordlist as *dh*, and there are differences in the way this sound is pronounced throughout the dialects of Bundjalung. It is variously pronounced like the *th* in English 'these', like English *j* and like the *zh* sound in 'measure'. The name of the Warrazambil Ranges in the New South Wales–Queensland border area reflects the *z*-like pronunciation in *wardham-bil* 'mythical monsters' — probably like the so-called rainbow serpent.

BUNDJALUNG WORDLIST

WORDLIST CATEGORIES

1. Body parts and products
2. Kin relationships
3. Human classification
4. Language, mythology and ceremony
5. Human artefacts
6. Food, cooking and fire
7. Topography
8. Elements
9. Mammals
10. Reptiles
11. Birds
12. Aquatic life
13. Insects and spiders
14. Plants
15. Physical qualities
16. Non-physical qualities
17. Motion
18. State
19. Vocalisation and thought
20. Bodily functions
21. Impact and violence
22. Holding and transfer
23. Location, direction and time
24. Interjections
25. Pronouns
26. Placenames

1. Body parts and products

bambam	bruise, swelling
baŋ-baŋ *(Y)*, gam-gam *(G)*, juŋ-juŋ *(W)*, jundhuŋ *(C)*	brain
baŋgim *(We)*, bawur *(others)*	head
binaŋ	ear
danar	rib
daŋgan *(Y,G,C)*, jambay *(W)*, yambay *(Wi)*	hand; finger(s)
darigan	bone
diraŋ	tooth
dulguh *(Y)*, dulgu *(W)*, jugul *(W,C)*, guldhu *(We)*	heart
dumirgan *(Y)*, bulun, miran *(C)*, walmir *(G,W)*	chest
durbin *(Y)*, gaŋgar *(C)*	nape of neck
gadhul *(Y)*, banyargan *(others)*	fat
gam *(W)*, guhndun *(others)*	hair of head

gaŋgil	arm
gindil	knee
gumar	blood
gunaŋ	faeces, shit
gurin	elbow
jalayn	throat, neck
jaŋgahn *(Y)*, nugal *(W)*	cheek
jaraŋ	leg; thigh; claw
jeyaŋ	mouth; beak
jibag *(Y)*, warehyn *(G)*, wari, juguŋ *(C)*	spit, spittle
jibiyn *(W)*, yilim(?) *(Y)*	eyebrow
jigay	sore
jinaŋ *(Y)*	foot; thumb; big toe
jurguŋ *(Y)*, yalayn *(others)*	tongue
miyi *(Y,G)*, jiyaw *(Wi,W,C)*	eye
mubar *(Y)*, muli *(G,W)*, mulih *(C)*, girar *(We)*	back, spine
muhŋ *(Y)*, muŋ *(G)*, mundu, mihran *(W)*, miran *(C,Wi)*, mundu *(C)*, gidhar *(G)*	belly, stomach
mulehŋ	vomit
muŋgar *(Y)*, buluyn, buluyn-buluyn *(W,Wi,C)*, yulumayn *(G,C)*	kidney
muruh *(Y)*, muru *(others)*	nose
nahr	tendon, vein
nugal *(Y,W)*, mibiyn *(G,Wi)*	face; cheek
ŋamah *(C,Wi)*, guruhm(bil) *(W,We)*	breast; milk
ŋihl *(W,Wi)*, ŋihr *(Y,We,C,B)*	forehead
walagan	shoulder
waŋayn	armpit
waram, warambil	left hand
wulu	ankle
wuru *(G,C)*, gaŋgar *(W)*	neck
yarayn	beard
yilŋan *(all)*, gandehgil *(C)*	liver
yulayn *(Y)*	skin, hide; feathers

2. Kin relationships

babaŋ *(Y)*, biyaŋ *(Y, Wi)*, bidhaŋdhar, bidhaŋbihyn *(G, W)*, mahmaŋ *(G, W)*, dahri *(W)*	father; uncle (father's brother)
bahbiyn	grandmother (maternal); grandmother (paternal *Y*)
banahm	brother or male cousin of female; younger brother of male (methods of calculating who is in *banahm* relationship differ for male or female ego)
buguy	parent-in-law
gaguhŋ	brother (older) of male; uncle; male cousin
gami	grandmother (paternal); grandmother (maternal *Y*)
guhŋdhar (gawaŋdhar?) *(Y)*, gawaŋ *(Y, C, W, G)*	uncle (mother's brother; mother's male cousin)
muyuhmdhar *(Y, Wi)*, muyum *(C)*, mudhum *(C, G, W)*	son
muyuhmgan *(Y)*, muyuhmdhargan *(Wi)*, muyumgan *(C)*, mudhumgan *(C, G, W)*	daughter
nanahŋ	sister of male; older sister of female
nyubuŋdhar *(Y)*, bani *(C)*, banidhar *(others)*	husband
nyubuŋdhargan *(Y)*, banigan *(C)*, banidhargan *(others)*	wife
nyuguhn	nephew, niece
ŋadhaŋ	grandfather
ŋaruyn	aunt (father's sister)
wabuhyn	sister (younger) of female
wadhuŋ *(Y, G, W)* (wadhuŋdhar, wadhunbiyn), mahmi (from 'mummy'?) *(W, C)*, gunihŋ *(We)*	mother; aunt (mother's sister)
yirbul *(Y)*, yirbuŋ *(others)*	cousin (cross-cousin)

3. Human classification

baliŋ	young man
balugahn	handsome man, mythical hero, Jesus Christ
bihbi (from English 'baby'), guŋ (boy), guŋgan (girl)	baby

dagay *(Y,G,C)*, yirili *(W)*, yirahli *(Wi,We)*	white man
ganilihgu *(Y)* (literally 'for tying up'), ganjibul *(others)*	policeman
gawuŋgan	beautiful woman, mythical heroine, Mary mother of Jesus
gidhuhm *(Y,G,C)*, gidhulum *(Y)*, dandaygam *(C)*	old man
jabuh *(Y,G)*, janagan *(W,C)*, janaŋgan *(Wi,C)*	boy
jabuyn *(Y,G,C)*, dubahdhar *(W)*, dubaydhihn *(Wi)*	young girl
jaguhr *(Y,G,W)*, jaŋur *(C)*	stranger
jahdham	child
jalgayn *(Y)*, dubay *(others)*	woman
jaw-jaw (from 'chow-chow')	Chinese
mibiyn *(G)*, baygal *(C)*	person (*Also means* face)
mibiyn *(Y)*, baygal *(all)*	adult Aboriginal man
miruŋ(gan) *(Y,G)*, miruhŋ *(W)*, waruŋ *(C)*	old woman
waymehrigan, waynmehrigan *(Y,G)*, yiriligan *(W)*, yirahligan *(Wi)*	white woman
wubin *(Y)*, wiyun *(others)*	clever man, expert

4. Language, mythology and ceremony

budherahm	myth, sacred story
buhl *(Y)*, nambuhl *(G) (and others, according to degree of initiation)*	bora ring
dagay *(Y)*, maguy, mawi *(C)*	ghost of dead Aboriginal man
dawargan	ghost of dead Aboriginal woman
gurgun *(Y,G)*, ŋuyay *(C,W,Wi)*	language; word; noise
nyari	name
ŋahri	play (used also in context of cinema, corroborees, etc.)
wamal	corroboree dance (leg-shaking)
yawar, yawahr	corroboree song

5. Human artefacts

behŋ (from 'bag')	bag
bilahr *(W,C)*, bilar *(Y)*, juwan *(Wi,C,G,Y)*	spear
bagay *(We)*, bagah *(others)*	shield

bagul (from 'bark')	canoe
bandahn *(Y,C)*, wagar *(Wi,C,W)*, mugim *(G)*	axe
baŋgu (literally 'for the bank') *(Y)*, nyaguhŋ *(others)*	money
bargan	boomerang (returning)
baruŋ	boomerang (for fighting)
bindan *(Y)*, dugul-duguhl *(W)*, warbi, warbigan *(C)*	dillybag
bin.geh *(Y,G,W)*, bawuŋdhin (literally 'pertaining to the head') *(W)*, bawurdhin *(C)*	hat
bugalihgu (literally 'for poking/writing')	pen, pencil
bugur *(Y,G)*, waguy *(C)*, ganilihgu (literally 'for tying up')	rope
burahŋ(dhin)	dress
diman (literally 'ashes') *(Y)*, waybar (literally 'fire') *(others)*	camp
dindihdh (from English 'tin dish')	dish
dugurgan	bag (man's)
dululbi, duluhlbi (literally 'rattling')	rifle, gun
galgan *(Y)*	bag (of swamp rush)
ganay *(Y,We)*	digging stick
ganyal	fishing line
gawarilihgu (literally 'for running'), gawarinyun (literally 'while running')	car
gayuhn *(Y)*, jaraŋgehyn/jaraŋgihn (literally 'pertaining to legs')	trousers
gulay *(Y)*, ŋarbayn	net for fishing or for trapping animals in a narrow pass
gulbili *(Y)*	bed (of grass)
gundul *(Y)*	boat
jahn	shirt
jandahlgan *(C)*	bag (woman's)
jinaŋdhin (literally 'pertaining to the foot')	shoe(s)
juŋur, nahy (from English 'knife')	knife
murundaŋ	club with knob on end
nyugam *(Y)*	basin, pot, billycan, bucket
ŋamahr *(W,C)*	axe; large stone
ŋumban *(Y,G)*, waynjigur *(W,C)*, wanyigur *(C)*	blanket

ŋumbiyn	house, humpy
wahrilihgu (literally 'for carrying')	basket

6. Food, cooking and fire

bulahwar (from English 'flour')	flour
burehn (from English 'bread')	bread
burehn.gu (literally 'for bread')	butter
burgar	sea; beach
dahmber (from 'damper')	damper
diman (literally 'ashes') *(Y)*, waybar (literally 'fire') *(others)*	camp, group of humpies
diman *(Y)*, muruhyn *(G)*, muruyn *(C)*	ashes
gabay (literally 'honey'), gadhalgahyn	sugar
gudha (honey of large bee) *(Y)*, gaba (honey of small bee) *(Y)*, gudha, gabay, jambulaŋ *(C)*	honey
guluy, guluhy, warehyn-warehyn (literally 'froth-froth')	beer
jalŋay (literally 'bright, shiny'), maŋur *(W)*	light, torch
jindi (dry leaves), gadhalgahyn (of liquid 'sweet')	tea
juhm	smoke, cigarette
nuŋayn *(Y, Wi)*, naŋayn *(G, W, Wi, C)*	food, tucker
waybar	fire; kindling; matches; cigarette lighter
yigam, bulah (from English 'bullock') *(Y)*, bulaŋ *(all)*	meat

7. Topography

balun	river, creek
bamay	plain, flat
bibu(h) *(GC)*, buyuhl, buruhl *(Y)*, dugun *(others)*	mountain
birman (from *birma-* 'yawn'?)	cave, hole
dalagar	mud
gahwaŋ	lagoon, swamp (*Also means* 'waterfall' in some dialects)
gudhiŋ *(Y)*	ochre, paint
gulgan	road, track; spoor
jagun *(all)*, ŋayil *(W)*	ground, earth, soil, land

jaru *(W,Wi)*, daraw, dehyu *(Y)*, jarul *(C)*	stone, rock
muli	hill, ridge; back(bone)
yaruŋ *(Y)*, guygum *(others)*	sand, beach (*Also means* salt)

8. Elements

bigi *(GC)*, nyaŋga(r) *(GC,Y)*, yalgan *(Y,others)*	sun
bube	dust
buluhlmaŋ *(Y)*, buhlmaŋ *(G)*, buyan-buyehn *(C)*, buhyn-buhyn *(W,G)*	whirlwind
bumbi *(Y)*, buŋbi *(G)*, walah *(G)*, bagay *(W)*, bundar *(C)*, budhar *(C)*	frost
dagam *(W,We,C)*	cloud
dihlbi *(Y)*, margan *(C)*	dew
dubayn *(W,G)*	fog
garaŋ	hailstones
gibam	moon
guŋ, guhŋ all, nyabay *(W,C)*	water
guwaŋ	rain: *guwaŋ badhi-* to rain (literally 'rain hit')
guwaŋdham (literally 'without rain')	drought
guyuhmgan	star
jan.gayn	lightning
juyn.gun *(Y)*, jun.gun *(G)*, buluyn-buluhyn *(W)*, gurbuŋ *(B)*	cloud, rain
mihŋbil *(W)*	thunder
mugar	storm
muli-mulih (name of Woodenbong community)	hilly
ŋulahr	flood
wagahn (literally 'crow')	Canopus (star)
wariŋehn	Pleiades
wariŋihn	winter
yargeh *(Y)*, buhyi-buhyi *(Y)*, buyan (buwiyan) *(W,C)*, burgiyn *(G,C)*	wind

9. Mammals

bahy	kangaroo rat
banjim (baynjim) *(G, Y, W)*	native cat
biŋ-biŋ (from reduplication 'pig-pig', from English)	pig
budhigehn, budhigahn (from English 'pussycat')	domestic cat
bulah *(Y)*, bulaŋ (from English 'bullock')	cattle
bunihyn *(all but We)*, jina-jina *(We)*, jena-jena *(all but Y, We)*	echidna, spiny anteater
burbi *(all)*, duŋgihr *(B)*	koala
gehruŋ, giruŋ *(Y)*, girman *(G, Y)*	flying fox
guruhman *(Y)*, guruman *(others)*	male grey kangaroo; kangaroo (general term)
guruŋgar	female grey kangaroo
guyahyn	possum; rabbit
jimbaŋ (from English 'jumbuck')	sheep
mani (general term for 'wallaby, kangaroo' in *W*)	wallaby
nyamul	baby or young animal
ŋagam *(all)*, dabay, dabahy *(Wi, W)*, ŋura *(Y)*	dog
wadham *(G, We)*, wayam *(Y)*, jihrmurul *(W)*	squirrel glider
yaguy	bandicoot
yaramaŋ, yaraman	horse
yurgiyn	dingo

10. Reptiles

bingihyn, biŋgiŋ	turtle
darahyn, waŋwaŋ *(C)*	frog
diruyn *(Y)*, ŋuhynba, ŋuhynbe *(others)*	snake
gabul *(Y, C)*, yambah *(G, W, C)*	carpet snake
gubagan *(Y, W)*	blue-tongue lizard
jiruhŋ	goanna (common)
jiwah	lace monitor
magil	water dragon
manalgam *(Y)*, mundhurgum *(Y, G)*	death adder
marun	goanna, possibly the sand goanna

nyaram	bearded jew lizard, frilled lizard (*Also means* 'vulva' in some dialects)
ŋamahl	ground goanna, burrowing goanna or tree goanna

11. Birds

balin-balihn, bim-bim, buluhm-buluhm *(Y)*, bilin-bilehn *(G)*, dihn-dihn *(W)*	peewee, magpie lark
bilin, bilin-bilin	parrot
budhabuyeh, budhabudheh, budhay-budhay *(Y)*	swallow
buyuhlgan, wuhrbuŋgan *(Y)*, wuhrbiyn.gayn *(G)*, guyguyŋyuŋgan *(C)*	curlew
deber-debehr, dibir-dibehr *(Y)*, dabe-dabehr	plover
dihndin *(Y)*, bihmbim *(Y,G)*	noisy miner, soldier bird
gabuyn, maŋarehm	egg
gagurim *(Y)*, gahgun *(all)*	kookaburra
galbuyn *(Y,G)*, bunbun *(C)*	lyrebird
gandal	wing
gehr, gehraŋ *(Y)*	sulphur-crested cockatoo
gilgil, muralman *(Y)*	brolga
ginihbi *(We)*, ginibi *(others)*, muru-gudhihyn *(W)*	swan; magpie goose
gulguruŋ *(Y)*, wudhwudh *(G)*	butcherbird
guŋgum, gumgum *(Y)*, mumbir-mumbir *(G)*	tawny frogmouth
gurahmburuhn *(Y,G)*, wurguluhm	magpie
jalwaŋ	tullawong
jindi	nest (*Also means* 'tea' in some dialects)
jinir-jinir *(Y)*, juni-junihr *(C)*	night owl
jiŋir-jiŋir *(W)*, jiŋgir-jiŋgir *(G)*, juynjulam *(We)*	Willie wagtail
jugi-jugi (reduplication 'chooky-chooky', from English)	domestic fowl
juŋgar, juŋar	pelican
mahr, mahr-mahr	black duck; duck (general term)
mibayn	wedge-tailed eagle
nuŋaynbil *(Y)*, yirihyn *(G)*, yiririhyn *(C,Wi)*, marahn *(C,W)*	bird (general term)

ŋadhaŋah (literally 'belonging to grandfather') *(Y)*	regent bowerbird
ŋawgan *(Y)*, mulayn-mulahyn *(C)*, mulanyin *(W)*, gurehlgam *(G)*	blue crane
ŋuruyn	emu
wagahn *(Y)*	crow
wayilahr	yellow-tailed black cockatoo

12. Aquatic life

buŋgu-buŋgu *(Y)*	soldier crab
dugu(h) *(Y)*, junam *(W,C)*, buygun *(G)*	cod
jalum	fish (general term); mullet: *jalum bira-* to throw a fishing line
jubi *(Y)*	mud crab
mugihm	perch
mulayn	crayfish, lobby
wagayn	catfish
wardham	shark, eel; mythical monster
winyum *(Y)*	sand crab
yugir *(Y)*, dugunum *(G,C)*, dugum *(W)*	shell, shellfish, cockle, mussel

13. Insects and spiders

banjalahm	butterfly, moth; winged insect (general term)
baran-barahn	spider
bayahr, bayar-bayahr	centipede
buhlam, wayam *(Y)*, wadham *(G,W)*, julur *(C)*	scorpion
dugul	big wasp
dulum	louse
gihyn *(W)*, ŋuyn-ŋuyn *(G)*	ant (general term)
ginyin	mosquito
gudhabuŋgal *(Y,C)*	black bee (a native sweet)
gudhalayn, giyn-giyn	small black ant
gulayn	tick
gumbu *(Y)*, wawar *(C)*	cobra worm or toredo (a delicacy)
gunuhm *(Y,G,W)*	ant, bull ant
jubar, jubal	witchetty grub (in wattle trees)
julgeh *(Y)*	earthworm
junbar *(Y)*	fly; maggots

muyi *(Y)*	bees' wax
nyanay *(Y)*	leech
nyugay *(Y)*, yala, gabay, jambulaŋ *(others)*	bee (general term)
nyugay/yugay *(Y)*, gabay *(others)*	Italian bee
wir-wir	flea
yirimbahm	cicada

14. Plants

badihda, barehda	potato
barwaŋ *(Y)*	burrawang palm, zamia
bigar	ironbark
bilaŋ, bilaŋgah	casuarina
bimbul *(Y)*	Moreton Bay pine, hoop pine
binahn (from English 'banana')	banana
bubiyn *(We)*, buy-buy *(others)*	angophora
budharbiyn	flower
budhe *(Y)*, walam *(G,W)*	cunjevoi (lily) (used as a poultice)
budheh	Moreton Bay fig
buhnyi	bunya pine or nut
buŋaw	bloodwood
buŋgul	mushroom
dihbin *(Y)*, gihmbi, gihmbigah	stinging tree
gaban *(Y)*, gabal *(others)*	rainforest, thick forest
gaban-gabahn *(Y)*, gabal-gabahl *(others)*	forest, light or dry
gabugahn	corn, corn-cob
garahbil	blady grass
gihmbi, guhmbi	stinging nettle
gundul *(Y)*, bagul	bark
guwayn, gurayn *(Y)*	Moreton Bay ash
jali	tree
mandarahm	blackberry, wild raspberry
murehr *(Y)*, yirahr *(Y)*, barbam *(W,G)*	spotted gum; grey gum
nuruy	vine
nyuhmin *(Y)*	walking-stick palm
ŋarul *(Y,G)*	boxwood, gum-topped box-tree
waran, wayan (literally 'hip')	root
wudheh *(Y)*, bihynbar *(G)*	red cedar
wurahŋ	leaf
yihdhaŋ *(Y)*, wulaŋ *(G)*, wudhaŋ *(others)*	grass
yihnaŋ	reed

15. Physical qualities

barbaŋ *(Y)*, balbaŋ *(G)*	flat, smooth
bargahn, deyul *(C)*, yargehyn *(C)*	thin
bidhaŋ	little, small
bugaw	rotten, stinking
bulah *(Y,C)*, buruhr *(G,C)*, bulahbu *(W,C)*	two
dalahn *(Y,G,C)*, deber *(W,C)*	white
dalbay *(Y)*, yirihŋ *(G)*, ŋambuhr *(W,C)*, ŋahmbir *(C)*	slow
daram *(Y,G,We)*, dalgahy *(W,C)*	dry
duhndun *(Y)*, ŋagu, jagabar	black
duhyiyn *(Y)*, duluŋ *(C)*, guyir *(W,C)*, guyihr *(We)*, dalaŋ *(C)*	fear; frightened
duwan *(Y)*, ŋandir, ŋagu *(others)*	dark
gaba *(Y)*, gaybe	another
galaŋ *(Y)*, galan *(G,W)*	sharp
gamay *(Y,G)*, gidhuhyn *(Wi,C)*, jehr *(W)*	big
gibar	white, off-white
gudhihn *(G)*, gudhihyn *(W,We)*, gudhihŋ	red
gugiyn/wugiyn *(Y)*, ŋabar *(W)*, jamgal *(C)*	fast, quick
gumbuyn (often pronounced *gumbunj)*	finished, complete, ended
gurahr	long, tall
jalŋay	shiny, bright; flame
jan.gahy, jaŋgay, jan.gay	wet
jan.gam *(Y)*, gadhaŋ *(G,W)*, dandur *(C)*, garahni *(C)*	hard, tough
jindihn *(Y)*, mabehr *(W)*, gumbi *(G, C)*	many
jundur *(Y)*, jumbur *(others)*	heavy
miyidham (literally 'without eye') *(Y)*, jiyawdham (literally 'without eye') *(C)*, gulaŋ *(G)*	blind
mul, mulgalaŋ	short
ŋuhn	hot (weather)
wariŋ	cold (weather)
wuhbi, binaŋdham (literally 'without ear')	deaf
yabur	one
yulu	smell, fragrance

16. Non-physical qualities

bugal	good
damgay, gahbuyn	greedy
gareŋgi (from English), jaŋ bawur (literally 'bad head')	cranky
gihdhar *(C)*, gidhir *(W)*	sad, sorry
jaŋ	bad
jaŋuy, ŋiriyn, gareŋgi	angry, bad-tempered
milge-milgi *(Y)*, midhuŋ *(W,C)*, naruyn *(G)*	happy
miyi-banja- (literally 'cover eye')	jealous
waŋal *(Y)*, jibayn *(Wi)*	deaf; disobedient
wubihn *(Y)*, wiyan, wuyan *(others)*, mindal *(G)*	clever
yirihŋ *(G)*	lazy

17. Motion

banja-, baynja-	to cover something
banma-	to dress, get dressed
bina-, bin.ga- *(W)*, bana-, ban.ga-, barwa- *(others)*	(of the sun) to fall, set; (of frost) to form
gahdha- *(G,W,C)*	to chase
gani-	to tie up
gawari-	to run
gayi-, gayeh-	to enter, go in, through
jambama- *(Y)*, jambaguni- *(C)*, guni- *(G,W)*	to try to do something
jigini- *(W)*	to do how, do with what
julba- *(Y,G,C,We)*, baramgah- *(W)*	to jump
juluhya-	to go down
minyaŋi- *(Y,Wi)*, nyaŋa-, nyaŋga- *(others)*	to do what, do something
numbuh-, numbih-	to return
nyumba- *(G,Wi)*, miyumba- *(W,C)*	to show, show how to do
ŋalawa-	to hunt, look for
wahŋma- (literally 'to cause to work', from English 'work')	to work
walaŋgi-	to crawl
wamgiyn-yan.ga- *(Y)*, yaŋguwa- *(C,We)*	to come
wandi-	to climb, go up

wayah-	to fly
yan- (yanba-, yan.ga-)	to go: *yanbali-* to walk around
yaruh-, gayi-	to swim

18. State

ganja-(li-)	to marry, get married
jahna-	to stand, stand up
ŋunda- *(G,W,Wi,C)*, wunda- *(G)*	to wait (for something/someone)
wuna- *(Y)*, wana- *(others)*	to leave (it), stop doing (it)
yahna-, yahn.ga- *(Y,G)*, yehna-, yehn.ga- *(W,Wi,C)*	to sit, sit down
yina- *(Y,G,C)*, yuna- *(W,Wi,C)*	to lie, lie down; to live at a place

19. Vocalisation and thought

duŋa-, duŋga-	to cry, weep
ganŋa-	to hear; to think; to know; to understand
gaŋga-	to call out (includes bird call)
guyirma- (literally 'to cause fear')	to frighten
minyi- *(Wi)*, minji- (miynji-) *(others)*	to laugh
munmuyhnba-	to murmur
nadhga(h)- *(G,W)*, naga- *(C)*	to whisper
ŋalawa-, ŋihmba- *(C,W)*, ŋaraynma- *(C)*, ŋihnba- *(Wi)*	to ask
wadhe- *(Y,C)*, giya-, wehya- *(Y,C)*, wihya- *(Y,C)*, gidha-, gudha- *(G)*, gihya- *(C)*, wayma- *(W)*, wadhi- *(W,C)*, wayi- *(Wi)*	to say, speak, tell
wiyn.guŋba-, wiynba-	to whistle
yaŋma-	to say wrongly, swear
yarbi-	to sing
yerehŋba-	to scream
yuŋba-	(of a dog) to bark

20. Bodily functions

bahna-, bahn.ga-, bahrwa-	to get up, arise
balahn *(C)*, gilaŋ *(Y,G)*	dead
balahn.ga- *(W,Wi)*, balahna-, balahrwa-, juluhŋgi- (euphemism, literally 'to go down') *(G)*	to die
baribunma-	to dream (about)

budhar-wana- (literally 'to become soft')	to be in love
burgal *(Y)*, barahyn *(G, Wi)*, jayuhm *(C)*	pain
buruhŋba- *(W)*	to snore
durahrwa- *(G)*, buyuhyn-wana-, gidhuhngan-wana-, jehr-wana- (literally 'big-become') *(C)*	to grow
gihyn-giyn, mandayn *(G)*, gidhi-gidhi *(C)*	itchy
ginyilga-, guluŋba- *(W)*	to cough
girihyn *(Y)*	tired
ja-	to eat
jaluba-	to urinate
jalubay	urination
juga- (literally 'to swallow') *(Y)*, ja- (literally 'to eat') *(Y)*	to drink
mamir *(Y)*, miriŋ *(others)*	alive
mula *(We)*, gabir, gaybir *(others)*	hungry
nugay, nuway	thirsty
nyah-	to see, look at
ŋahynbir *(noun)*, ŋahyn bira- *(verb*, literally 'to throw yawn') *(G)*	yawn
ŋurahm, ŋurahm yuna-, yina- *(all)*	asleep
wuhbi, binaŋdham	deaf
yalyal, yaldhal *(Y)*, yadhal *(G)*, gibiŋ *(W,C,Wi)*	sick
yulu *(noun) (G)*, yuhlu *(noun) (W)*, bandi- *(W,C)*, bandeh- *(verb) (C)*, gaŋŋa- *(verb) (C)*	smell

21. Impact and violence

baguna- *(We)*, galga- *(others)*	to chop, cut
bawga-	to build
bayi- *(Y)*, badhi- *(G)*, naba- *(Y)*, buma-/bumba-	to hit
bira-	to throw
buga-	to poke with a sharp object (*Also means* to write)
buma-, bumga-	to kill; to hit, fight
duwa-	to dig; to bury
gahŋa-, yanihndi- *(G)*	to take

gawa-	to break something
gawga-	to cut
guyba-	to cook; to burn
manda-	to scratch, scrape
yiŋa-, yiŋga-	to bite

22. Holding and transfer

buhwi-, buhyi-	to pull
jawa-	to send
madhima- (literally 'there-make')	to put there
nama-	to hold; to touch
wahri-	to carry; to wear
wuhbi-	to lose
wula-	to give
wulima-	to find
yaɲini-, yanihndi- *(G)*, yaɲini- *(others)*	to bring

23. Location, direction and time

babargam (literally 'above', that is 'upland', 'inland')	west
baginjai, bagiynja *(W,C)*	nearly
bahŋa-, barga-	(of the sun) to rise; to get up; to appear
bala(y) *(Y,Wi,C)*, bale *(G)*	below, underneath
bayahyn	now, today
bundagahl *(Y,G)*, garin *(W)*	near
buram, buram (*burambah* locative case) *(Y,C)*, numbihl (*numbihla* locative case) *(W,Wi,C)*, nimbihl *(We)*	behind
dihlbi-dihlbi (reduplication 'dew-dew', from English, referring to dew in the early morning) *(Y,G)*, mulagan *(G,W,C)*	dawn, morning
dugun(dah) *(Y)*, babar *(others)*	above, on top
gadhi	here
gah	there (far)
gahbe	that (yonder unseen)
-gahl	after
galgiwa- *(Y)*, gehgi- *(W)*, gaywa- *(C)*	(of the sun) to set
gali, gale	this (here, visible)

gawul(ah) *(Y)*, bagar *(G,W)*, gayuhynbar *(W,Wi)*	far
gili, gile	that (yonder, visible)
guhgin *(W)* (compare 'north'; not listed in other dialects)	east
gunah	this (unseen)
guriyahbu, gurihyabu	a long time ago
juwi	down; below
madhi	there (close)
mali, male	that (there, visible)
munah	that (unseen)
numgir	daytime
nyuŋgulgan *(Y)*, ŋuhn.gahla (literally 'is hot') *(Y)*, ŋuhn.gu	summer
ŋandir	night
ŋaway *(W)*, gugin (literally 'people of north') *(G)*	north
ŋubu	tomorrow; yesterday
ŋululŋmay	soon
wahŋgan, dunam *(W)*, waŋgahn, birihn *(C)*	south
yawun	afternoon
yili, yile *(Y)*, yile, yila *(others)*, jiyah *(C,W,Wi)*, wiynji *(Y)*	where
yinjahgan *(Y,G)*, nyali *(C)*	when

24. Interjections

guram, gurambeh	perhaps
guway	come here
je *(G)*	hey!
ŋabi, ŋabu	off you go!
ŋeh, yaway	yes
yugam, yugambeh *(Y,Wi)*, yagam, yagambeh *(G,C,W)*	no, not

25. Pronouns

janabaŋ *(Y)*, nyulamaŋ, nyulaŋam *(others)*	they
minyaŋ *(Y,Wi)*, nyaŋ *(others)*	what
nyulagan *(Y,G)*, nyahn.gan *(Wi,W)*	she
nyulaganah *(Y,G)*, nyahn.ganah *(Wi,W)*	her (possessive)

nyulagani *(Y,G)*, nyahn.gani *(Wi,W)*	her (object)
nyulaŋah	his
nyulaŋi	him
nyuli, nyule *(Y,G)*, nyule, nyula *(others)*	he
ŋadhu *(W)*, ŋayu *(others)*	I (ergative)
ŋahn *(Y)*, ŋehn *(G,C)*, ŋihn *(C,W,W)*	who
ŋali	we
ŋaliŋah	our
ŋaliŋi	us
ŋaliwahlu *(Y)*	we (you and I)
ŋanyah	my
ŋanyih *(Y)*, ŋanyi *(others)*	me
ŋay *(also* ŋaw *Y)*	I (nominative)
ŋirihmaŋ *(Y,G,Wi)*, bula *(B)*, blagan *(W)*	you (plural nominative)
wahlu *(Y,G)*, wiya *(Wi)*, wuhye *(B)*, wudha *(W)*	you (singular nominative)
wehlu *(We)*, wahlu *(others)*	you (singular ergative)
wihnyi *(W)*, wahnyi *(others)*	you (singular object)

26. Placenames

Bilihnadhihl (literally 'once belonged to a parrot')	Billinudgel
Gamigal	Evans Head
Manal, Manaldhahli (Manandhahli) *(Y)*, Yilbagan *(Y)* (present name of Beaudesert Racecourse)	Beaudesert
Dahbalam, Jabilum	Tabulam
Damgay (literally 'greedy')	Tomki
Duluhm, Duluhmi	Tooloom
Gundulgunbi *(Y)*	Mt Ladybrook (where the two stone dogs are)
Gurigay	Coraki
Jahdham (literally 'child')	Tatham
Jalgambuyn	Mt Lindesay
Jenehŋmam	Casino
ŋudhumbuyn	Woodenbong
Waŋalbuŋ *(Y)*	Mt Tamborine
Wulumbiyn (compare 'Murwillumbah', nearby)	Mt Warning

1. Bundjalung

Grammatical notes

Unlike most other Aboriginal languages in the broad Pama-Nyungan family which covers most of Australia, Bundjalung had genders, so there are different pronouns for 'he' and 'she'. In addition, adjectives used to have endings to show whether they referred to males, females, trees or things (everything else). As you will probably have noticed, in the preceding lists a number of words for females end in *-gan*, a feminine suffix. It does not occur on 'woman', 'girl', etc., but does occur on kin terms, 'old woman', etc., as well as on some stars. Apart from 'he' and 'she' and these endings, only a few traces of this system are used now.

Like most Aboriginal languages, Bundjalung uses suffixes to show such things as who is doing an action, who or what is the recipient of the action, what instrument is used for the action, where the action occurs, who benefits from the action, 'from' or 'out of', purpose, and possessor. The purposive suffix *-gu* and the benefactive suffix *-baya* don't change with the word they are added to, but the other suffixes do change to 'blend' with the last sound of the word.

One set of suffixes, *-Du* (transitive subject or instrument), *-Da(h)* (location), and, in the northern dialects, *-Dih* (location in the past), generally add:

> a matched (or homorganic) stop (*b*, *d*, *j*, *g*) before the vowel
> *u/a/hih* to words ending in a nasal (*m*, *n*, *ny*, ŋ)
> *y* before the suffix vowel after a vowel
> only the vowel to words ending in *l* and *r*

The other suffixes, *-Ni* (object), *-Nu* ('from'), and *-Nah* (possessor) insert:

> ŋ before the vowel in the suffix after a vowel
> *n* after *l* or *r*
> only the suffix vowel after nasals

Suffixes for transitive subject (ergative — see page xvii) and for object are generally only used on words for large animals, such as humans, kangaroos, dogs, etc. For example, the following sentence

> *jabuhyu ŋuhynba nyahni*
> 'The boy saw the snake'

involves the ergative form of *jabuh* 'boy', but in

> *wir-wir yiŋgahla ŋagami*
> 'Fleas are biting the dog'

the word for 'flea', *wir-wir* does not take this suffix.

Verb suffixes do not change form with different verbs. However, some suffixes have slightly different meanings in different dialects, and some suffixes are different in form in the different dialects. The northern dialects only had two tenses (as well as the imperative mood): past and non-past, whereas the others had three: past, present and future. There is also a suffix *-li* which shows continuous action. Other suffixes can show such things as action in the remote past, habitual past action, the reliability of the statement (whether the speaker saw it happen), or if the action was done for a reason.

2

Ngiyampaa

TAMSIN DONALDSON

The name 'Ngiyampaa' literally means 'word-world', from *ngiya* meaning 'word', 'talk' or 'the law', and *-paa* which means something like 'world'. Similarly, the word for 'country' is *ngurrampaa*, which is literally 'camp-world', from *ngurra* 'camp' and *-paa.*

The Ngiyampaa speakers who taught me their language so that it could be written down for the future belong to the last generation to grow up camping about in their own country, living in their own world of words, and following, as far as it was still practicable, *mayingku ngiya,* the law of the people, 'the blacks' law'. Their camp-world was the dry, riverless country between Sandy Creek and Willandra Creek in the geographical centre of New South Wales, with Cobar the nearest town to the north and Ivanhoe to the south. The oldest amongst them were born close to the turn of the century.

Younger people of Ngiyampaa descent have all grown up speaking English as well as Ngiyampaa, or with English dominating. In the 1920s the Ngiyampaa were gathered together in the centre of their country at Kirraawara (Carowra Government Tank). In 1933 the people at Carowra were shifted by the Government to Menindee, in Paakantji country; and in 1949 those still at Menindee were shifted again to Murrin Bridge outside Lake Cargelligo, in Wiradjuri country. Relatives now live in places all over south-eastern Australia and further afield.

Though Ngiyampaa is the most widely remembered name for the language, there is another name, Wangaaypuwan (often spelt 'Wongaibon' in anthropological literature). This name is one of a set of names by which speakers of a group of languages to the west of the Great Dividing Range, for roughly its whole length in New South Wales, distinguished themselves from one another. Each of these names starts with the word for 'no' in the language concerned, followed by its suffix meaning 'with' or 'having'. For example:

Wangaay-puwan	the people who use *wangaay* for 'no'
Wayil-wan	the people who use *wayil* for 'no'
Gamil-araay	the people who use *gamil* for 'no'
Wiradjuri	the people who use *wirraay* for 'no'

These 'no-having' languages were all quite closely related to one another, and shared quite a lot of vocabulary, either with exactly the same forms having the same or similar meanings, or with the recurrent forms having systematic small differences from language to language. For instance, *pilaarr* occurs in both Ngiyampaa and Wiradjuri. In the former it is the name of the casuarina tree called 'belah' in English, in imitation of this word. In Wiradjuri it is the name of another casuarina found in Wiradjuri country. The Wiradjuri word for 'quandong' (from which the English word comes) is exactly the same as the Ngiyampaa word *kuwanhthaa*, except that it has an additional *ng* sound at the end. The same goes for the word for 'head', and a number of others.

The closest of the 'no-having' languages to Wangaaypuwan in both grammar and vocabulary is Wayilwan. Both have the word *ngiya* and the ending *-paa*, so Wayilwan too has the alternative name Ngiyampaa, though it is pronounced a little differently, which has led to some people writing it as Ngemba.

The selection of Ngiyampaa words listed below were learnt from a local group of Ngiyampaa people 'with *wangaay*' calling themselves *pilaarr-kiyalu* 'people from the belah country' east of Ivanhoe, as opposed to the *nhiilyi-kiyalu* ('people from the nelia tree country') to the west. Some grew up around Trida Station and some around Keewong Station. There are occasional vocabulary differences between these two groups. Where this is so, both Trida and Keewong words are listed.

Spelling and pronunciation

Each distinct sound in Ngiyampaa is represented by a single letter or pair of letters, as follows:

a, aa, k, i, ii, l, m, n, ng, nh, ny, p, r, rr, t, th, ty, u, uu, w, y

All Ngiyampaa words, except for a few borrowed from English, end in a vowel, or in *y*, *l*, *rr* or *n*.

NGIYAMPAA WORDLIST

1. Body parts and products

kanaa	shoulder: *Kanaanhthi tyu kiyi, kaathiingku thii winanganhi* My shoulder twitched, my sister was thinking of me
karra	phlegm
kiil	urine
kii	heart
kilkin	armpit
kuna	shit, faeces
kurraluu	liver
kuthal	fat
kuway	blood
mara	hand, finger; five; upper grindstone or handpiece

marrkun	ankle
mil	eye (*Also means* seed)
munuukaa *(Keewong)*	elbow
murruthaa	nose; beak
muwa	body hair; fur; feathers
ngalki	little finger; little toe
ngamu	breast, milk: *Ngamunhthi tyu kara, purraathu thii ngiyara* My breast is twitching, my kid's talking about me
ngantal	mouth
ngimpi	bone: *thakal ngimpi* jawbone; *pala ngimpi* skull
ngulu	face, forehead
ngunuukaa *(Trida)*	elbow
nhiinmay	penis
nhukii	throat, front of neck
nhurru	upper arm; foreleg; wing
pala	head
pana	flesh, muscle; lean meat
parraan	rib: *maku parraan* new moon
pii	forearm
pirri	chest
puntay	knee
purrpi	stomach, belly, paunch; tripe
puru	testicles
thaka	faeces, shit, esp. while still inside the body
thakal	cheek, jaw
thalay	tongue
thalparr	shoulder
tharra	thigh, lap; hindleg
thina	foot, toe
thun	tail
waangan	kidney fat, caul fat
walya	vagina
wirra	tooth
wurran	hair of the head
wurru	back of the neck, bones of the neck, nape
wutha	ear
yarray	beard, whisker
yulay	skin; peel
yulu	nail of finger or toe, claw, talon; hoof

2. Kin relationships

kaakaa	brother; cousin-brother
kaathii	sister; cousin-sister
kunii	mother
paapaa	father
purraay	child, son, daughter

3. Human classification

kuuy	white man
mayi	person, Aboriginal person
ngupaan	spouse, lover
pukaayangkaa	old person of either sex
thuurrkala	(initiated) man
tyiirr	spirit (of dead person)
waatyin	white woman
warungan	spirit (of living person)
winarr	woman
wirringan	doctor, clever person
wulman	old man
wultuman	old woman
yuungin	companion, mate

4. Language, mythology and ceremony

karrii	truth
katharay	respect for punishment
kurikuta	sky-being
kuthi	song
kuyan	shame
ngiya	word, talk; the law
ngiyampaa	word-world, language
ngiyangkaraa	story, speech, harangue
ngurra	camp, home; bed
ngurrampaa	camp-world, country
nguuya	special familiar of *wirringan mayi*, such as a mouse or possum
nhanya	persistence
purrpa	ceremony for making boys into men
puupuu	being associated with initiation ceremonies
thiitu	bundle of goods for exchange
thuwii	being that lives in caves, hairyman

tyirr	spirit of dead person
waaway	being that made the rivers, rainbow serpent
wanta	scary being (literally 'ugly')
warangun	spirit animating live person
yuwi	name

5. Human artefacts

kanay	digging stick, crowbar
katurr	windbreak
katyal	water container, bucket
kulay	net bag
kunytyi	house
mawirr	cord, string
mukirr	hunting net
muntupa	anything made of iron or steel
murra	spear
nganu	mia-mia
palkaa	boomerang
pampuu	shoe
paparr	wooden shovel with pointed handle
parrima	gun
pata	dress, skirt, clothes
patik	fence
pawaarr	skin rug
punti	club
thapil	ball for throwing games
thupu	hat
wakarr	axe
wiiyampay	headrest, pillow
yapa	track, trace, (including hand stencil on rock; all creatures and objects blown by the wind can make *yapa*)
yukaaywa	mattress

6. Food, cooking and fire

maynykiyamali	to cook, light a fire, etc., without success (literally 'fail-with fire')
munkurrmali	to break an animal's joints before cooking
muunkiyamali	to burn up

ngalan	flame, light
ngalanmali	to light (a fire, etc.)
nhama	ash
pankali	to burn something
thanpali	to cook in the ashes
wayumali	to mix, e.g. flour and water (literally 'move in circles-with hand')
wayungkali	to stir, e.g. tea (literally 'move in circles-pierce)
wii	fire, firewood, match, lighter

7. Topography

kalkaay	gilgai, waterhole
karul	stone (*Also means* money)
kuparr	raddle, ochre
mingka	burrow
mirrka	cave
munil	narrow hole, crack
ngurunhu	crabhole, swamp
paki	water's edge
punan	dust
thakun	earth, dirt, sand, ground
thirraan	rise, mound, sandhill
thirrama	hill

8. Elements

kali	water
kapataa	moon, month
kirralaa	star
kuntaa	cloud (not thundery or streaky)
kurrumin	shadow, reflection, image, picture, photograph
miyarr	wind
nganira	loom, lightness in night sky before sun or moonrise, over distant fire or town
ngawu	night, darkness
palima	sky
panturr	thunder
papilaa	fog
thakarr	cold weather; frost, ice

thalkuri	storm cloud
tharriyal	warm weather
thuni	sun; day
thuni kurunhapa	west (literally 'where the sun goes in')
thuni patharapa	east (literally 'where the sun comes out')
thuraay	streaky cloud
winytya	mud, silt
wirrangkara	hailstone
yangki	(Halley's) comet
yurru	rain

9. Mammals

kima	stick-nest rat
kirrpatya	kangaroo (grey)
kunarr	pademelon
kurakay	brush-tailed possum
kurrukun	cattle (bull, cow, steer, heifer, etc.)
kurruu	bandicoot
marrawul	marsupial mouse, common dunnart, house mouse
marrawuy	kangaroo (red)
mirri	dog
nhanikuut	goat
papilaa	native cat
parrpay	rock wallaby
pathaaypaala	bat
pikipiki	pig
pilikuut	billygoat
pilpi	bilby
puuluraam	ram
thikarrpila	porcupine, echidna
thingkaa	animal, meat, a person's 'meat' or totem
thumpa	sheep
thunpaka	mouse, perhaps *Sminthopsis crassicaudata*
wirruu	wallaby, little scrub kangaroo
wuupa	mouse, perhaps *Planigale tenuirostris* and/or *Planigale gilesi*
yarraaman	horse
yuki	dingo, wild dog
yurraapat	rabbit

10. Reptiles

kaluu	bogghi, scrub shingleback lizard
karrakila	plain country shingleback lizard
kuukaarr	tree goanna
panturr miimalmiimal	'flycatcher' skink (literally 'thunder holder')
thulii	sand goanna
thurru	venomous snake
yapaa	carpet snake

11. Birds

kapukaa	egg
kilaa	galah
kulukaaru	crop of bird, craw
maliyan	eaglehawk
miithumiithuka	miner or soldier bird
muthi	nest
ngurruy	emu
pakay	shell of egg, mussel, tortoise etc
pirrikirraparaay	redbreast
pirrumpirruu	rainbow bird
purangun	black duck
thipi	bird (emu is generally regarded as *thingkaa* rather than *thipi*)
thuthupay	honeyeater
tyirrityirri	Willie wagtail
wiyu	black jay
wungka	emu young
yuru	thrush

12. Aquatic life

kuya	fish
muumparaay	big spotted frog
pakay	shell of egg, mussel, tortoise, etc.
pintuukay	mussel
yingka	yabby

13. Insects and spiders

kamukin	mosquito
kapu	'any small creature you haven't got a name for', insect, creepy-crawly
kapul	louse
maramaraka	spider (because he's 'all hands')
murruu	grasshopper
muwampi	bag shelter moth caterpillar, 'itchy grub'
nhukuy	maggot
pankay	jumper ant
purimal	fly
purruungkaa	bull ant
thakapila	bag of bag shelter moth caterpillars
thinil	nit
thunpay	scorpion
wangkay	meat ant

14. Plants

karrpakurr	basin in fork of tree
kirraa	leaf
kurrawin	flower
kukurr	tree, stick, (object made of) wood
mali	mallee
maluman	lerp (sweet edible white scale on eucalypt leaves)
mukarr	any prickly or burry plant, as porcupine grass
ngaarrka	wait-a-while bush
ngarrkaray	leopardwood tree
nhaalya	fallen leaf litter
nhiilyi	nelia tree
nhuna	grass seed
paka	vine of wild banana
pilaarr	belah
pili	gum, pitch, resin
thiku	emu bush (important for medicine)
thirriil	cumbungi, 'bamboo'; (reed) spear
thutirr	lignum
walu	loose (strip of) bark flying

warriyarr	warrior bush, wild currant (burnt to ward off rain)
wilkarr	wilgah
yuwan	vegetable food, bread

15. Physical qualities

kama	cool
kapurr	rotten (wood)
kiityan	green, blue
kirraparaay	red, yellow
kiruu	warm
kukun	lame, crippled
kuyungan	(one's) own
maki	unripe, raw
makuu	one, single, alone
mankarr	scaly, wrinkly
marrayipiya	old
mathaa	wet, damp
mukaa	asleep
nguurraa	light (weight)
paamirr	long, tall
pangkapa	white
pankay	dry, dead (tree)
papirr	big
parraay	fast, quick
parurr	failing to grow
puka	stinking, rotten, dead
pulakarr	two: *pulakarrpu* both
puluy	black
pumpaa	short
pungku	many: *pungkupu* all
pupay	small, short
thalangay	fresh, new
thintarr	bald
thirrangkal	smart, flash
wakunpi	someone else's
waral	stiff (muscles)
wiki	ripe; cooked
wirriwal	heavy
yarrurr	slow, steady

16. Non-physical qualities

mayaal	incompetent, ignorant
pukil	pleased, happy
tharrmay	clever, knowledgeable
thukaay	really; a lot
warraay	bad
yarrmal	mischievous
yatama	good
yuuthi	too much

17. Motion

kumpikirri *(Trida)*	to swim
kupali	to chase
kurungakirri *(Keewong)*	to swim
kurungkirri	to enter, put on (clothes)
manapikirri	to go hunting
manmili	to follow
ngupungkikirri	to dive
paarangkirri	to jump, hop
parrangkirri	to fly, rise, get up
pathali	to come, come out, appear
pipuwakirri	to run, drive in a vehicle, travel
thuwakirri	to fall
wakakirri	to dance
wakapali	to run fast, flow swiftly; boil
walkakirri	to climb
wanaparakirri	to leave someone, something
yanakirri	to walk, go, move along: *Thaay yanaa!* Come here!
yapali	to track

18. State

kali	to be
kurukakirri	to be in
ngityali	to rain: *ngityangityali* to drizzle
thiirrpakirri	to know
warakirri	to stand; grow
wiikirri	to sit, sit down, stay, live: *wiimali* to marry (literally 'to make sit down')
yuwakirri	to lie: *mukaa yuwakirri* to sleep

19. Vocalisation and thought

kintakirri	to laugh
kipayali	to reply (literally 'exchange-speak')
kunuyali	to shout, talk loudly, sing out (literally 'with energy-speak')
ngiyali	to speak, say, tell
palayali	to speak in a whisper (literally 'with little energy-speak')
pinpali	to shout at, rouse on
wakaymali	to sing
walinytyali	to be lonely (for someone)
winangakirri	to think (about), remember
winangali	to hear, listen
yalamakirri	to be tired, lazy, apathetic
yungakirri	to cry

20. Bodily functions

kaapili	to vomit
karulpali	(of snakes) to rear before striking, get power to poison from the big snake in the Milky Way
kathali	to bite (literally 'break-with mouth')
kirrampili	to be sick, feel pain
manunhthali	to eat stolen food, to steal (e.g. of a dog)
ngaakanmakirri	to feel (cold, fed-up, etc.)
ngaakirri	to see: *ngaayaka thu nuu!* See you!
ngaarungkirri	to drink
ngamali	to feel (literally 'test-with hand')
ngamumali	to give birth, lay an egg
ngamungkirri	to suckle
ngathali	to taste (literally 'test-with mouth')
nhukali	to swallow
palathali	nibble (literally 'with little energy-do with mouth')
palungkirri	to die
pirrapili	to be hungry
puthakirri	to smell something
putharrpakirri	to kiss
puumpili	to blow
thali	to eat
wuruuntali	to suck out, e.g. poison (literally 'move out-with mouth')

21. Impact and violence

kamali	to break, break up, grind, grate (literally 'break-with hand')
kapili	to cut, cut off, cut out (literally 'break-away')
kathinmali	to smash (literally 'break-hit')
kipaympili	to give in return, give back, throw back (literally 'exchange-away')
kunungkali	to dig, sew, etc., hard (literally 'with energy-pierce')
kurukali	to put in
mali	to make, do
mamali	to get, catch, seize
mayngkali	to spear, sew, etc., unsuccessfully (literally 'fail-pierce')
miimali	to hold
mulanmali	to repeat, do over and over (literally 'repeatedly-do with hand')
mulanthinmali	to hit repeatedly
muthili	to hammer, pound, thrash
ngakali	to poke a hole to see what's there (literally 'test-pierce')
ngathili	to try for a foothold (literally 'test-with foot')
ngimali	to rub, paint
nhimali	to pinch
pakali	to dig
palpali	to scrabble, dig lightly
pantali	to tie: *purrpangku pantali* to initiate
pumali	to hit: *pukaku pumali* to kill
purrpali	to pluck (hair, feathers, etc.), uproot
thurri	to spear, pierce, prick (*Also means* to write)
waamali	to skin
wamali	to build
wantarrmali	to mislay
wirrityinmali	to knock down, e.g. quandongs (literally 'move down-hit')

22. Holding and transfer

kaangkirri	to carry, bring, fetch
manumali	to steal
muunpili	to give, throw, etc., all
ngaaraymali	to show
ngukirri	to give
thirrakali	to dip for water (literally 'move up-pierce')
thirramali	to lift, pick up (literally 'move up-with hand')
wanangkirri	to throw
wuruunmali	to pull out (literally 'move out with hand')

23. Location, direction and time

kakirr	back, area behind
kampirra	a day either side of the reference time, that is, yesterday or tomorrow
kurraarr	far away
kuwayu	for a long time: *kuwayupu* always
marrathal	a long time ago: *marrathalpu* as far back as possible, in the beginning (called 'dreaming' in some other languages)
milan	neighbourhood, vicinity
murru	front, way ahead; road
nhirriin	outside, edge
pawu	centre, middle
pinku	tip, point
thalan	just then, directly: *thalanpu* now
warra	right close

24. Interjections and particles

kaapu	sh!
karraapu	don't!
minya?	what? (say it again)
ngaawaa	yes
wangaay	no, not
yakarraay	ouch! take that!

25. Onomatopoeics

karrwa	crackle: *karrwapali* to go *karrwa*, to crackle; *karrwamanya* crackly
ngampurr	rumble, as approaching thunder, whirlwind
ngap	phut, sudden silence
thanthan	throb, as an infected wound
thup	note of robin redbreast
yilkirr	rustle

26. Determiners and pronouns

minyawaa...?	what...?
ngathii, -thii	me, my
ngaanhthiwaa...?	who...?
ngalii, -lii	we, us (two)
ngana	that
ngani	there
ngathu, -thu	I
ngina	this
ngini	here
ngintu, -ntu	you (singular)
nginuu, -nuu	you (object), your (singular)
ngiyani *(Trida)*	we, us (more than two)
ngiyanu *(Keewong)*	we, us (more than two)
wanhthawaa...?	which...?
wanthalawaa...?	where...?
wityuwaa...?	how...?
yaay	thus, that's it

27. Placenames

Kaliyarr	Lachlan River
Kirraawara	Carowra
Kunampityaal	Trida
Kuparr	Cobar
Paawan	Barwon River, Darling River
Yakarrarray	Keewong

Grammatical notes

A sample list of around 500 words with only English glosses to demonstrate their meanings cannot go very far towards representing a language that has been used to speak whole lifetimes of a different way of life. It is especially important to bear this in mind now that the quality of those very different lives is remembered only at a distance, and by so few.

Readers may look up all the vocabulary in the brief text that follows and so guess at some of the ways in which the grammar allows words to be used in talk.

Waaway winytyaka yananhi. Kaliyarr waawathu miyi, Paawan yanpii. Palunhila thirramaka. Kali luku nginilaa wampanha kuwayupu. Wangaay ni thirramathi kurunhi. Yapa luku nganilaa kurinya.

Waaway travelled through the mud. Waaway made the Lachlan River, the Barwon and the Darling too. Then (he) died at the hill. His water still rises at this place. He couldn't get through the hill. His tracks are there.

This is a shortened version of a story told by Eliza Kennedy, and given in full in Donaldson (1980, pp 316–17). In that book grammar is analysed in detail, and there is a full index of affix forms.

A lot of meanings that are dealt with in English by separate words are dealt with in Ngiyampaa by attaching a suffix or a whole string of suffixes to another word. For example, *-ku* in the phrase *mayingku ngiya* 'the law of the people', means 'of'. This happens most dramatically with verbs. For instance someone commented after I had driven through the night, pulling up only for a take-away hamburger, 'She ate as she was going along in the dark, poor thing!'. Her comment took the form of a one-word sentence, with the meanings which require eleven extra words in English all being tacked on to the verb 'eat':

Thal-way-ngapi-kuwa-nhi-na!

That is, piece by piece:

Eat-while going along-at night-*expression of sympathy-past*-that one.

Two other grammatical devices make for fewer separate words than in English to express certain kinds of meanings. Reduplication and the compound verb system provide analytical and generalising short cuts that relate together meanings usually indicated by different words in English. The verb *ngityali* is listed here meaning 'to rain'. The reduplicated form *ngityangityali* means 'to drizzle'. *maka* means 'other', *makamaka* means 'all sorts of', or in Aboriginal English 'different different'. All the compound verbs ending in *-kali*, glossed here as 'pierce' cover the whole range of 'piercing' actions indicated by various English verbs such as 'sew', 'dig', 'spear', etc., while their beginning parts are easiest to translate by a separate adverb or adverbial phrase.

2. Ngiyampaa

References

Donaldson, Tamsin 1980, *Ngiyambaa the language of the Wangaaybuwan*, Cambridge University Press, Cambridge

Donaldson, Tamsin 1985, 'From Speaking Ngiyampaa to speaking English' *Aboriginal History*, vol. 9, pp 126–147

Hercus, L A and Peter Sutton 1986, *This is what happened*, Australian Institute of Aboriginal Studies, Canberra

Johnson, Doreen, Eva Longmore, Eliza Kennedy, Horace King, Lena Parkes and Mamie King 1981, *Ngiyampaa Alphabet Book*, with audiocassette. Western Readers, revised edn 1985, Development and Advisory Publications of NSW, Dubbo

3

Paakantyi

LUISE HERCUS

The name 'Paakantyi' comes from the word *paaka* 'river' and literally means 'belonging to the river', the river being the Darling. People along the Darling were able to understand one another from near Bourke down to Wentworth; they also had the same social system, the same division into the two matrilineal moieties Makwara and Kilpara (see page xvi above). This basic similarity was noted long ago by Curr (1886, p. 167) who stated that

speech varies so little amongst the several tribes that some of my correspondents are under the impression that there is but one language on the Darling.

The people used to call themselves by different names according to their different groups, but they all spoke what were basically dialects of the one language. The unified name 'Paakantyi' has now become more and more prevalent among the people themselves for all the 'River' groups, and we therefore use the term in this same collective sense.

The Paakantyi language group extended over a wide area into the dry lands away from the river, as far as the Willandra to the east and a long way into South Australia to the west, to the Canegrass and further north past Olary. Although there was great similarity, there was not uniformity: although they spoke dialects of one language the people had allegiance to their own separate group. The dialects did not form a continuous chain but belonged to two main branches. The situation can be summarised by the following diagram:

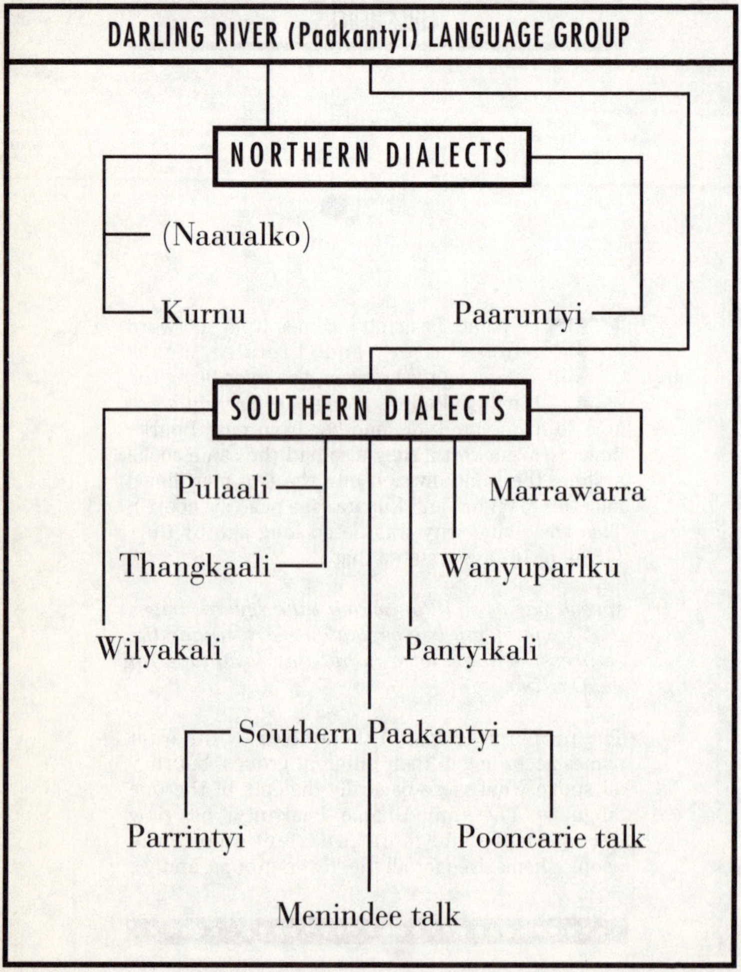

Unfortunately we have only limited knowledge of many of the dialects. For example, Naaualko (*Nhaawu-parlku*), once spoken upstream from Wilcannia, was lost very early. It was mainly the dialects belonging to areas away from the river that disappeared: we have no recordings of Thangkaali, nor of Pulaali to the west, nor of Parrintyi from the south-east, for example.

Fortunately, Tindale (1939) was able to transcribe — with brilliant accuracy — a long text and some vocabulary in Marrawarra, the language of the Wentworth area. If one knows the Pooncarie type of Paakantyi one can clearly follow every word of Tindale's transcription, provided one makes allowances for what were obviously the dialectal differences. Marrawarra became extinct in the 1940s with the death of 'Auntie Polly', who had been looked after by other Paakantyi people, especially the Lawson family. By the late fifties there was still a speaker of Wilyakali, Dougal Macfarlane, and of Paaruntyi, Mrs Quayle: they both gave information to S A Wurm. George Harrison, a speaker of Wangkumara, had some knowledge of Paaruntyi too. George Dutton was the last speaker of Pantyikali (which was apparently almost identical to Wanyuparlku) and he recorded myths and stories for Jeremy Beckett and some linguistic material for Luise Hercus shortly before his death in 1969. The remarkable Grannie Moisey, who lived to the age of 100, maintained her knowledge of Kurnu and a deep interest in traditional matters.

The present vocabulary is abridged and modified in spelling from that published in the grammar by Hercus (1982). It is confined to Southern Paakantyi, and is based on information from the late Jack 'Gunsmoke' Johnson, the late Kate Bugmy and Gertie Johnson, with much assistance from Elsie Jones. Without them this wordlist simply would not exist.

Spelling

A standard orthography has been employed for writing Paakantyi, using the following letters, which have their usual values for Australian Aboriginal language orthographies (see page xxvii above):

a, aa, i, ii, k, l, ly, m, n, ng, nh, ny, p, r, rl, rn,
rr, rt, t, th, ty, w, y

PAAKANTYI WORDLIST

WORDLIST CATEGORIES	
1. Body parts and products	15. Physical qualities
2. Kin relationships	16. Non-physical qualities
3. Human classification	17. Motion
4. Language, mythology and ceremony	18. State
5. Human artefacts	19. Vocalisation and thought
6. Food, cooking and fire	20. Bodily functions
7. Topography	21. Impact and violence
8. Elements	22. Holding and transfer
9. Mammals	23. Location, direction and time
10. Reptiles	24. Interjections and particles
11. Birds	25. Demonstratives and pronouns
12. Aquatic life	
13. Insects and spiders	
14. Plants	

1. Body parts and products

kaantarra	blood
kananya	stomach
kangarra	sweat
karraya	thigh, upper leg
karta	shoulder
kiparra	urine
kirli	ankle
kuna	faeces; bowel
kunkuku	cold, flu
kuntu	belly, 'guts'
kupu	elbow
kuukurru	ribs; body (general term)
kuuranya	muscles
maanpa	flesh
mara	hand, fingers
mara-kirli	wrist (literally 'hand-ankle')
marni	fat
marnku	lower arm
miiki	eye
mili	nail; claw
mimi	lips

minta-ulu	nose
mirri	face
mulu	lower back
munhu	upper lip
ngaka	tears
ngaltya	spit, phlegm
ngama	breast; milk
nganti	teeth
ngarli	cheek
paathingki	kidney, kidney fat
paltha	skin; bark
parnpa	neck, throat
piku	forehead; face (general term)
pirnha	bone
puna	chest
puumpa, puumpa-puumpa	back of neck
thalka	lungs, lights
tharlinya, tharlanya	tongue
tharna	back
thartu	head (*Also means* cap of eucalypt seed vessel)
thartu-parti	brain (literally 'head-egg')
thikinya	armpit
thiltya	sinew
thina	foot
waka	jaw
wangkarra	arm, upper arm near shoulder
yalka	mouth
yalku	lower leg
yuri	ears

2. Kin relationships

kaakutya	brother (elder)
kampitya	father
kany(i)tya	grandmother (maternal)
kiingkutya	nephew (sister's son, man speaking; brother's son, woman speaking)
kumpaka	wife
kuratya	grandmother of opposite moiety; old woman
marli	man, husband, male
mungkatya	aunt (father's younger sister)

ngamaka	mother; female of animal
ngarlu, ngarlutya	mother-in-law (woman speaking); father's oldest sister
nguntatya	brother-in-law
nguulka	grandfather (of opposite moiety)
parlutja	sibling (younger)
wanka	matrilineal totemic descent line (*Also means* meat)
wapanya	grandchild
wimparra	son or daughter (man or woman speaking)
wirtuka	sister (elder)

3. Human classification

katyumpaka	young woman
kuratya	old woman (literally 'grey hair having'); grandmother of opposite moiety
marli	man, male
marli-parlu	boy
marta	old man, big, large, important person, tribal elder
muni-muni, munityiri	policeman (literally 'tie up')
muurrpa, parlu	child
nhuungku	woman
puurri	ghost: 'The *puurri* is white because he fancied himself and put on kopi' (*Also means* white people)
wiimpatya, wimpatya	man (general term), person, generally used now to denote an Aboriginal as opposed to a white person

4. Language, mythology and ceremony

kupatya	kopi (white gypsum powder used for painting)
Kurlawirra	Ancestral Being of great importance, 'God' (said to have walked up into the sky at Mootwingee where his last footsteps before he went up into the sky can still be seen.)
maarni	corroboree
miki, nhiiki	name

munta	secret-sacred, forbidden
ngalpa	habit, use, custom; appearance, colour
parlku	language: *Paakantyi parlku* the Paakantyi language
thunka	cemetery, burial ground
yarnku	song, ritual song

5. Human artefacts

kalkurru	spear (with barb)
kampi	shirt, clothes
karniyala	bark dish, coolamon
karnka	yamstick
kulyi	hut, humpy
kulyparra	shade-hut, shade
kutyurru	waddy (a long throwing stick with a knob at one end)
malka	net, fishing net, stringbag
mira	bag, skin bag
nhantu	windbreak, shelter
parlka	string, fibre
pirla-pirla	net bag, dillybag, swag, belongings in general
pirra	waddy
pulthurru	boat
wakaka	tomahawk, stone-axe
wana	boomerang (a fighting boomerang of the non-returning kind)
yangku	shield
yapara	camp
yuurraka	paddle

6. Food, cooking and fire

kanya	cooking stone, stone put in the fire for griddling and for heat retention
kunika	fire, firewood
kunika-kuku	firestick
kunikalpa	fireplace, oven
mawala	coals

nganya	flame, light; name of the famous Paakantyi man from Cutheroo Station who ran away to Thangkaali country and founded the Nganya tribe
nhiki	charcoal
palpa	ashes
puntu	smoke (*Also means* train)

7. Topography

karnu	stone, rock
kiirra	country, place, ground
marnti	soil, ground
mingka	hole, deep hole in the ground, cavern
paaka	river, the Darling in particular
parla	mud, wet clay
parlara	plain, bare open area
pilthi	yellow ochre
pini	soakage: *pini nguku* soakage water
thiiri	sand
thiltakarra	lake
thumpi	deep waterhole, permanent water
yapa	track, footprint
yaparla	claypan
yuthurru	road, path

8. Elements

karkanya	sky, high up
kuntyirri	shadow, reflection
kuulyi, kuulyi-kuulyi	winter, cold season: *kuulyi-kuulyina* in the winter
kuurlurku	mirage
makarra	rain
nganinya	fog
nginta	cloud
nguku	water
paatyuka	moon, month
pinti	lightning, thunderstorm
purli	star
putharra	dust-storm
putyi-putyi	hot weather time: *putyi-putyina* in the summer

thungka	night, darkness
thuulpa	flood
yantantyi, yantinya	whirlwind
yartu	wind, gale
yuku	sun, daylight, day

9. Mammals

kaangkaru	horse (*kaangka-* means 'to ride')
karli	dog
kirpatya	black kangaroo, the western grey
kurti	bilby, rabbit-eared bandicoot
manku	mouse (*Sminthopsis* species)
muuluru	water-rat
pilta	possum
tharlta	red kangaroo
thintili, wantaali	echidna
yarrantyi	possum
yuururru	euro

10. Reptiles

kaani	lizard (borrowed into English as 'carney')
kaltu	sleepy lizard
karkumparayititya	Jacky lizard
muna	green snake
murlatya	tadpole
ngaarnurru	black goanna
ngarruka	frog, large green frog
ngatyi	water-snake, mythological rainbow serpent
paanmulu	knob-tailed gecko
parna, thaakurlu	yellow-brown goanna, Gould's goanna
pumarla-puka	turtle, 'stinking' turtle
thaangkuru	black snake
thurru	snake (general term)
wirlu-wirlu	brown snake

11. Birds

kalkara	stormbird (probably the oriental pratincole)
kalku	bald coot
kalthi	emu
karkirri	waterhen
katha-katha	Major Mitchell cockatoo
kawampa	nankeen crane
kiiku	sulphur-crested cockatoo
kiingki	white cockatoo, corella
kilampa	galah
kulthapa	duck (teal)
kuluruku, kulurharru	magpie
kunarli	wood duck
kurarli	jay, 'lousy Jack', white-winged chough
kuukakaka	kookaburra
kuukunya	dove
maltharra	feather
manparra	black duck
munityara	top-knot pigeon
murlaru	bronze-wing pigeon
ngartatya	black cormorant
paawuka	screech-owl
parti	egg of bird or insect
pilyara	eaglehawk
pulyki	feather, down, fur, hair
thiilyana	ring-necked parrot
thiirri	mudlark, the Ancestral Mudlark which created the Darling River
thirri-tyirri	Willie wagtail
thiyara	black cockatoo
thuulkika	turkey
waaku	crow
walpanya	stormbird, swallow
wanganya	nest, of bird or sticknest rat
wapuka	mopoke owl
watya	corella
wirrupa	quarrion, cockatiel
yungkuuli	black swan

12. Aquatic life

kunpali	yellow-belly
nhaampa	bony bream
parntu	Murray cod, the most important food fish in the Murray-Darling system
thilyila	perch
yamaka, yamatya	catfish

13. Insects and spiders

kaalpi-kaalpika	moth
kaanti-kuntarra	scorpion
kalkirri	bull ant
katyunya, kathunya	crayfish (cf. *kungkulu*)
kiilka	centipede
kungkulu	crayfish (*Cherax* species), differs according to Paakantyi speakers from *katyunya* in the position of the lower segments of the claw
kunti	mosquito
kutarti	maggots
kuunpu	caterpillar (hairy)
mara-maraaka	spider
munhi	green ant (known for its vicious bite)
ngutu	lice
nhaapa	edible grub (general term)
piityarla	tree grub, large witchetty grub
piinti	grasshopper
piipuru	ant, a large species of ant, also used as general term
pilyu-pilyuka	butterfly
purlarrra	fly, blowfly
thumuuli	wild honey
watarta	mussels
wiithi	shrimp
wingurru	fly (general term), ordinary bush-fly

14. Plants

kaaki	prickle, burr
kaarima	mallee
kaarima-kaarima	scrub, bush-country, mallee-scrub
kakarla	wild banana creeper (both the root, which was called *ngarnti*, and the fruit were popular food)
kalutyu	'spinach' (probably *Calandrina* species)
kamurru	river red gum
karlku	belah
karnpuka	quandong
karti	gidgee
kula	hollow tree
kulta	grass, green ground vegetation in general
kulu	butt of a tree: *kuluna* beneath a tree, at the butt of a tree
kumparla	coolabah
kurkurru	black box
kuyamarra	sandalwood (the male totemic tree)
maanta	water-weed, water-plants
marlka	mulga
mukirli	wild orange
ngartu	nardoo
paapa	grass seed, edible seed
parlkara	root
pinpa	pine tree
puuwuru	leaf
thapi	mistletoe
yarra	stick, piece of wood, timber, tree (general term)

15. Physical qualities

karlpi	clear: *karlpi nguku* clear water
karrangka	sharp, pointed
karratya	round
kathi, kathika	sour, bitter-tasting
kathuka	short
katyiluku	narrow, small, little

kukirika, kukirka	black
kumbatya	big, large
kurkanya	sweet, sweet-tasting
kurnku	wet
maki	raw, uncooked; unripe
matha	hard, dry: *matha manhu thayayika* they eat dry bread
mingku-pantatya	blind
mukutya	short, small
murlintyi	new, fresh
ngalkina, ngalkirka	red
ngitya	one
ngurni	dirty
nguungki	cooked, ripe
nhintatya	thin, skinny
nhumparka	green
nhurrani	right (as opposed to left)
paaluru	long
paatyirka	white, light coloured
parkulu	two
puka	dead, rotten, smelly
purrinya	alive, living
putyarla	sharp, pointed
thakuli	heavy
tharla	dry
tharmanya	light, not heavy
thurlaka	bad, ugly
wankaraaka	right, right-hand side
wapirlka	hot, boiling
warli	state, condition
wilka-wilka	hungry
wirtu-	old, big, important
yaki	cold, chilled
yalkutya	left, left-hand side
yalthi	straight; long, tall
yamirri	shallow: *yamirrina ngukuna wirkataapa* I shall swim in the shallow water
yarni	short
yungkaaku	alone, on one's own
yuri-nhapatya	deaf (literally 'having closed ears')

16. Non-physical qualities

kaaru	other, different
kurlika	angry, wild (with someone)
kuta	other, other people, the rest
kutanya	all, everybody
marri	true, real
matala-tya	satisfied: *matalatyaapa* I've had enough
mathirri	much, many
matya, matyitya	bold, game, daring, tame
miikika	clever: *miikika wimpatya* a clever man
mingku, mingku-mingku	mean, refusing to give food to a hungry person
ngati	wrong, against the rules
nhurrinya	hard, tough; loud
palirika, paliira	nice, good, beautiful
paltha	shame
paninya	jealous
parnti	full, complete
walpinya, walpunya	stubborn, naughty
wanpa	silly, ignorant
withulu, withunya	all, everything
yarla	own, proper, true
yungka	own, personal

17. Motion

iika-	to float
kaangka-	to ride
kaanpa-	to wade across a river
kaanya	to fall over, collapse
kala-	to look for something, search
kalya-	to run
kapa-	to follow
karpa-	to feel, grope for something
karrampara-	to dance with leg-quivering
kurta-, kurti	to touch, reach right up to
manta-	to wait, lie in wait for somebody
mari-ma-	to look after, care for
muni-, muni-muni-	to tie: *muni-munithu karlina* he is tying up his dog
ngantyi-	to leave, abandon

ngarta-	to light a fire
ngulya-	to wash: *ngulyathu kampiri* he is washing clothes
nguuwa-	to cook
nhaarta-	to catch fish, go fishing: *parri-tyaapa nhaartala* I went fishing
nhapa-	to lock up, imprison
paka-	to perform a corroboree, dance
papu-	to come out; (of the sun) to rise up
parnka-	to crawl; to creep up on someone
parra-	to run, to hurry; to travel
parri-	to go, to walk
pilka-	to run away (downwards), to go downhill, or downstream; (of the sun) to set
thalpa-	to stand or stay around: *minha-manti thalpimpa* why are you standing around?
thika-	to return, go home, come back
wampi-	to fly
wapa-, wapu-	to come, arrive, come out
winka-	to find
wirka-	to swim

18. State

(ng)iingka-	to be, sit
(ng)ima-	to rest, lie down
(ng)ipa-	to lie down, stay
pumpa-, pumpara-	to rest, sleep
tharri-	to stand upright

19. Vocalisation and thought

kanka-la-	to growl, get wild
kantha-	to run someone down, spread gossip about someone
karka-	to cry out, scream
karnpa-	to tell lies
kiinta-	to laugh
kirka-	to show, teach
kulpa-, kulpi-	to tell, talk, speak
muuya-	to have a row, abuse someone
nganyi-, ngaantya-	to ask for something, beg

nguuya-	to fear, to be frightened: *nguuya-laapa!* I am scared!
paki-	to sing
thangki-	to be pleased, be happy
waanta-	to know: *kila waantathu ngiikina* I don't know his name
wanta-	to forget: *wantaana parlku* forgetting the language
wayu-	to be sorry; to grieve over someone
yanta-	to cry out, call
yurri-(la)-, yurringka-	to listen, know, understand

20. Bodily functions

kalhika	sick
kunka-	to swallow
malma-	to die, pass away (only used for humans): *malmatyi* he died
marnta-	to vomit
miika	pain, illness: *kuntu-miika* stomach-ache; *thartu-miika* headache
miikatya	sick, ill, a sick person (literally 'having pain')
pami-	to see
pami-la-	to look at, watch
puka-la-	to die (humans and animals)
puunta-	to smell, sniff
thalti-	to hear, listen: *kila thaltila* he won't listen
thayi-	to eat
thunti-la-	to suck
thupa-	to spit
wiitya-	to drink
yarka-	to be thirsty; to perish

21. Impact and violence

malpa-	to throw something at somebody, pelt someone (with stones)
manga-	to make, build; to fix up, cure: *mangatyu wanganya* he built a nest
ngarpa-	to build, make, establish, create
palka-palka-	to beat
panta-	to strike with any pointed weapon
parta-	to sting, bite; to write

puupa-	to blow, blow a fire; to shoot with a gun
thaka-	to pierce, spear; to write
thampa-	to dig
wanti-	to burn
yaaka-	to break

22. Holding and transfer

kaanta-	to fetch
kaanti-	to take away, remove something far away, carry
kaanti-nya-	to have
kaantipa-	to send, direct
karnma-	to steal, 'shake', take away
kuuripa-	to hide (an object), conceal something
mangka-	to hide, 'plant', hide oneself
muuma-	to pick up, lift up
ngaarta-	to throw
(ng)ipi-	to put down; to lay (eggs)
nguuka-	to give
wapi-	to return, give back

23. Location, direction and time

ilaaku	yesterday
itha-mari	this way, in this direction
itharra	here
itharra-watharra	here and there
kaantinya	old; a long time; long ago: *kaantinyantu* from long ago, of old
kalypu	soon, by and by, later on
karringki	tomorrow
maawulu	slowly
malaaka	the other side, across the river, 'to the other side'
miputa	completely
murrarta	fast, quickly
ngantarra	behind, later
parityirri	far away, distant
pitya	outside, out of doors: *pityana* on the outside
thalypa	near, close by
thulu	close together, adjoining

thunturru	now, immediately
warra	side, direction
watha, wathana, wathaka, watharra	there (in the middle distance)
yaamaka, also kangaka	right here
yaamari	this way, here in this direction: *yaaamari parri!* come here!

24. Interjections and particles

-alpi	like: *parntu-alpi* like a cod
ilaakuayi	oh dear! goodness! (literally 'my yesterday')
-ili	now, immediately
kali	only
kila	not (used in both statements and prohibitions)
kinurtili	enough now! stop it!
ngaatha	no, nothing
ngarratya	together, in company
ngata	perhaps, maybe: *ngata manthaltaapa* perhaps I'll wait
ngim, ngii	yes
nhantama, nhantara	again, all over again
palya palyarta	directly; wait!
-purra	indeed (emphatic added to verbs)
-tya	having, owning
walya	not, don't
-wanki	mainly, in the first place: *ngintu-wanki wantima* you are the main one that wants something
wara	then, furthermore (linking particle)
wintya	where? which?
yarlinya	too much, a lot

25. Demonstratives and pronouns

(k)iki, (k)iiki	this, this right here
(k)inha, (k)inhi) (k)inhu	that one
(k)ithi, (k)ithu	this one quite close
minha	what?
ngali	we two
ngapa	I (subject of intransitive verb)
ngathu	I (subject of transitive verb)
ngimba	you (singular, subject of intransitive verb)

ngina	we (plural)
ngintu	you (singular, subject of transitive verb)
ngupa	you two
ngurta	you (plural)
nhananya	how? which?: *nhananya warna ngimpa* or *nhananya ngiingkimpa* how are you?
nhantharra	how many?
watha, wathu	that one further away
wintyika	who?
yuna	that (far away), there (in the distance); then

Grammatical notes

The Paakantyi language as exemplified by Southern Paakantyi has a complex grammatical system.

Nouns show the following case distinctions which are marked by suffixes added to the stem:

Case	Suffix	Example	English
Absolutive	—	*yaparra*	camp
		muurrpa	child
Ergative	*-thurru*, *-nhurru*[1]	*muurpa-thurru*	by this child
		muurpa-nhurru	by that child
Dative-Allative	*-ri*	*muurpari*	to the child
		yaparra-ri	to the camp
Instrumental-	*-na*	*muurpana*	in (or by means of) the child
Locative		*yaparrana*	in (or by means of) the camp
Ablative	*-(u)ndu*	*muurpandu*	from the child
		yaparrandu	from the camp
Purposive-Benefactive	*-mandi*	*muurrpamandi*	for the child
		yaparramandi	for the camp
Comitative	*-ambala/-umbula*[2]	*muurpa-ambala*	in company with the child

[1] These suffixes are based on case forms of demonstratives, *-thurru* referring to something close at hand, and *-nhurru* to something further away.

[2] The form *-umbula* is used with nouns ending in *-u*.

3. Paakantyi

The absolutive is used for the subject of an intransitive sentence and the object of a transitive sentence; it is also the form used in this list. The ergative is used for the subject of a transitive (but not intransitive) sentence. See page xvii in the Introduction for a full explanation of the different types of case.

In Paakantyi, possession is expressed by possessive markers which immediately follow the noun. Thus the first person singular possessive marker is *-ayi* , the second *-(u)ma*, the third *-na*, and the first person plural possessive marker is *-inana.* Using the word *kiira* 'country' as an example, one would therefore say:

kiirrayi	my country
kiirrama	your country
kiirrana	his country
kiirinana	our country

The case markers follow these possessives. Hence *kiirrayiri* means 'to my country', and *kiirrinanari* 'to our country', *yaparrayindu* means 'out of my camp' and *yaparramana* 'in your camp'.

The verbal system is complex. Subjects and objects are both added as suffixes to the verb root, and tense is shown by suffixes. The marker for the present is zero (that is, no suffix is added), the past is expressed by *-ty-* and the future by *-t-* while the first person intransitive subject marker is *-aapa* as in:

ngiingka + *aapa*
sit + I
'I sit'

ngiingka + *-ty-* + *aapa*
sit + *past* + I
'I sat'

ngiingka + *-t-* + *aapa*
sit + *future* + I
'I shall sit'

Subject and object incorporation is shown in the following examples:

watu + *-ty-* + *ika* + *(a)yi*
take away, rob + *past* + they + me
'They robbed me'

palka + *-t-* + *athu* + *uma*
hit + *future* + he, she, it + you
'He'll hit you'

References

Hercus, L A 1982, *The Bágandji language*, Pacific Linguistics, Series B, no. 67, Canberra

Tindale, N B 1939, 'Eagle and Crow Myths of the Maraura Tribe, Lower Darling River, N.S.W.', *Records of the South Australian Museum*, vol. 6, no. 3, pp 243–261

4

The Sydney Language

JAKELIN TROY

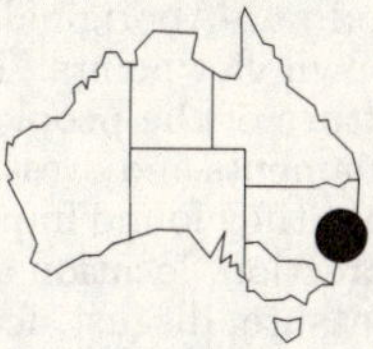

The language discussed in this chapter was spoken by Aboriginal people in the Sydney district at the time of the arrival of the First Fleet of British colonisers in Sydney Cove, Port Jackson, on 26 January, 1788. It is called here simply 'the Sydney language' because there is no record of the name given to the language by its speakers and no word recorded meaning 'language'. However, the names 'Iyora' and 'Dharug' have been used by linguists as names for the language or its coastal and inland dialects respectively. *Iyora (yura)* is the Sydney language word for 'person' and was first used in the mid-twentieth century as a language name. *Dharug* has never been given a meaning and was first used in the late nineteenth century.

Unfortunately, there are no living speakers of the Sydney language. However, many words were borrowed from the language into English by early settlers. A number of the words and placenames are still in use today and can be easily recognised in the wordlist, for example, *warada* 'waratah', *dingu* 'dingo', *wumara* 'woomera', and *baramada* 'Parramatta'. (Only a selection of placenames are given in the wordlist below.)

The wordlist contained in this chapter was reconstructed from eighteenth and nineteenth century documents which record the observations of people who had first-hand experience of the language. There is enough evidence in these sources to allow a reconstruction of the main features of the grammar of the language (see Troy 1994). This reconstruction demonstrates that it is a typical south-eastern Australian language which shares many features of grammar, vocabulary and phonology with its neighbours.

In addition to linguistic information, the sources also provide a record of some of the earliest conversations between Aboriginal people and the colonisers from England. They provide us with insights into the attempts by Aboriginal and non-Aboriginal people to understand each other and to explain their own viewpoints. The wordlist below provides an introduction to the culture of the people, their social relationships, the food they ate, their ornaments and dress, weaponry and implements and their manufacture, what they found important in the natural world, their ways of indicating direction, location and time, and some of their informal expressions of pleasure, disgust, fear or surprise.

Much information about the Aboriginal people of Sydney and their culture and lifestyle can be gained from reading accounts written by First Fleeters. Early colonial artists also produced many paintings and sketches of the people, their artefacts and way of life, the environment of Sydney and its flora and fauna. The written and pictorial descriptions, when studied together, bring to life the world of the Aboriginal people who were the first to have extended contact with the English colonisers. Recent analyses of the historical and the archaeological record provide further insight into the world of the Sydney Aboriginal people. It is not possible to provide more than brief comment here about the people. However, further information can be found in the references cited at the end of the chapter.

The Sydney people lived well on the products of the sea and shoreline. They were expert at fishing and braved the water in canoes made from sheets of bark bunched up and tied at the ends and sealed with gum. Fish were even cooked in the canoes on open fires. It is interesting that the word for a person fishing, *man*, was the same as the word for 'ghost' or 'apparition', which may be suggested by distance or night fishing by firelight. Fish, fishing and the artefacts of fishing figure prominently in the vocabulary of the Sydney language.

A plague with symptoms similar to smallpox devastated the Aboriginal population in 1789, killing large numbers of people and leaving the survivors weakened physically and emotionally. Subsequently, many Aboriginal people became permanent residents in and around the settlement, increasingly dependent on help from the colonists. The food and goods of the colonists were an attraction to the Aboriginal people and they coined new words in their language to describe some items, including *dalangyila* 'window', *nangyila* 'telescope' and *nanangyila* 'reading glass'.

The traditional cultural and social life of the Sydney people perpetuated itself within the settlement until the early 1800s and the people became very familiar with the colonists.

> the natives were become very familiar and intimate with every person in the settlement; many of them now took up their rest every night in some of the gentlemen's houses (Hunter 1968, p. 143)

They were often seen staging corroborees and physical contests in the open spaces reserved as common ground for use by all the colonists in Sydney. Aboriginal people also entered into the commerce of life in the colony by bartering fish for bread, rice, vegetables and salt meat (Phillip 1968, p. 352; Collins 1975, vol. 1, p. 137).

Study of the Sydney language was a popular pastime with the literate First Fleet officers and it is to them that we owe most of our knowledge of the language. Very few studies of the language exist from the nineteenth century, and by the twentieth century what little research was being undertaken was based entirely on nineteenth and eighteenth century records. The group of languages to which the Sydney language belongs is called Yuin-Kuric by linguists. It is now functionally extinct and our knowledge of the languages is based entirely on documents made by people who had an early interest in Aboriginal languages.

Spelling

The vocabulary in the wordlist below has been written using an orthography devised to overcome the problems of great variation in the sources used to reconstruct the language (for further comment and discussion of the orthography see Troy 1994). This orthography uses the following letters:

a, b/p, d/t, dj/dy/tj, g/k, i, k, l, ly, m, n, ng, nh, ny, r, rr, w, y

THE SYDNEY LANGUAGE WORDLIST

WORDLIST CATEGORIES

1. Body parts and products
2. Kin relationships
3. Human classification
4. Language, mythology and ceremony
5. Human artefacts
6. Food, cooking and fire
7. Topography
8. Elements
9. Mammals
10. Reptiles
11. Birds
12. Aquatic life
13. Insects and spiders
14. Plants
15. Physical qualities
16. Non-physical qualities
17. Motion
18. State
19. Vocalisation and thought
20. Bodily functions
21. Impact and violence
22. Holding and transfer
23. Location, direction and time
24. Interjections
25. Demonstratives and pronouns
26. Placenames

1. Body parts and products

banarang	blood
barangal	throat
barrang	belly
barrangal	skin
biba	rib
budbut	heart
bugai	fat (human)
bunang, guruk	knee
bung	buttocks
bura	testicles
dalang	tongue
damara	hand
dara	tooth
darra	leg, thigh
djarrung	shoulder
djiwarra	hair
dyara	bone
gabara	head
gadlyang	nape, neck
gadya	penis
galgala	smallpox-like disease
garaga	mouth

garungan	fingernail
gidigidi	armpit
gumirri	vagina
gunat	hair matted with gum
guni	faeces, shit
guri	ear
mai	eye
manuwi	foot
marbal	chest
midyung	sore
nabang	breast
naga	liver
ngulun	forehead
nuga	nose
una	elbow
walu	shin
wiling	lips
yarring	beard
yilabil	urine, piss

2. Kin relationships

babana	brother
biyanga	father
damali	namesake
djambing	sister-in-law
djurumin	sister
durung	son
duruninang	daughter
dyinmang	wife
gabami	intermediary in disputes
gamarada	friend, comrade
gulang	widow while in mourning
guman	grandfather
guwalgalyung	elder sister
guwalgang	elder brother
mubi	mourner at a funeral
mugung	lover
mugungalyi	marital partner
mulamang	husband
ngalaiya	ally
ngaramada	younger brother
ngarangalyung	younger sister
wiyanga	mother

3. Human classification

dyin	woman
dyinuragang	old woman
gaiyanaiyung	old man
gaiyara	name
garadyigan	doctor
guragalung	young man
guragalungalyung	young woman
gurung	child, baby
maiyal	stranger
man	fisherwoman (*Also means* ghost)
mani	fisherman
mula	man
waruwi	girl
wawura	rascal
wiring	female
wungarra	boy
yura	person

4. Language, mythology and ceremony

biyani	curative operation performed by women to cure illness in other women
buduwai	ritual for preventing children from becoming thieves by scorching their fingers
djanaba	laughter
garabara	a dance
malgun	woman with two joints of the little finger on her left hand removed ritually
man	ghost (*Also means* fisherwoman)
nanga mai	dream
nanung	piercing of the nasal septum to receive a bone or reed decoration
yabun	music made by singing and beating time
yalabi daiyalung	bora ceremony
yulang yirabadjang	tooth extraction initiation ceremony for young men

5. Human artefacts

aragung	shield for war (large and solid)
bangada	ornaments
bangala	water-carrying vessel made from bark tied at each end
barra	fishhook
barrin	apron-style covering worn by unmarried girls made from spun possum hair tied in cords from a possum-hair belt
budbili	possum rug
bumarit, wumarang, bumarang	boomerang for fighting
damang	cap
darral	feather ornament for the head
duwal	spear (short, with two barbs)
galarra	fish harpoon (5–7 m long, with four barbs)
gamai	spear (general name)
garradjun	fishing line made from bark
gulima	basket made from the knot of a tree
gunang	spear for hand-to-hand combat
guni	yamstick
gunya	dwelling made by people
guwariya	fish harpoon for children
muding	fish harpoon (small)
mugu	stone hatchet
narawang	paddle, oar
ngalangala	club with a mushroom-shaped head
ngamul	sinker for a fishing line made from a small stone
ngurra	camp
nuwi	canoe
wigun	spear thrower made from heavy wood with one end rounded to be used as a digging stick
wuda, wudi	club shaped from a long piece of wood thicker at one end
wumara	spear thrower about one metre long, with a shell scraper at one end made from a *gadyan* (Sydney cockle)
yalga	barb of a spear
yilimung	shield for parrying

6. Food, cooking and fire

djarraba	firestick; gun
gadjal	smoke
ganalang, yuruga	heat
garuma	blubber
gili	flame, light
guwiyang	fire
ngarrun	fat of meat
nggununy, badalya	food

7. Topography

bulga	hill
buruwang	island
dyiral	shoal water
ganing	cave
garagula	ebb tide
garrigarrang	sea
gumirri	hole
guru	deep water
marrang	sand, beach
muru	road, path
nura	country, place

8. Elements

badu	water
bamal	earth
barabung, minyimulung	dew
baragula	flood tide
birrung	star
buduwangung	Magellanic Clouds
burra, garrayura	sky
danagal	ice
duruga	falling star
garaguru	cloud
giba	stone
gura	wind
gurbuny	fog
guwara	high wind
guwing	sun
marri yanada	full moon
mungi	lightning

murungal	thunder
walan, bana	rain
warriwul	Milky Way
yanada	moon

9. Mammals

badagarang	eastern grey kangaroo
banggarai	swamp wallaby
buduru	potoroo
bugul, wurra	mouse, rat
bungu	flying phalanger
burumin	possum
dingu	dingo
djubi	sugar glider
dun	tail
ganimung	Gaimard's rat-kangaroo
marriyagang	tiger cat
mirrin	brown marsupial mouse
wanyuwa	horse
wirambi	bat
wiring	female animals
wubin	feather-tail or pygmy glider
wulaba	rock wallaby
wularu	wallaroo
wumbat	wombat

10. Reptiles

bayagin	leaf-tailed gecko
daning	death adder
gan	reptiles (snake, goanna or lizard)
malya	diamond python
ngarrang	bearded dragon
wirragadara	bandy-bandy

11. Birds

binit	tawny frogmouth
binyang	bird
bubuk	boobook owl
buming	redbill
bunda	hawk
bunyarinarin	masked lapwing

burumurring	wedge-tailed eagle
djamuldjamul	whistling kite
dyaramak	sacred kingfisher
dyuralya	brolga
gaban	egg
garadi	glossy black cockatoo
garrangabumarri	pelican
garrawi	sulphur-crested cockatoo
girra-girra	seagull
gugurruk	black-shouldered kite
gulina	rufous night heron
gulungaga	red-browed finch
guma	king parrot
guriyal	parrot, parrakeet (general term)
guwali	shag, cormorant
marrigang	sittella
mulgu	black swan
munu	bill
murradjulbi	singing bushlark
muruduwin	fairy wren
ngunyul	feather
ngurra	birds' nest
nuwalgang	magpie goose
urwinarriwing	eastern curlew
wangawang	ground parrot
wilbing	wing
wirgan	noisy friarbird
wugan	crow
wungawunga	wonga pigeon

12. Aquatic life

badangi	Sydney rock oyster
baludarri	leather-jacket
barung	yellowtail kingfish
baruwaluwu	dolphin
burra	eel
dainya	mud oyster
dalgal	mussel
daringyan	stingray
gadyan	Sydney cockle
gaguni	toadfish

garuma	black bream
gawura	whale
ginari	shovel-nosed ray
guruwin	grey nurse shark
magura	fish
marumara	zebra fish
walamai	snapper
walumil	Port Jackson shark
waragal	mackerel
yara	crab

13. Insects and spiders

babunang	black ant
burudyara	butterfly
djuni	scorpion
dyulibang	maggot
dyura	mosquito
gilbanung	grasshopper
gunalung	caterpillar
gunyagunya	beetle
malagadang	body louse
miyanung	fly
muna	louse, flea
mung	ant

14. Plants

bugi	bark
burumarri	brown gum
buruwan	rock lily
daguba	creek or brush cherry
damun	Port Jackson fig
daranggara	cabbage tree
diramu	tree
djirang	leaf
djuraduralang	bark used to make fishing lines
gadigalbudyari	Christmas bell
galun	grasstree stem
ganugan	vegetable (edible)
gulgadya	grasstree
gurgi	bracken fern root
midiny	yam

midjuburi	lilly pilly
ngalangala	mushroom
wadanggari	banksia
wadi	wood
wagaldarra	great dendrobium
waraburra	false sarsaparilla
warada	waratah
yagali	grasstree seed head

15. Physical qualities

badjal	sick
bali	thirsty
barrabarri	empty
binya	pregnant
bula	two
bulgaga	green
burara	dry
buruk	full
buruwi	three
daidyai	painful
didyiriguru	enough
dugara	cold (weather)
dugarang	straight
durumi	left
dyarrbi	short
dyirra	white
gadalung	hot
gangat	bald
ganunigang	old
garungal	hard
garungarung	pretty
gudjibi	decayed, rotten
gunai	burnt
gungun	dead
gunimarra	rotten, stink
gurara	long, tall
guwidbanga	itchy
madyung	torn
malung	dark
marana	first
marrai	wet

marri	many, great, large; very
mudai	soft
mudjil	red
mudung	alive
ngana	black
ngarang	small, little; younger or junior
wugul	one
yanbat	tired
yarragal	yellow
yuru	hungry

16. Non-physical qualities

baragat	afraid, frightened
djirun	coward
guirgurang	glad
gulara	angry, cross, displeased, ill-natured
madung	brave
mangi, malarra	married
marama	bored
marri	big, great; very
wiri	bad, wrong, malignant, pernicious
wurabada	anger
wural	bashful, ashamed

17. Motion

bangga-	to paddle or row
bugi-	to swim, dive, bathe
bunga-	to make or do
bunya-	to kiss
dyargali-	to scratch
gaba-	to dip for water
galuwa	to climb
ganga-	to wash
guma-	to dig
man-	to find
narri-, warrawi-	to stand
ngalawa-	to sit, lie, remain, live
ngalbunga-	to go
ngarra-	to tie
walama-	to return
wumara-	to run; fly
yana-	to walk
yini-	to fall

18. State

buyi-	to die
dyarrba	to tire
dyirun	to fear

19. Vocalisation and thought

baiya-, djiadi-	to speak
baraya-	to sing
bilya-	to laugh
dunga-	to cry
gama-	to call
guwanyi	to tell
wanya-	to lie
wingara-	to think
wumi	to scold
wurgya-	to whistle

20. Bodily functions

bada-	to eat
buyi-	to die
daba-	to yawn
djanga-	to chew
dula-	to bite
gani-	to smell it
garri-	to cough
naa-	to see
nanga-	to sleep; asleep
ngaina-	to breathe
ngara-	to hear or listen
wida-	to drink or suck

21. Impact and violence

baiyi-	to kill, strike, hit, beat
djura-	to spear
galabidya-	to cut
gana-	to burn
ginyi-	to crack between the nails, as a flea
gudba-	to break
yiri-	to throw

22. Holding and transfer

barrbagi-, wuri-	to lose
garama-	to steal
mana-	to get, take, gather, fetch, collect
ngairi-	to carry
nguwiya-	to give
wiyana-	to put down
wuna-	to throw away

23. Location, direction and time

barani	yesterday
barawul	far (a long distance)
barrabugu	tomorrow
baruwa	near
burawa	above, upwards
duriyumi	left
gamarruwa	day
guwagu	presently
inyun, gadi	down, below
ngairaigal	soon
ngarrawan, warawara	far, distant
nguwing	night
nung	now
warrangi	right

24. Interjections

biyal	no, not, do not
didyai didyai	you hurt me!
gamungali	term of affection used by girls
gugugu gugugu gugugu!	stop! leave me alone! away! no no!
gunin bada	shit-eater! (a favourite term of reproach)
guribuni	no ears! (said to a person not answering a call)
guwi!	come here!
jiriyai!	a warcry
minyin?	what?
murama, ii	yes
umun!	sh!
wari wari!	stop, stop!

wawu?	where?
wuru wuru!	go away! (an exclamation of defiance)
yanu!	I go!
yuwin	indeed!

25. Demonstratives and pronouns

dali	this (nearest)
dyi	here
iniya	there
mungan	that
ngala	we (dual)
ngana	who?
ngaya	I, me
ngindu	you (plural)
ngyina	we (plural)
ngyini	you (singular)

26. Placenames

Banarung	Rose Bay
Baramada	Parramatta (formerly Rose Hill)
Barrawari	Inner South Head
Bayinguwa	Garden Island
Buridyawugali	Breakfast Point
Daliyungi	Bradley Point
Daralbi	South Head
Daruwiya	Sydney Cove (west point)
Dubuwagali	Sydney Cove (east point)
Gabagaba	Middle Head
Gamai	Botany Bay
Garangal	North Head
Gayimai	Manly Bay
Gayumai	Collins Cove
Gumura	Long Cove
Madala	Camp Cove (west point)
Wann	Parramatta district
Wariyama	Cockatoo Island
Warran	Sydney Cove
Wuganmagali	Farm Cove
Yira yirara	Farm Cove (east bank)

References

Anon 1790–91, Vocabulary of the language of N.S.Wales, in the neighbourhood of Sydney. (Native and English, but not alphabetical), manuscript, Marsden Collection, School of Oriental and African Studies, London

Capell, Arthur 1970, 'Aboriginal languages in the south central coast, New South Wales: fresh discoveries', *Oceania*, vol. 41, pp 20–27

Collins, David 1975 [1798], *An account of the English colony in New South Wales with remarks on the dispositions, customs, manners, etc., of the native inhabitants of that country*, (2 vols) A H & W Reed, Sydney

Dawes, William 1790, Grammatical forms of the language of N.S. Wales, in the neighbourhood of Sydney, by — Dawes, in the year 1790, manuscript, Marsden Collection, School of Oriental and African Studies, London

Dawes, William 1790–91, Vocabulary of the language of N.S. Wales, in the neighbourhood of Sydney. (Native and English), by Dawes, manuscript, Marsden Collection, School of Oriental and African Studies, London

Hunter, John 1968 [1793], *An historical journal of events at Sydney and at sea 1787–1792, by Captain John Hunter, Commander H.M.S. Sirius; with further accounts by Governor Arthur Phillip, Lieutenant P.G. King and Lieutenant H.L. Ball*, Angus and Robertson, Sydney

King, Philip Gidley, Journal, in Hunter 1968, pp 196–298

Mathews, R H 1903, 'The Dharruk language' *Journal and proceedings of the Royal Society of New South Wales*, vol. 35, pp 155–160

Osmond, Meredith 1989, A reconstruction of the phonology, morphology, and syntax of the Sydney language as recorded in the notebooks of William Dawes, unpublished manuscript, Department of Linguistics, Australian National University, Canberra

Phillip, Arthur, Journal, in Hunter 1968, pp 299–375

Ridley, William and John Rowley 1875, 'Language of George's River, Cowpasture, and Appin', in Ridley 1875, pp 103–108

Ridley, William 1875, *Kimilaroi, and other Australian languages, second edition, revised and enlarged by the author, with comparative tables of words from twenty Australian languages, and songs, traditions, laws and customs of the Australian race*, Thomas Richards, Sydney

Tench, Watkin 1979, *Sydney's first four years. A narrative of the expedition to Botany Bay, and a complete account of the settlement at Port Jackson 1788–1791*, Library of Australian History, Sydney

4. The Sydney Language

Troy, Jakelin 1990, 'Australian Aboriginal contact with the English language in New South Wales: 1788–1845', *Pacific Linguistics* B-103

Troy, Jakelin 1994, *The Sydney language*, Jakelin Troy, Canberra

5

Wiradjuri

SALLY McNICOL and DIANNE HOSKING

Wiradjuri was one of the largest language groupings in New South Wales, being spoken over much of the central southern region of the state. Wiradjuri country (*nguurrambang*) appears to have included some of the larger river systems of New South Wales: the Murray, the Murrumbidgee, the Lachlan and the Macquarie. The Wiradjuri language is closely related to Ngiyampaa, which is spoken in the region west of Wiradjuri country; it is less closely related to Gamilaraay, spoken to the north-east.

The names of these languages are derived from their separate words for 'no', combined with the comitative suffix (meaning 'with' or 'having'). For instance the name Gamilaraay is composed of *gamil* 'no' and *-araay* 'having' (Austin 1993, p. 3). For a discussion of the meaning of the language name Ngiyampaa see the chapter by Donaldson in this volume. So, for Wiradjuri, *wirraay* means 'no' or 'not', and the comitative suffix is *-dhuurray* (northern dialect) or *-juurray* (southern) meaning 'having'. The Wiradjuri are the people who have *wirraay* for 'no'.

Over 60 different spellings of the language name have been recorded in the past 150 years, including Wiradjuri, Wiradhuri, Waradgeri, Wooragurie, Wirrathuri, Wiraiari. It is likely that there were at least two dialects of the Wiradjuri language — roughly speaking, the northern and southern. As mentioned above, the northern dialect used *-dhuurray* for the comitative suffix ('having, with'), while *-juurray* was used in the south. Although a standardised spelling system has been developed and adopted in this volume for Wiradjuri words in general, the spelling of the language name itself, *Wiradjuri* , has general acceptance and therefore has been maintained.

The Wiradjuri people's first contact with Europeans was in 1813, when the Blue Mountains were first crossed by the new settlers. Being the nearest people on the western side of the mountains meant that the Wiradjuri were in constant contact with white people from that time. By the 1890s few Wiradjuri were living independently from white inhabitants, which posed an ever increasing threat to their culture and language.

Due to the opening up of the area for farming and gold prospecting, less and less land was accessible for the Wiradjuri to live on and more and more cultural practices were lost. The language fell into decline so that by the early 1900s the children were no longer learning Wiradjuri as their first language. This means that it was the parents of today's oldest people who were the last of the Wiradjuri to speak their language fluently. However, this is not to say that Wiradjuri is dead. Many Wiradjuri people today know vocabulary from their language and use it in everyday speech. Even some English words they use express unique Wiradjuri concepts, so that an English speaker might understand what is said, but not necessarily the nuance of the utterance.

About the wordlist

The wordlist below is a small sample of the list of approximately 4000 words which ultimately we will be able to reproduce. Words from historical sources which were included in this work were, with one or two exceptions, those for which we had at least two sources (and preferably more).

In some cases a word is spelt in more than one way. The different spellings represent variant pronunciations. We have offered the alternatives because we are not able, in all cases, to say what the original word was like. Often a word has undergone a sound change and the reconstructed word differs slightly from the way it is spoken today.

Sometimes there are alternative words offered for the same English gloss. This may reflect a dialect difference. Alternatively, the words may have meant something slightly different, but the distinction was not noted by the early recorders of the language and unfortunately now the subtle differences have been lost. Another explanation might be that a word with the same or similar meaning was borrowed from another dialect or language.

The early collectors may have believed that a word they were told was the generic word for all 'kangaroos', 'rocks' or 'wood', whereas they may well have been told the words specifically for, say, 'grey kangaroo', 'stone suitable for flaking' (there are many words for kinds of stone in Australian languages) or 'firewood' as opposed to 'wood for artefact making'.

For all animals, plants and other things in the natural and man-made world there would have been words to talk about everything which people needed to talk about. A word would have existed for every species of creature in the Wiradjuri area and for each specific natural feature.

When talking about children, for instance, there were probably several names for babies in various stages of growth, for example, 'new-born', 'not yet weaned', 'not yet crawling', 'crawling', 'toddler' and so on, and for children in varying stages of development and similarly for teenagers and adults, just as in English. In the case of body parts, body products and functions, it is likely that the alternative words are euphemisms as in languages the world over. It would not be surprising to find that there were several words for, say, the genitals of each gender.

Some things translate easily from one language to another (although linguists usually argue that it is not possible to ever translate precisely). There are many concepts, however, which are very difficult to translate between languages. A good example is the Wiradjuri word *dhalaay* or *dhalay* . It is variously said to mean 'angry', 'sad', 'sorry', 'sudden excitement', 'passion', and 'shame'. There are a couple of possible explanations for these different meanings. We could infer that some people did not know the 'real' meaning of the word or that the same word has unique meanings in different regional dialects. What we believe to be the case, however, is that *dhalaay* is a very complex concept (as emotions tend to be in all languages) and it does not correspond to any one emotion that we can name for English. It is very likely that it is an emotion which all humans feel in certain situations, the difference is that the Wiradjuri language allows its speakers to express the complex emotion they are experiencing as 'feeling *dhalaay*'.

Verbs

Verbs in the wordlist are presented in the infinitive form. As in English, Wiradjuri verbs are mainly used in their inflected forms. The following are some examples of Wiradjuri verbs with their infinitives and inflected forms listed:

gindhaay to laugh (*gindhanha* laughing; *gindhanhi* laughed; *gindhagirri* will laugh)

baluung to die (*baluuna* dying; *baluu, baluuni* dead, has died; *baluunggirri* will die) buudaay to smell (*buudanha* smelling; *buudadha* smell!; *buudanhi* smelt; *buudagirri* will smell)

buumal to hit, strike, beat (*buumarra* hitting; *buumaay* has hit, struck; *buumala* hit!; *buumalgirri* will hit)

wangal to dig (*wangarra, wangali* digging; *wangaay* dug; *wangala* dig!; *wangalgirri* will dig)

Spelling and pronunciation

The following letters are used in writing Wiradjuri:

a, aa, aay, ay, b, dh, ee, g, i, j, l, m, ng, nh, ny, oo, rr, uu, w, y, yn

There is an explanation of the pronunciation of many of these letters on page xxvii of the Introduction, but there are one or two that require attention here.

The sequence *aay* is pronounced like the English word 'eye', *uu* is like the sound in 'book' or 'put', and *oo* is like that in 'mood' or 'spoon'. *ny* is similar to the sound in the middle of the English words 'onion' and 'canyon'. However, when this sound occurs at the end of a word, it is written *yn* in order to avoid confusion caused by English spelling conventions which might lead people to want to pronounce this *ny* sound as in English 'many'.

WIRADJURI WORDLIST

WORDLIST CATEGORIES

1. Body parts and products
2. Kin relationships
3. Human classification
4. Language, mythology and ceremony
5. Human artefacts
6. Food, cooking and fire
7. Topography
8. Elements
9. Mammals
10. Reptiles
11. Birds
12. Aquatic life
13. Insects and spiders
14. Plants
15. Physical qualities
16. Non-physical qualities
17. Motion
18. State
19. Vocalisation and thought
20. Bodily functions
21. Impact and violence
22. Holding and transfer
23. Location, direction and time
24. Interjections and interrogatives
25. Demonstratives and pronouns
26. Placenames

1. Body parts and products

balang	head
binij	vagina
binji	stomach
birra	back (*Also means* tired)
birring	chest
buubuul	buttocks, anus
buulbeenj	pregnant (probably from *buurbiyn* 'belly')
buunggayn, buunggang	knee
buunjalang, buunggalang	testicles (see *garra, buurruu*)
buurray	fart (compare *buurraay* 'baby, child, boy') (see *nyirrij*)
buurrbiyn	stomach, belly; abdomen; intestines
buurruu	testicles (see *buunjalang, garra*)
dhabal	bone
dhalayn	tongue
dharrang	thigh
dharrarr	ribs
dhuula	anus, backside
dhuuluubi	bone marrow
dhuumba	saliva, spittle (see *giyalang*)
dhuun	penis (*Also means* tail of an animal) (see *gabeeyn*)
dhuun-dhuung	female genitalia or reproductive organ, exact reference unclear (appears to be a reduplication of *dhuun* 'penis')
gabeeyn, gabeenj	penis (see *dhuun*)
gabuuga, balang gabuuga	brain (*Also means* egg)
gadhaay	throat
gana	shoulder
ganang	liver (see *guurraluung*)
garra	testicles (see *buunjalang, buurruu*)
geel	urine, piss
geen	heart
gijang	hair of head; animal hair; wool
gilgeen	armpit; hair under the arm (*Also means* the fins of fish)
giyalang	saliva, spittle
guunang, guunuung	faeces, shit

guurraay	fat, possibly kidney fat (see *wamuu*)
guurraluung	liver (see *ganang*)
guuwanbila	menstruation
guuwayn	blood
jinang, dhinang	foot
jirri, dhirri	grey hair
marra	hand (*Also means* to do or make)
marrin	body
mil	eye
muula	sore, ulcer, boil
muulang	vomit
muuluudin	moustache
muurruudha, muurruu	nose
ngamuung	breast; breast milk; milk
ngayn	mouth
nguuluung	forehead
nguuna	elbow
nhan	nape of neck
nyaandi	menstruation (euphemistic — *nyaandi* means 'thingummyjig' or 'what's its name') (see *guuwanbila*)
nyili	snot (see *nyuugam*)
nyirrij	fart (probably a Cowra word) (see *buurray*)
nyuugam	snot (see *nyili*)
wamuu	fat, grease, fat person
wuudha	ear
wuurranbaay	very hairy
wuurrang	hair of head
wuurruu	neck
yarrayn, yarrang	beard; hair on head; chin
yirang	tooth
yuulayn	skin
yuuluu	fingernail

2. Kin relationships

baadhin, baayjin	grandmother
babeen	father
gaagang	older brother
galmayn, galbuumayn	younger brother
guuni	mother
minggan	older sister
muugan	sister
ngamuurr	daughter
nguuban	husband; wife; spouse
wuurruumayn	son

3. Human classification

balaan	woman; aunt; white woman
baluubuunildaayn	murderer (The verb 'to murder' is *baluubuunil*, and *-daayn* is a suffix which corresponds to the '-er' in English, changing a verb into the person who does the action, such as 'singer' from 'sing'.)
barramaldaayn	policeman (literally 'one who grabs (people)')
bijaa, bijarr	man; boss; old man
buudhang	Aboriginal person, Koori (*Also means* the colour black)
buurraay	baby, child
gabaa, gaba	white man (possibly an English loan word from 'governor')
ganjan, ganjang, ganyan	policeman (probably from the English word 'constable')
geeyn, geenj	pervert (extended from the meaning 'to stare')
gibirr	man; mankind; outsider
gibirrgang	young boy (uninitiated)
guudha	child
guudhingan	composer of songs
guuwiyn	white man (In the NSW south coast languages of Dharawal and Dhurga, *guuwiyn* means 'ghost', which is what white men were initially thought to be. It has also been recorded as meaning 'he', probably referring to outsiders, 'someone else who is not one of us'.)

inarr	woman (*inarr* was probably *yinarr* originally, but by 1838 Wiradjuri seems to have dropped *y* before *i* and *w* before *u* in most cases.)
inarrgang	girl
jirribang, dhirribang	old man (from *jirri* or *dhirri* grey hair)
marragirr	widower
marraguunggang	widow
marrambang	friend (*Also means* very good)
mayn	Koori person (probably refers only to Wiradjuri people in the same manner in which other groups refer to themselves as *nungga, yolngu, murri, nyungar* and so on. Despite this word's resemblance to the English word 'man' it is a Wiradjuri word and not a loan word.)
migay	girl, woman, marriageable young woman
migay-gang	young woman (unmarried)
muuj, muuji	friend
ngaarrabang	poor thing, poor fellow
waajin, waayjin	white woman (from English 'white gin')
walwee	young man
wanggaay	baby, child
yaambuuldaayn	liar, teller of yarns

4. Language, mythology and ceremony

bageeyn, bageenj	clever man, doctor (*Also means* ghost; magic)
birik	ghost, spirit, floating ghost comes out of the mist at you (from English 'spirit')
buurrbang	ground and ceremony for making boys into men
guudhi, guuji	song (style unknown)
mirriyuula	ghost dog with a clever man's head, which comes when the curlew calls him
nguurrambang	country, home, place of birth

wandang	ghost, spirit, a bad spirit (a mythological being said to cause illness) (*Also means* ugly man)
Wirraayjuurraay	Wiradjuri (the name of the language, derived from *wirraay* 'no, not' and *-juurray* 'with, having'. The Wiradjuri are the people who have or use the word *wirraay* for 'no')
yuuwiyn	name

5. Human artefacts

badhang, bajang, bajan	clothes (*Also means* kangaroo hide; blanket)
bagaay	spoon made from shell
barrgan, balgaang	boomerang
biyaga	tobacco (*biyaga* is probably a direct loan from English 'tobacco') (see *gadhal*)
buundha	cigarette (from *buundhuu* 'smoke')
bundhi	club
dhambaang	hat
dhawiyn	axe
dhuubuu, dhuuba	hat, net cap
dhuuluu	spear (*Also means* straight)
gadhal	tobacco (*Also means* smoke) (see *biyaga*)
ganaay	yamstick
girri-girri	red wine (*Also means* the colour red)
guulaay	net bag; fishing net (see *narrbang*)
guunji	house, hut
mareeyn	canoe (*Also means* coolamon) (see *warrgang*)
marrgaa	shield
narrbang	dillybag; fishing net (see *guulang*)
nguurrang	camp (*Also means* nest)
walang	money (*Also means* stone)
wamarr	spear thrower, woomera
warrgang	canoe
weejali	alcohol
wuugi-galiyn	whiskey (literally 'hot-water')

6. Food, cooking and fire

buunan	ashes, dust
buundhuu	smoke, rising vapour, dust
dhaaguun	ashes (*Also means* earth; soil)
dhangang, dhangaan	food, bread (originally 'bread made from seeds')
dhiyn, jiyn dhinggaa	meat, flesh (see *ngali*)
gadhal	smoke (*Also means* tobacco)
geewal	cook, to cook: *geewali* 'cooked', *geewarra* 'cooking'
ngalan	flame, light
ngali	meat, flesh (some animals are called *ngali*, probably signifying that they are edible) (see *dhiyn*)
weeyn	fire, flame
wigay	bread, vegetable

7. Topography

bila	river
bilabang	billabong
dhaaguun	earth, soil (*Also means* ashes)
dharrang	creek
dhirrayn, jirrayn	mountain, hill
galiyn, galing	water
garraay	sand, sandhill
gawal	swamp
guubarr	red ochre
guunang-guunang	yellow ochre (see faeces)
guunigal	plain, level ground
mirruul	white clay
muurrang	mud
muurruu	path, road (see *yabang*)
walang	stone (*Also means* money)
yabang	path, track (see *muurruu*)

8. Elements

birrang	horizon (*Also means* far)
galimbang	rainy weather
galiyn, galing	rain; water (see *yuubal, yuurruung*)
girralang	star (see *mima*)
girralang buundinya	falling or shooting star

girrarr	wind
giwang	moon
guunama	snow; hailstones
guunanggalang	sky
guurraman	shadow
guuwang, gwang	mist
maarruu	lightning
maarruu-muuna	sheet lightning
migee	a bolt of lightning
mima	star (see *girralang*)
muurruubarraay	thunder
nguurruung	night
yirri, yirra	sun (*Also means* face)
yuubal	to rain
yuuluubirrgiyn	rainbow
yuurruung	cloud and rain

9. Mammals

balbuu	kangaroo rat
bandharr	kangaroo (species unknown)
barrandhang	koala
barrbaay	rock wallaby
buudharruung	flying fox
dhuun	tail (*Also means* penis)
ganuurr	kangaroo species unknown
ganyi	echidna, porcupine (possibly southern dialect)
gindaayn	ringtail possum
guulang	wombat (see *wambad*)
mabi	native cat
mirri, mirrigan, mirrigaa	dog
ngali	meat, flesh; used when referring to a specific animal to signify that it is edible
ngarradan	bat
walarroo	black wallaroo
wambad	wombat (see *guulang*) (*wambad* is a loan from the Sydney language Dharug)
wambuuwayn	kangaroo, probably the large grey kangaroo (see placenames)
wandiyali	echidna, porcupine (possibly northern dialect)

wilay	possum
wilay bijarr	buck possum (*bijarr* is a word for 'old man')
wilay guunal	doe possum (*guunii* is the word for 'mother')
yuugi	wild dog, dingo
yuuluuma	kangaroo (species unknown)

10. Reptiles

dhuuliyn, dhuuleeyn	ground or sand goanna
dhuumin	death adder
dhuurruumang	young snake
dhuurruung	snake (general term)
gadhi	snake (general term)
galiynjuuliyn	red-bellied black snake
gandhalwaa	turtle (perhaps long-necked)
girrawaa	tree goanna
guudhamang	turtle (perhaps striped)
nharrang	lizard (possibly frill-necked)
warralang	brown snake
yaba	diamond or carpet snake

11. Birds

bilirr	black cockatoo
buubil	feather; wing
buudhanbang	black duck
buujaan	bird (general term) (see *dhibilaayn*)
buurralgang	brolga
dhibilaayn	bird (general term) (see *buujaan*)
dhinawan	emu (nth dial.) (see *nguurruuyn*)
dhuundhuu	black swan
gabuuga	egg (*Also means* brain)
gambal	bustard, plains turkey
garruu	magpie
gawuurra	feather
guuguubarra	kookaburra
guulirrji	peewee, mudlark
guunaarruu, guunaarruung, guunaarra	wood duck
guurribang	curlew
jirri-jirri, dhirri-dhirri	Willie wagtail
malyan	eaglehawk

muurrayn	sulphur-crested cockatoo
nguuguung	tawny frogmouth, mopoke
nguurrang	nest (*Also means* camp)
nguurruuyn	emu (see *dhinawan*)
waagan	crow
yuunggaay	mallee hen, scrub turkey

12. Aquatic life

bagaay	shell
barrgaayn	leech
binduugayn	mussel
dhanguurr	catfish
guulaangga	frog
guuya	fish (general term)

13. Insects and spiders

buuga	blowfly (*Also means* maggot; rotten)
buugabanha	flystruck
buuga-buuga	very maggotty, very rotten
buuja-buuja	butterfly
buurrimal	fly
dhuunbayn	scorpion
dhuundhin	louse nit (egg)
dhuurruuy	ant (species unknown)
gabayn, gabang	grub (not witchetty)
galang-galang	locust, cicada
ginma	caterpillar
giyan	centipede
guulan	louse (see *muunhuu*)
marrarr	spider (species unknown)
muugiyn	mosquito
muunhuu, muunha	louse
muurruung	grasshopper
ngarruu	honey
warruu	wasp, hornet

14. Plants

bilarr	swamp or river oak
birrguu	scrub, the bush
birri, birrigan	white box
buugarruu	grass (species unknown)
buuguuwin	grass (species unknown)
buurree	wattle, weeping myall
dhani	wattle (species unknown)
geegal	tree, firewood; windbreak, shelter
girrang	leaf
guurrawin	flower
gwandaang	quandong tree, native plum or cherry
madhan	tree (general term)

15. Physical qualities

baamirr	long, tall
babirr	big
baluudaay	cold
barra-barra	white (see *gaban*)
barrdhang, barrjang	bitter, unpleasant to taste or smell
barrgan-barrgan	crooked (*Also means* the moon when forming a sickle)
binaal	big (*Also means* eldest; *also* many, much, all)
birra	tired (*Also means* back)
birra-birra	very tired, lazy
biyang	many, much, all
buubaay	small
buubaayjuul	very small
buudhang	black (*Also means* Koori)
buuga	rotten, meat when tainted
buuga-buuga	very rotten, blackish colour of meat when rotting
buula	two
buula-buula	four
buula-nguunbaay, nguunbaay-buula	three
buunguu	many, much, all

buunguu-galang, biyang-galang	everything, a great many (It is not possible to explain the subtle difference in the meanings which would have existed between *galang, buunguu, biyang* and *binaal.* However, note that they may be reduplicated or combined to emphasise the quantity)
buunguul	short
buunya	soft, elastic (see *muurraay*)
buurrang	dry (probably used generally, as for dry leaves, branches, honeycomb, riverbeds, etc.) (see *yalguu*)
dhalbal	to wet
dhamba-dhamba	very soft; hollow sounding
dhuuluu	straight (*Also means* spear)
gaban	white
galang, galang-galang, buunguu-buunguu	many, much, all
galiyn-galiyn, galing-galing	wet
gambil	uneven, crooked
giluung	sharp
girri-girri	red (*Also means* red wine)
guumba	unripe
guunang-guunang	yellow (ochre)
manarr	wide
muuguu	blunt
muula-muulang	to be very sick (reduplication of *muulang* 'to vomit', or a compound of *muula* 'sore, ulcer, boil' and *muulang* 'to vomit')
muunuun	big
muurraay	soft, elastic
muurruun	alive, life
ngarran	hungry
nguunbaay	one
walan	strong, hard
wali-wali	crooked
wuugil, wuunggi	hot, heat
wuura	weak
yuurruurr	hungry
wuurruurr	full, sated with food

yalguu	dry (possibly specifically a dry dead tree)
yinggil	sick, ill

16. Non-physical qualities

dhalaay, dhalay	angry; sad; shame (This word obviously cannot be directly translated into English. Different languages encode concepts in different ways. Thus *dhalaay* was probably a strong personal emotion which embodied aspects of the English concepts of 'shame', 'sadness' and 'anger'.)
gadhang	happy, glad
gajag	horrible, disgusting
giyal-giyal	fear, shame
guuweenda, gweenda	shame
gwaangi, gwaang-gwaang	mad, silly, stupid, lunatic (probably from *giwang* 'moon', like English 'lunatic' from 'lunar'; people were said to become insane with changes in the moon, especially during the full moon)
maaligan	mad, insane
marrammuubang	bad (see *wirraay marrambang*)
marrang	good (*Also means* friend)
mirringgan	dog-like, thievish, wicked
wandang	ugly (extended from the meaning 'bad spirit')
wangguun	bad
wanjibaayn	naughty
wirraay marrambang	bad (*marrang* means 'good', -*bang* is an ending which means 'very', so *marrambang* means 'very good'; *wirraay* means 'no' or 'not'. So the compound means 'without much goodness' or 'not much good'.) (see *marrammuubang*)
yaambuul	nonsense, a lie

17. Motion

baambee	to swim, float
barraay	to fly

buunbaay	to run
buundee	to fall
dhanyanaay	to come: *dhanyadha* come (here)!
galiyaay	to climb
gindhaay	to play, be playful; laugh
guumbee	to wash, bogey, bathe
wagaay, wagaji	to dance
wuubuungee	to dive
yanaay	to go, walk: *yanadha* go!
yarrabi	to go, walk, go away

18. State

giyal	to be afraid; be ashamed
warraay	to stand
wee	to sit, stay, live (somewhere)
wirree	to lie down

19. Vocalisation and thought

dhuuluu-yala	to talk straight
gindhaay	to laugh; to play
guudhi, guuji	to sing; song (style unknown)
nyimli	to cry
winanggaay	to know, to think, to understand
yal	to speak
yuunggaay	to cry

20. Bodily functions

baluung	to die
buudaay	to smell
dhal	to eat
dharril, dhuurril	to give birth
dhuurri, dharri	sexual intercourse
geeyn, geenj	to stare (*Also* extended to mean 'pervert')
muugeeyn, muugeenj	to be blind
muulang	to vomit
ngaaga	to see, watch, observe
ngaay	to see
ngamrri, ngangarri	to sleep
weejal	to drink
winanggal	to hear
wuudha-muuga, muuguu-wuudha	to be deaf (literally 'without ears')
yuurraay	to sleep, be asleep

21. Impact and violence

badhal	to bite
baluubuunil	to kill, murder
banggal	to cut
buumal	to hit, strike, beat
ganaay	to burn
marra	to do, make (*Also means* hand)
wangal	to dig

22. Holding and transfer

barramal	to get, carry, fetch, bring, give, take, hold
birrambal	to throw: *birrambalanha* throwing at each other
buunji	to share, sharing; cadge, bludge
gaang	to get, carry, fetch, bring, give
manggi	to steal
ngaaminya	to find
nguung	to give, get, carry, fetch, bring (Although it is not possible to say what differences in meaning there are between *barramal, nguung* and *gaang* it appears that *nguung* has a predominant meaning of 'give'.)

23. Location, direction and time

bilagal	down, downhill (towards a creek)
birra	away from (*Birra* means 'back'. If your back is toward something then you are either 'turned away from' or 'moving away from' it.)
birrang	far
dhalan	soon
galiyaaynbal	up, above
guugin	near
guuwaay	by and by
marradhal	long ago
ngana	there, that
nganayn	over there (in the distance)
ngina	here, this
nguunbaay ngangarri	one day (literally 'one sleep')
nguurruunggal	morning; tomorrow; dawn; early)
yandhal	now

24. Interjections and interrogatives

dhadhi?	where from?
dhaga?	where at?
dhaguu?	where to?
gaja!	don't! get away!
gajag!	horrible! disgusting!
garriya!	don't!
minyang?	what?
ngaawaa	come here!; to beckon
ngaawaa, nga, ngaayn	yes
ngandhi?, ngandhiwaa?	who (is)?
ngandhuu?	who (does something)?
ninggi! ninggi-ninggi!	look! look out!
waay!	look out!
warrguu?	why?
way!	look out! be quiet!
wijuungga?	when? How?
wirraay	no; not
yaala	yes

25. Demonstratives and pronouns

ngadhi, ngaji	my
ngadhuu, ngajuu	I
ngali	we two (dual)
ngana	that, there
nganayn	that over there (in the distance)
ngina	this, here
ngинduu	you (singular)
nginduu buula	you two (dual)
nginduugirr	you (plural)
nginuu	your, yours
ngiyani	we more than two (plural)

26. Placenames

The following are tentative explanations only.

Cabramurra	possibly derived from *gambirra marra*: *gambirra* to be crooked, and *marra* hand
Cootamundra	probably derived from *guudhamang* turtle: Cootamundra is said to mean 'place of turtles'

Narrandera	probably derived from *nharrang* frill-necked lizard. One of the stories of the area is that at this place a man speared a frill-necked lizard.
Tumbarumba	possibly derived from *dhamba dhamba* very soft
Wagga Wagga	probably derived from *waagan waagan* which would mean 'a lot of crows'. *Waagan* is 'crow' and Wagga Wagga is said to mean 'place of many crows'.
Womboin	probably the large grey kangaroo *wambuuwayn*

Borrowed words

Whenever groups who speak different languages have prolonged contact, words are often borrowed into one or both languages. Wiradjuri has added a richness to the English language. Many places in New South Wales have Wiradjuri names like Cootamundra and Wagga Wagga. Many common words for natural features, animals and birds were also borrowed into the English language from Wiradjuri. Examples are *billabong*, *quandong* and *wallaroo*.

Similarly, words were borrowed into Wiradjuri from neighbouring languages and English. Wiradjuri people sometimes express concern that a particular word may be from another language or from a different dialect of Wiradjuri and therefore somehow not quite correct. However, a look through an English dictionary will reveal how many English words are originally from other languages. Furthermore, film and television have brought many current American and British English words into Australian English. Words become part of everyday language by being commonly used and understood by other members of the speech community. They are not incorrect because they did not originate in a particular language, and a language should not be judged to be impure or corrupted simply because it contains words from other languages.

Reduplication and extended meanings

Reduplicating (doubling) a word is a common feature in languages the world over. In Wiradjuri, reduplication sometimes changes the grammatical part of speech of a word. For example, from *galiyn* (*galing*) 'water' we have *galiyn-galiyn* (*galing-galing*) 'wet'. In this instance the reduplication has made a noun into a stative verb or adjective and has also added a sense of emphasis to its meaning. In other cases the effect is to intensify the original meaning of a word, as is done in English by the word 'very'. Reduplication can also change the meaning of the original word altogether while at the same time retaining some sense of the original meaning, for example, from *guunang* 'faeces' we have *guunang-guunang* 'yellow ochre'.

But the meaning of a reduplicated word is not always closely related to the meaning of the original word. For example, *mirri-mirri* meaning 'bad person', 'wicked', 'dog-like' is derived from *mirri* 'dog'. And *birra* 'tired' reduplicates as *birra-birra* 'very tired' as might be expected; this word, however, can also mean 'lazy'.

It is common for languages to name things according to the way they sound (onomatopoeia), as in English 'quack' and 'crunch'. In Wiradjuri, birds are often named in this way: for example, *jirri-jirri* 'Willie wagtail' sounds like the Willie wagtail's call.

The meanings of words are sometimes extended: *birra* 'away from' is an extension of *birra* 'back' (if your back is to something then you are turned or moving away from it). (Body part nouns are used with extended meanings in many languages.) Another example is *walang* which used to mean 'stone' (and possibly 'hard'). This meaning was extended to 'money' and today *walang* is one of the words still used by Wiradjuri people to mean 'money' while the original senses have been lost. Similarly, *weejal* originally meant 'to drink' but now means 'alcohol'.

References

Austin, P 1993, *Gamilaraay, an Aboriginal Language of Northern New South Wales*, La Trobe University, Melbourne

Coe, M 1986, *Windradyne — a Wiradjuri Koorie*, Blackbooks

Dixon, R M W 1980, *The Languages of Australia*, Cambridge University Press, Cambridge

Hosking, D and S McNicol 1993, *Wiradjuri*, Panther Publishing

McNicol, S 1989, A Salvage Description of the Phonology & Morphology of Wiradhuray, BA Honours thesis, ms no. 2790, Australian Institute of Aboriginal and Torres Strait Islander Studies library, Canberra

Read, P 1988, *A Hundred Years War: The Wiradjuri People and the State*, ANU Press, Canberra

Threlkeld, L 1834, *An Australian Language*, Sydney Revised ed. (ed. John Fraser), Government Printer, Sydney, 1892, Appendix D 'Grammar and vocabulary of the Wiradhari dialect in New South Wales', pp 56–120 (from Rev. James Gunther)

6

Wembawemba

LUISE HERCUS

Wembawemba was one of the so-called Kulin languages, to use the name given by W Schmidt in his classification of Australian languages (Schmidt 1919). These languages are all related, and shared the word *kuli* 'people', on which the language group name is based. The western Kulin languages were once spoken over the whole of western Victoria except for the southern coastal areas west of Melbourne and sections of the Murray valley down from Robinvale. With over 75 per cent common vocabulary, the relationship between the western Kulin languages was particularly close. Indeed, they must be regarded as dialects of one language, as has been made clear by Dixon (1980, p. 259).

The dialects are named according to their word for 'no', and belong to three main groups:

1. The Werkaya group, consisting of Werkaya of north-western Victoria, and probably also Yardwadjali of the far west of the state,

Djadjawurrung of the Wimmera, as well as Wadawurrung from further south. We have modern data only for Werkaya.

2. The Wembawemba group, including Wembawemba and Perepaperepa of the Loddon and Campaspe rivers, and the Murray between Swan Hill and Echuca, and across into the Riverina, as well as Narinari from Booligal to near Balranald (Hercus 1978, pp 119–131). Perepaperepa, which adjoined Wembawemba to the east, was practically identical to it. By the turn of the century, the two groups had begun to regard themselves as one; they shared their most important places of abode at Kerang and Lake Boga, and Moonacullah Mission near Deniliquin in Perepaperepa country became a centre for both groups. Mathews' brief grammar (1902) of 'Bureba-bureba' (Perepaperepa) is applicable to Wembawemba except for a few differences such as the first person singular pronoun.
3. The Mathimathi group, which consists of Mathimathi of the Balranald area, Watiwati from downstream of Swan Hill, Letyiletyi from near Robinvale, and probably also the adjacent Wekiweki and Yariyari for which we have no adequate data.

Spelling and pronunciation

The following letters are used in writing Wembawemba:

a, b, e, i, k, l, m, n, ng, ny, p, r, rl, rn, rr, rt, t, th, ty, u, w, y

As in the majority of Aboriginal languages there is no contrast between voiced and unvoiced consonants (see page xxviii above). In this chapter the unvoiced consonant letters have been used, as they are closer to the actual pronunciation. Hence we write:

t, rt, ty	*not*	d, rd, dy
p	*not*	b
k	*not*	g

The only exception to this is after nasal consonants, because here the consonants are strongly voiced and to write, for instance, *wempa* for *wemba* ('no') would grossly distort what we know of the pronunciation. We therefore write *nd, rnd, ndy* not *nt, rnt, nty*; *mb* not *mp*; and *ngg* not *ngk.*

Ng is pronounced the same as in English, but this sound often occurs at the beginning of words. When *ng* is followed by *g* we have simply used the spelling *ngg.* For those rare cases where an ordinary *n* or *rn* is followed by *g* we have inserted a dot between *n* and *g* so that it is clear that it is not *ng*, but *n* + *g* or *rn* + *g*, as in *tarn.ga* 'to put on (clothes)'.

WEMBAWEMBA WORDLIST

This Wembawemba wordlist is mainly based on material recorded in the sixties by Luise Hercus from Nancy Egan, Stanley Day and John Taylor. This wordlist would not have been possible without the years of encouragement and support on fieldwork from the late Graham Hercus, nor without the recent help of Val Mitchell, Melva Johnson, and Nick Thieberger.

WORDLIST CATEGORIES

1. Body parts and products
2. Kin relationships
3. Human classification
4. Language, mythology and ceremony
5. Human artefacts
6. Food, cooking and fire
7. Topography
8. Elements
9. Mammals
10. Reptiles
11. Birds
12. Aquatic life
13. Insects and spiders
14. Plants
15. Physical qualities
16. Non-physical qualities
17. Motion
18. State
19. Vocalisation and thought
20. Bodily functions
21. Impact and violence
22. Holding and transfer
23. Location, direction and time
24. Interjections
25. Demonstratives and pronouns
26. Placenames

1. Body parts and products

kanak	heel
kar	leg
karep, kareput	thigh
karr	nose
kathap	armpit
kir	urine
kunenyuk	guts; faeces (his)
kurn	throat
kurratyuk	fat (other than kidney fat) (his)
kurrk	blood: *wira kurrkuk* (literally 'his blood is running fast') he has a fever
kurrmbuk	breast; milk (her)
larinjuk	lungs (his)
larnginyuk	ribs (his)

lerri	claw, (finger)nail: *lerrinyuk* (literally 'its claw') the claw of any animal or bird, or any hard shell, as of a crayfish
liya	teeth
manye	hand
marangin	second finger (your)
merkuk	ankle (his)
merterruk	bone (his)
mir	eye: *mirnuk* his eye
mityuk	skin (his) (*Also means* the bark of a tree)
mula	hip
mum	bottom, rump
munyi	hair (body)
munyi-wurru	moustache
munyuk	elbow (his)
murrekuk	cheek (his)
murreng	head: *tyakinyarr tyalinyuk* (literally 'good head-his') he is clever
ngani	beard
ngarre	hair
nyani	neck
pap-kune	large intestine (literally 'mother of guts')
pap-manya	thumb (literally 'mother of hand')
parka-minandap	third finger
pathingguk	knee (his)
pengguk	meat (literally 'its body')
perk-perk	prickles, as of an echidna
pili	stomach (external)
pirmpuk	marrow (his), the marrow of a bone
pirre	bald head, with just a few tufts of hair
pirrkuk	tail (his)
pun	testicles
purap	leg
put	groin
thathakuk	arm (his); wing of a bird
thather	shoulder
tunep	little finger

tyalingin (*also once* tyalinin) — tongue (your); language, speech. The word for 'tongue' was also used in the sense of 'food' in some idiomatic expressions: *tyakinyarr tyalinyuk* you will eat his food; *wembanda tyakiny tyalingin*! I won't eat your food!

tyang — chest: *tyangin* your chest

tyina — foot, footprint

wirimbula — ears: *wirimbuluk* its ears, scalp

wurru — mouth, lips: *wurrenyuk* his mouth

yalep-yalep — first finger

yiren, yiren-yiren — eyebrows: *yiren-yirendin* your eyebrows

yulp — right hand, straight: *yulpin* your right hand

2. Kin relationships

kuka — grandmother (both maternal and paternal); grandchild (reciprocal term): *kukandandak* my grandchild

kurri — cross-cousin, male or female

kutning-kurringek — late younger brother (mine)

kutninyuk — younger brother (his): *kutningek* my younger brother

kuyinggurrin — mother (your): *kuyindrruk* his mother (also used as a general term for 'female': *kuyindrruk wirrengen* a female dog)

mam — father

mathimuk — wife (his)

mim — grandparents (paternal); old people in general

minggayin — daughter (your)

mituk — husband (her)

ngaluk — aunt (father's sister)

nganyityuk — husband, lover (her)

ngapa — maternal grandfather (this term, even in recent times, included the brothers of the maternal grandfather)

ngapundek — grandchild (mine) (said by the maternal grandfather)

ngark	uncle, father's side
nyalentyin	mother-in-law (your) (addressed to a man)
parrem-parrem	great-grandfather (paternal)
tyarrembayin	uncle (your) (mother's brother)
tyatyin	elder sister (your)
tyaty-kurringin	late elder sister (your)
tyinanity	nephew
wa-kurringin	late elder brother (your) (cf. *wawin* your elder brother)
wathip, watyip	son
wawin	elder brother (your)

3. Human classification

kare-kare-kurrk	a number of young women; the Pleiades (stars)
karri-kurk	girl, teenager
karriyapert	single man
kuli	people, crowd
kulingulang	shy person
kulken	youth, teenager (up to about 15 years)
kuthalthana-kurrk	widow (literally 'they pity the woman')
kwe	friend! mate! (also used by husband and wife to address each other)
lerrk	woman, female
lerrk-payingkuk	girl, female child
marruk-marru-ngurak	chief, headman
mukundity	single woman
ngalembert	champion dodger, an expert at dodging spears
nganinyuk	bearded man
Ngarri-paluk	name of the group of Wembawemba people which included those at Lake Boga (literally 'the Bull Oak people')
ngunyim-kurrk	old woman (literally 'shrivelled up like an empty waterbag')
nyarremben	old man
nyernik-nyernik	senior local person
pambi-mum	coward (literally 'scared-bottom')

pangel	witchdoctor, clever man (*Also means* eagle, because witchdoctors identified with the eaglehawk and could turn themselves into eaglehawks)
payingguk	child: *pembengguk* children
peligmen	policeman (loanword from English)
peng	man, human being, body; self (used in reflexive constructions: *penggandak* to myself, *tyilpendinggat penggandak* I banged myself)
pen-wurru	big-mouth (literally 'someone who has a mouth as big as a hollow tree')
pepeny	baby
puliwarl	youth, late teenager
puny-wil	quick, smart person; fast runner (both this and the synonym *milak-wil* are based on the idea of a person running with hot ashes to light a new fire)
tyunggi-kurm-kurrk	woman with swelling breasts, young marriageable woman
tyurunggi-pili	big-belly, a grossly fat person
wam	stupid person, idiot
warengin	left hand (your)
watypala	white man (from English 'white fellow')
wilkil-mir	squint-eyed (literally 'eye continually turning around')
windyentap	dwarf
wurreker	message carrier
wurretyil-manuk	executioner; apart from lighting the *wurretyil* to kill offenders against traditional law, it was also his duty to kill hopelessly malformed babies whom he stifled soon after birth
wurrpa	youth (about 15 to 18 years)
wuthu	man, male
yawirrek	enemy (my) (literally 'that which is meat for me')
yukal	friend: *winyarr yukalin* who is your friend?

4. Language, mythology and ceremony

kathel	sound of knocking: limbs of trees knocking together, banging of the time-sticks, clapping of hands
katy-katy	evil magic
lety-lety	mythical, spotted and dog-like animal (this could refer to the thylacine)
murrup	ghost
ngatha	name of a mythical being, a small creature that lived in reed-beds. The *ngatha* was regarded as harmless; he would appear at dusk and sometimes even talk to people in their own language and camp near them, particularly if they had caught lobsters, his favourite food.
nyanyimen	omen, bad omen foreshadowing the death of a close relative. Such an omen takes the form of a person's ancestral animal, *parrembuk*, in odd surroundings, such as a kangaroo walking right up to the dogs of a person whose totem was a kangaroo, or a possum coming in daytime into the camp of a person whose totem was a possum: *nyanyimen kinya wile pirnin* it is a bad omen that this possum came; *nyanyimen* was also used as an exclamation, 'what's up?', 'what's wrong?'
tanggel	bunyip, mythical water creature
tarn	ball game played with a ball made from possum skin
warrang-warrang	songs, corroboree
warrpa	wailing, funeral song
weyi	song
yemin-yemin	burial ground, graves
yemurraki	Dreamtime, the distant past, Dreamtime legend

5. Human artefacts

kalingality-karren	necklace made from cane grass
karn	dress (from English 'gown')
karrek	spear thrower
karem	spear-shield
kare-tyak	walking stick (literally 'leg on ground'); this was the main and very effectively used weapon of the old women at Moonacullah
kerning	bone awl
kulk	large drag net
kuyen	stabbing spear
lar	camp, home, bark shelter: *larnuk* (literally 'his home') the nest of a bird
liyangi-kure	necklace made from kangaroo teeth
malka-pula	time-sticks (two); these were beaten together (and not against the ground) and were used only by men. Wembawemba women usually clapped in accompaniment to the men's singing or to their own singing.
malkarr	waddy shield
manyenyuk	necklace made from crayfish claws
marap-marap	grinding stone, used for the grinding of stone tomahawks
matyem	possum-rug; Wembawemba people sewed possum skins with kangaroo sinew
ngatuk	possum cloak
nyelin-nyelin	small dragnet
nyil-kalk	woman's waddy, covered with porcupine quills and poisoned
pakap-tyarem	short throwing spear, made of mallee
paring	track: *paringguk* his track
pert-pert	needle, netting needle
pilp	drum, made from wood
pinwurrayi	stone tomahawk with long handle, used only for fighting
purrk	windbreak, shelter
tilak	wooden barb of a spear
titandi	knife

wan	boomerang
waten	stone knife
weny-weny	clothes

6. Food, cooking and fire

kuma	raw food
lerep	manna from scale insects (this word has been adopted into English either from Wembawemba or from a closely related language, whence 'lerp insects')
letwil	kindling wood, small sticks
lil	manna, sweet resin
lukal	oven, midden
milak	ashes, dust
ngamety	tea
panem	damper, bread
puliny	spark
puny	hot ashes, from which one can relight a fire
purt	smoke
purtuk	tobacco
tyakuwa, tyakuwala	to feast, celebrate
tyendel	firestick, flame
tyirrem	bushfire
wanap	fire, firewood: *kalpindak kinyam wanap!* cut up this firewood!

7. Topography

kawa	mountain, large mountain
kurang pirr	river
kurrek	sand
kuthap	stone
luthak	waterhole
marang-marang	mirage
nyirring	steep slope, the steep sloping edge of a river
nyirringdela	creekbed
pety	quartz stone
pirr	stream, running water
prri-tya	claypan, bare ground
prrim	spring; native well

punyul	mountain
terik-terik	gravel
tumawan	gully
tya	ground, soil, land
tyangek	my own place, my birthplace
tyekil	lake

8. Elements

karrthi	summer
katen	water
kurre-wil	the star Sirius (literally 'kangaroo-having')
marndar	thunder
mareng, marng	dark cloud
marrik-marrik	wind, cold wind
merriny	wind
mithiyen	moon, month
mithek	rain
mula-ngert	the star Venus
ngak	shade, shadow (*Also means* covered shelter; photograph)
ngalu	springtime
parnbandilang	rainbow (literally 'shining in many colours')
partikalang nyawi	sunset (*Also means* west)
pathak	hailstone
payika-turt	shooting star
perrp	morning
tanbil	cumulus cloud
terning	ice
tirril	sky, heaven, up above
tyarrang	blue sky
wayinlarr	lightning
wit	winter
wit panyalu	autumn

9. Mammals

kali	dog
kama	black swamp wallaby
kurre	grey kangaroo
lipkwil	echidna
nganuty-nganuty	bat

pana	ringtail possum
parra	red kangaroo
parre	kangaroo rat
perrity	native cat, quoll
pirmity	joey, young kangaroo
tharre-mum	rabbit (literally 'white-bottom')
tuwang	flying possum, glider
tyambek	sheep ('jumbuck')
tyawer	pouch of marsupial
tyerrika-wirimbul	rabbit (literally 'stand-up ears')
wile	brush-tailed possum
wilkar	dingo
yareman	horse
yurn	native cat, tiger cat

10. Reptiles

kaliya	sleeping lizard
ken	frill-necked lizard
kurnwil	reptile (general term); black snake
lirrk	death adder
mir-wil	mallee snake (literally 'eye-having', probably from the yellowish tear-drop mark round the eye)
mirndayi	mythical maned snake
ngakangina	worm snake
pip-ngatha	gecko
tyalung	brown snake
tyuling	big black tree goanna
watha	brown sand goanna

11. Birds

kalalek	Major Mitchell cockatoo
karndeli	butcherbird
kathekarr	white cockatoo, corella
kawir	emu
kunawar	swan
kurng-kurng	kookaburra
kuthun	brolga
lawan	mallee hen (this word has been borrowed into English as 'lowan')
lim	ringneck or mallee parrot

mert-meril	large black cormorant
ngakak	magpie goose
nganggerrel	black-billed spoonbill
ngare	black duck
ngarrawu	bustard
ngathang-wil	nankeen crane (literally 'crayfish-having')
pandelang	whistling eagle
pirrimpirr	bee-eater
pulerrn-pulerrn	lyrebird
purunggi	little quail
tun	bellbird
tyali-kurrkuk	red-capped robin (literally 'red-tongue-his')
tyinap	sulphur-crested cockatoo
tyir-katen	darter (literally 'tearing the water')
tyune-tyunety	tawny frogmouth
tyurung-wil	emu (literally 'the long one'; this is an instance of the use of a nickname which presumably replaced an older word for 'emu' in Wembawemba. The use of nicknames helps to account for the particularly great diversity in the words for birds in Victorian and other Australian languages.)
wa	crow
wanggerrel	large black-and-white cormorant
wilek-wilek	galah
wiran	black cockatoo
wuk-wuk	boobook owl
yerratety-kurrk, yerratethkurrk	owlet-nightjar (this bird was the female totem)

12. Aquatic life

kurrumeruk	Murray cod of great size
kurumburt	water-rat
lip-lip-wil	crayfish (literally 'spike-spike-having')
man	small land-leech
mapiyal	platypus
ngumel	Murray trout

nirnak	frog
nyim	short-necked turtle (has a less pleasant taste than the long-necked species and was not generally eaten)
pandyil	Murray cod
pility	large water-leech
pil-wil lernget	broad-shelled turtle
pirre-wil	catfish (literally 'tuft of hair having')
pithen	mussel
tuk	bull frog
walen	crayfish (soft)
yawirr	fish (general term) (*Also means* flesh of any edible creature)

13. Insects and spiders

kukal	caterpillar, sawfly larvae in clusters on tree
lirri	mosquito
liyek-wil	bull ant
marra	meat ant
munggin-munggin	midges
munya	louse
parruyity	house mouse
pathang	large black ant
pithik	fly, blowfly
puluwang	wattle goat moth, carbuncle grub in box trees
puruny	green-headed ant
tirri-tirrit-puriny	cricket
tyak-tyak	white ant
tyilep-tyilep	small stinging ant
tyina-waruk	centipede (literally 'having a lot of legs')
wininyuk	mouse, pouched mouse
wirimbeliny	spider
wirimbeliny tyeliwil	red-backed spider
withe-kama	scorpion (literally 'little wallaby')
wiyit	caterpillar sawfly larvae
yurru-wil	moth

14. Plants

karren	lignum
kiwarra	broombush
kuthu	bitter quandong
marrung	Murray pine
mirrwan	yam
mityern	white box
ngarreli	water-weed
ngarri	bull oak
ngunity-ngunity	native pear
ngurrel	'dogwood' *Myoporum platycarpum* (this name has gone into English as 'ngural')
pep	white gum
pithikal	quandong
piyal	red gum; tree (general term); stick
prrityirrim	resin from the Murray pine, used as a glue
pungurt	wire-rush used for basket-making
purrung	small mallee with dark wood inside
purren	grass seed; dry seed of a species of *Panicum* which was ground and made into flour
purtity	root of reed-mace or cumbungi (a favourite food)
talem-talem	nardoo
tyulern	saltbush
wityerrum	waterlily (large); this probably refers to the Darling lily
wurt-wurt	bulrush
wutya	sap, resin of wattle trees
yalem	mushroom, may perhaps refer to a subterranean fungus of the 'blackfellow's bread' type

15. Physical qualities

kepin	one
kepin manye	five (literally 'one hand')
kepin manye pa kepin	six (literally 'one hand and one')
kepin manye pulety	seven (literally 'one hand and two')
kepin manye pulety pa kepin	eight (literally 'one hand and three')

kepin manye pulety pulety	nine (literally 'one hand and four')
kepin pa kalepul	three (literally 'one and two')
kethawil	many, a vast number
kunatyila-wil	dark, dark-coloured
kurranduk	big (*Also means* large grinding stone)
kurrk-kurrkuk warrawil	red (literally 'having the colour of blood')
lambrruk	many, a vast number
latyuk	naked
lithayatang	sharp, pointy
liyewil	jagged (literally 'teeth-having')
ngak	shade, shadow; covered shelter, shade hut (*Also means* photograph: *tirndiny ngakin* he will take your photograph)
pakuwinyawil	bright, very brightly coloured
pamba-wil	frightened, shy
parruk	many, a lot
pathip-pathip	few, a small number
puletya	two
pulety manye	ten (literally 'two hands')
pertayatang	dry
pilerrmatang	white, light coloured, yellowish
pumbilang	cold
purt-purt-warra-wil	blue (literally 'smoke-coloured')
puwang	stinking
tharretayil	white, shiny white
tirtenayuk	new, fresh
tyalang	hot
tyelimatayil	red
wathentyen	dead (a euphemistic term used for humans only; *wiken* was the general term)
wiken	dead
witheyuk	small, little
wurkatang	black
wutya-wutya	sweet, sweet resin
yathaminyuk	bad, nasty, ugly, deformed

16. Non-physical qualities

kuli-wutyup	savage, fierce (literally 'hatred in the belly')
ngil	noise
ngunggurr-wil	wild, furious
telkuk	good, beautiful
wakatang	determined, obstinate

17. Motion

kawenda	to crawl
milpila	to twist
nyetenya	to play, run around
parenga	to run after, chase
payika	to get up; to rise in flight, fly: *payiki, werrki kinya peng!* get up, quick, there is a man coming (said as a joke among a group of girls)
perrepa	to climb (trees)
perrmila	to go sneaking round, seek to kill by stealth
piyalanggila	to run along the edge of a river below the actual bank (literally 'where the roots of the red gum trees are')
putheka	to come in, as to a camp: *putheka larnangin* he's going into your camp
puthekila	to dive into the water
titya	to shift, change places
tyarrepa	to shut; *tyarrepak ninyam!* shut this door! *tyarrepak ninyam tumikal!* shut this tent!
waletyuwa, waletyuwana	to come very close
wara	to walk, to come (used mainly in the fixed phrase *nyuka wari!* come here!)
wariwa	to go away
wawa	to follow
weraya	to be slow
werrka	to hurry
wilka	to turn round
wirraka	to swim
wirreka	to run, hurry

withewa — to return, to go home: *nyatyerruwarr withewiny?* when will you go home?

wurrengala — to chase away, e.g. to whisk away flies

yangga — to walk

18. State

kalina — to love

katyina — to be unable: *katyinanda nyaka* I can't see

katyina nyernda — deaf (literally 'he can't understand')

katyina wurraka — dumb (literally 'he can't speak')

kungaya — to keep quiet: *wemba-kat kungaya* he is never quiet

kurrumbaya — to be jealous: *kurumbaya-kat kinya lerrk* this woman is jealous

merentyemen — cold

mulpaya — to be weak

ngupa — to be full, satisfied: *ngupanda-kat* I've had enough

nyakamuna — to be careful, look out: *nyakamuni!* look out!

nyemberra — to wait for

nyengga — to sit

pamba — to be frightened

parngga — to be thirsty

pilepileta — to shine, glitter

pira — to be bald, bare

pumba — to be cold

tyalanga — to be hot

tyileka — to be sick: *tyilekanda* I am sick

tyipen — fresh, happy, uplifted

wakatanga — to be obstinate: *wakatangarr* you are an obstinate person

wika — to be hungry, starve, die: *wikanda* I am hungry; *wikinyanda* I will starve, I will die

yathangga — to be bad, ugly, cruel or just unpleasant

yathanggaya burpuk — to be silly (literally 'head becoming bad')

19. Vocalisation and thought

kalaya	to ask, question: *kalayak kinyam peng* ask this man
karnda	to shout, yell
karrkara	to cry out for help, scream
kiya	to speak: *nyanyarar kiya?* what are you saying?
kulingula, kulingulaya	to feel shy
kurtemila	to whinge, keep complaining
kutha	to pity, be sorry
ngarngila	to pretend, tell lies
nyaka	to see, watch; to think of, consider
nyarna	to worry over, regret
nyarrepa, nyarrepila	to sing, chant a curse, point the bone
nyernda	to know, understand (*nyernda* is clearly connected with *nyerna* 'to hear'. This derivation, implying that 'hearing is knowing', is common in Australian languages.)
nyernila	to listen
nyumila	to think: *nyinga nyumilin, nyanya kila* then he thought, what is this now?
perrmeraya	to betray (used particularly in connection with birds such as the noisy miner, who gave away any person sneaking after game)
tyalila	to abuse, swear at, call someone names
tyarrmba	to yell at, scare off
tyurra	to speak ill of
warrangga	to sing
wurreka	to speak
yakuwa	to dream
yarka (*in song* yareka)	to search for, expect: *yarka pepeny* she is expecting a baby
yawirra	to dislike, hate

20. Bodily functions

kanyengka	to cough
karrma	to vomit

kirityila	to urinate
kumba	to lie down, sleep
kupa	to drink
milpa mirnuk	to wink (literally 'to bend his eye')
murpa	to kiss
ngarupa	to smell: *ngarupanda kinyam pengguk pengen* I can smell this rotten meat
numila	to cry, weep
nyakila	to look, watch
purnburnwilang	swelling, sore
purngga	to blow, blow a fire: *purnggak kinyam wanap!* blow that fire!
purrenga	to snore
tyaka	to eat
tyarpa	to yawn, open one's mouth wide
tyinangeta	to sneeze
tyiyel	to lust
tyurnda	to spit
waripa	to dance, take part in a corroboree
wekuwa	to laugh loudly, make a cackling sound like a possum
wirta	to whistle
yarkuwa	to look for, search for over a long distance: *yarkuwanda wilkarr* I am looking around for dingoes

21. Impact and violence

kalpa	to cut, break
karta	to kick
keninga	to tie up
lepuwela	to hunt up, chase
lithkuna	to sharpen to a point; to splinter
nyanga	to burn: *nyanga-kat kinya nyawi* the sun is burning; *nyangen* burnt
pangga	to dig
paraya	to hunt
parka	to poke or prod something; to poke in the bed of a stream with a spear looking for turtles
punda	to bite
pungga	to spear

puyika	to fall down
taka	to hit, smack, strike with the hand; to kick
taktyerra	to fight, hit one another
tawa, tawila	to hit (with a weapon), so as to injure a person
thandela	to poison
tirndila	to sew (a possum rug)
tyilpa-tyilpa	to hit repeatedly, flog
tyira	to tear
tyirrpa	to strip a canoe
warema	to scratch so as to hurt (as opposed to *kurema* to scratch to relieve an itch)
wurruwila	to clean up; to tidy and roll wool

22. Holding and transfer

kanintya	to steal
kanya	to breathe
karrenga	to pour out, spill
karrka	to grab, catch
katima	to have (from English 'got'): *wembanda katima panem* I haven't got any bread
kirrpa	to pull
larrpa	to throw
munga	to do, make: *mungak kinyam wanap* make this fire
mutya	to pick up, take
nyinga	to wipe, wipe off
nyipa	to bury
pertaya	to dry: *pertayak ninyam kan* dry that dress
pulpa	to roll something on the ground; to heap up (stones or sticks)
tarnega	to put on (clothes)
tyapa	to hide or 'plant' something
tyarrwila	to wash thoroughly, clean up
tyayipana	to drop, let fall
tyemula	to find (after a search)
werrpana	to pull out; to catch (a fish): *werrpaninanda kinyam wirrenggal* I caught this perch
yuka	to paint, smear with fat

23. Location, direction and time

karrelkuk	tonight
kathang	afterwards, later
kilamerrr-malamerrr	here and there
kilayitya	long ago
kiluwity	today
kiwa	right now, immediately
kiyawety	this way, hither: *kiyawety-mayewety* hither and thither
kunakal, kunyikal	underneath
malamen-tya	distant place, a faraway country
malamerr	over there (distant)
malamiya	long ago
maye	over there, in the middle distance
ninya, nyinya	this one right here
nyarri	now
nyulmiyakun	long ago
nyuwa	here, near
partikalang nyawi	west (literally 'sunset')
perrpuk	tomorrow
pirnang nyawi	east (literally 'the rising sun')
puyikalang tern	south (literally 'frost or dew dripping down')
tyelik-tyelik	yesterday
tyerri-mumuk	upside down (literally 'stand up bottom')
wembaken	never

24. Interjections

kayi kuthap	I'm sorry (exclamation of sympathy)
kikwa	right then
kuthap, var kuthap-kayi	what a pity!
malamen	shut up! (a threatening exclamation, probably originally 'that far! (and no further)')
manmulakaty	shame on you!: *nya manmulakaty!* how disgusting!
ngatha	really! my word! *ngatha kinya tyurpa!* goodness, it is absolutely pouring! *ngatha-kat yathaminyuk kinya payingguk* my word, this is a naughty child!
ngayi	oh! (usually translated by 'crikey')

ngunyami	sorry! poor thing!
nya	really, indeed
parayi	well! (an exclamation of pleasure and surprise, also used as an exclamation calling for attention)

25. Demonstratives and pronouns

ngaliyuk	our two, belonging to both of us
ngin	you (singular, subject)
ngindeyuk, ngindayuk	yours (singular)
ngin-guli	you three (subject)
nguteyin	you people
nguteyuk	yours (plural)
walakandak	ours
walangandak	we
walangandakana	us
walangek	I
walanggin	you (singular)
walanyuk	he, she, it
waleyuk	yours (belonging to you two)

26. Placenames

Kunert-kunert	Round Lake near Kerang (literally 'lot of cottonweed')
Kurrm	the Lake Boga area
Kutyewap	Lake Tatchewop, near Kerang
Merterruk-pert	Swan Hill
Mile	Murray River
Muyi-mir	Lake Boga
Nyuranggal	Boga Long Lake Hill
Tuwang	Long Lake, near Kerang
Tyalkul	Dry Lake, near Kerang
Tyarrm	Lake Charm, near Kerang

Grammatical notes

Like all Australian languages, Wembawemba has a complex grammar. Here we mention just a few grammatical features that are particularly relevant to the wordlist.

To indicate that an object is someone's possession, the noun is marked with a possessive suffix referring to the owner. The singular possessive suffixes are:

	After nouns ending in consonants	After nouns ending in vowels
my	*-ek*	*-ngek*
your	*-in*	*-ngin*
his	*-uk*	*-nyuk*

The following examples illustrate these suffixes:

wutyup	stomach	*tyina*	foot
wutyupek	my stomach	*tyinangek*	my foot
wutyupin	your stomach	*tyinangin*	your foot
wutyupuk	his stomach	*tyinanyuk*	his foot

There are, however, many further and more complex rules relating to the indication of possession. In the wordlist above we have given the most frequently occurring form, namely, if available, the third person singular (all genders).

There is no single part of speech corresponding to the notion of adjective in Wembawemba. Descriptive words implying a fairly permanent quality — for example, 'good', 'bad', 'little' — usually consist of noun bases followed by various attributive suffixes. Thus *telk-uk* 'good' could be interpreted literally as 'goodness belongs to it', and *tirtenayuk* 'new' as 'newness belongs to it'. Personal qualities are very often expressed by means of nouns with the 'having' suffix *-wil*, such as *liya-wil* 'sharp' (literally 'teeth-having') and *kurraty-wil* 'fat' ('fat-having'). Terms denoting colour can be formed with the suffix *-yil* which seems to be similar in function to *-wil*, and may in fact be derived from it, for example, *tharratayil* 'white'. An alternative suffix is *-(t)ang* which marks a present participle — for example, *tharratang* 'being white'.

Wembawemba uses stative verbs to express temporary conditions such as 'to be hot', 'to be sick', 'to be frightened'. These stative verbs are listed in the wordlist under the heading State.

Verbs are given in this wordlist in the present base form in *-a*, which also serves as third person singular. This is the most commonly used form of the verb. Other parts of the verb can also occur as separate items of vocabulary:

Original Function	**Form**	**Example**	**Vocabulary Translation**	**Function**
Present Participle	+ *ang*	*kulayatang*	wet	adjective
Past Participle	+ *an*	*waran*	covered	adjective
Purposive	+ *ap*	*kuthap*	for pitying!	exclamation

Previous work on Wembawemba

It is very fortunate that for Wembawemba there is very early, though limited, documentation. The collection by Smyth (1878) contains two short lists, by Godfrey and by Munro. The collection by Curr (1886–87) contains four lists, one by Fawcett from Boga, another by Curr himself from 'the neighbourhood of Boga, probably Moorerbat (Murrabit) and the lower Loddon', a third by J McCarthy from Gonn Station and a fourth from the magistrates at Moulamein. These early sources are generally consistent with each other and with the modern recording.

The early sources do not contain any grammatical analysis; however almost four pages are devoted to the grammar of 'Wambawamba' in a paper by R H Mathews (1903, pp 184–188). This grammar was discussed with speakers of Wembawemba in 1962: they did not consider the Mathews material to be Wembawemba and thought it was either Watiwati from Swan Hill or the closely related Mathimathi from the Balranald area, and this is confirmed by data from these languages.

There is one major work on Wembawemba vocabulary. This was published in 1911 by A C Stone, who had been baker at Lake Boga for eighteen years. It is a detailed and most important contribution. The orthography is based on English, and there is therefore some confusion. Because of his special relationship with people at Lake Boga, Stone was able to gather the kind of data on material culture and traditional matters that no casual observer could have noted, and he wrote down his findings with great care; his work is unique in Victoria.

No further work appears to have been done on Wembawemba until Tindale compiled a short vocabulary in 1938, and then nothing further until Stan Day spoke to the writer in 1962.

References

Curr, E M 1886–1887, *The Australian Race*, 4 vols, Melbourne

Dixon, R M W 1980, *The Languages of Australia*, Cambridge University Press, Cambridge

Hercus, L A, 1969, *The languages of Victoria, a late survey*, Australian Institute of Aboriginal Studies, Canberra

Hercus, L A 1978, 'A note on Narinari', *Papers in Australian Linguistics*, no. 11, pp 119–131, Pacific Linguistics, Canberra

Hercus, L A 1986, *Victorian languages, a late survey*, Pacific Linguistics, Canberra

Mathews, R H 1902, 'The Aboriginal languages of Victoria', *Journal and Proceedings of the Royal Society of New South Wales*, vol. 36, pp 71–106

Mathews, R H 1903, 'Some Aboriginal languages of Queensland and Victoria', *Proceedings of the American Philosophical Society*, vol. 42, 243–253

Schmidt, W 1919, *Die Gliederung der australischen Sprachen*, Vienna

Smyth, J Brough 1878, *The Aborigines of Victoria*, (2 vols), Melbourne

Stone, A C 1911, 'The Aborigines of Lake Boga', *Royal Society of Victoria, Proceedings*, vol. 23, 433–468

7

Diyari

PETER AUSTIN

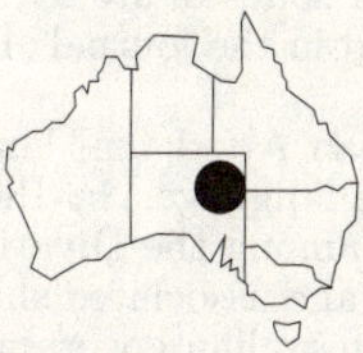

The Diyari language was traditionally spoken in the far north of South Australia, to the east of Lake Eyre. The southern boundary of Diyari country lay along a line between the present-day township of Maree and Mt Freeling in the northern Flinders Ranges. Their country went as far east as Lake Blanche and Lake Gregory, north to Lake Perigundi and Lake Howitt, and west towards Lake Eyre. Here they met up with the territory of their neighbours, the Thirrari, who occupied the eastern shore of Lake Eyre. Diyari country is traversed by the lower reaches of Cooper Creek – a mostly dry watercourse that runs from western Queensland through Innamincka (of Burke and Wills fame) and into Lake Eyre. The Birdsville Track also passes through Diyari country. This is one of the driest and hottest regions of Australia with an average annual rainfall of about 100 mm (or 4 inches) and summer temperatures regularly reaching 45 degrees; however the whole of the area was exploited by the Diyari and is covered with placenames and mythological sites.

7. Diyari

The Diyari's neighbours were the Thirrari and Arabana (to the west), the Kuyani and Adnyamathanha (south), the Yandrruwandha and Yawarrawarrga (east), and the Ngamini and Wangkangurru (north). The Diyari language is quite similar to Thirrari and Ngamini — speakers could understand one another easily. These languages also seem to be related to Yandrruwandha and Yawarrawarrga, with which they share much common vocabulary. The other languages to the west and south are quite different, however.

When they were first contacted by white settlers in the 1860s, the Diyari probably numbered over 1000, but today there are only two people alive who can speak the language fluently. One of these, Mr Ben Murray (whose traditional name is *Parlku-nguyu-thangkayiwarna*), was born in 1893 and is also the very last speaker of the Thirrari language. His life history, including a series of stories told by him in Diyari and Thirrari has been published in the journal *Aboriginal History* (see References below).

Unlike many Australian Aboriginal languages, Diyari has a long history of use as a written language. In 1869 German Lutheran pastors established a mission among the Diyari at Lake Killalpaninna on Cooper Creek; the mission and associated sheep station flourished until its closure by the South Australian government in 1914. The missionaries studied the Diyari language and used it in their work and their daily lives, including preaching in Diyari and teaching it in the mission school. They prepared primers, school books, dictionaries and grammars of Diyari, and translated a large number of Christian works into the language, including hymns and the Old and New Testaments. The Diyari were taught to read and write, and we know from written records that they used the language in their letters from the turn of the century until about 1960. Ben Murray regularly read his copy of the New Testament until his eyes became weak some years ago.

One of the most remarkable missionaries, the Rev. J G Reuther, not only translated the New Testament into Diyari, but also compiled a 14-volume manuscript on Diyari language, culture, mythology and history that includes a massive 4-volume dictionary. This manuscript was translated into English by Rev. P Scherer in 1981 and stands as monument to Reuther's dedication to the Diyari people. Recent research on Diyari began in the 1970s when tape recordings and notes were made by Luise Hercus, David Trefry and myself. I wrote my doctoral thesis on Diyari and published a grammar of it in 1981, and am currently working on a dictionary and collection of stories told by the last speakers.

About the wordlist

Diyari has a vocabulary of many thousands of words, and is especially rich in words describing the environment, human beings and relationships. It has many words for animals and plants of the arid desert country in which the Diyari lived, and lots of words for everyday activities, such as carrying:

waltharna	to carry on the head
pardarna	to carry in the hand
thukarna	to carry on the back

or moving about:

waparna	to go
wirarirna	to walk about
parlkarna	to go on a journey
purrkarna	to wade through water

In the wordlist below, only the most basic words are listed. To get the full meaning of words it will be nécessary to look at a full Diyari dictionary.

When the Diyari came in contact with Europeans, they adapted their language to the new environment and new objects around them, sometimes extending the meanings of their own words, and sometimes taking words from English. So, Diyari *dakarna* 'to pierce with a pointed instrument' was extended to mean 'to write', *warraparna* 'to tell a story' was widened to mean 'to read'. Sometimes English words were taken and adapted, as *rapiti* 'rabbit', *walypala* 'whiteman' (from 'white fella'), or *wilparra* 'any wheeled vehicle' (originally 'wheelbarrow', but extended to cover any vehicle with wheels, including what Diyari call *thurrhu wilparra* 'train', literally 'fire vehicle'). In this way, present-day Diyari speakers could talk or write about anything in their daily lives, including both traditional and contemporary topics.

Spelling and pronunciation

Like many other Aboriginal languages, Diyari has just three vowel sounds:

i, u, a

There are 23 consonants:

d, j, k, l, lh, ly, m, n, ng, nh, ny, p, r, rd, rl, rn, rr, rrh, rt, t, th, w, y

Diyari has a number of unusual features in its consonants, including a difference between *t* and *d*, and *rt* and *rd* in the middle of words, as in *karti* 'raw' versus *kardi* 'sister's husband, brother-in-law'. The letter *d* is always followed by a rolled *rr*, sounding something like the Scottish pronunciation of the beginning of 'dram'. As well, Diyari has three *r*-sounds: a glide *r* similar to an American 'r', a short flap *rr* (pronounced very quickly, like the 'd' in the middle of Australian English words — Diyari *kirri* 'clever' sounds like English 'kiddy'), and a strongly rolled *rrh* pronounced like a Scottish 'r'. The difference between the 'r's' is important for meaning: compare *thararna* 'to go up', *tharra* 'thigh', and *tharrharna* 'to fly'.

Diyari has five *n*-sounds: *n*, *nh*, *ny*, *ng* and *rn* (see page xxviii for a discussion of these symbols), and four *l*-sounds: *l*, *lh*, *ly* and *rl*. Again, the differences between these sounds are important for meaning, as in: *nganha* 'me', *ngana* 'to be', and *nganya* 'to muck around'.

The letters *n* and *nh*, and *l* and *lh* can be optionally preceded by *d* when they occur as the second consonant of a word — speakers sometimes pronounce the *d* and sometimes omit it. Some examples are: *widlha* or *wilha* 'woman', and *thidna* or *thina* 'foot'.

All words in Diyari must end in a vowel, and all words begin with a consonant.

DIYARI WORDLIST

WORDLIST CATEGORIES

1. Body parts and products
2. Kin relationships
3. Human classification
4. Language, mythology and ceremony
5. Human artefacts
6. Food, cooking and fire
7. Topography
8. Elements
9. Mammals
10. Reptiles
11. Birds
12. Aquatic life
13. Insects and spiders
14. Plants
15. Physical qualities
16. Non-physical qualities
17. Motion
18. State
19. Vocalisation and thought
20. Bodily functions
21. Impact and violence
22. Holding and transfer
23. Location, direction and time
24. Interjections and particles
25. Demonstratives and pronouns
26. Numbers
27. Introduced items
28. Placenames

1. Body parts and products

dapa	sore
darla	skin
kadlhu	liver
kangu	sweat
kapurrha	armpit
karlu	testicles
kidni	penis
kipara	urine
kirla	vagina
kuja	eyelash
kumarrhi	bone
kuna	faeces
mandrra	stomach
mangathandrra	head

mara	hand
marna	mouth
marnathandrra	tooth
marni	fat
milki	eye
mimi	lip
muku	bone
mulha	face; nose
murnampirrhi	chest
ngalja	saliva
ngama	breast
ngara	heart
ngarnka	beard
ngarnkajandrra	chin
ngulhu	forehead
nguna	arm
ngurrhamuku	shin
pangkithirrhi	rib
panja	knee
parlku	body
parra	hair
pilpa	eyebrow
pilpiri	shoulder
pirda	navel
pirrhi	fingernail
tharli	tongue
tharlpa	ear
tharra	thigh
thidna	foot
thilja	sinew
thinthipirri	elbow
thuku	back
wakarrha	back of neck
wilyirrhi	bottom
yurlku	throat

2. Kin relationships

kadnhini	mother's mother
kaka	mother's brother
kaku	elder sister
kami	father's mother
ngandrri	mother
ngapiri	father
ngardarda	mother's father
ngathata	younger sister or brother
nhiyi	elder brother
nhuwa	spouse
papa	father's sister
yanku	father's father

3. Human classification

kanku	boy
karna	person
kupa	child
mangawarrhu	widow
mankarrha	girl
matharri	man
pinarrhu	old man
widlha	woman
wilhapina	old woman

4. Language, mythology and ceremony

kararrhu	moiety name
mardu	totem
matharri	moiety name
murramurra	ancestral being
pinya	revenge expedition
tharla	name
thidnanipa	man on revenge expedition
warda	corroboree headdress
wima	corroboree, ceremony, song
yawarrha	word, language

5. Human artefacts

kalthi	spear
katu	windbreak
kirra	boomerang
ngurra	camp
pirli	dillybag
punga	hut, humpy
thurla	chisel
thurrhu manya	firestick
wadna	yamstick
wirrpa	pubic tassel
yakutha	bag
yama	fishing net

6. Food, cooking and fire

kanya	ashes
nganthi	meat, edible animal
ngapa	water
ngunku	tobacco for chewing
pandrra	cooked, ripe
pijirrhi	native tobacco
pirla	coals
puka	vegetable food
purda	unripe
thupu	smoke
thurrhu	fire
wayi-rna	to cook

7. Topography

daku	sandhill
jili	spring
karirrhi	river
karrku	red ochre
kurdu	hole in ground
marda	rock, stone, hill
mingka	hole
mitha	ground, sand
palthu	road
pantu	lake
parru	yellow ochre
pulyurrhu	mud
thaka	clay

8. Elements

diji	sun
dijithandrra	star
kunmi	mist
ngarrhimatha	flood
paraji	light; lightning
pariwilpa	sky
parlku	cloud
pira	moon
thalara	rain
thinka	night
wathara	wind
wijikura	whirlwind

9. Mammals

jukurrhu	kangaroo
kadnungka	spectacled hare wallaby
kantu	rock wallaby
kapitha	bandicoot
kinthala	dog
mayarrhu	marsupial mouse; marsupial rat
palyarra	kangaroo rat
pildrra	possum

10. Reptiles

kadni	stumpy tail lizard
kalta	blue-tongue lizard
kapirrhi	goanna
pirrhinti	perentie
thandrripila	brown snake
wama	carpet snake
wanku	snake

11. Birds

darurdarrhu	seagull
kardarrhungka	white cockatoo
karlathurrha	wild turkey
karrhawara	eaglehawk
kawalka	crow
kilankila	galah
kujikuji	blue long-tailed wren

kukunka	hawk
kurrparu	magpie
kuti	swan
mulhaparra	pigeon
munyi	owl
murlpa	crane
paya	bird
purrhalka	brolga
tharrhalku	teal duck
thindrrithindrri	Willie wagtail
warrhukathi	emu
wirluru	curlew

12. Aquatic life

kilaparrha	bony bream
kintha	shrimp
kunkithirri	crayfish
kurri	mussel
marrkara	yellow-belly
murlu	crab
ngankanthi	catfish
parrhu	fish
thidnamara	frog
yurndayurnda	tadpole

13. Insects and spiders

karlipilhi	butterfly
kata	louse
kudnapinjinarra	sandfly
kunthi	mosquito
marankarrha	spider
miriwiri	maggot
mirrka	ant
munju	fly
munjurrhunga	blowfly
panga	caterpillar
pindrri	grasshopper
thilthirri	centipede

14. Plants

kantha	grass
kaparrha	root
karlku	bulrush
malka	mulga
ngamangama	milkweed
patharra	box tree
pirta	tree
thangkaldrri	sweet millet
tharlpa	leaf
warta	butt
yawa	wild onion

15. Physical qualities

dampu	round
danthu	soft
jarrkara	sharp
kaldrri	salty
karti	raw
kilpa	cold
kurdukurdi	crooked
kurnu	one
madlhanji	bad
malkamalka	spotted
malthi	cool
mandrru	two
mardi	heavy
marnka	slow
marrhalyi	red
marrhu	wide
marrpu	many
maru	black
mikiri	deep
murnamirri	full
muya	dry
ngapajangka	wet
ngapu	quiet
ngawa	light
ngumu	good
ngurrhu	hard
nhurrhu	quick

nyarni	blunt
pandrra	cooked; ripe
parda	wet
parrjarna	all
parrkulu	three
payirrhi	long
pirna	big
pirrhapirrha	flat
purda	unripe
putha	shallow
tharlku	straight
thungka	rotten
waka	small
waldrra	hot
wardu	short
warrhu	white
wuldrru	narrow

16. Non-physical qualities

kirrhi	clever
mawa	hunger
mirrja	noisy
muka	asleep
nguyuni	greedy
nharri	dead
partiparti	stupid
puju	blind
thardi	thirst
tharlpa kurrhu	deaf
thipi	alive
yunka	jealous

17. Motion

durnka-rna	to emerge, come out
karri-rna	to climb
karr-rna	to chase
kathi-rna	to climb
kurlkunga-rna	to jump
kurrha-rna	to put down
marrka-rna	to crawl
mindrri-rna	to run

ngapunga-rna	to swim
ngari-rna	to go down
pardaka-rna	to carry
pirrhikuthi-rna	to dive
pirrki-rna	to play
purri-rna	to fall
tharrhaka-rna	to float
tharrha-rna	to fly
thika-rna	to return
wadni-rna	to follow
wakara-rna	to come
waltha-rna	to bring
wapa-rna	to go
wirrhi-rna	to enter, go in
yinpa-rna	to send

18. State

ngama-rna	to sit, stay, camp
parra-rna	to lie (of inanimates)
tharrka-rna	to stand
thurrara-rna	to lie, sleep (of animates)

19. Vocalisation and thought

danka-rna	to discover
darni-rna	to bid farewell to
jampa-rna	to be very fond of
karrka-rna	to call out
kilparri-rna	to disbelieve
kingka-rna	to laugh
kurrutharrha-rna	to forget
ngundrra-rna	to think
nguyama-rna	to know
wangka-rna	to sing
warrapa-rna	to tell
winpa-rna	to ask repetitively for, pester
yakalka-rna	to ask
yatha-rna	to speak
yindrra-rna	to cry

20. Bodily functions

kajakaja-rna	to hurt
kipara-rna	to urinate
kudna-rna	to defecate
kundrrunga-rna	to snore
marna thapa-rna	to kiss
marna tharrka-rna	to yawn
ngana-rna	to be
nganja-rna	to want
ngapija parda-rna	to dream
ngara-rna	to hear, listen
nguku warra-rna	to vomit
ngundrra-rna	to think
nguyama-rna	to know
nhayi-rna	to look at, see
pali-rna	to die
panthama-rna	to smell
parnima-rna	to smell
pulka-rna	to blow
thadni-rna	to copulate
thapa-rna	to drink
thayi-rna	to eat
yingki-rna	to give
yurlka-rna	to swallow

21. Impact and violence

daka-rna	to pierce, stab
dama-rna	to cut
karrha-rna	to tie
kilja-rna	to peel
milka-rna	to pinch
nandrra-rna	to hit
paku-rna	to dig
palka-rna	to split
thirrhi-rna	to fight
thurrpa-rna	to twist, spin; to tease
thuti-rna	to bury
wakarripa-rna	to break
warrkamandrra-rna	to tie, tangle
wirrhipa-rna	to paint
yarrki-rna	to burn

22. Holding and transfer

mama-rna	to take away from, snatch
mandrra-rna	to grasp
nhanga-rna	to pour
parda-rna	to hold, carry in hand
thardupa-rna	to push
thuka-rna	to carry on back
waltha-rna	to carry on head
warra-rna	to throw
yika-rna	to squeeze
yinpa-rna	to send
yirrpa-rna	to pull

23. Location, direction and time

diji	day
karakara	near
karrari	today, now
kilpa	winter
kilpa waldrra	year
kudnankarri	south
ngunyari	right
pira	month
thangkuparna	tomorrow
thidnankarra	north
thirrhiwa	east
waldrra	summer
waldrrawirti	yesterday
warrhanganju	left
warrhitha	far
warru	long ago
yantakarra	west
yarra	that day
yarrha	this way

24. Interjections and particles

kaparrhawu	come here!
kapawu	look out!
kawu	yes
kawuwarna	that's correct!
mayi	well then, all right
nganha	oh yes, is that so

nganjalu	good job!
nguyala	poor thing
purrhu	hey!
walya	wait a minute!
yakayayi	hooray!

25. Demonstratives and pronouns

ngakangu	to me
ngakarni	my
ngaldrra	we two (including you)
ngaldrrangu	to us two (including you)
ngaldrrarni	of us two (including you)
ngali	we two (excluding you)
ngalingu	to us two (excluding you)
ngalirni	of us two (excluding you)
nganhi	I
ngayana	we all (excluding you)
ngayanangu	to us all (excluding you)
ngayanarni	of us all (excluding you)
ngayani	we all (including you)
ngayaningu	to us all (including you)
ngayanirni	of us all (including you)
nhaka	there
nhangkangu	to her
nhangkarni	her
nhani	she
nhawu	he
nhingkirda	here
nhungkangu	to him
nhungkarni	his
pudla	they two
pudlangu	to them two
pudlarni	of them two
thana	they all
thanangu	to them all
thanarni	of them all
warangu	to who?
waranha	who?
warni	whose?
yidni	you
yingkangu	to you

yingkarni	your
yudla	you two
yudlangu	to you two
yudlarni	of you two
yurra	you all
yurrangu	to you all
yurrarni	of you all

26. Introduced items

japuli	shovel
jipijipi	sheep
juka	sugar
mutuka	car
nhantu	horse
pakutha	fox
pipa	paper, book
rapiti	rabbit
tharra malka	policeman
thirti	tea
thurrhu wilparra	train
walypala	white man
warli	house
wilparra	wheeled vehicle
witiminirri	hat
yakayita	gate
yawarrha yingkirnayija	missionary

27. Placenames

Durlkaninha	Dulkanina Station
Kaparrhamaranha	Kopperamanna
Katithandrra	Lake Eyre
Kirlawirlpaninha	Killalpaninna
Kudnarrhi	Cooper Creek
Malka mandrru	Mulka Station
Mangurrhani	Mungerannie Station
Maramulhurrunha	Muloorina Station
Marndawardunha	Mundowdna Station
Marnpiawi	Murnpeowie Station
Mayarrhu mitha	Mira Mitta Station
Pantu pirna	Lake Hope
Pirikurnti	Lake Perigundi
Wayikalkunha	Clayton Creek
Winthamingkanha	Frome Creek

Grammatical notes

Like all the languages of this book, Diyari has a rich grammatical system with fine distinctions of meaning indicated by changing the form of words. In Diyari all such grammatical meanings are expressed by suffixes, that is word endings. This can result in somewhat long and complex words, such as:

thurraripipalumayi

This can be analysed as:

thurrari-pi-pa-lu-mayi
lie-cause-for another-two-order
'You two make him lie down for me!'

Nouns in Diyari are suffixed for case — case marking is of the 'split ergative' type, where:

1. some pronouns have one form for intransitive and transitive subject (nominative) and a different form for transitive object;
2. common nouns have one form for intransitive subject and transitive object (absolutive) and a different form for transitive subject (ergative);
3. all other nouns and pronouns have three forms for the three functions.

In addition, there are case affixes for dative (possessor), locative (location at), allative (location towards) and ablative (location from). Here are some examples:

Kupa	*mindrri-yi*	*ngurra-ya*	*daku-ndrru*
child	run-*present*	camp-*allative*	sandhill-*ablative*

'The child is running to the camp from the sandhill.'

Karna-li	*widlha*	*nhayi-yi*	*walypala-ya*	*warli-nhi*
man-*ergative*	woman	see-*present*	whiteman-*possessor*	house-*loc.*

'The man sees the woman in the whiteman's house.'

Notice the order of words in the Diyari sentence: subject comes first, object next and finally verbs are toward the end of the sentence.

Adjectives (quality words) follow the noun in Diyari, unlike English where they precede the noun. Thus we find *karna pirna* 'a big man' (literally 'man big') and *widlha waka* 'a small woman' (literally 'woman small'). When these are used in a sentence, the adjective takes the case suffix and nothing is added to the noun. So, compare the following to the example above:

Karna	*pirna-li*	*widlha*	*nhayi-yi*	*walypala-ya*
man	big-*ergative*	woman	see-*present*	whiteman-*possessor*
	warli	*waka-nhi*		
	house	small-*loc.*		

'The big man sees the woman in the whiteman's small house.'

Diyari has pronouns for first, second and third persons, and distinguishes between singular (one), dual (two) and plural (more than two). In the first person dual and plural there is a difference between inclusive (including the person spoken to) and exclusive (excluding the person spoken to). Diyari is different from most other Aboriginal languages in that it marks a difference between male and female in the third person singular: *nhawu* 'he' versus *nhani* 'she'.

Unlike in most other Aboriginal languages, Diyari verbs are not divided into conjugations — all verbs take the same sort of endings. The endings show the time when something was done, or express ideas like making an order. Here are some examples (see also above):

Nhawu	*pinarrhu*	*pali-ya*	*kudnarrhi-nhi*
that	old man	die-*past*	Cooper Creek-*locative*

'That old man died on Cooper Creek.'

Wata	*mindrri-ya*	*nhaka*
not	run-*command*	there

'Don't run there!'

Diyari also has auxiliary verbs which follow the main verb and show the time when something happens (English also has auxiliaries but they come before the verb, as in 'will go', 'have gone', 'is going'):

waparna wanthiyi	went (long ago)
waparna wapayi	goes (habitually)
waparna warrayi	went (recently)
wapalha nganayi	will go (future)

Here are some examples:

Thana-li	*muka*	*kurrharna*	*wanthiyi*	*mudlha-nhi*
they-*ergative*	bone	put	*long ago*	nose-*locative*

'They used to put bones in their noses long ago.'

Ngaldrra	*yathalha*	*nganayi*	*thangkuparna*
we two	talk	*future*	tomorrow

'We will talk tomorrow.'

Diyari also has a special feature of verbs that is found in many central Australian languages: an ending is placed on some verbs to show that their subject is the same or different to that of another verb. This is called *switch-reference*, and is seen especially with verbs indicating a purpose ('in order to ...'). If the purpose action is done by the same subject then *-lha* is added, but if the purpose action is done by a different subject then *-rnanthu* is added. Here are some examples:

Ngathu	*nganthi*	*wayi-yi*	*thayi-lha*
I	meat	cook-*present*	eat-*purpose:same subject*

'I am cooking meat (for me) to eat.'

Ngathu	*nganthi*	*wayi-yi*	*kupa-li*	*thayi-rnanthu*
I	meat	cook-*present*	children-*ergative*	eat-*purpose: different subject*

'I am cooking meat for the children to eat.'

In English when the second subject is the same, it can be left out ('I am cooking meat to eat'). In Diyari *-lha* shows this sameness of subject explicitly. Imagine how this could be useful when it comes to sentences like 'I bought some ice cream to eat' — in Diyari you can tell if I am going to let anyone else eat some ice cream too!

Further reading

A technical description of Diyari for an academic audience may be found in Austin (1981). For stories in Diyari see Austin and Murray (1981), and Austin (1986). There is a discussion of Diyari literacy in Austin (1986). The biography of Ben Murray is to be found in Austin, Hercus and Jones (1988). The Reuther manuscript was published as Reuther (1981). For information on Rev. Reuther and the Killalpaninna mission, see Jones and Sutton (1986). A history of the mission by Christine Stevens is to be published by Oxford University Press.

References

Austin, P 1981, *A grammar of Diyari, South Australia*, Cambridge University Press, Cambridge

Austin, P 1986, 'Afghan story' and 'Paradise crossing', in *This is what happened*, eds L A Hercus and P Sutton, pp 129–132, 293–296, Australian Institute of Aboriginal Studies, Canberra

Austin, P 1986, 'Diyari language postcards and Diyari literacy', *Aboriginal History*, vol. 10, pp 175–190

Austin, P, L A Hercus and P Jones 1988, 'Ben Murray *Parlku-Nguyu-Tangkayiwarna*', *Aboriginal History*, vol. 12, pp 115–188

Austin, P and B Murray 1981, 'Afghans and Aborigines: Diyari texts', *Aboriginal History*, vol. 5, pp 71–79

Jones, P and P Sutton 1986, *Art and Land*, South Australian Museum, Adelaide

Reuther, J G 1981, *The Diari* Australian Institute of Aboriginal Studies, Canberra

8

Kaurna

ROB AMERY and JANE SIMPSON

IN COOPERATION WITH KAURNA PLAINS SCHOOL PROJECT AND LEWIS O'BRIEN

Kaurna is the name currently given to the language of the Adelaide Plains. It consists of several closely related dialects spoken from Crystal Brook in the north to Cape Jervis in the south and bounded on the east by the Mount Lofty Ranges and on the west by St Vincent's Gulf. Linguistically, Kaurna is closely related to Narrunga, Nukunu, Barngarla, Adnyamathanha and other languages to the north and west. In fact, Kaurna speakers could probably understand Narrunga almost as easily as Australians can understand American English. The languages to the east are rather different. Without training, Kaurna speakers could not have understood Ngarrindjeri, a neighbouring language to the east, just as English speakers cannot understand Spanish without training. However, there were, and still are social ties between the Ngarrindjeri and the Kaurna people.

The Adelaide Plains provided the inhabitants with a variety of foods, both plant foods (tubers, wattle gum, berries and others) and animal foods (birds' eggs, white ants, grubs, possums, kangaroos, fish, lizards, emus and other game). They met the cold winters by wearing possum skin clothes and building huts roofed with bark, or making use of fallen trees.

With the establishment of the colony of South Australia in 1836, and the city of Adelaide, the Kaurna were rapidly dispossessed of their lands, despite reasonably amicable relations initially with the settlers. The first recorded numbers of Kaurna people are not large — about 310 in 1841, and only 150 in 1843. This probably has to do with the arrival of diseases ahead of the settlers. Many died in the smallpox epidemics of 1789 and 1829 which spread from eastern Australia. Two observers of the effects of the tragedy wrote:

> They [Aborigines] universally assert that it [smallpox] came from the east, or the Murray tribes, so that it is not at all improbable that the disease was at first brought among the natives by European settlers on the eastern coast. They have not suffered from it for some years; but about a decennium ago it was, according to their statement, universal; when it diminished their numbers considerably, and on many left the marks of its ravages, to be seen at this day. They have no remedy against it, except the *nguyapalti,* [...] the smallpox song, which they learnt from the eastern tribes, by the singing of which the disease is believed to be prevented or stopped in its progress. (Teichelmann and Schürmann 1840, p. 34)

In 1838, two missionaries of the Dresden Lutheran Missionary Society, Christian Teichelmann and Clamor Schürmann, arrived in Adelaide. They studied the Kaurna language and culture, publishing a description of the language in 1840 after just eighteen months work. In 1839 they established the Native Location School on the banks of the Torrens River. They taught children to read and write in their own language in this school until 1845. Official work on the Kaurna language stopped in the 1840s, but in 1857 Teichelmann sent an extensive vocabulary of the language to George Grey, then Governor in South Africa, which has never been published. There are other records of the Kaurna language (e.g. Wyatt 1879), but these two are the most significant and most accurate, and it is from these that we have derived the wordlist.

The Kaurna population declined rapidly, and those that remained retreated to the fringes and small towns outside Adelaide. In 1850, the Poonindie Training Institution was established near Port Lincoln and a number of young Kaurna were sent there, along with other people from the Murray River and other districts. In 1865 Cawthorne wrote 'Of this tribe [Adelaide Plains] at the present moment I believe not 5 individuals exist, 4 years ago, as well as I could ascertain, there was but one family living'. Upon the closure of Poonindie in 1894 the Aboriginal people were sent to Point McLeay near the Murray mouth or to Point Pearce on Yorke Peninsula. The last fluent speaker of Kaurna, Ivaritji or Ibaritji (Mrs Amelia Taylor), died in 1929.

Despite claims or pronouncements of imminent extinction, Kaurna people have survived. Several thousand Nungas (Aboriginal people) in Adelaide today are able to trace their Kaurna ancestry. These people typically also have Ngarrindjeri and/or Narrunga ancestry with which they usually identify more closely because of their ties with the Point McLeay and Point Pearce communities respectively.

In the intervening period, the Kaurna language has remained documented in the historical record. The vocabulary recorded provides a snapshot of some aspects of Kaurna life 150 years ago. A few Kaurna words borrowed into English in the early contact period continue to be used (e.g. *wurley* from Kaurna *wodli* 'hut, house'). More importantly, Kaurna is enshrined in many place names in and around Adelaide. Maps of Adelaide suburbs and the Adelaide Plains reveal distinctive Kaurna placenames, such as Aldinga (*Ngultingga*), Onkaparinga (*Ngangkiparringga*), Noarlunga (*Nurlungga*), Willunga, Myponga, Yankalilla, Uraidla (*Yurreidla*), etc.

There are many interesting aspects of Kaurna history, life, language and culture to be discovered from looking at the historical records. For instance, they used birth order names for female and male children, up to the ninth born. These were used as terms of address and reference.

	Female	Male
First Born	*Kartanya, Kartiato*	*Kartammeru*
Second Born	*Waruyu*	*Waritya*
Third Born	*Kudnato*	*Kudnuitya*
Fourth Born	*Munato*	*Munaitya*
Fifth Born	*Midlato*	*Midlaitya*
Sixth Born	*Marruato*	*Marrutya*
Seventh Born	*Wanguato*	*Wangutya*
Eighth Born	not recorded	not recorded
Ninth Born	*Ngadlaato*	*Ngadlaitya*

The Kaurna today

In recent years there has been renewed interest in the Kaurna language. Some Aboriginal organisations and institutions (for example, the Tandanya Centre) have drawn their names from Kaurna vocabulary. In 1990, several songs were written in Kaurna (and other Nunga languages). Some of these songs are becoming very popular among Nunga children and in the Nunga community. Kaurna Plains School, an Aboriginal school established in 1986, has embarked on a Kaurna language program. Stories have been written and other materials produced. The program has received unanimous support from the school staff, parents and students (demonstrated by the Education Review

Unit findings in June, 1992). A senior secondary Kaurna language program commenced nearby at Inbarendi College in 1994.

Staff and children are beginning to relearn the language and to use the language creatively again. To do this, words need to be created for the new things and ideas that have come in since the language was recorded. Fortunately, Teichelmann and Schürmann (1840) list many words for new concepts, and these show different ways of creating new words. These processes include expanding the meaning of an existing word (e.g. *pari* 'rice' from *pari* 'maggot'); compounding words together (e.g. *makki-tau* 'window' from *makki* 'ice, glass' and *tau* 'hole'); doubling words (e.g. *tadlitadli* 'frypan' from *tadli* 'spit'); making nouns from verbs (e.g. *nurlitti* 'key' from *nurlendi* 'to turn, twist'); adding endings (e.g. *turtiana* 'shirt' from *turti* 'arm' and the ending *-ana* 'belonging to'); cutting words down (e.g. *kappi* 'tobacco' from *kappendi* 'to vomit') and translating parts of an idea (e.g. *gadlapindi* 'hell' from *gadla* 'fire' and *pindi* 'pit').

These terms provide us with a useful resource to make new words for new concepts by analogy, and some new words (e.g. *padnipadnitti* 'car' from *padnendi* 'to run', *karrikarritti* 'aeroplane' from *karrendi* 'to fly' and *muka muka karndo* 'computer' from *mukamuka* 'brain' and *karndo* 'lightning') have already been introduced. Fortunately, the language was documented well enough to allow for a significant amount of linguistic reconstruction to be done. Moreover, we can use ideas about expressing new concepts found in related languages which are still spoken (Adnyamathanha and Pitjantjatjara for instance) to meet contemporary needs.

The Kaurna language is currently fulfilling an important role in the formation of Nunga identity. Many Nungas are keen to retrieve and revive their linguistic and cultural heritage (Gale 1991).

About the wordlist

The words listed in this compilation come mostly from Teichelmann (1857), with some extra information from Teichelmann and Schürmann (1840). For reasons of space, only 500 of the several thousand words in the sources have been included. We have departed from the format of many of the wordlists in this volume by increasing the coverage of words in the areas of thought, learning, social relationships, relationship with land, and feelings. We have also tried to include Kaurna words that are similar to Narrunga words still used by Nungas. The Narrunga words come from Doris Graham (Graham and Graham 1987).

For space reasons also, we have shortened the dictionary entries so that they now consist of word, variant spellings and the original definition. Additional comments have been left out and the expression has sometimes been made more modern if the original is confusing. The full entries, especially those in Teichelmann (1857), contain a great deal of linguistic, cultural and historical information. Here is part of a full entry from Teichelmann (1857):

Kundo, the chest, whereas *ngarnmi* the female breast;
2. anything projecting similar as the chest
3. as the seat of several passions, as
kundo wilta, brave, bold; fearless;
kundo punggondi, to dislike, hate; [...]
kundo punggorendi, to be concerned about; to be sorry;
kundo punggorendaii ngaityo yungakko, 'I am concerned about, or long for my elder brother.' [...]

We have included some botanical identifications of plants which were kindly provided by Beth Gott, or were taken from Clarke (1985, 1988). The bird identifications are those from Condon (1955). The mammal and reptile identifications are based on those given for the corresponding words in Adnyamathanha in McEntee and McKenzie (1992) and Tunbridge (1991).

Spelling and pronunciation

Working out how to pronounce the words of a language is not easy when there are only written records — no fluent speakers and no tape-recordings. We have to find out what the sounds of the language are, and how those sounds correspond to the letters used by the people who wrote the language down. For Kaurna we are fortunate in that it appears to resemble other southern South Australian languages, such as Nukunu, spoken to the north. Luise Hercus recorded on tape the late Gilbert Branfield speaking Nukunu. She has prepared a dictionary from this (Hercus 1992) using a practical spelling system which represents the different sounds of Nukunu. Some Kaurna words can be matched with similar Nukunu words, and we can gain some idea of the sounds of Kaurna from this.

However, the pronunciation of sounds written with *t, rt* or *tt* are hard to work out precisely, because, while there were three *t* sounds other than the *ty* sounds, Teichelmann and Schürmann do not systematically distinguish them. We know from comparing Kaurna with Nukunu that what Teichelmann and Schürmann write as *kalta* 'sleepy lizard' had an alveolar /t/ (Nukunu *kalta*), whereas *milte* 'red ochre' probably had an interdental /th/, (Nukunu *milthi*). Like the *t* sounds, the *n* sounds and *l* sounds tend to be confused (Kaurna *karndo* 'thunder or lightning' Nukunu *karntu* 'storm'; Kaurna *parndalla* 'spine', Nukunu *pantila*). Probably there were three *r* sounds, as there are in Nukunu. Teichelmann and Schürmann use *rr, r* and rarely *r* with a dot under it to mark different *r* sounds. However, their use of *r* and *rr* do not correspond systematically to the three different *r* sounds in Nukunu (Kaurna *wirri* 'shoulder blade', Nukunu *wiRi;* Kaurna *wirri* 'club', Nukunu *wirri;* Kaurna *wirra* 'forest', Nukunu *wira*).

There were probably six vowel sounds in Kaurna, three short and three corresponding long vowels. Teichelmann and Schürmann used five letters, *a, e, i, o, u,* as well as marks on these vowels, and combinations of vowels, to represent these sounds. Thus their *mena* 'eye' corresponds to Nukunu *miina,* and their *kauwe* 'water' to Nukunu *kawi.*

In the wordlist we have used the original spellings of Teichelmann and Schürmann, rather than attempt to create a more accurate spelling system for Kaurna. However, we have chosen to use the Teichelmann and Schürmann spellings for two reasons. First, these spellings are quite well established; their spellings have been used to name institutions and buildings in the Adelaide area. Second, even if comparative work with other languages were done, the results would be at best partial, since many Kaurna words do not correspond directly to words in other languages.

Variant spellings have been included from both the 1857 and the 1840 dictionary, because we do not know exactly how the words were pronounced, and because the variants give us an idea of the range of pronunciation. However, we have not included variants beginning with *b* and *g.* This is because it does not seem to change the meaning if words starting with *p* are pronounced with *b* or *p,* or if words starting with *k* are pronounced with *g* or *k.* However, if a word is only found starting with *b* or with *g* in the dictionaries, it is spelled with a *b* or a *g* here too.

KAURNA WORDLIST

WORDLIST CATEGORIES

1. Body parts and products
2. Kin relationships
3. Human classification
4. Language, mythology and ceremony
5. Human artefacts
6. Food, cooking and fire
7. Topography
8. Elements
9. Mammals
10. Reptiles
11. Birds
12. Aquatic life
13. Insects and spiders
14. Plants
15. Physical qualities
16. Body states
17. Feelings
18. Values
19. Motion
20. State
21. Vocalisation and thought
22. Bodily functions
23. Impact and violence
24. Holding and transfer
25. Location, direction and time
26. Interjections
27. Social activities and property
28. Learning, schools and education

8.1 ______________ Kaurna ______________

1. Body parts and products

bakkurta	cuts on the body when healed, the dots on the chest and back of the Aborigines
bulta	heart in man and beast
gurlte	cough, catarrh, expectorated matter; a cold
kandarla	perspiration, sweat
kanti	thigh, leg, as of mutton, etc. (Narrunga: *kanti* thigh, *gunthi bultha* pants, undies)
karlto	heart; possibly also the lungs or the pit of the stomach
karro	blood
kartakka	shoulder
karti	human blood
malta	beard in general; cheekbone
mamba, matta	knee (Narrunga: *muthi*)
manka	elevated scars on the chest or back produced by incisions
mannando	lower arm
mannuworta	occiput, neck
marra	finger; hand (Narrunga: *murra*)
mena	eye (Narrunga: *mina*)
moka *or* muka, mukamuka, ngarro moka *or* ngarru muka	brain
mokarta *or* mukarta	head
mudla	nose (Narrunga: *moothla*)
mūndo	anus, that where you sit upon (Narrunga: *moornta*)
munto, mūrlo	belly, abdomen
murki	face; forehead (Narrunga: *moorlki*)
nando	upper arm (Narrunga: *arntu*)
ngammi	female breast (Narrunga: *ngammi*)
ngammi ngarro *or* ngammi ngarru	milk
ngaratta *or* ngarratta	spine
ngokurra	joint of the shoulder
ngulta	cuts on the back and chest
ngurra, minti	scar, cicatrice
nukke	mucus of the nose; a cold (Narrunga: *nookee*)
parndalla	spine, lumbar region

parpa	skin of the human body; skin generally; foreskin
pureta *or* purita	loins; kidneys
tadlanya	tongue
ta-yappa	mouth (Narrunga: *thubra*)
tia	tooth, row of teeth; edge (Narrunga: *thea* lips)
tidli	region round about over the hip bones, waist, abdomen, stomach; hunger, hungry
tidna	foot, footmark, track of men or animals (Narrunga: *thidna*)
tidngi	elbow
tinninya	rib
tittinda	line of hair running from the pubes to the umbilicus
tundanda *or* tundondo	heel; ankle bone
waltu *or* worlto	nape, neck, termination of the spine where the neck commences
wangki	throat
wirri	shoulder, more particularly the part towards the back
yärko *or* yerko	leg (Narrunga: *yarlkoo*)
yärkunda	whole neck between shoulder and head (*Also means* prop, pillar)
yärla, yellamuka	calf of the leg
yurre	ear (found in the placename *Uraidla*, literally 'two ears', referring to Mount Lofty and the adjoining point)

2. Kin relationships

bukkianna	ancestors, forefathers
ipiti	one who has lost his mother, motherless orphan
kakka akka	lover, spouse
kanggallanggalla	parent
karto	wife
maityukka	girl whose father is dead
muranye	mother whose child has died
ngaityaii	my mother, 'mamma'
ngaityerli	my father, 'pappa'
ngangkimeyu	one who is in the relation of a mother to; female parent, mother

ngangkita *or* ngangkitta	mother; used of father-in-law too
ngubba, yärlinna *or* yerlinna	husband
panya *or* panyappi	younger brother or sister
tuinya	widow
wārnpi, warrinya	one having lost his father, fatherless orphan
wikandi *or* wikkarndi	father whose children are dead
yakkana *or* yakkarna, yakanata, yakkanilya	sister, older sister
yampinna	widower
yangarra	wife
yärli meyu *or* yerli meyu	father
yunga, yungalya, yungata	elder brother

3. Human classification

burka *or* buṛka	old; complete tattooed Aborigine, being now a full-grown man and admissible to all secrets and privileges
mankarra	girl, young woman
meyu	man
meyu worta, yertameyu	countryman
nepo	neighbour, companion
ngammaitya	woman (general term), wife
ngangki	female (general term) (found in the river name *Ngangkiparringga*, literally 'on, at or upon the river associated with women', written as 'Onkaparinga' in English) (Narrunga: *ungki*)
pappa	youth who has undergone the ceremony of circumcision
pinde *or* pindi meyu	European (from *pinde* hole, pit, grave)
pinde wadli *or* pindi wadli	past childbearing; old woman
wakowako *or* wakwakko	child (general term), little one
yärli *or* yerli	male, masculine

4. Language, mythology and ceremony

-burka *or* -buṛka	affixed to names of districts, indicating person who is the proprietor and inhabitant of

	the district, or who originated there or whose home it is. Thus *Mullawirra-burka*, 'old man of the dry forest' (on the east side of Aldinga Plain), was the name of an Aboriginal man called 'King John' by Europeans
kangarlta *or* kangkarlta	surname
kuinyo	dead person, skeleton, death personified (probably the source of the word *goonya* for 'white person') (Narrunga: *goonya* white person)
kuinyunda	sacred, forbidden
kurri *or* kuri	play; corroboree
narri	name
pindi	habitation of souls before birth and after death (*Also means* hole, pit, grave; *also* European)
towilla	soul, spirit, ghost
warra	speech, word, language, etc.
wārrāra *or* wārrawārra *or* worrarra	Aboriginal doctor, sorcerer, etc.; the spell of the sorcerer
yammaiamma	Aboriginal doctor, sorcerer, teacher

5. Human artefacts

bakke-bakketi *or* bakketti	stone knife
biltatti *or* biltitti	pair of scissors (from *biltendi* to cut)
budni worta	light, quick running vehicle, a gig (probably from *budnandi* come + *worta* behind)
kadlotti	girdle made of the threads spun of man's hair, worn round the waist, only by adults
kaiya *or* kaya	small spear, which is thrown with the *midla*
kandappi	Aboriginal chisel, made of flint or glass (*Also means* the preparation of a kangaroo or other skin for a bag or cloak)
karpa	support, prop, pillar
karra birri	bedstead (from *karra* high + *birri* scaffold)
katta	heavy stick to fight with, club

kondolli gadlaieri	oil-lamp (from *kondolli* whale + *gadlaiere* light)
ku	shelter
kudnawodli	water closet, privy, toilet (from *kudna* excrement + *wodli* hut, house)
kuintye *or* kuntye	fringe of string worn by the female sex around the waist, apparently from the time of puberty to the time of first pregnancy
kuntoro kattitti	umbrella (from *kuntoro* rain + *kattendi* carry)
kuri	circle, compass
kurotura	parasol (from *kuro* crown of head + *tura* or *turra* shade, shadow)
mānna *or* manna	crosscut saw (from *mandi* to draw, pull)
maikarnkarnkatti	spoon (from *mai* food + *karnkarnkatti* lifter)
maiwondawondarti	plate, dish etc. (from *mai* food + *wondandi* to put down)
makki	glass (*Also means* ice)
makkitau	window (from *makki* ice, glass + *tau* hole)
makkitura	looking-glass, mirror (from *makki* ice, glass + *tura* or *turra* shade, shadow)
maltapirratti	razor (from *malta* beard + *pirrandi* to shave)
memakki	spectacles (from *me* eye + *makki* ice, glass)
midla	propelling stick of the spear, which gives the power to the spear
minde *or* minti	net for fishing and for catching game
mokartianna *or* mukartiana	covering of the head, hat, cap (from *mukarta* head; the word *mukarti* for 'hat', found in many other Aboriginal languages, probably comes from this word)
mullabakka	shield made of dry bark
munta	large net for catching emus and other game
mutyerta	clothing, covering (probably from English 'my shirt')

nainmainmatti	pair of pincers, scissors (from *nainmandi* to press or keep together)
narna	door
ngarra papalto *or* ngarra pappalto	stool (*Also means* tree stump)
ngarruwodli	whitewashed house (from *ngarru* white substance + *wodli* house)
nukkeana	pocket-handkerchief (from *nukke* mucus of nose)
paitpurla gadlaiere	candle (from *paitpurla* grease, fat, oil + *gadlaiere* light)
parndàpure	ball, bullet; gun, musket (from *parndendi* to crackle, sparkle, or perhaps *parnda* limestone + *pure* stone)
parupammamatti	fork (from *paru* meat + *pammandi* to pierce)
pïki worli	pig sty (from *worli or wodli* hut, house)
pirri *or* biṛṛi	fish hook, or any other hook (*Also means* fingernail, claw)
rabbitti worli	rabbit hutch (from *worli or wodli* hut, house)
puiyu *or* puiyo	tobacco-pipe (*Also means* smoke) (Narrunga: *booya* cigarette)
purno	net bag
tadlitadli	frying pan, pot, etc. (from *tadli* spittle)
taingyedli *or* tainkyedli	rush bag
tammiammi	plate (from *tammi* flat, plate-like)
tando	bag made of kangaroo skin
ta nurletti	key (from *ta* mouth + *nurlendi* to turn)
tawirti	grinding stone
tia turrota	stout hand-saw (from *tia* tooth + *turrondi* to saw)
tia wirrota	cross-cut saw (from *tia* tooth + *wirrondi* to plane)
tidnabalta	shoe or boot (from *tidna* foot + *balta* covering) (Narrunga: *thidna bultha*)
tikiana *or* tikianna	waistcoat (from *tiki* rib area)
tikketikketti	chair, seat (from *tikkandi* to sit)
tindo	watch, clock (*Also means* sun)

tipogadla	gunpowder, matches (from *tipo* spark + *gadla* fire)
tipongatpangatpatti	ramrod (from *tipo* spark + *ngatpandi* to put into)
tura nakko nakkoretti	looking-glass (from *tura* shadow + *nakkorendi* to see oneself)
turnki *or* turngki	cloak, cloth, any covering of the body
turnki marngo *or* turnki titta	button (from *turnki* body covering + *marngo* small globular thing or *titta* knot, tie)
turtiana *or* turtianna	jacket, coat, shirt (from *turti* arm)
tutturto	circle; compass; wheel
wadna *or* wādna	short stick formed at one end like a chisel used for climbing up trees
wātpa *or* waātpa	covering, skin; cloak
winda	large spear, thrown by hand
witoturlo	cylindrical object, such as a telescope, flute, etc.; cylinder
wityo	needle, consisting of a thin pointed bone from the hindleg of a kangaroo, used as an awl or dagger
wodli *or* worli	hut, house (probably the origin of the word *wurley* in Australian English)
worki, workitti	pair of pincers (from *workendi* to pinch)
yammaru *or* yammāru	bag to take food in, knapsack, provision bag
yärko balta *or* yerko balta	stockings, etc. (from *yerko* leg and *palta* covering)
yerkoana, kantiana	pair of trousers (from *kanti* thigh or from *yerko* leg)
yoko	large bark tray; bark canoe, ship, boat
yudna	male pubic covering

6. Food, cooking and fire

burta	flame of the fire, blaze, red-hot embers
gadla	fire, fuel, wood (Narrunga: *karla*)
kambandi	to burn, roast, bake, cook: *kambaritti worli* oven
kanyayappa	hole for steaming game or vegetables

mai *or* maii	all sorts of vegetable food (Narrunga: *mai*)
meri	salt (*Also means* hail)
moka *or* muka	egg (Narrunga: *mooka*)
murromurro	flour, bread (from *murro* ashes, dust)
ngadlendi	to take fire, to burn
pari	rice (*Also means* maggots)
parrandi	to light a fire in the Aboriginal way by rubbing two sticks together
parru *or* paru	flesh (general term), animal or game meat, all sorts of animal food (Narrunga: *bardoo*)
pinyatta	sugar; honey from the grasstree or flower of the indigenous honeysuckle tree *tarnma*
warrondi	to roast under hot ashes

7. Topography

iṛi	belonging to the country; vernacular; homeborn, etc.
kaṛko *or* karko, milte	red ochre
kauwe	water
kopurlo	seawater (*Also means* alcohol) (Narrunga: *goo-billa* alcohol)
mokurta *or* mukurta	hill, mountain
ngarro *or* ngarru	pipe clay, chalk, or any white substance, such as white ochre, chalk, lime, etc.
nurlo	corner, or turn of a river (found in *Noarlunga*, which is incorrectly given as *Ngurlo-ngga* in the published dictionary)
pangkarra	country, district, fatherland; district or tract of country belonging to an individual
parnda	limestone, lime
parri	river, creek, gully (found in the river name *Onkaparinga*, literally 'at the women's river')
pudna	waterhole, Aboriginal well
pure	stone
tappa	path, road, track
tarni	saltwater, seawater; surf, sea

toka	mud, dirt; mortar
yärnbanna *or* yernbanna	purple ochre, a species of red ochre
yärta *or* yerta	earth, land, soil; country
yerlo	sea

8. Elements

biturro, karndo	thunder and lightning (*Karndo* is also the name of a large bird, said to be the author of the thunder)
kakirra *or* kakkirra, marrero, piki	moon
kudlilla	rainy season, winter
kuranye	rainbow
makko	cloud
manya	cold, rainy (Narrunga: *munya*)
ngaiera	air, sky, the firmament
ngulti	darkness, night
parnatti	autumn
purle	star
tindo	sun; day
tura *or* turra	shadow, shade
waitpu, warri	wind
willutti *or* wiltutti *or* wilutti	spring
woltatti	hot season

9. Mammals

burko-burko	common grey mouse
kadli	wild dog, when tamed (Narrunga: *gudli*)
kurka	kangaroo rat (probably the bettong)
kurlo	white female kangaroo (male: *tarnda*)
mabo	native cat
maityomaityo	bat
muntotakanna	goat (from *munto* abdomen + *takanna* wide, broad) (possibly from *mundo* anus)
nanto	male grey kangaroo (female: *wauwe*)
pilta	black-tailed possum

(pindi) nanto	horse (from *pinde* or *pindi* European + *nanto* kangaroo; *nanto* or *nantuwu* became the word for 'horse' in many other Aboriginal languages) (Narrunga: *nunthoo*)
pingko	a small animal with a white tail that burrows in the earth (taken into English as 'pinkie', describing a bandicoot, possibly the rabbit-eared bandicoot or bilby)
tarnda	large reddish kangaroo species (female: *kurlo*)
warto	wombat (Narrunga: *whartu*)
wauwe	female grey kangaroo (male: *nanto*)
wirappi	animal living in hollow trees, native squirrel
wirka	dog, dingo

10. Reptiles

ilya	black poisonous snake
kadno	large lizard species, possibly the central bearded dragon
kalta	goanna species eaten by the Aborigines, probably the sleepy lizard (Narrunga: *culta*)
kanto	bullfrog
paitya	reptile, vermin, any dangerous or disliked animal (Narrunga: *bucha* snake)
yura	large snake, or other monstrous and imaginary being

11. Birds

kari	emu
koa *or* kua	black crow
kudlyo	black swan
kurraka	native magpie
kurraki	white cockatoo
marnpi	wild pigeon
murtaannaitya	European hen (from *murta* excrement of animals)
ngungana	kookaburra, laughing jackass

parriparu	bird (general term)
pitta	native goose: *pinde pitta* English goose (from *pinde or pindi* European)
tiwu	black cockatoo
willamba *or* willampa	black cockatoo with yellow or white feathers in the tail
wilto	eagle species
winnaityinnaitye	birds collectively, poultry
winta	large owl
wolta	wild turkey
yao	seagull
yeltu	pelican
yutika	black cockatoo with red feathers in the tail and under the wings

12. Aquatic life

kakirra	small black river mussel
kondolli	whale (as *condolley*, this word was used for 'whale blubber' by early settlers in South Australia)
kunggurla	crawfish, river crawfish
kuya	fish (general term) (Narrunga: *guhyar*)
nakkudla *or* nakudla	shark
ngaltaitya	small crawfish species, the river crawfish
parraitya *or* parraitye	seaweed
tarnipaitya	sea-crab

13. Insects and spiders

barti	grub or insect in general, every grub before it turns into a chrysalis (found in many southern languages, and has been taken into English as 'bardy')
gadlabarti	native bee
kadngi	ant species
kudlo	black native louse (Narrunga: *goodlu*)
kunte paitye *or* kunti paitya	mosquito
ngarrulta *or* ngarrutta	centipede species

parraitpa *or* paraipa	locust
pinde kudlo *or* pindi kudlo	European louse, European flea (from *pinde* or *pindi* European + *kudlo* native louse)
tappo	common fly
tiwa	native honey
wako	spider

14. Plants

bakka	dry bark of trees; husk, peel; skin of man and beast
birira *or* biṛiṛa	native vegetable, resembling when dressed the cabbage, a vegetable growing near rivers (possibly New Zealand spinach)
birkibirki	peas (probably from *birki* a bit, small piece)
kandara	native vegetable resembling radish
kappi	tobacco (from *kappendi* to vomit)
karra	red gum tree
kundanye	native honeysuckle flower; the water in which the flower has been soaked
kurru	grasstree
narno *or* narnu	indigenous pine
ngurreka *or* ngurrēta	flower, blossom in general
parnappi	mushroom
parngutta	bulbous native root, used as a substitute for potatoes
tarnma	native honeysuckle, blossom cone of honeysuckle
tidli	bark of trees while green
tutta	grass, hay
wilya	foliage, leaves; small branches, young branches, brushwood (found in the placename *Patawalonga*, literally 'at the *patta* gum foliage')
wirra	forest, grove, wood, bush
wita	peppermint tree
wito	common reed
yakko	kind of gum (as from grasstree or from pine), used for hafting tools (may be the origin of the word 'yakka' for 'grasstree' in South Australian English)

yulti	stringy-bark tree
yutuke	sweet sap of the grasstree

15. Physical qualities

bika	soft, pliable
bitoka	soft, swampy
burtunna	old, aged, worn out
karalta	green; blue
karrokarro	red
kitya	bitter, brackish, salt, etc.
koma *or* kuma	one
kumatpi	quick, quickly
kurlto	short
kutyondi	little, small, but few
madurta	soft, smooth, even, not rough, even
maityukka	quick, active; attentive
mantikatpa	slow, lazy
marnkutye	some; three
minno ninnona *or* minnuninnuna	shining, smooth, slippery, like the gum of the *minno* wattle (probably *Acacia pycnantha*)
muinmo	more; farther; go on
nadli	short, compact (person)
ngamma	heavy, great, bulky, stout
paltarta	light, not heavy
partanna	all, nothing but
parto	thick, big
perkanna	bright, white, of light colour
pintya	softly, gently, slowly
piri	enough, sufficient, no more
pulyo, pulyonna	dark, black
purlaitye	two
purrutye	all, the whole
taltarni	red, yellow red
tarnba tarnbarni	firm, hard
tauatta	many in number
tiarka	sharp (*Also means* toothpick)
tiatinna	blunt
toku	small, little
topa	whole, all, entirely
towinna	long, stretched, extended

turtpa	small, narrow, tight, and thereby long
wilta	hard, firm; tenacious
wirranniranna *or* wirrannirranna	yellow, yellow brown
wirrilla	quick, quickly, rapidly
worta burro	all, altogether
yärnda	wide, large
yärra *or* yerra	different, distinct, separate; both (expressing the notions of individuality and reciprocity)
yärrabula *or* yerrabula	four, each two different ones
yellakkiana	new; fresh
yerrabularlukko	four times
yokunna	crooked, bent
yurnti	heavy, strong

16. Body states

bulti	asleep
manti	to be unable
medo	sleep
munturndo	pregnant (Narrunga: *moonthana*)
nakkarra	awake
padyotti *or* paityotti	blind; a blind person
purro, purruna	whole, sound, healthy, well; alive, living
taingi, tiltya	strength, power, might (*Also means* sinew)
taityo, tidli bakka	hungry
tungki	of a bad smell, offensive, rotten (Narrunga: *thoongka* smell)
wārrangko *or* worrangko	ill, sick, unwell
yurretinna	deaf (*Also means* disobedient) (literally 'earless')

17. Feelings

karnkendi	to laugh
kundo	chest, breast; the seat of several emotions: *kundowārponendi* to wish, desire
kurru	bashfulness: *kurru karri* to be ashamed (Narrunga: *gooroo*) (*Also means* crown of the head)
kurturendi	to be or look sad, sorry, dejected, to sit having the head drooping

maingki *or* mengki	laughter, joy, smiling
mangkulaiendi	to be embarrassed; to fear
marngu	anger, crossness; jealousy, envy
muiyo	feelings, inclination, attachment, love
nguinya *or* nguinye *or* ngunya	joy, pleasure, delight
padlondi	to desire, wish, long, covet (*Also means* to die)
pidlingga	stingy, parsimonious, niggardly
tangka	liver; the inner part of anything; desire, longing, the seat of the feelings: *tangka mankorendi* to have compassion, or to be, feel attached to, to be friendly towards
tangkarro	fright, horror, violent rage, excessive passion
turla	angry, excited, provoked, enraged; serious
waii	fear
yitpi	heart, soul; will, inclination (*Also means* any small central single seed): *yitpi manni* to be friendly, inclined to a person; *yitpi ngandandi* to feel aversion or antipathy

18. Values

marni	good (*Also means* fat, rich)
numa	good, well, right, etc.
wadli *or* wādli	not good, bad, awkward, disliked
wakkinna	bad, wicked, naughty, morally and physically bad

19. Motion

budnandi	to come, appear
karrendi	to rise, stand up and getout of the way, make room, etc.
kumbandi	to disappear, not be present; being gone, gone away
makkandi	to shake, quiver with the legs as in dancing
murrendi	to go, walk, travel
ngatpandi	to put into; dip, dive, go down, enter in, etc.

padendi	to swim
padmendi	to jump, leap, skip
padnendi	to go, depart
perkendi	to come out (of birds hatching or a boil opening)
purtpurendi	to jump, as the kangaroo
tanendi	to come forth, appear (of the sun, of seeds, of rising from the dead)
tattendi	to ascend, climb up; to go towards
warrendi	to look for, seek; to pick up
warriappendi	to seek, pick up, find (used as the name of Warriappendi Alternative School)
worndandi	to soar, like a bird
yakkandi	to chase, pursue
yudlondi	to push, shove; to push on; to drive or herd sheep, cattle, etc.
yurrondi	to creep, sneak, steal upon

20. State

bidnandi	to stay, delay, hesitate; to refuse
-nendi	to become (suffix: creates verbs denoting that a person or object is about to exist in a new form or condition)
tikkandi	to be or live somewhere; to sit, rest, etc.
wandendi	to lie down; to locate or dwell
yärnkandi	to be hanging, hang on someone; to infect
yuwandi	to stand, stand upright; to stand still

21. Vocalisation and thought *See also section 28*

ingarnendi	to look about; to enquire
kaltendi	to ask, demand, command, to give orders
karlta mandi	to sing
malyopartanna	joking, funny
manta	untruth, a lie
moka bandi *or* muka bandi	to think of, remember
mokandarendi	to forget
murka	weeping, lamenting, crying

ngartendi *or* ngattendi	to ask after, inquire
nguttandi	to intimidate, frighten, threaten, more particularly by telling untrue reports
niko, yurro	joke, jest
takkandi *or* tarkandi	to name, call; to say
tampendi	to know, understand, perceive, to recognise, be acquainted with
tangkuinya	dream
tiati yailtyandi	to believe that it is true
tiatti warra	truth
tirkandi	to know, understand, perceive, conceive with the mind, learn
turkondi, turkorendi	to inform, tell
wānggandi	to speak, say, utter; to converse, chat, talk, etc.
witte wittendi	to wish, desire, ask, demand
yailtyandi, yailtyarendi	to believe, think, suppose, to be of opinion
yärrarendi	to be uncertain, in doubt

22. Bodily functions

kanggandi	to bear, bring forth
kappendi	to vomit
kudnatendi	to evacuate the bowels
kumbotendi	to make water
kungarendi	to cause a scent or smell, to smell
madlendi	to be no more, to die
maiendi	to eat
mailtyandi, mailtyamailtyandi	to taste
marto	smell, scent; taste, flavour
mudlendi	to smell
nakko nakkondi	to look at, examine, inspect
nakkondi	to see, look; to know
nantandi	to eat vegetable food along with meat
ngarkondi	to eat, drink, enjoy, etc.
ngarrambulandi	to be tired, fatigued, sluggish, dull
padlondi	to die, perish, starve
paiandi	to bite, chew (*Also means* to understand)
paintyappendi	to touch, feel

parta	sexual intercourse (polite term); *parta mangkondi* (of women), *parta yungkondi* (of men)
tarkondi *or* tarnkondi	to devour, eat, gormandise (impolite term)
tipparendi	to feel pain, ache
tira tartandi	to hide; to cover, shelter
warra inggarnendi	to listen, hear when one is speaking (literally 'to expect the word' or 'wait for it')
wordnendi	to be born (*Also means* to fall, drop)
yurre inggarnendi	to listen

23. Impact and violence

bakkandi	to dig out roots, etc.
bakkendi	to cut with a flint or stone knife
battendi	to throw a spear, a stone, etc.; to let go, untie, etc.
biltendi	to cut off, pinch off
kadlondi	to tread upon, press down with the foot
kundandi	to strike, beat, fight, kill by striking
madondi	to stroke, pat, fondle, etc.
midlendi	to pinch, crush, grind
nayandi	to fasten one thing to another, sew
paltandi	to throw, strike
pammandi	to spear; to touch upon, to bound, as two countries, etc.
tartandi	to cover, shut up, etc.
tattondi	to kick
tittappendi	to tie, fetter, etc.
wirkandi	to rub, scratch
yärtandi	to break

24. Holding and transfer

kabba kabbandi	to send off (a beggar), cast out, etc.
kanggandi	to carry about with you; to accompany about
karnkondi	to raise up, lift, heave; to draw out water, etc.
kattendi	to carry, bring, fetch

mandi	to draw off, pull off, take off
mankondi	to take hold of, touch, take
mettendi	to steal, take away
minnondi	to make, create, do, etc.
pintyandi	to make, produce, create
wondandi	to put, lay down; to leave behind; to give over working
yärkandi	to spread and extend a skin on the ground for the purpose of preparing it for use
yunggondi	to give, to hand over to, etc.

25. Location, direction and time

būki	formerly, in time past
bukilyelo	yesterday
karra *or* kaṛṛa	high
karradlo	far, distant
kawanda	north (found in the placename *Cowandilla*, literally 'in the north')
kura	near, close by, here
mari *or* marre	east
muna	before; front
narta	now, at present
padba *or* patpa	south
paninggolo	tomorrow, morrow
tarkari	in future, at a later period
tarna	backside, the back of
trukko	inside, interior
tudno	entirely, forever, continually
wakkurti	perhaps, likely, it may be (always supposing certainty)
warro	out, outside, at large
wongka	west
worta	end; last; behind
yakki	deep, below; valley
yangkadli	afterwards, at a later time
yella	present time, today

26. Interjections

kawai	come!
ko, kopiri	expressing assent: well; you may do so
madlanna	no, not
ne	yes; so it is (merely affirms the statement contained in another person's question, while *tiati* asserts and contends if the thing should be disputed: *Paintya ninna wandeota? Ne yaintya.* There will you sleep? Yes, here.)
paia	interjection of wonder, surprise, etc.
paitya	astonishment, amazement (stronger than *paia* which expresses agreeable surprise)
tamurti *or* tamurtiko	astonishment and surprise
tamurti paitya	used at any disappointment; the answer to it is *waburti*
tiatto	affirmative, yes, thus it is
waburti *or* wāburti	answer to *tamurti* or *tamurti paitya*
yakka alya	alas! oh! dear!
yakka	expressive of dislike, unpleasantness, disagreeableness, etc.
yakkaitya	highest degree of despair or rage, etc.

27. Social activities and property

banba-banbalyarnendi	introducing of one tribe to another and the following conference, when they pointed out to each other their respective relationship; used today for 'hold a conference'
birko mankolankola	messenger, ambassador
birko worta	ensign, one who accompanies the messenger
iando	visit
inbarendi	to meet one another (used as the name of Inbarendi College)
ira, wirra	fight, battle
kudla	alone, by itself
kumangka	together, in one, in company

kumarta — own, belonging to oneself
mattanya — owner, proprietor; master
ngaiyandi, ngayandi, ngayarendi — to play, joke, tease
nguiya nguiya — moral pustule between two parties, a difference, a sore between them
taikurri — with, in company, also
tanda — exchange, barter, the place where the barter takes place
tira mankondi — to interfere, mediate
wadu — communion, partnership; together, in commune
wārpulaendi *or* worpulaendi — to work, exert oneself, be active; to care or work for others
wirringga — together, in common with
yaitya — own; native, indigenous; proper; fresh
yaityarna — natives belonging to the country
yerlteriburka — counsellor, adviser; commander

28. Learning, schools and education

bultarrappendi — to draw along a mark, as with a lead pencil, which another has prescribed
karltakarltanya — calling, as the church bell; crying
malta ngaitya — not eloquent, speaking badly or incorrectly
malta wilta — eloquent, speaking the language correctly and fluently
marka — trace, track, mark (*Also means* writing slate)
marka markandi — to count, number (*Also means* to mark out; to set a copy)
markarendi — to beat the time, as in music
mokarta manni — good head (for learning)
mokarta worpo — retentive head, of good memory
mokatinna — stupid, silly, without intellect
ngutto atpandi — to teach, instruct
parndo — ball to play with
pepa — paper, letter (from English 'paper'): *Ninna ngannaitya yellarra yakko pepaitya budni.* Why did you not come to school (literally, 'for paper') today? *Nindo ngadlu nintini pipangga nakkolyerniappeta?* Will you let us again look upon the paper (that is, instruct us)?

pepa worli	school house
perkulaiendi	to produce a noise, sound; to sound the letters in spelling
tarlti	pen (*Also means* wing; feather)
tirkallirkalla	an intelligent, wise person
wakkarendi	to be ignorant, stupid, foolish; to forget (*Also means* to err, go astray, lose oneself, etc.)
wallara	clear-headed, intelligent, clever
warra mailtyandi	to imitate one's language or speech when spoken incorrectly
warra markandi	to imitate one's speech
warra paiandi	to understand the language, speech, etc.
warte ngatpandi	to instruct in knowledge
wirromandi	to divide, part in two
wonba wonbandi	to number, count
yamma	ignorant, simple, foolish, stupid, silly
yammaiamma	a doctor, teacher, etc.
yerthoappendi	to rear, bring up, educate
yerrakartarta	scattered, disorderly, without design, at random
yurre paiandi	to pay attention; understand
yurrirka	attentive; obedient

References

Amery, Rob 1993, 'Encoding new concepts in old languages: A case study of Kaurna, the language of the Adelaide Plains', *Australian Aboriginal Studies*, 1993, no. 1, pp 37–47

Clarke, P A 1985, 'Fruits and seeds as food for southern South Australian Aborigines', *Journal of the Anthropological Society of South Australia*, vol. 23, no. 6, pp 2–12

Clarke, P A 1988, 'Aboriginal use of subterranean plant parts in southern South Australia', *Records of the South Australian Museum*, vol. 22, no. 1, pp 63–76

Condon, H T 1955, 'Aboriginal Bird names — South Australia', *The S.A. Ornithologist*, vol. 21 (6–7 July 1955), pp 74–88; vol. 21, part 8 (14 October 14 1955), pp 91–98

Gale, Peter 1991, 'Nunga and Proud of it' Aboriginal languages in Adelaide: From the loss of 'Mother-Tongue' to language revival, BA Honours thesis, Flinders University, SA

Gara, Tom (ed.) 1990, *Aboriginal Adelaide*, special issue of the *Journal of the Anthropological Society of South Australia*, vol. 28, nos 1 and 2

Graham, Doris May and Cecil Wallace Graham 1987, *As we've known it: 1911 to the present*, South Australian College of Advanced Education, Aboriginal Studies and Teacher Education Centre, Underdale, South Australia

Hemming, Steve 1990, '"Kaurna" Identity: a brief history', in Gara (ed.), pp 126–142

Hercus, Luise 1992, *A Nukunu Dictionary*, Australian Institute of Aboriginal and Torres Strait Islander Studies, Canberra

McEntee, John and Pearl McKenzie 1992, *Adynya-math-nha English Dictionary*, John McEntee and Pearl McKenzie, Adelaide

Moorhouse, Matthew 1843, Annual Report of the Aborigines Department for the year ending 30th September 1843, reprinted in Gara (ed.), pp 54–62

Ngarrindjeri, Narrunga and Kaurna Languages Project 1990, *Narrunga, Kaurna and Ngarrindjeri Songs*, Kaurna Plains School

Simpson, Jane (forthcoming), 'A Grammar of Kaurna', to appear in R M W Dixon and B J Blake (eds) *Handbook of Australian Languages*, Cambridge University Press

Sutton, Peter and Michael Walsh 1979, *Revised linguistic fieldwork manual for Australia*, Australian Institute of Aboriginal Studies, Canberra

Teichelmann, C G 1857, 'Dictionary of the Adelaide Dialect', manuscript no. 59, Bleek's Catalogue of Sir George Grey's Library dealing with Australian languages, South African Public Library

Teichelmann, C G and C W Schürmann 1840, *Outlines of a Grammar, Vocabulary, and Phraseology of the Aboriginal Language of South Australia, spoken by the natives in and for some distance around Adelaide* (facsimile edition 1982), Tjintu Books, Largs Bay

Tindale, N B 1974, *Aboriginal Tribes of Australia*, ANU Press, Canberra

Tunbridge, Dorothy, in association with the Nepabunna Aboriginal School 1991, *The story of the Flinders Ranges mammals*, Kangaroo Press, Kenthurst

Watson, W, C G Teichelmann and M Moorhouse 1842, Report on the Aborigines of South Australia, *Transactions of the Statistical Society*, printed in the *South Australian Register*, 8 January 1842. Reprinted in Gara (ed.), pp 40–53

Wyatt, William 1879, 'Vocabulary of the Adelaide and Encounter Bay tribes, with a few words of that of Rapid Bay', in J D Woods, *The Native Tribes of South Australia*, Adelaide, pp 157–182

9

Nyungar

ALAN DENCH

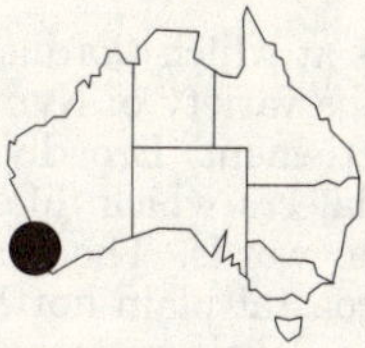

Nyungar is the name used for what was originally a collection of dialects of one language spoken in the south-west of Western Australia. The full extent of Nyungar territory covered a wide range of ecosystems. The people of Perth exploited the seas, the Swan estuary, and the extensive system of freshwater lakes on the sandplain between the coast and the Darling scarp. Further south and east, people lived off the resources of the tall karri and jarrah forests. The southern coastal people built fish-traps, hunted turtle and feasted on beached whales. And to the north and east, Nyungar people lived in the semi-arid regions of what is now the wheat belt. Just how far east Nyungar-speaking people ventured is not known, though they probably travelled into the fringes of the Western desert region, through the goldfields region around Kalgoorlie and Norseman, and south-east along the coast to the edge of the Great Australian Bight. As with all the lists collected together in this dictionary, the Nyungar wordlist gives some small insight into the detailed knowledge Nyungar people had of their environment and the uses to which they put the abundant natural resources available to them.

Although it is clear that Nyungar was originally spoken in a variety of dialects, detailed knowledge of the names and original distribution of the dialects has been lost. But while there are now very few speakers of Nyungar, their knowledge of the language is complemented by a wide range of historical sources — many early European settlers made wordlists of their local languages. The remaining Nyungar speakers are predominantly of the eastern dialect region (see below) and so the original Perth dialect, for example, is only salvageable from historical sources.

Dialects

From the different locations at which wordlists were collected it is possible to build a picture of the variety of Nyungar dialects as they were spoken before European settlement. Broadly speaking, there appear to have been three distinct dialects which differed mainly in their varying pronunciations of similar words. The Northern dialect was spoken around Perth and on the coastal plain north to the Moore River and inland to New Norcia. The South-western dialect was spoken in the south-western corner of the state, from the Murray River south to the Blackwood River. The Eastern dialect covered the largest area: from Denmark and Albany in the far south, east probably as far as Esperance and Ravensthorpe, and north through what is now the wheatbelt. The following words illustrate the common pattern of differences among the three dialects:

	Northern	**South-western**	**Eastern**
tooth	*ngarlku*	*ngorlka*	*ngorlak*
throat	*wardu*	*worda*	*wort*
hip	*kulka*	*kwelka*	*kwalak*
kidney	*djubu*	*djuba*	*djuup*
woman	*yaku*	*yoka*	*yok*
bandicoot	*kurndi*	*kwernda*	*kwernt*
quokka	*kuka*	*kwoka*	*kwok*
ringtail possum	*ngurra*	*ngwarra*	*ngwarr*
bardie grub	*bardi*	*berda*	*bert*
spear	*kidji*	*kitj*	*kidja*
skin bag	*kudu*	*kuda*	*kut*

Of course, sometimes dialects have completely different words rather than variations on a single word:

	Northern	**South-western**	**Eastern**
forehead	*yurdu*	*yimang*	*yimang*
cheek	*nyuritj*	*ngalak*	*kalykart*
kingfisher	*kanyinak*	*kanyinak*	*birangku*
charcoal	*murrar*	*yirrak*	*yarrkal*

In the wordlist below, a number of abbreviations are used to indicate roughly the regions in which particular words are found. These are:

- N mainly around Perth but also north to New Norcia and east to York, Beverley and Mekkering
- NE the northern wheatbelt area
- SW from the Murray River, south to the Blackwood and including Bunbury, Bussleton, Margaret River and Bridgetown
- S including the lower southwest and the south coast, Albany (King George's Sound) and Denmark
- SE around Albany, Denmark and north to the Stirling Ranges
- E the Eastern dialect, from Albany and Denmark to the south and north through the wheatbelt
- gen a word which appears to have been in general use across the whole Nyungar region

Some words have no dialect label. These were recorded in a number of locations but do not appear to be obviously restricted to one definable area and are not common enough in the sources to be considered general terms.

Spelling and pronunciation

Not surprisingly, the early European settlers were not trained linguists and each of them used their own method of spelling to write down the words of a language very different to their native English (or French, or Spanish). So, for example, the following spellings have all been used for the word which means 'emu': *wach*, *wagi*, *wegar*, *wad-jee*, *wagie*, *wegie*, *wadge*, *wait*, *weid*, *wadgi*, *waitch*, *weitj*, *wadgie*, *watcha*, *wej*, *wadji*, *waygee*, *weja*, *wadye*, *we-ja*, *wet*, *waga*, *wēj*, *wetch*, *wage*, *wēja*, *wid-jee*, *wagee*, *wedge*, *widjee*, *wager*, *weeche*, *widyee* and *waggy*.

In many cases now, Nyungar people do not remember the words found in these lists and so a standard spelling must be reconstituted from the historical lists. Linguists are able to do this by comparing the varying spellings with one another, checking the internal consistency of the individual lists and making informed guesses based on their knowledge of other Australian languages and on the patterns of pronunciations of modern speakers of Nyungar.

The spellings represented in the Nyungar list given here are a regularisation of the spellings which occur in the many sources (for example, the words given for 'black duck' are based on an analysis of over fifty distinct spellings in the sources). It is quite likely that some of these words will not be recognised by today's Nyungar speakers — either because the word has been forgotten, because the pronunciation of the word has changed over the past 150 years of contact with English, or simply because I, the linguist, got it wrong. However, this list represents my best guesses, to date, of the meanings and pronunciations of words collected by the earliest recorders of the Nyungar language.

The spelling system used in this list is based on a practical orthography agreed upon by Nyungar people at two language conferences held in the south-west in 1986 and 1990. It differs in having a series of interdental consonants (made with the tongue tip between the teeth — see page xxvii of the Introduction) and in representing long *e* and *o* vowels using a colon (*e:* and *o:*). Thus the spelling system uses the following symbols:

a, aa, b, d, dh, dj, e, e:, i, ii, k, l, lh, ly, m, n, ng, nh, ny, o, o:, p, r, rd, rl, rn, rr, rt, t, th, tj, u, uu, w, y

Notice that the spelling system distinguishes *p* and *b*, *t* and *d*, etc., which are normally not distinguished in Australian languages (see page xxviii above). The voiceless sounds are written at the ends of words, the voiced sounds elsewhere. Other versions of the standard Nyungar spelling system use *oo* for *u* and do not show vowel length.

Younger speakers of Nyungar have a pattern of pronunciation which has been influenced by English. The most important differences are worth noting here:

First, when the *ng* nasal sound occurs at the beginning of a word, it is usually replaced by simple *n* for younger speakers, resulting in *nobilyang* for *ngobilyang* 'red'; *nangk* for *ngangk* 'mother'; *nalku* for *ngarlku* 'tooth'.

Second, interdental consonants, which for many words varied with palatal consonants (see the wordlist below), have been replaced by alveolar consonants for all but the oldest speakers. Some palatals are also replaced by alveolars: *dwongk* for *dhwongk* 'ear'; *daa* for *dhaa* 'mouth'; *dalan* for *dhalany* 'tongue'; *nungaa* for *nhungar/nyungar* 'person'; *nint* for *nhint* 'tail'.

Third, from the historical sources it appears that Nyungar had a contrast between the two 'r' sounds (*rr* and *r*). Some of the oldest speakers retain the contrast but in most cases the *rr* flap has merged with either the continuant *r* or with the alveolar stop *t/d*: *mangkat* for *mangkarr* 'hair'; *n(g)aril* for *ngarrily* 'rib'; *maran* for *marrany* 'vegetable food'; and *maa(r)* for *marr* 'wind, cloud'.

NYUNGAR WORDLIST

WORDLIST CATEGORIES

1. Body parts and products
2. Kin relationships
3. Human Classification
4. Language, mythology and ceremony
5. Human artefacts
6. Food, cooking and fire
7. Topography
8. Elements
9. Mammals
10. Reptiles
11. Birds
12. Aquatic life
13. Insects and spiders
14. Plants
15. Physical qualities
16. Non-physical qualities
17. Motion
18. State
19. Vocalisation and thought
20. Bodily functions
21. Impact and violence
22. Holding and transfer
23. Location, direction and time
24. Interjections

1. Body parts and products

baany *(E)*, banya *(W)*	sweat
biily *(E)*, bilya *(N,SW)*	navel
biip *(E)*, biba *(SW)*, bibi *(N)*	breast
birrak *(SE)*, birrka *(N)*, badjang *(N)*	boil, sore
birt *(SE)*, birda *(N,SW)*, kwirrak *(E)*	sinew
bukal *(E)*, bukala *(SW)* kungk *(E)*, kungka *(SW)*, kungku *(N)*	back, backbone
bunitj, bwonitj *(E)*	knee
dhaa *(gen)*	mouth
dhaarnt *(E)*, bilka *(N,SW)*, belak/balkat *(E)*	ankle
dhalany *(gen)*	tongue
dhawul *(gen)*	thigh
dhe:ly *(S,E)*, dhelya *(N)*	saliva
dhwongk *(E)*, dhungka *(N,SW)*	ear
djen *(E)*, djina *(N)*, djena *(SW)*	foot (*Also means* track)
djirang *(gen)*, bunya *(N)*, bwony/bony *(SW,S)*	fat
djumbar *(SE)*, djawany *(N,E)*, djaw *(E)*	fur, downy hair
djuup *(E)*, djuba *(SW)*, djubu *(N)*	kidney
kaat *(E)*, kada *(N,SW)*	head

korbal/kobral *(gen)*, kaburla *(N)*	stomach, guts
kurt *(E)*, kurdu *(N)*	heart
kuump *(E)*, kumbu *(N)*	urine
kwalak *(E)*, kulka *(N)*, kwelka *(SW)*	hip
kwan *(E)*, kuna *(N)*, kwona *(SW)*	faeces
kwenily *(E)*, dharrkart *(NE)*	windpipe
kwetj *(E)*, kwedja *(SW)*, kudji *(N)*, djula *(NE)*	bone
maar *(E)*, mara/marra *(N)*	hand
maat *(E)*, mada *(N,SW)*	leg
mangkarr *(SW,E)*, mangkarra *(N)*	hair
marak *(E)*, marrka *(N)*	(lower) arm
mar biirr *(E)*, mara birri *(N)*, mara birra *(SW)*	fingernail
mar ngangk *(E)*, mara ngangka *(N)*, mar kayang *(S)*	thumb
mayar *(gen)*, mayara *(N)*	liver
mert *(E)*, mirda *(W)*	penis
miin	lip
mininy	moustache
mop *(E)*, moba *(SW)*, mabu *(N)*	skin
mungk *(E)*, mungku *(N)*	shoulder
muru *(N)*	buttocks
muuly *(E)*, mulya *(N,SW)*	nose
myaal, mayel	eye
ngalak *(S)*, yuratj/nyuritj *(N)*, kalykart *(E)*	cheek
ngaly *(E)*, ngalya *(N)*	armpit
ngambarn	scar, cicatrice
ngarnak *(E)*, ngarnka *(N)*	beard
ngarnak *(E)*, ngarnka *(N)*, ngarnitj, ye:t *(NE)*	chin
ngarrily *(gen)*, nyamitj *(SE)*	rib
ngorlak *(E)*, ngarlku *(N)*, ngorlka *(SW)*	tooth
ngornt *(E)*, ngurnda *(SW)*, ngurndu *(N)*, minka *(N)*	chest
ngu:p *(E)*, nguba *(SW)*, ngubu *(N)*	blood
ngurditj *(NE)*, ngontj *(NE)*, mo:n *(SE)*, djina ngardu *(N)*, djen ngort *(E)*, djena ngorda *(SW)*	heel

nguy(ang) *(E)*, nhukatj *(N)*	elbow
nhanka *(W)*, nhanak *(E)*	back of neck
nhint *(E)*, nhinda *(SW)*, nhundi *(N)*	tail
walyal *(gen)*	lungs
warnak *(E)*, warnku *(N)*	upper arm
wort *(E)*, wardu *(N)*, worda *(SW)*	throat
wulitj *(gen)*	calf
yaatj *(E)*	thighbone, femur
yimang *(S,E)*, yurdu *(N)*	forehead
yoitj *(E)*, yadju *(N)*, yodja *(SW)*	testicle

2. Kin relationships

dhem(an), murran	grandmother; daughter
djuk *(E)*, djukan *(N)*, djuka *(SW)*	(elder) sister
kambart *(gen)*	niece
kardang *(SW)*	younger brother
kongk *(E)*, kangku *(N)*, kongka *(SW)*	uncle, mother's brother
kort *(E)*, kardu *(N)*, korda *(SW)*	spouse
kowat *(N,SW)*	younger sister
kubang *(gen)*, babin *(N)*	friend
kurlang(a)	son (*Also means* child)
kwarat *(gen)*	daughter
maam *(SE)*, maman *(N,SW)*	father
maan-yok/maam-yok *(SE)*, maman yok *(N,SW)*	aunt, father's sister
mayar *(gen)*	nephew
murran, dhem(an)	grandfather; son
ngangk *(E)*, ngangka *(N,SW)*	mother
ngulyar *(gen)*	brother; sister-in-law
ngunt *(E)*, ngundan *(N)*, ngunda *(SW)*	(elder) brother

3. Human Classification

djanak *(E)*, djanka *(N)*, wiyarn/wern *(S) Also* nyurlim *(gen)*, mulard(a) *(N)*, kadjin *(NE)*, kaanya/keny *(N)* (nhotj *(SE)*: literally 'dead')	spirit, ghost, devil
kulamandi/kulambidi *(gen)*, wiyabindi *(SE)*	young man

kurlang(a) *(gen)*	child
maandi *(SE)*, mandika(ra) *(N,SW)*	young woman
malka(r)karrak *(gen)*, bulyakarrak *(gen)*	doctor, magic man
manatj *(gen)*	policeman (literally 'black cockatoo')
mandjang *(S)*, djirralak *(N)*, baditj *(S,SW)*	old man; old woman
nhop, nhoba *(SW)*	baby
nyungaa, nhungaa, yungaa, mamarap *(N)*	man, person, human
wadjala, nyidiny *(E)*, nguyuwa(r) *(E)* (*Also* djanka *(N)*, djanak *(SE)*, kadjin *(NE)*: literally 'devil')	white person
yok *(E)*, yaku *(N)*, yoka *(SW)*	woman, female

4. Language, mythology and ceremony

bindibindi, nyindjin, ngulyinak, yirrarlang	peeled stick hair ornaments
dhardarr *(gen)*, djundaly/dhundaly *(N)*, dhurnt *(SE)*, dhurnda *(SW)*, dharram *(SE)*	white clay, white
djuwar/dhuwar *(gen)*, bwayil *(SE)*, djunya *(SW)*, djuny *(E)*, mardarr *(SE)*, wilki *(N,SW)*, wilak *(S,E)*	red ochre, clay
dwerda dhaya/dhwert dhaya	dog tail hair ornament
kandjin	yellow ochre, clay
kwely *(S,E)*, kwelya *(N,SW)*	name
mulyart	nose ornament
nhulbarn *(gen)*	hair belt
wangka *(N,SW)*, wangk *(S,E)*	word, story, language
wukarri	hair band
wundu	hair string
yidi *(N)*, yida *(SW)*	song

5. Human artefacts

bilarra *(N)*	double barbed spear
burdan *(gen)*	long spear
burraly/bworrily *(gen)*	quartz headed spear
bwok *(S,E)*, buka/bwoka *(N,SW)*	skin cloak
dhaba *(N,SW)*, dhaap *(S,E)*	knife
dharra *(N,SW)*, dharr *(S,E)*	barb of spear

dhawak *(gen)*	throwing stick
kerl *(S,E)*, karli *(N)*, kerla *(SW)*	boomerang
kitj *(S,E)*, kidji *(N)*, kidja *(SW)*	spear
kodj *(S,E)*, kadju *(N)*, kodja *(SW)*	stone axe
kut *(S,E)*, kudu *(N)*, kuda *(SW)*	skin bag
mangkar *(gen)*, warratj *(N)*	fighting spears
mirr *(S,E)*, mirru *(N)*, mirra *(SW)*	spear thrower
wan *(S,E)*, wana *(N,SW)*	digging stick, staff
wurnda *(gen)*	shield

6. Food, cooking and fire

ben *(S)*, bina *(N)*, benang *(SW)*	light
birru *(E)*, bidal *(N)*	sparks
buyu *(N)*, buya *(SW)*, buyi/buwi *(S)*, kirri(k) *(N)*, kirra *(NE)*	smoke
dhatj *(S,E)*, dhadja *(N,SW)*	meat, meat food
karl *(S,E)*, karla *(N,SW)*	fire, firewood (*Also means* country, homeland, camp)
koba *(E)*, kop *(S)*	coals
marrany *(gen)*	vegetable food
yarrkal *(SE)*, murrar *(N)*, yirrak *(SW)*	charcoal
yuwart *(S,E)*, yuwarda *(N,SW)*	ashes

7. Topography

barnatj *(SE)*, warlu *(N)*, warla *(SW)*	flat country, plain
bil *(S,E)*, bilu *(N)*, bila *(SW)*	river
bindja(rr) *(gen)*, bworra *(N,SW)*	swamp country
boy/bwoy *(S)*, buyi *(N)*, boya/bwaya *(N,SW)*	rock, stone
budjar *(gen)*	ground, earth, land
dhombarn *(N,S, E)*, karrap *(SW)*	hole
kaat *(S,SW)*, kata *(N)*	hill, mountain
karl *(S,E)*, karla *(N,SW)*	country, homeland, camp (*Also means* fire, firewood)
kont *(S,E)*, konda *(N,SW)*	cave
kuyarra *(N)*	sand
kwongkan *(N,E)*	sand plain
mamart *(SE)*, wadarn *(N,SW)*	sea
maya *(N,SW)*, may *(S,E)*	shelter, hut, house
nhorn *(E)*, nharnu *(N)*, nhorna *(SW)*, babi *(S)*	muddy, swampy ground
yalya *(SW)*, yaly *(S)*	dirt, sand, clay

8. Elements

balyap *(SE)*, balyan *(N)*, mirritj *(N)*	dew
bindarri *(S,E)*, yida *(N,SW)*, yet *(S,E)*	lightning
dhelkar *(S,E)*, nhaku *(N)*, nhaka *(SW)*, nhaak *(E)*	frost
dhwely/dhwoly *(E)*, dhulya *(N)*, dhwalya *(SW)*, djindi *(N)*	mist, fog
djindi *(S)*, djindang *(SW)*, ngangkar *(N)*	star
kaip/ke:p *(SE)*, kabi *(N)* kaba *(SW)*, kap *(S)*	water, rain
kidalak *(SW)*, kadiyak *(SE)*	night
malkarr *(N,SW)*	thunder
marr *(gen)*, marra *(N)*	sky; cloud; wind
miak *(E)*, mika *(N,SW)*, yawiny *(SE)*, marrardak/marrardang *(N)*	moon, month
mol *(S,E)*, malu *(N)*, mola *(SW)*, murdak *(E)*	shade
ngangk *(E)*, ngangka *(N)*, ngangkarn *(SW)*, djatj/dhatj *(S)*, yokat *(S)*	sun

9. Mammals

burdi	burrowing rat-kangaroo, boodie
dhalkatj	rabbit-eared bandicoot, dalgyte, bilby
dhama(r)	tammar wallaby
dhanart	marsupial mouse, dunnart
dhudhiny *(SW)*	joey kangaroo
dhwert/dhurt *(SE)*, dhurda *(N)*, dhwarda *(SW)*	tame dog
djuditj	native cat, chuditch
kumal	brush-tailed possum
kwaar/kwer *(E)*, kura/kwura *(N)*, kwera *(SW)*	brush kangaroo
kwernt *(E)*, kurndi *(N)*, kwernda *(SW)*	southern brown bandicoot
kwok *(E)*, kwoka *(SW)*, kuka *(N)*	quokka
maal *(E)*, mala *(N)*	small bandicoot, marl
mandarda	western pygmy possum, mundarda

murt *(E)*, mardu *(N)*, murda *(SW)*	yellow-footed marsupial mouse, mardo
ngort *(gen)*	horse
ngulbungar	honey possum, noolbenger
ngwarr *(E)*, ngurra *(N)*, ngwarra *(SW)*, wamp *(E)*	black/ringtail possum
nhumbat	numbat, banded anteater
nyingarn *(NE)*	echidna
warr *(E)*, warru *(N)*, wurra *(SW)*	female kangaroo
warrang	nail-tailed wallaby, wurrung
woly *(E)*, walya *(N)*, wolya *(SW)*	rat-kangaroo, woylie
yakany *(gen)*, mokany *(SE)*	dingo
yongkar *(gen)*, yungkara *(N)*	kangaroo

10. Reptiles

dhukatj	dugite
djurrang *(SW,E)*, kalari *(N)*	lizard (general term)
karda	black, race-horse goanna
kilang *(E)*, buyi *(N)*	turtle
kuya, kwiya	bullfrog
kwont *(E)*, kunda *(N)*, kwanda *(SW)*	black snake
manar	long-tailed goanna
muluwarr	horned lizard
nhorn *(E)*, nhurna *(N,SW)*	black snake
waakal	carpet snake
wort, yaam, madjak, dhundjar	edible frog (various)
wurrkaly	frog
yakany	freshwater turtle
yuwarn *(E)*, yuwarna *(N)*, yorna *(SW)*	stump-tailed goanna

11. Birds

barnangar, mayadang	blue-belly parrot
budalang *(N,E)*, bilabang *(S)*, nyirrimba *(N)*	pelican
darilbart *(SW)*	yellow-belly parrot
dhabarn *(N,SW)*, djabarn *(SE)*, biil *(SE)*, bela *(SW)*, djirlak *(N)*	shrike
dhandu *(N)*, djurnda *(SE)*, minmin *(SE)*	fish hawk

dhangkarak *(N,E)*, wadjalak *(SW)*	wattler
dhawaran, dhamalak, djalyap, dhunyart	twenty-eight parrot, ringneck parrot
dhulangart *(E)*	dove
djakal-djakal *(N)*	sulphur-crested cockatoo
djet *(E)*, djida *(N)*	bird
djididjidi, minidjit, nyidangitj	wagtail
djilyan *(SE)*	sea-eagle
djirraly, djilak, kanap *(S)*	feather
kadarr	musk duck
kalyang	teal duck
kambigur *(SW,E)*	owl
kanyinak *(N,SW)*, birangku *(SE)*	kingfisher
karlbarnang	black shag
karrak *(gen)*	red-tailed black cockatoo
karrkany *(SW)*, djildjil *(gen)*	chicken-hawk
kawarr	rosella
kudap *(NE)*	little eagle
kuraka/kurak *(N,SW)*, kwarabarnt *(S)*, wakarn *(SW)*, wakarrang *(SE)*, nyamarak *(S)*	mountain duck
kurbardi *(SE)*, kulbardi *(N,SW)*	magpie
manatj *(gen)*	white cockatoo
marli *(gen)*, kuldjak *(N,SW)*, wilarr *(SE)*	black swan
midi	black-and-white shag
ngakarl	seagull
ngalyin *(E)*, kulim/kwilam *(N)*	coot
ngaw *(gen)*	mallee fowl
ngulya *(NE)*, ngulak/ngulyak *(S)*	white-tailed black cockatoo
ngunan *(E)*, ng(w)unana *(N,SW)*	black duck
ngurrak *(E)*, ngurrku *(N)*, ngurrka *(SW)*, boya *(SW)*, boy *(S)*	egg
nhiyan *(SW)*	sparrow hawk
nyiil *(S)*, djila *(N)*, kanba *(W)*	wing of bird
waarlatj *(E)*, waldja *(N,SW)*	eaglehawk
wardang *(gen)*, kwakan *(SW)*	crow
wayan *(N,SW)*, madu *(N,SW)*	heron
we:tj *(E)*, wadji *(N)*, wedja *(SW)*	emu
wudha/wadha *(N,SW)*, muritj *(SE)*, ngambin *(SE)*	pigeon

12. Aquatic life

bamba *(N,SW)*	stingray
bidawa *(gen)*	pearlshell
djilki *(N)*, djilka *(SW)*	gilgie, freshwater crayfish
djundula *(S)*, jindulu *(SW)*	flounder
djung *(E)*, muyart *(SW)*	freshwater cobbler
kalkart *(E)*, kalkarda *(N,SW)*, mardarang *(S)*	mullet
karr *(N)*, karraly *(SW)*, marrimarri *(S)*	crab
karraly *(N,SW)*	saltwater cobbler
kartarn *(SW)*, ngawily *(S)*	groper
kunak *(gen)*	koonak
maadjat *(S)*	shark
manyin	seal
marralya *(gen)*	mussel, oyster
marran *(gen)*	marron
marrkany *(N)*, bulyan *(SW)*	rock cod
mimang *(N)*, mamang *(SW,S)*	whale
mundu (SW,SE)	tiger shark
ngarri *(SW)*, milak *(SW)*, warrak *(E)*	salmon
ngumatj *(SW)*	jewfish
nharalang *(SW)*	herring
warnang *(SW)*	blue shark
warranang *(N)*, kayala *(SW)*, dhwerdabangarn *(S)*	porpoise
yidjarap *(N)*, kodjarrak *(S)*, kodjakarrak *(SW)*	snapper
yukil	sea-shell

13. Insects and spiders

bardi *(N)*, berda *(SW)*, bert *(E)*	bardy grub
bilibili *(N)*, bila *(E)*, birr *(SE)*	beetle, cockroach
bindibindi *(N)*, bentbent *(SW)*, marmar *(NE)*	butterfly, moth
budjin, burdak, karrart, dhudula, kwalak *(S)*/kwelka *(N)*	ant
djidaly (N,NE)	grasshopper, mantis
djingkitj *(N)*, dhurdatj *(SE)*, ngurrkalitj *(S)*, nhurrka/nyurrka *(SW)*, nyiwaring *(N)*	mosquito
kanbar *(E)*	march fly

kanbarr *(N)*, kanbarra *(SW)*, djirraly *(NE)*	centipede
karr/kar *(E)*, karra *(N)*	spider
kilil (N,NE), kirdirra/kirdal *(S)*, kulang *(E)*	sergeant ant
kuul *(E)*, kulu *(N)*, kula *(SW)*	louse
mint	tick
mirramirt *(SE)*	jumping ant
mulatj *(E)*	white ants/termite eggs
nenim *(N,SW)*, won *(SE)*	leech
nharna *(N)*	caterpillar, worm
nhurda/nyurda *(SW)*, nhurdu *(N)*, nhurt/nyurt *(E)*	fly
wiit *(E)*	white ant, termite
yingkarn *(W)*	cricket/cicada

14. Plants

baat*(S)*, bada *(N,SW)*	rush grass
balka (N,NE), balak *(S)*	blackboy, grasstree (*Xanthorrhoea* species)
balkar *(N)*, mangkara *(N)*, mangka *(NE)*, kuril *(S)*	branch of tree
biyak *(S)*, bika *(SW)*, biriny, kodjap, dhadhaba *(N)*, dhurdin *(S)*	blackboy, grasstree (*Xanthorrhoea* species) resin
borr *(E)*, barru *(N)*, borra *(SW)*, barrar *(S)*	rough blackboy, grasstree (*Xanthorrhoea* species)
boy *(E)*, bayu *(N)*, boya *(SW)*	zamia nut
bungkara *(N)*, bwongkar *(S)*	banksia
burn *(N)*, djakat *(S)*, kugany *(N)*, kwardany *(S)*, miin *(gen)*, djabak *(SW)*/dhabak *(N)*	edible roots
burn *(S,E)*, burnu *(N)*, burna *(SW)*	tree, wood
burt *(S,E)*, biditj *(S)*, buda *(SW)*	bark of tree
bworr *(S)*, wanal *(N,SW)*	root of tree
dhwart *(E)*, dhwarda *(SW)*, dhurda *(N)*	York gum
djanda *(N)*	hakea
djarraly	jarrah
djilba *(N,SW)*, djelap *(S,E)*, djep *(S)*, wotj *(S)*	grass
djirridj *(E)*, djirrdji *(N)*, djirrdja *(SW)*	zamia palm

kalkaly *(W)*, yurlak *(N)*, yiman *(N)*	blackboy species (*Xanthorrhoea*)
kalyang *(gen)*	wattle tree
kardan *(N,SW)*, marri *(SW,S)*, kalyin *(E)*	redgum, marri
karri	karri
kulart *(N)*	blue gum
kulbuku (NW), benya *(NE)*	fig tree
kwel *(S,E)*, kwela *(SW)*, kwerdal *(NE)*	sheoak
kwonart	jamwood seeds
madjarak *(N)*	fruit of fig
mangart	jamwood
mangkatj *(gen)*	banksia flower
marrany *(gen)*	vegetable food
mayarr *(E)*, dhilbi *(N)*, dhudjba *(S)*	leaf of tree
me:n *(S)*, mena *(SW)*, mina *(N)*, ngarla *(SW)*	edible gum
mitj *(E)*, midju *(N)*, midja *(SW)*, madjang *(S)*, barratj *(N)*	banksia cone
mudjarr *(gen)*	Christmas tree, *Nuytsia floribunda*
mudurt *(N)*, yubarl *(S,SW)*	tea-tree
ngok *(S,E)*, nguka *(N,SW)*	honey from banksia
wang *(gen)*, djak *(NE)*	sandalwood
warrak *(E)*	salmon gum
warrany *(N)*, yuk *(S)*	yams
wornt *(E)*, warndu *(N)*	white gum, wandoo
yandjaitj *(N)*, karrat *(S)*	type of rushes
yumbak *(N)*, yorla *(SW)*, yorl *(S,E)*, yalu *(N)*	tea-tree bark

15. Physical qualities

balyan *(N,SW)*	wet
bony/bwony *(SW,E)*, bunya *(N)*	fat
bul *(S)*, bula *(N)*, bularang *(E)*	many
dhandjal *(N,SW)*	shallow
dhardal *(SE)*, dhardang *(N,SW)*	raw, uncooked, alive
djilap *(N,SW)*	sharp
djurta/dhurt *(SW)*	blunt
kany/keny *(gen)*, dhumbart *(N)*	one
karap *(SE)*, djalum(a) *(N)*	salt, bitter

karlarak *(gen)*	hot
kert-kert *(gen)*	fast, quick
kop *(SE)*, muwarn/murn *(N,SW)*	black
kudjal *(gen)*	two
kumbar *(gen)*	big
kunyak *(gen)*	soft
kurart/kwerart *(SW,E)*, kurarda *(N)*	short; straight
kwap *(E)*, kwaba *(N,SW)*	good, well
kwedjalarr *(SE)*, bwonyburt *(N,SW)*	thin
mow *(E)*, mawu *(N)*, mardany *(SW,S)*, warrang *(N)*	three
murdak *(gen)*	deep
murdatj/murditj *(gen)*	hard, firm, strong, solid
ngelan *(SW,E)*, ngalin *(N)*	crooked
ngiding/nyiding *(gen)*, nhaka *(N)*, kurrkany *(SW)*, malkarn *(E)*	cold
ngobilyang *(N,SW)*	red
ngunyang *(gen)*, nguku *(N)*, ngok *(S)*	sweet
nhop *(SE)*, budhany/bodhany *(N,SW)*	little
nhotj *(E)*, minyi *(N)*, minya *(SW)*, badjak *(E)*	rotten, stinking
nhotj *(modern gen)*, wen *(E)*, wena *(SW)*, wening *(N,SW)*, winatj *(N,SW)*	dead
warra/werra *(gen)*, wakany *(SE)*, windang *(N,SW)*	bad
wurri *(SW,E)*, walyardi *(N)*	long
yinyang *(gen)*	new, fresh

16. Non-physical qualities

bidabap *(SW,S)*, bidababa *(N)*	weak, tired
bidjar *(gen)*, bidji *(N)*	asleep
burdanyak *(gen)*, bandany *(N)*, wirrart *(SW)*, yulap *(gen)*	hungry
dhabalkan *(gen)*	slow, quiet
dhwongk-bart *(E)*, dhwongka-bart *(SW)*	deaf
kaditj *(gen)*	knowing, clever
kaditj-bart *(gen)*	stupid

karrang *(gen)*	wild, angry
kulmerang *(gen)*	shame
mandjang *(gen)*, djirralak, baditj	old
minditj *(SW,E)*, mindatj *(N)*, berrak *(E)*	sick, sore
miyal-bart *(gen)*	blind
murrart *(gen)*	full, sated
nhakal *(N,SW)*	tame; kind
wangka-bart, maya-bart, dhalany-bart	dumb
wayarn *(gen)*	afraid, frightened; dead

17. Motion

bardang	to jump; to fly; to step
dhabat, ngurnt kurl	to fall down
dhandang	to climb
dharrbu, wayarri, warri	to swim
kirt kurl, murditj kurl	to run, go fast, go strongly
korr kurl	to return
kurl	to go
kwadjat kurl	to go forward
waba	to play
wart kurl	to go away
yan	to walk, go
yirra kurl	to go up, ascend, get up
yuwal kurl	to come

18. State

ngurnt	to lie
nhanap	to stop
nyin, ngin	to sit
yuk	to stand

19. Vocalisation and thought

bardap, kulyam	to tell a lie
kadatj, dhungka, dhwongk	to hear, listen
mirru, mirra, marri, melyarn	to call out, sing out
nhaku, djinang	to see, look at, look for
wangka, wongk	to speak, talk, tell, ask
yirra kwert, kedining, ketarding	to sing

20. Bodily functions

bakan	to bite
boban, bwaban	to blow
dhankan	to yawn
kawin	to laugh
ngany, waka	to breathe
ngarn, nhalku *(SW)*	to eat; to drink
nyindjan *(N)*, bunyan	to kiss
wal, wel	to cry
wen	to die

21. Impact and violence

bam, boma	to hit
bin, ben	to dig, scratch, scrape, cut
dhakarn	to break, cut
dhan, dhorn	to stab, pierce, spear
dhukarn	to cook, burn
nyirang	to scratch
yudarn	to tie

22. Holding and transfer

barrang	to grab, take, get, hold
barrang kwert	to push
kanka	to carry, bring
kwert	to throw, drop
mal	to pull
yungka	to give

23. Location, direction and time

barr, barra	astray
benang	morning; tomorrow; day
birak	summer
biratj	midday, noon; day
bordak *(S,E)*, barduk *(N)*	close by, near
burnur(u), wardanak	autumn
buyang, wurrar	far
kadakadak, kadiyak, kadik, karrimbi, marrart-marrart	evening, dusk
kadakany, karranya, karram, yinya	yesterday
kakarr, yirra *(SW)*, mornang *(E)*	east
kalarak, karrbalak, karramak	afternoon, evening

korr	back, return
kwadjal	in front, forward
makur(u)	winter
mardak	behind
marrak, kaniyang, winak(al), ngardi *(SW)*	west
marrart(ang/ak), kidalak	night
minangal, djilba	spring
mirnang *(SW,E)*, buyal *(SW)*	south
ngardi	down
wart	away
wulul(an), manya(na)	tomorrow
yabaru *(SW,E)* djirral *(N,SW)*, wiil/wilu/wila	north
yirra	up
yuwal	this way, hither

24. Interjections

kaya, kay, kwa	Yes!
yuwad(a)	No!

Grammatical notes

Like other Australian languages, Nyungar marks subjects and objects with case suffixes. However, because of the lack of data it is still unclear exactly what rules governed the choice of subject and object marking. Word order in Nyungar is typically Subject-Object-Verb. The following examples illustrate this:

yok	*nhunga-rr-any*	*nyin*	*djinangany*
woman	man-*plural-obj*	sit	watching

'The woman was watching the men.'

kongk-al	*mayar*	*wangkany*
uncle-*subject*	nephew	telling

'Uncle was telling his nephews.'

As will be quite clear to the reader, the wordlist gives very little detail of Nyungar verbs. There are two reasons for this. First, the early settlers were more interested in recording the names of things than recording sentences or stories in Nyungar, and so very few verbs are listed in old wordlists. For the same reason, I have not given dialect details for the verbs — the information is simply too sketchy.

Second, it appears that Nyungar was a language that managed to do a great deal of work with very few verbs. To describe complex actions, a series of verbs were linked, often together with one or more of a set of adverbs which qualified the manner, the time or the direction in which some action was occurring. The Motion section of the wordlist gives some clear examples of adverb + verb combinations. The following two sentences also illustrate this:

kany	*wart*	*kurliny*	*dhadj*	*kurl*	*ngardangany*
one	away	going	meat	go	hunting

kurl	*djinangany.*	*karl-inariny*	*kurl*	*kurl*	*djinangany*
go	looking	fire-begin	go	go	looking

'One is going off hunting meat, going along looking. The fire is starting as (he) goes along looking.'

References

Douglas, W H 1976, *The Aboriginal languages of the South-West of Australia*, 2nd edn, Australian Institute of Aboriginal Studies, Canberra

Moore, G F 1884, *Diary of ten years eventful life of an early settler in Western Australia, incorporating a descriptive vocabulary of the language in common use amongst the Aborigines of Western Australia*, facsimile edn 1978, University of Western Australia, Nedlands

10

Gooniyandi

WILLIAM McGREGOR

Gooniyandi is spoken by around 100 Aboriginal people in Fitzroy Crossing (Kimberley, Western Australia) and a number of outstation communities in the river areas between there and Halls Creek. The language is in a relatively weak state, and it is not being passed on as a full language of communication to the children, who are learning the language Kriol (a creole variety of English spoken in this area and across to north-western Queensland) as their mother tongue. However, since 1982, there has been concern about this situation, and over the years various programs have been developed to teach the language to children in the schools at Yiyili, Gogo and Fitzroy Crossing.

Gooniyandi is a non-Pama-Nyungan language (see page xi above). The only closely related language is Bunuba, which was traditionally spoken to the north-west. Together the two languages form what is known as the Bunuban family; they are about as alike as French and Italian. Gooniyandi shares around 45 per cent of its basic vocabulary items with Bunuba, but only a little over 20 per cent with Walmajarri and Djaru, the abutting Pama-Nyungan languages.

Other spellings of the language name include Gunian, Goonien, Kunian, Konean and Guniandi; it must, however, be distinguished from Gunan, which is a Northern Kimberley language spoken in the vicinity of Kalumburu.

As in other Aboriginal groups, kin relationships play a prominent role for the Gooniyandi, and this is reflected in the number of kinship terms in the language. Even when people are not related by 'blood', they can establish a kinship tie by reference to the system of 'skins' (or subsections, as anthropologists call them). Everyone belongs to one of eight skin groups, and this determines who they can marry, and what skin their children will belong to. By knowledge of their respective skins any two people can work out their kin relation to one another. For further discussion of this very complex system see McGregor (1990, p. 15). The main point is that it is the nature of the kinship tie between two people which governs how they interact with one another. Some relationships, notably the mother-in-law relationship, require utmost circumspection, while others are quite unconstrained. There are also differences in speech: when speaking to one's mother-in-law, one should speak circumspectly (the Gooniyandi term is *goon-* 'speak shamefacedly'), and a number of special words are used such as *balija* 'man' instead of the ordinary *yooloo*; *gamalg-* 'speak, tell, say', instead of ordinary *miga-* and *jag-*; and *girrbi-* 'go, walk' instead of ordinary *ward-*. (For a longer list, and further discussion of this style of speaking, see McGregor 1989.)

Spelling and pronunciation

Gooniyandi spelling has undergone a number of changes over the years as more speakers are becoming literate. The system used here is the one currently being used in literacy materials produced by David Street at the Karrayili Adult Education Centre in Bayulu. The following letters are used:

a, aa, b, d, rd, g, i, j, l, rl, ly, m, n, rn, ng, nh, ny, r, rr, th, oo, w, y

In this system, *oo* stands for the vowel sound like the *oo* of English 'fool', usually written *u* in Aboriginal languages, as well as for the long version of that sound.

As usual, *ng* stands for the sound represented by these letters in English words such as 'sing'. Gooniyandi also has the sequence of sounds *n* followed by *g*. To keep this distinct from *ng*, a dot is used to separate the letters. Thus *n.g* stands for the sequence *n* followed by *g*, while *ng* is a single sound. (See also notes on pronunciation on pages xxvii–xxix of the Introduction.)

GOONIYANDI WORDLIST

WORDLIST CATEGORIES

1. Body parts and products
2. Kin relationships
3. Human classification
4. Language, mythology and ceremony
5. Human artefacts
6. Food, cooking and fire
7. Topography
8. Elements
9. Mammals
10. Reptiles
11. Birds
12. Aquatic life
13. Insects and spiders
14. Plants
15. Physical qualities
16. Non-physical qualities
17. Motion
18. State
19. Vocalisation and thought
20. Bodily functions
21. Impact and violence
22. Holding and transfer
23. Location, direction and time
24. Interjections and particles
25. Demonstratives and pronouns
26. Introduced items
27. Placenames

1. Body parts and products

barndi	arm
birdi	thigh
boolga	grey hair
digi	boil
dooloo	heart
doomoodoo	chest
gaji	sore
gamoo	breast; milk
garajbi	body
garli	jaw
garndagarndadi	throat
garrawooloo	shin
garri, garrwi	armpit
gawoo	lungs
gimani	knee
girlinggi	penis
gooji	bone
goonggoodoo	saliva
jaabi	nape of neck
jawoorloo	calf
jilywiri	guts

10.1 Gooniyandi

jinyjili	navel
joonggoo	elbow
joorloo	stomach (external)
joowadi	sweat
lawadi	shoulder
limimi	chin
linggali	ankle
lirri	guts
man.ga	ear
manili	nose
marla	hand
marliwidi	lip
marnba	buttocks, bum
miljarndi	fingernail; toenail
milyilyi	brain
min.ga	fat
minyjoo	tooth
mirali	hip
mirli	liver
mirra	head
mooloo	face; forehead
moonda	stomach (internal)
moordoo	cicatrice (ceremonial scarring)
moorloo	eye
ngalyadi	testicles
ngirrirli	cheek
ngoonyjoongoonyjoo	moustache
ngoorroorndoo	pubic hair
nyaninyi	vagina
roo	faeces
thaaliya	semen
thaawoorroo	beard
thalanyi	tongue
thangarndi	mouth
thinga	foot
waarri	blood
walamboo	rib
wiliwili, wingarri	neck (exterior)
wilmirri	kidney
wirla	back
yambarra	hair of head
yilaa	urine

2. Kin relationships

garingi	wife; wife's sister
garingilangi	husband and wife pair
gilagi	grandfather (father's father)
jaja	grandmother (mother's mother)
jaminyi	grandfather (mother's father)
lambadi	father-in-law (wife's father)
marna	older brother
marni	older or adult sister
marriyali	mother-in-law (wife's mother)
ngaboo	father; father's brother
ngaja	younger brother or sister
ngaliganyi	daughter
ngalinyi	son (of a woman)
ngaloowinyi	son (of a man)
ngarranyi	mother; mother's sister
ngawi	father's sister
ngawiji	grandmother (father's mother)
ngoombarna	husband; husband's brother
nyaanyi	mother's brother

3. Human classification

barndanyi	old woman
booga	baby, child
boogalangi	poor fellow
boolga	old man
galara	widow
galardingarna	avenger, someone who avenges the death of a relative (literally 'dweller of white ochre': avengers adorned themselves with white ochre before setting out on their revenge expedition)
galinda	adolescent girl
gambayi	uncircumcised boy (not yet initiated)
ganayinggi	person bereaved of son or daughter
gijali	dead person, dead body
gimangarna	'bushman', person not knowledgeable in white ways (literally 'bush-dweller')
goornboo	woman
jaliji	friend, ceremonial mate

10.4 Gooniyandi

jalngangoorroo	doctor
joogoo	child
malooga	ceremonial manager (*Also means* boss)
marlara	girl
maroowa	killer, murderer
mawoolyi	children, little ones
mayara	circumcised adolescent
narroogoo	namesake, person with same name
nawoornga	bereaved of a (distant) relative
nganyandi	dead person, dead body
ngoolyoongoolyoo	circumcisor
yarrbanyi	initiand (person going through initiation)
yooloo	person, Aboriginal person, man

4. Language, mythology and ceremony

bamboo	didgeridoo
barawoorroo	fighting ground
bilyji	red ochre
birlirri	ghost, spirit of a person
darroogoo	sacred, secret
galardi	white ochre
garnana	tree burial platform ('Calvary')
garnbag	clapsticks
garndaarra	yellow ochre
gooni	dream
goowaa	news or word of someone's death
jarndirri	inquest stones; these were placed under the burial platform, each stone representing a possible killer — the killer was determined by which stone that was marked by liquid from the corpse
joonba	song
thangarndi	language
yingi	name

5. Human artefacts

baali (*occasionally* gaali)	path, road
binyjawinyja	pearlshell pendant
boorlba	things, material possessions
burnduwarli	headband
galwaya	canoe
gananyi	digging stick
garli	boomerang
garroona	shield
gilarla	tobacco
goorra	grinding stone
goorroo	fire saw
gri	fish poison
jagooli	pearlshell pendant
jalandi	belt of human hair
jamayina	axe
jinali	spear
moorroo	club
ngawali	woomera, spear thrower
ngoonyjoo	tobacco
ramboorra	fishing net
riwi	camp
than.gindi	fighting spear
wirinyi	hut
yamadi	coolamon

6. Food, cooking and fire

birri	charcoal
dili	flame, light
doonggooloo	prohibited or taboo food
garanyi	hot cooking stones (*Also means* bullet, rifle)
garooroo	ground oven
gawoondoo	ashes (cold)
langa	salt
maa	meat
manyi	vegetable food; flour, bread
wan.gi	smoke
wayandi	fire, firewood
woob	to cook

7. Topography

banda	ground, dirt
birndirri	plain (*Also means* bald)
doo	cave
gima	bush
goomooloo	a place that should be avoided by a person because a close relative (e.g. spouse, child or parent) died there recently
goorrgoo	hole in ground
joodoo	dust
ngaarri	hill, rock, stone, pebble, money
ngarrali	pebble
walyarra	sand
winamoo	cliff

8. Elements

birrinyi	sky
galamanda	mud
gamba	water, liquid, alcoholic beverage; waterhole
girngali	wind
jaalinyi	moon
jarlangga	creek
jimilooroo	lightning
jiwirni	cyclone
joomoo	soak, soak water
lanygiya	daytime, midday
maningga	night
mirri	sun
mirriyindi	rainbow
naya	thunder
ngaaloo	shade
ngalangala	bank of river or creek
ngoomoorroo	cloud
warda	star
warlibirri	river
warramba	flood, floodwater
winhthi	spring water
yiwindi	rain

9. Mammals

barawoo	female kangaroo
binjirrmi	bat
ginyma	flying fox
girlinggoowa	male of a species
goomboorna	plains country wallaby
jamarra	male kangaroo
jambiyindi	possum
marranyi	dingo
minaji	echidna
ngamari	female of a species
nyawa	tail
tharra	tame dog
thirroo	kangaroo (general term)
wanyjirri	river kangaroo
woombanoongoo	rock wallaby

10. Reptiles

barlanyi	snake (general term)
garrbala	mountain devil
giwili	water goanna
joonggoorra	water-snake
lalanggarra	a type of freshwater crocodile
loomoogoo	blue-tongue lizard
manggoola	ta-ta lizard
nganthamany	brown snake
nyarlangarri	king brown snake
walwarrangga	a type of freshwater crocodile
wawanyi	goanna (general term)
wawooloo	frill-necked lizard
wilirrabi	long-necked turtle
yilimi	carpet snake

11. Birds

balnganyja	sulphur-crested cockatoo
barlara	topknot pigeon
bija	nest
bin.gidi	feather
booloogoo	kite hawk
diyadiya	peewee
doomboo	owl

10.12 Gooniyandi

galamooda	bustard
gambinyi	egg
garnanganyja	emu
garnbirra	eagle
garranggarrang	diver bird (cormorant)
girlinygirliny	galah
girramala	black cockatoo
goorralga	brolga
goorranggool	butcherbird
jadiyadi	spoonbill
jawawoodoo	kookaburra
jindiwirrinyi	Willie wagtail
jirigi	bird
joorrgina	bowerbird
lawarla	black duck
marrawi	peaceful dove
mayarda	pelican
thiligi	tawny frogmouth
wanggiri, wanggana	crow
wilimooroomooroo	chicken-hawk
wirndoo	curlew
wirndoo	scrub turkey

12. Aquatic life

balga	barramundi
gawi	fish
gilyjirrjgi	tadpole
goolamangarri	catfish
jarramba	crayfish
jarrja	shell
jirragi	frog
ngawaya	mussel
woogoo	frog

13. Insects and spiders

baarndi	spider (general term)
bilinyi	tick
birrinyooloo	wasp
biyirndi	maggot
ganbadi	centipede
gooradooroodoo	termites

goorlinyi	mosquito
jangalangala	red ant
lagarndi	grubs (witchetty)
lawinyjina	green ant
malimali	butterfly
migi	ant (general term)
milaloowa	scorpion
ngalinya	sugarbag, honey
ngawagoo	antbed
ngirrinyi	fly
nyanggi	lice
wida	bee
yoorroo	spider web (*Also means* telephone wire, telephone; air-route on which an aeroplane travels)

14. Plants

baga	bindi-eye (burr)
balma	fork of tree, junction of creeks
bilirndi	red gum
birla	yam
birlnga	bark
garringarri	waterlily
gilirni	grass
girili	tree, stick
goonthoorrngarri	limestone country yam
goorroomba	paperbark
jiga	flower
joowidiyidi	bohemia tree
langgagooloo	hollow log
larrgardi	boab tree
mawoorroo	bloodwood tree
moogoorloo	grass seed
nyirri	spinifex
warrgarli	wattle
warriyayi	a lerp (an edible white substance found on leaves of certain gum trees)
warrwili	coolabah
yimarrarra	leaf
yirrali	root
yoonggoo	scrub

15. Physical qualities

balyadi	smooth, flat (of ground)
binyidi	hard, strong
booladi	dry
boordbara	hot (weather)
dagoorladagoorla	rough (of ground), pot-holed
damarda	blunt; deaf; blind
galyba	soft
gambi	sick
garndiwa, garndiwangoorroo	many
garndiwirri	two
garrirndi	fat
girrabingarri	long
giyi	wet
goornga	raw (meat)
gooroogooroo	black
jalgoodoo	sharp (point)
jiginya	small
joodoo	straight, right
joorloongarri	sated with food
labawoo	white
lambardi	small
larrbi	thin, skinny
lawagimana	white
maadi	cold (weather)
mooyoo	asleep
ngamoonhingi	old
ngarloodoo	three, a few
ngayirla	thirsty
ngirrinyjila	hungry
nyamani	big
nyarna	deep (of water)
ramboorra	light (weight)
tharidi	heavy
thigi	short
thirrgirli	straight (as of a line)
thiwa	red, person
thoorndoo	rotten
wan.ga	alive
yanoonggoo	new
yoowarni	one

16. Non-physical qualities

binarri	clever
ganybili	ashamed
joornanygarra	good
thirri, thirrimili	wild, angry; fight
wangmarra	insane
yijgawoo	bad, stupid
yoowa	frightened, cautious

17. Motion

bar	to climb up
barn	to return
bayal	to swim
bij	to emerge, arrive; to rise (of the sun)
boorij	to dance
boorlooboo	to follow
dirib	to enter
gard	to fall
gird	to go away
girrar	to run, go quickly
goornag	to turn around, turn over
jarrg	to jump
joorra	to chase
laja-	to ride (e.g. a horse)
marorr-	to muster, gather together
moow	to search for, look for
thinggil	to dive into water
thood	to climb down, descend
thoorloog	to stand up
ward	to go, walk; to carry
widag	to pass by
yood	to sit down, put

18. State

bagi	to be lying
balib	to go out (of fire), extinguish
liga	to wait
loombarrany	to float
wara	to be standing
warang	to be sitting

19. Vocalisation and thought

baa	to shout
binarri	to learn
binarrig	to teach someone
galgal	to laugh
goon-	to speak shamefacedly or respectfully in presence of taboo relative (especially a mother-in-law); speak respectfully of the dead, or when a close relative has died
gooni	to dream (of someone)
goowaj-	to name someone or something by name, tell
jag	to tell, say
jijag	to speak
miga	to tell, say
narda	to cry, weep
ngalany	to sing a song, sing (bewitch) a person
ngoorrab	to shout
yag	to promise
yan.gin	to ask for something

20. Bodily functions

danymili	to hear, listen
gij	to wake up
mila	to see, look
moorniny-	to copulate with
nang	to die
ngab	to eat, consume, burn
nginoong	to lick
ngoorloog	to drink
nhar	to urinate
niyig	to swallow it
thirraj	to defecate, void, eject
wab	to smell it, to smell
wird	to bite
woorloorl	to ache
yooroog	to vomit

21. Impact and violence

boorr	to rub
dij, garoong	to break it, be broken
doorn	to cover it
gaj	to cut it
gard	to hit, kill, fell
goorday	to grind
jany	to squeeze
joog	to hunt kangaroos by chasing them
mird	to tie up
ngarag	to make, construct
nyag	to pierce
nyoomboorl	to bathe
nyoon	to rub
thirrirt	to yandi (to winnow grass seeds from husks in a coolamon)
thoorlng	to kick
wirrij	to dig, scratch
woob	to cook

22. Holding and transfer

booroo	to hide it
doow	to take it, get it, catch it, fetch it
gad	to leave it
galiny	to carry
garloo-	to find nothing
gilba	to find it
goorij	to hold
lig	to listen for news of someone's death
loow	to push along
ngang	to give it
nyin	to lose it; to leave, forget something
thard	to hang up (on peg)
waj	to throw
yood	to put down

23. Location, direction and time

baabirri	down, below
balyoowa, balyjoowa	behind
barrangga	summer, hot season (pre-wet season)
boorroo	north
garrwaroo	yesterday; afternoon
gindiwa	upstream
graa	near, close by
jibirri	downstream
laandi	up, above
liya	west
marnangoorroo	far
moongayayoo	tomorrow; morning
munggoowarla	cold season, 'the dry'
ngamoo	before, already
ngarranggarni	long ago, Dreamtime
ngila	east
ngirndajiya	here
ngiyi	south
ngoorriya	there
wamba	later on
wilangajarri	ahead
yalawa	near, close by
yaningi	now, today
yidirla	'the wet'

24. Interjections and particles

ba	come on, let's go
gaj	OK, you can go
mangarri	no, not
marlami	no, nothing, none
nya	here you are
warawoo	ouch! ow!
warriwarri	sorry, shame (on hearing an inappropriate word)
yoo, yoowayi	yes

25. Demonstratives and pronouns

bidi	they, them
birrangi	their, theirs
gidi	you (to more than one person)
girrangi	your, yours (to more than one person)
jaji	what
ngaanggi	your, yours (to one person)
nganyi	I, me
ngarragi	my, mine
ngidi	we two (me and you, me and someone else); we more than two (excluding you)
nginyji	you (to one person)
ngirndaji	this
ngirrangi	belonging to us two (me and you, me and someone else); belonging to more than two of us (excluding you)
ngoonyiya	where (at)
ngoonyiyirra	where (to)
ngoorndoo	who
ngoorroo	that
nhoo	his, hers, its
niyi	he, she, it
yaabja	some
yaadi	we more than two (including you)
yaanya	other
yarrangi	belonging to us three or more (including you)

26. Introduced items

bilanggidi	blanket
booloomani	cow, cattle
dimana	horse
doowa	store
gardiya	white person
googoonyjarri	sheep
limba	policeman
magarda	hat
maja	boss, manager
malngarri	white person

mayaroo	house
milimili	paper, letter
minyawoo	cat
mirnmirdgali	policeman (literally 'tie-up-er')
nayoo	knife (European)
nyirraji	bull
wajbali	white person
wiliwili	fishing line
yawarda	horse

27. Placenames

Bamathithi	Gogo station (the name Gogo comes from Gooniyandi, but is not a placename. It seems that the prominent hill near Gogo homestead was a sacred site (*darroogoo*) and children were warned away from it, being told that it was inhabited by Gugu (probably a bogey man). The area where the homestead stands was never before referred to as Gogo; this is what white people called it, from what children were told about the place
Bayulu	the Aboriginal community on Gogo station, named after a billabong nearby
Danggoo	Geikie Gorge (a popular tourist attraction not far from Fitzroy Crossing, located in Bunuba country); also the name of a creek in the desert south of Christmas Creek, Tonka Springs, in Walmajarri country
Janjoowa	hill in Fitzroy Crossing where mission was located, which gives its name to the nearby Aboriginal community, Junjuwa
Mooloorrja	waterhole on Margaret River, on Fossil Downs station, which gives its name to Mulurja community
Ngoomban	cliffs on main road to Halls Creek, about 80 kms from Fitzroy Crossing

Yiyili — waterhole on Margaret River, on Louisa Downs, which gives its name to Yiyili community

Grammatical notes

To speak Gooniyandi you need to know more than just words — you need to know how to put them together into sentences, particularly because the rules for doing so are very different from English. In English the basic rule for constructing a sentence is that you put the subject first, then the verb, and finally the object (if the sentence is transitive). The order of the words is important — there is a big difference between *The woman saw the man* and *The man saw the woman.* In Gooniyandi you could put the three words *goornboo* 'woman', *yooloo* 'man' and *milanga* '(s)he saw him/her' in any order without changing the meaning. The difference between 'the woman saw the man' and 'the man saw the woman' is carried not by the order of the words, but by the forms of the two nouns: if the woman is subject, the form *goornboo-ga* is used; if the man is subject, *yooloo-ngga* is used:

goornboo	*-ga*	*yooloo*	*milanga*
woman	-by	man	(s)he-saw-him/her

'The woman saw the man.'

yooloo	*-ngga*	*goornboo*	*milanga*
man	-by	woman	(s)he-saw-him/her

'The man saw the woman.'

The order of words in these two sentences could be changed in any way without affecting the meaning. The subject is identified by the suffix -*(ng)ga*, while the object always comes without a suffix. Note that, as is the case for most Aboriginal languages, there is no word for 'the' (or 'a') in Gooniyandi.

However, the subject of an intransitive sentence (one without an object) takes no suffix at all, just like the object of a transitive sentence:

goornboo	*waranggiri*
woman	(s)he-is-sitting

'The woman is sitting down.'

Other meanings that are expressed by prepositions in English are expressed by suffixes on nouns in Gooniyandi. There are, for example, suffixes meaning 'in, at, on', 'towards', 'away from', 'for', etc.:

-ya 'in, at, on' (locative case)

goornboo	*waranggiri*	*riwi*	*-ya*
woman	(s)he-sits	camp	-at

'The woman is sitting in camp.'

-yirra 'towards' (allative case)

goornboo	*wardji*	*riwi*	*-yirra*
woman	(s)he-went	camp	-to

'The woman went to camp.'

-nhingi 'from, away from' (ablative case)

goornboo	*wardji*	*riwi*	*-nhingi*
woman	(s)he-went	camp	-from

'The woman went away from the camp.'

-yoo 'for' (dative case)

goornboo	*-ga*	*ngaarri*	*-yoo*	*moownga*
woman	-by	stone	-for	(s)he-looked

'The woman looked for the money.'

One area of particular complexity in Gooniyandi grammar is in its verb forms, which change depending not just on the time the action occurred, but also according to who was or is doing it, and to whom. Thus, an intransitive verb like *ward-* 'go' has scores of different forms, while a transitive verb like *mila-* 'see' has hundreds. Some appreciation of the structure and complexity of Gooniyandi verbs may be gained from the following forms for these two verbs, respectively, which represent but a small fraction of the different forms of each:

ward-ngi	I went	*ward-ji*	(s)he went
ward-ngiri	I am going	*ward-giri*	(s)he is going
ward-bingi	I will go	*ward-bi*	(s)he will go
mila-la	I saw it	*mila-loona*	I saw them
mila-ala	I see it	*mila-aloona*	I see them
mila-wila	I will see it	*mila-wooloona*	I will see them
mila-nga	(s)he saw it	*mila-wina*	(s)he saw them
mila-a	(s)he sees it	*mila-ana*	(s)he sees them
mila-wa	(s)he will see it	*mila-woona*	(s)he will see them

It should be observed that no distinction is made according to the gender of the subject or object: the same form is used irrespective of whether the subject or object is male, female or neuter.

These brief remarks only scrape the surface of the complexity of Gooniyandi verbs. The reader may have noticed that the above forms for *ward-* 'go' all end in *i*, whereas those for *mila-* 'see' all end in *a*. This is not accidental: the ending *i* is mainly found when the verb is intransitive; *a* when it is transitive. There are an additional ten such endings which may be used, each having a different meaning, and going with different verbs. Some examples are *-bini* as in *gard-bini* '(s)he hit him/her', *-ani* as in *gardbani* '(s)he fell', *-bindi* as in *rarriny-bindi* '(s)he got thirsty', and so on.

Perhaps one of the most fascinating things about Gooniyandi grammar is the pronouns. Instead of the usual distinction in the first person between 'we (including the hearer)' and 'we (excluding the hearer)' (see page xix), Gooniyandi has the pronoun *yaadi* meaning 'we more than two (including you)' and *ngidi* for any other 'we' — that is, for 'me and you' and 'me and one or more others but not you'.

A detailed description of Gooniyandi grammar can be found in McGregor (1990), which also contains a short wordlist and three texts. This work is, however, suitable only for trained linguists, and there is unfortunately no non-technical description available of the language. See McGregor (1988, pp 27–30) for further general information on the language, including information on language programs and an extensive bibliography. Kimberley Language Resource Centre (1993) contains another Gooniyandi wordlist.

References

Kimberley Language Resource Centre 1993, *Gooniyandi Wordbook*, KLRC, Halls Creek

McGregor, W 1988, *Handbook of Kimberley languages. Volume 1: General information*, Pacific Linguistics, Canberra

McGregor, W 1989, 'Gooniyandi mother-in-law "language": dialect, register, and/or code?' in *Status and function of languages and language varieties*, ed. U Ammon, pp 630–656, Mouton de Gruyter, Berlin and New York

McGregor, W 1990, *A functional grammar of Gooniyandi*, John Benjamins, Amsterdam

Street, D and T Chestnut 1984, 'We spell it Gooniyandi: notes on the new Gunian orthography', *Aboriginal Languages Association Newsletter*, vol. 6, no. 4

11

Yindjibarndi

SUE SMYTHE and NICK THIEBERGER

Yindjibarndi is one of the languages spoken at Roebourne, in north-western Western Australia. Its speakers originally came from the tableland area of the Pilbara, around the Fortescue River near Mount Pyrton, north to the Upper Yule River and east to Mungaroona Range. This includes what is now the Millstream-Chichester National Park, an area that contains many significant sites for Yindjibarndi people. Several hundred people still speak Yindjibarndi, and there is a program to teach the language in Roebourne Primary School.

Other spellings for the language name are Injibandi, Ingibandi, Jindjiparndi and Jindjibandji.

As language is both a mirror and a vehicle for culture, it is necessary to know something of Yindjibarndi cultural life to appreciate the differences between it and the dominant European society in Australia.

Each Yindjibarndi person is born into one of four 'skins' or 'sections'. These sections determine marriage partners, and allow someone to know how they are related to anyone else, even if they have never met them before. The four sections are called Banaga, Burungu, Balyirri and Garimarra. A Banaga man marries a Burungu woman and they have Balyirri children. A Garimarra man marries a Balyirri woman and they have Burungu children. As soon as you know what section someone belongs to and what generation they are, you can work out their relationship to you. Some relationships involve special restrictions. For example, all people who are classed as a man's brother-in-law must be avoided by him; he should not talk to them, or be present in the same place as them. In addition, speakers of Yindjibarndi have a 'respect' vocabulary, a set of words that they must use when a man is in the presence of his mother-in-law. For example, the respect word for 'dog' is *yuurru*, while the normal, or everyday word is *wanyja*. Some more examples are shown below.

Everyday	Respect Vocabulary	English
bayiwanarra	*bargarranygaa*	plains kangaroo
yirdiya	*mardiya*	road
gunayi	*babu*	father
gananggarri	*warba-gu*	come
gankala	*minkaa*	on top
barrimirndi	*thurru*	sea serpent

The reader will notice, in the last section of the wordlist, that to use the pronouns of Yindjibarndi you must know if the people you are referring to are of the same or different generation levels. As generations are regarded as being cyclical, there are only two, alternating, generation levels in the Yindjibarndi system, one's own, and not one's own. People of the same generation level, for example, are two brothers, a man and his sister-in-law, a grandchild and its grandparent. People of different generation levels are, for example, a parent and their child, a child and its aunty, a child and its great-grandparent.

About the wordlist

Some of the words in the following list are derived from English. This is especially the case for introduced items, animals, clothes, and so on. Notice that the words for bullock (*buliman*), lamb (*yilam*), shoe (*jujigu*) and cat (*buthi*) are adapted to the sound system of Yindjibarndi. Another way of dealing with naming new things is by extending the meaning of existing words. For example, *barbarrnyungu*, the word for 'bird', has also become the word for 'aeroplane', and *marba*, the word for 'cajuput' (a type of tree) has become the word for 'money'.

11.1 Yindjibarndi

Spelling and pronunciation

The spelling system presented below has been used in the dictionary of Yindjibarndi written by Bruce Anderson. (See the notes on pages xxvii–xxix in the Introduction for a guide to pronunciation).

a , aa, b, d, g/k, i , ii, j , l, lh, ly, m, n, ng, nh, ny, r, rd, rl, rn, rr, th, u , uu, w, y

YINDJIBARNDI WORDLIST

WORDLIST CATEGORIES

1. Body parts and products	13. Insects and spiders
2. Kin relationships	14. Plants
3. Human Classification	15. Physical qualities
4. Mythology and ceremony	16. Non-physical qualities
5. Human artefacts	17. Motion
6. Food, cooking and fire	18. State
7. Topography	19. Vocalisation and thought
8. Elements	20. Bodily functions
9. Mammals	21. Impact and violence
10. Reptiles	22. Location, direction and time
11. Birds	
12. Aquatic life	23. Pronouns

The item in brackets following the verbs listed below indicates the class to which the verb belongs. For an explanation of verb classes, see Grammatical notes *following the wordlist.*

1. Body parts and products

barraa	shoulder
barruu	kneecap (*Also means* grinding stone)
birrirdi	fibula (small bone of lower leg) (*Also means* small boomerang)
biwi	breast, teat (*Also means* mother's sister)
bularda	heart (*Also means* pump, piston)
bulha	head
burdungu	chest
gawurn	skin
gulhi	bone
gurga	ear

jawurda	facial hair, beard, moustache
jina	foot(print)
jirli	arm
mararra	index finger, thumb (*Also means* first child)
marda	blood
marnburr	knee
mirga	crotch (*Also means* fork of tree)
munyju	ornamental scar, cicatrice
mutha	nose; tip, end
ngaji, nhanka	neck
ngamarri	liver
nganggaanyu	big thumb, toe
ngardanyungu	kidney
ngarlu	stomach
nhuurga	ankle
nyidbingga	on the hip
nyirndid	waist
thaa	mouth, beak
thambi	rib
thanggina	plaited hair
tharba	body
thurla	eye (*Also means* peg on woomera)
wanga	armpit
wanggarr	throat
warga	womb
warla	heel (*Also means* butt end of stone knife)
warli	lip
warnkurla	elbow
waurda	armpit hair
wirrarli	collarbone
wulu	thigh
yathuu	tongue
yirndi	forehead
yirra	sharp tooth; edge
yirrga	fingernail, toenail
yurrurn	hair, fur

2. Kin relationships

Note that kin terms in Yindjibarndi can have a number of equivalent terms in English.

babu	father
babui	woman's brother's child; woman's child's spouse; husband's sister's child
binhuma-gu *(Vl)*	to be correctly related
binhumarri *(Vo)*	to interrelate properly in Yindjibarndi law, greet each other cordially, etc.
binthi	woman's sister-in-law; woman's husband's sister; brother's wife; father's sister's daughter; mother's brother's daughter
biwarra	child and mother's sister
biwi	mother's sister (*Also means* breast, teat)
gamayi	stepmother; mother's younger sister; father's younger brother's wife; aunt (some, not all)
gananyuwarra	woman and her husband's sister
gawarli	man's father's mother; daughter's daughter; woman's son's daughter
gayaa	older brother
gurdaarra	man and his younger sibling
gurndad	man's daughter; brother's daughter; woman's sister's daughter
gurndagarra	mother's brother and his sister's son
mararra	first child (*Also means* index finger, thumb)
marndiyarra	father and child
marraa	younger brother
marrganhu	brother-in-law
marrganhuwarra	man and his wife's brother
mayi	younger sister
mimi	mother's brother; father's sister's husband; spouse's father
ngangga	mother
nhuwa	man's eligible spouse; mother's brother's daughter; man's father's sister's daughter; woman's mother's brother's son; woman's father's sister's son

nyirdi	mother-in-law; father's sister; mother's brother's wife; wife's mother; woman's brother's child
thamii	man's son's son; woman's mother's father; daughter's son
thurdu	older sister; father's older brother's daughter; mother's older sister's daughter
yarungu	man's wife's sister; brother's wife; woman's husband's brother; sister's husband
yayu	stepmother; mother's older sister; father's older brother's wife
yumini	stepfather; father's older brother; mother's older sister's husband

3. Human Classification

barninybarniny	baby (just having learnt to sit)
birirri	man (18 years and older)
buyama	orphan
gubiyarri, mangurlarra	children
gurnda	respect, shyness
gurnmairdi	good hunter
gurri	young girl ready for marriage
guwarduwarra	baby (just crawling)
jayira	fasting boy (12–14 years), youth
juju	mature, old (person)
juna	ritual assassin, kurdaitcha man, evil spirit
marndamarangga	police, handcuff (literally 'rock-hand')
marru	widow(er)
mawarnkarra	native doctor, magician
mirnumaa	teacher
mithi	white woman
murlawaya	one who always has meat
murrurru, wardirra	unmarried adult, bachelor, spinster
ngaarda	Aboriginal man
nyambali	boss, chief
nyirdingu	youngest child; last in a series
nyurdun	girl (about 2 years)
nyurnda, nyuju	recently initiated
thamunu	uncircumcised
thathaarlaa	liar, smart aleck

thugu	boy (about 2 years)
wanggawaji	bad speaker, one who speaks broken English
warliwi	boy (3–12 years)
wathurri	girl (3–16 years)
wilanngardi	baby (just having learnt to walk)
yithiyarra	brothers being initiated at same time

4. Mythology and ceremony

barri	devil
birdarra	ceremonial feast concluding initiation
birduwanguma-gu *(Vl)*	to capture for initiation
jawi	song
jinyji	wage, murder contract, payment, brideprice
jirda	ritual gift, as in ceremonial feast
mawarn	magic power
Minkala	Aboriginal God, deity, Jesus Christ
nyarna	soft chalky white stone used for paint
nyujuma-gu *(Vl)*	to initiate
thalu	increase site (a place where plants or animals can be increased by performing a ceremonial ritual, see Daniel 1990 for more detail)
thunggari	grave
wiligarri	female nymph, sprite

5. Human artefacts

bankirdi	short spear with smooth untanged point
barruu	grinding stone (*Also means* kneecap)
barumaya	mia-mia, spinifex house
bidbagurra	spear with forward tangs and four-edged point
birda	elevated burial platform
birdu	chisel
budbu	blade, axe
burliwarni	bullroarer
burruu	hair belt
gaju	metal axe, tomahawk

gayii	blunt training spear
gayirrwara	loincloth
gilirr	ornamental headband decoration, bullroarer
gurrardu	walking stick
gurriyarda	long two-piece spear with tanged point
jilungarda	firestick (*Also means* drill)
jinabuga, jujigu	shoe, footwear
jumbirirri	knife
marbamaya	paperbark house
marliyarr	headband
marndamaya	stone house
maurndu	spear for duelling and punishment
maya	house
mirlimirli	paper, letter, book
mirriji	string, rope
mujairdi	nose plug
mulu	blade attached to woomera handle, adze
ngalhandangu	mill slab
nyankardurdu	man's kilt
thanbardan	enamel basin, bark basin, coolamon
thardu	yandy, winnowing machine
tharra	twig hook used to snag bardy grubs
thaurra	fishing net
thurubu	trough
wajirr	fish spear
wambu	throwing stick with two points
wanbirnbuntharri, jurna	club, nulla-nulla
wanu	fighting stick used by women
warbarra	woomera, spear thrower
warlanu	long fighting stick
wilgurdu	spear with forward cutting tangs and three-edged point
wiliwili	fishhook
wirra	boomerang
wubu	box, container
wunggu	windbreak
yarra	shield
yatha	bough-shade, canopy
yuyu	music

6. Food, cooking and fire

bawa	fresh water
biyaandaa-gu *(Vr)*	to make jerky, preserve meat by cooking and drying
burgu	tobacco for chewing
buunyngu	honeycomb in rockholes
buyawirdu	firestick bush
galangu	sugarbag, honey sack
gamba-gu *(Vl)*	to burn something, cook something
gari	poison, alcohol
gurna	charcoal
gurndu	milk
jami	medicine
jirnda	hot coal, ember
mardumirri	damper
mirrin	stone hearth
mulhu	cold; winter; year
munda	blood pudding, baked clotted blood
murla	meat; animal
nyarranyarra	bought bread, vegetable food
nyilaardi	drink, native mead, honey and water spiced with lemon grass
waranu	sweet substance on leaves of river red gum
yawandaa-gu *(Vl)*	to place cooking stones (e.g. inside kangaroo)
yiwarda	ashes
yurraji	flame, tinder
yurrama	a soak for obtaining water

7. Topography

bargu	hill
jardungu	rockhole
marnda	rock, mountain, metal, hard material, money
marndamarnda	stony ground
ngamarlangu	cave

8. Elements

barbarr	sky
barndurrarna	Morning Star (Venus)
birndirri	star
burnngaarri	cyclonic cloud, running cloud
garuwarra	meteor, shooting star
mulhuwa	winter
tharnardi	ocean, sea
wilarra	moon, month; crescent-shaped mark in rock
wirrwi	wind, air
yundu	rain
yurra	sun, morning, day

9. Mammals

bajarri	hill kangaroo, euro
bayiwanarra	plains kangaroo
buliman	bull, cow
buthi	pussycat
gugurnjayi	sheep
gurdi	red marsupial mouse
jardunmarra	rock wallaby
jirriwi	echidna
mujira	dingo
ngaja	marsupial mole
nganggungu	old boomer kangaroo
wanggarrwanarra	camel (literally 'throat-long')
wanyja	dog
yawarda	horse
yilam	lamb

10. Reptiles

baliirri	blue-tongue lizard
banthawayi	giant savage goanna, perentie
bayamalu	king brown snake, mulga snake
guluwirri	brown snake
gurrumanthu	male goanna, bungarra, Gould's sand monitor
jagajagara	knob-tailed gecko, barking gecko
marndangatha	ridge-tailed goanna, ridge-tailed monitor
marniyarra	carpet snake

mayitha	water-snake, water python
muntha	lizard, ring-tail dragon
thawu	house gecko
warlu	snake
warndawarnda	tree snake, children's python
warrururga	black goanna, monitor
winkaru	stripe-tailed goanna

11. Birds

bararrji	seagull
barbarrnyungu	bird (*Also means* aeroplane)
bardu	feather other than emu's
bardurra	plains turkey, bustard
bargarrawarduwardaa	bush lark
barnbarn	ringneck parrot
batharra	budgerigar
baularri	night heron
birdirra	little corella
birrubirru	sacred kingfisher
bitharndi	galah
burnanyirunyiru	red-capped robin
buwaa	little black cormorant
gabagurda	spotted nightjar
gagarlurlu	crested pigeon
gujibirubiru	rainbow bird
gurluu	black duck
gurrarnkurrarn	mulga parrot
gurrwaru	pied butcherbird
gurrwiny	darter bird
jandindi	wild fowl with black tail
jarburrungu	wedge-tailed eagle, eaglehawk
jarnkurna	emu (*Also means* dark spot in Milky Way
jirrijirri	Willie wagtail
jiruna	pelican
judi	white-plumed honeyeater, native canary
jurdairri	red-backed kingfisher
jurlaurdu	spinifex pigeon (has topknot)
mardunkura	ibis
marnbi	bronze-wing pigeon

minbirrirri	kestrel
nyardu	emu feather
nyilinyilingga	welcome swallow
nyimayi	zebra finch
tharraji	bowerbird
thuli	tawny frogmouth
wagurra	crow
warluwurru	bird down
warndurla	magpie
warrinyin	painted finch
wiirrirri	blue wren
wilumarra	bush stone-curlew
winyamarangga	sea-eagle
wirndiwirndi	collared chicken-hawk, hawk
wiru	cockatiel
wurda	emu chick
yarnkarra	brolga, Australian crane
yilimbirraa	mudlark, peewit
yuya	quail

12. Aquatic life

barrimirndi	sea serpent
bijbarrara	milkfish, jumper bream
birrabirra	shell
bunyji	native yellow perch, black-barred grunter
galuburlu	spadefoot toad
gawi	fish
gurnkurn	blowfish
guuthu	tadpole
jangga	burrowing goby fish
jarraarn	burrowing river frog
jilanggurr	water-holding frog, spinifex frog
jiurra	bony bream
marndamirraa	eel
milinja	spangled perch
milyinkura	mangrove jack, red snapper
minyjiarri	hairback herring, bony silky bream
nyamina	dugong
thatharruga	sea turtle
yardiwi	carp-gudgeon (a tiny fish)

yarramirdangga	ox-eye herring
yarrwarlanygaa	large tandan (eel-tail catfish)
yathumba	flathead
yirratharnangga	shark

13. Insects and spiders

binbila	grasshopper
birna	bug
ganbarr	spider
gawarliwarli	butterfly
gumbujuja	cockroach, spinifex roach
gumirn	mosquito
jarnangu	bardy grub
jarru	march fly
marndaambirr	firefly
minarrangu	centipede
mirriminyja	common caterpillar
mirrinmirrin	cricket
thala	large black-and-yellow carpenter bee, native bumblebee
tharnku	bull ant
wanbayi	honeybee
warrurnbarrurn	blowfly, bluefly
waruma	common ant
yirrila	cicada

14. Plants

bajila	turkey-fruit, banana caper
barra	indigestible leaf, tea, tobacco
baru(urru)	any kind of spinifex, especially hard buck spinifex
birditha	dry or dead leaf
birnkardangu	tobacco species
bunaangu	bloodwood
bungaa	currant tree, raisin bush
burdardu	sandalwood (nut-bearing tree)
burlaala	fruit
burrga	spinifex resin, wax
jambirlangu	sweet dry sap from river red gum, etc.
jirriny	Millstream fan-palm

marba	paperbark, cajuput (*Also means* paper money)
marruwa	snakewood
mina	soft spinifex
minjurlu	spinifex gooseberry (a very sweet prickly tomato)
ngaluwany	water chestnut, a rush
wirbinygaa(wirdi)	tall river spinifex (plural)
wirndamarra	mulga tree
wirranggaa	river red gum
yali	spinifex ear
yarrwayi	wild tobacco growing near water

15. Physical qualities

marduurraa	flat on one's back
waji	bad, evil; foul, sour
warru	black, dark, night
mirduwarra	very brainy, intelligent
baya	fight, battle
galanggu ngarri	lie with legs flexed
yirdinygarra	lined up, queued up, in a row
wanarra	long, tall
maru	many, much
yiyangu	new, fresh
yurlu	nothing, none
gunyjirri	one
mardamarda	red
guda	short
jarruwirdi	three
gulharra	two

16. Non-physical qualities

bantharra	jealous
burrutha	sad
jaja	rubbish, worthless; ignorant; ugly
marli	lazy
mathid	languid, inactive
mayumarri *(Vo)*	to make peace with one another
minggalhu-gu *(Vl)*	to protect
ngajaarra	helpful, not lazy
thathamarnda	greedy, mean

thurlaburnu	nosy
thurnda-gu *(Vl)*	to roll something
thurrurd	true; straight to, direct
waba, maagurra	good
wirrard	feelings, emotions, spirit
wirrima-gu *(Vl)*	to play
yinjirrma-gu *(Vl)*	to be cruel
yurndiri	nasty, in a foul mood, sulky

17. Motion

banggarri *(Vo)*	to go
barnda-gu *(Vl)*	falling (as rain)
bininggarri *(Vo)*	to run, go fast
guriwaardarri *(Vo)*	to circle back, spin around
gurrawayi-gu *(Vn)*	to swim
jinama-gu *(Vl)*	to track
mirrunggama-gu *(Vl)*	to load woomera
muugarri *(Vo)*	to smoke (a pipe, tobacco, etc.)
tharrwa *(Vo)*	to enter, go in
thumburdankarri *(Vo)*	to flip, somersault, dive
waarra-gu *(Vr)*	to follow closely, track, hunt
wirdany	path, especially made by kangaroo
wiyanu	hunting
yarra-gu *(Vr)*	to chase
yindi *(Vo)*	to descend and remain in sight
yuni *(Vo)*	to descend and disappear (as the sun)

18. State

barndanyarbirri *(Vo)*	to sit cross-legged
barni *(Vo)*	to sit, stop, be
bayawirri *(Vo)*	to become vicious, become savage
mulhuwarni *(Vo)*	to turn cold, become winter
thardaankarri *(Vo)*	to sit with knees bent and parted and heels dug in

19. Vocalisation and thought

birni-gu *(Vn)*	to swear (at)
burlunyja-gu *(Vl)*	to nod, agree
gaardu	to shout
gurganyja-gu *(Vl)*	to think; to remember; to believe in
jawarlarlarri *(Vo)*	to whisper
mirnu	to know
mirnuma-gu *(Vl)*	to teach, show, direct
mirra *(Vo)*	to call out
muurnkarri *(Vo)*	to hum
nyurnima-gu *(Vl)*	to joke, tell a joke
thula-gu *(Vl)*	(of a dog) to bark
waalhu-gu *(Vl)*	to say goodbye to
wangga *(Vo)*	to speak, talk (about), ask; speech, talk, story, language, word, sentence
wanggayinyjarri *(Vo)*	to talk together, converse
wanyaarri *(Vo)*	to hear, listen, understand
wararrwarni *(Vo)*	to tease
yagayinygarri *(Vo)*	to groan, call out in pain, moan
yirraama-gu *(Vl)*	to sing
yurni-gu *(Vn)*	to call over

20. Bodily functions

bamba	sleep
bunha	sexual desire
buntha *(Vo)*	to wash oneself, bathe
buntha-gu *(Vl)*	to wash something, water something
buwarri	dream
buya-gu *(Vl)*	to kiss
gajardaa-gu *(Vl)*	to tickle
gubiyarrima-gu *(Vl)*	to cut in little pieces
gunayi-gu *(Vn)*	to defecate
jandi *(Vo)*	to cough
jiniyarri *(Vo)*	to get sick, be hurting
mija-gu *(Vl)*	to drink
ngalhi *(Vo)*	to cry
ngarrgu *(Vo)*	to eat
nyurndiwarni *(Vo)*	to die
thumbirraarri *(Vo)*	to fart, break wind
thurla nyimba *(Vo)*	to wink, blink

wilhanggaa-gu *(Vl)*	to spit
wirnawarni *(Vo)*	to tire, become tired
yarrwatharri *(Vo)*	to sweat
yathurndaa-gu *(Vl)*	to lick
yurrurnkarlaarri *(Vo)*	to grow hair or fur

21. Impact and violence

barbaa-gu *(Vl)*	to cure by massage
guthanyma-gu *(Vl)*	to squash, mash
jinka-gu *(Vr)*	to carve, whittle, chisel
mirndinyma-gu *(Vl)*	to shoot
nyirra-gu *(Vr)*	to cover, paint
nyurndima-gu *(Vl)*	to kill
thaardama-gu *(Vl)*	to split open
thani-gu *(Vn)*	to chop
tharlaa-gu *(Vl)*	to kick
thuwayi-gu *(Vn)*	to spear by throwing
waama-gu *(Vl)*	to scare, frighten
wajba-gu *(Vl)*	to detach, take off
wanayi-gu *(Vn)*	to clean
wanbi-gu *(Vr)*	to hit with a held instrument, beat, pound
wirndarn	cut
yirrima-gu *(Vl)*	to chop out a section from (a tree)
yirrwa *(Vo)*	to scratch
yurndaama-gu *(Vl)*	to crush, smash into tiny pieces
yurra-gu *(Vr)*	to dig up or out
yurrwi-gu *(Vn)*	to scrape, shave

22. Location, direction and time

balamu	long ago, a while ago; already; yet
Bambanyaa	Sunday; week
biila	outside, in the open
binggayi	holiday
birri	late afternoon
ganalili	dawn
gayilarni	from the south
jambu	left hand(ed), left side
jinggarni	from upstream
minkaa	on top

tharurru	sundown
wardandarni	from the north
warrunggamu	tomorrow
warruurraa	evening, last light, twilight
wirrwiwurraa	upwind
wularni	from the west
yaarni	from the east

23. Pronouns

ngalharndu	my, mine
ngali	you and I (same generation level)
ngaliuu	us and you (same generation level)
ngaliya	we two (same generation level)
ngaliyauu	us three or more (same generation level)
nhurnuulha	they two (same generation level)
nhurnuwi	they two (different generation level)
nhurnuyarndu	his, hers, its, of this
nyinda	you
nyindaulha	you two (same generation level)
nyindauu	several of you
nyinkaarndu	your
nyinku	to or for you
nyinkuwi	you two (different generation level)
wala	he, she, it, that (mid-distant)
walaagulha	they two
walaardu	that one

Grammatical notes

Unlike many of the other languages in this book, Yindjibarndi identifies the subjects of all sentences in the same way, regardless of whether they are transitive or intransitive. It is one of a group of languages in the Pilbara that do this, part of what linguists call the Ngayarta subgroup (after the word for 'Aboriginal person' in the languages).

To put a sentence together you need to know more than just words. In common with many Australian languages, Yindjibarndi uses suffixes to show such things as tense on verbs and case on nouns. Objects of sentences in Yindjibarndi carry suffixes (*-yi*, *-ngu*, *-gu*), and there are a number of other cases also marked by suffixes.

If you want to say that something happened at a certain place (the locative case), you need to add one of the following suffixes: *-ngga*, *-la*, *-rda*, *-d*, *-yu*, depending on the noun they are to be attached to.

Warnda *garri* *bargu* *-ngga*
tree stand hill *-locative*
'The tree is on the hill.'

To talk about moving away from something (the ablative case) you need to add one of the following suffixes: *-nggangu*, *-langu*, *-rdangu*, *-yungu*, depending on the noun they are to be attached to.

bargu *-nganggu*
hill *-ablative*
'from the hill'

Wanyja *bininggarri* *-nha* *mama* *-langu*
dog run *-past* father *-ablative*
'The dog ran from father.'

To talk about moving towards something (the allative case) you need to add one of the following suffixes: *-(g)arda*, *-nguwarda*, *-bathaa*, *-burraa*, *-(ng)uurraa*, *-gurru*, *-yuurru*, once more depending on the noun they are to be attached to.

Ngayi *banggarri* *maya* *-arda*
I go *-present* house *-allative*
'I am going to the house.'

There are a number of other cases with their own case suffixes which are not discussed here.

Note also that there are different forms of the pronoun depending on whether it represents the subject, object or indirect object of the sentence. In addition, a distinction is made between 'we' that includes the hearer, and 'we' that excludes them.

You may have noticed from the above examples that the order of words is similar to English, with the subject first, then the verb, then the object. This is not always the case, and many Yindjibarndi sentences have the subject first, then the object, then the verb. For example:

Manggurla *wanyja* *-yi* *nhawu*
child dog *-object* see *-present*
'The child sees the dog.'

Verbs belong to one of four classes (or conjugations). The table below illustrates some of the suffixes used for each conjugation. When a verb is listed in the wordlist above, it has *Vo*, *Vl*, *Vr* or *Vn* after it to indicate which class it belongs to. For example, *jandi-* is the basic form of the verb 'to cough'. It is in the Vo class, so to say 'coughed', you would add *-nha*, to make *jandinha*, to say 'was coughing', you would add *-ngu* to make *jandingu*.

Tense suffixes by verb class

	Vo	Vl	Vr	Vn
Present	-0	*-gu*	*-gu*	*-gu*
Past	*-nha*	*-rna*	*-rna*	*-na*
Imperfect	*-ngu*	*-rnu*	*-rnu*	*-nu*
Imperative	*-ma*	*-nma*	*-rnma*	*-nma*

Below are some examples of the above classes:

Vo

Wanyja	*ngarrgu*	*-nha*	*buthi*	*-yi*
dog	eat	*-past*	cat	*-object*

'The dog ate the cat.'

Vl

Yundu	*barnda*	*-gu*	*marnda*	*-a*
rain	fall	*-pres*	mountain	*-object*

'The rain is falling on the mountain.'

Vr

Wanyja	*yarra*	*-rna*	*manggurla*	*-wu*
dog	chase	*-past*	child	*-object*

'The dog chased the child.'

Vn

Ngani	*wala*	*wanyja*	*barndi*	*-gu*
what	that	dog	smell	*-pres*

'What is that dog smelling?'

For a full description of Yindjibarndi grammar, as well as a dictionary and a series of texts, see *The Yindjibarndi Language* by Frank Wordick (1982).

References

Anderson, B 1986, *Yindjibarndi Dictionary* (photocopy)

Brandenstein, C G von 1970, *Narratives from the North-West of Western Australia in the Ngarluma and Jindjiparndi languages*, vols 1–3, (with audio-disc), Australian Institute of Aboriginal Studies, Canberra

Daniel, D 1990, *Thalu Sites of the West Pilbara*, Department of Aboriginal Sites, WA Museum, Perth

Wordick, F J F 1982, *The Yindjibarndi Language*, Pacific Linguistics, Series C, Canberra

12

Dätiwuy

MERRKIYAWUY GANAMBARR

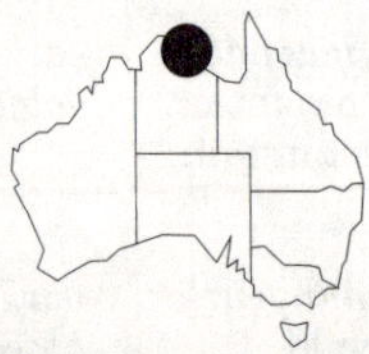

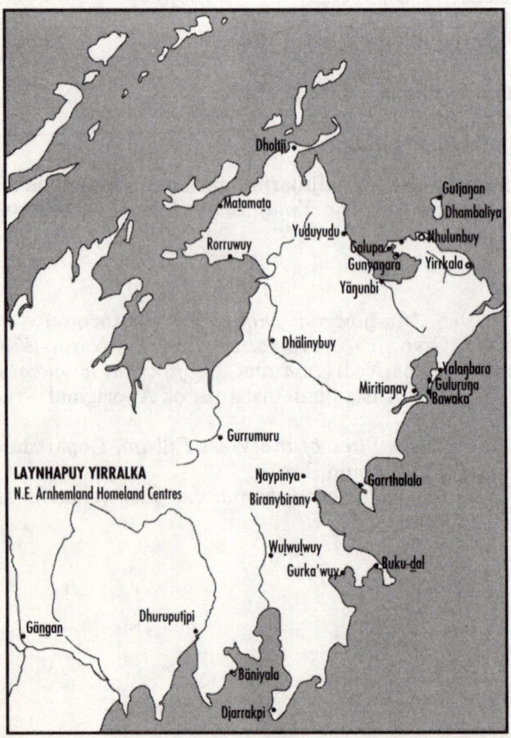

ŋarrany yurru l̲akaram nhumalaŋ dhäwu dhiyakuy nhä dhuwal ŋayi yothu yindiny. Mak linygun nhuma marŋgin ŋurikiyiny yolŋuw rock band-gu Yothu Yindiw. ŋunhiny yukurra lakaram yuwalktja gurrut̲u yolŋuny, gurrut̲u wäŋany ga gurrut̲u nhä malanynha dhuwal ŋanapurr yukurra nhäma, nhä malanynha ŋorra marrtji balanyar bitjan wäyin, dharpa, wata, gapu ga bulu wiripu ga wiripu nhä malanynha.

I want to explain to you what *yothu yindi* really means. You have probably heard about the rock band Yothu Yindi. *Yothu yindi* is really a relationship term. The relationship holds for people, land and all that we see about us, for things such as animals, plants, wind, water and many more.

Yo, yothu ga yindiny mayali' dhuwal balanyar bitjan ŋän̲d̲i ga yothu wo wiripuny yothu ga ŋän̲d̲i. ŋarrany dhuwal mala mit̲tji D̲ät̲iwuy. Dhiyak mit̲tjiw D̲ät̲iwuywuny ŋän̲d̲i wo yothu Wangurri. ŋayi yurru Wangurri ŋän̲d̲i wo yothu D̲ät̲iwuywu. Lakaramany yukurra mad̲ayin'thun gapuy ga wäŋaynha.

Yothu means 'child' or 'baby' and *yindi* means 'big' but in the expression *yothu yindi*, *yindi* refers particularly to the mother. This expression always involves two things in a relationship to each other. So if I am someone's or something's *yothu*, they are my *yindi*. I am in the D̲ät̲iwuy clan. For the D̲ät̲iwuy clan the Wangurri clan can be the child (*yothu*) or the mother (*ŋän̲d̲i*) (and vice versa). This relationship is shown to us by the mingling of the waters from two rivers coming out from the Wangurri and D̲ät̲iwuy lands.

We can use *yothu yindi* to talk about relationships between different things, about people, tribes, ceremonies, land and so on. For example, I am the *yothu* ('child') of the tribe Gumatj. Gumatj is the *yindi* ('mother'). Why? Because my mother is a Gumatj woman. So all Gumatj people are my *yindipulu* (*-pulu* is a suffix used to describe people, clans, etc., related through the mother's side). Also I am the next *yindi* ('mother') for my *yothu* ('child'), but I am also *yindi* for anyone who has a D̲ät̲iwuy mother. So we see how the relationship extends from the immediate family to cover whole tribes. Because of this, men are also considered *yindi* ('mother') and men can be *yothu yindi* to each other. All the members of the rock band Yothu Yindi are in this relationship to each other, and that's why they chose the name.

I would like to thank Melanie Wilkinson for her help in producing this chapter. Thanks also to Oscar Whitehead and Bandapuy Maymuru.

12. Ḏäṯiwuy

Another group of people who are closely linked with the *yothu* and *yindi* are those we refer to as *märipulu* (grandmother's group — in the kinship system *märi* refers to our grandmother on our mother's side and all her brothers and sisters). The *märi* is the 'head' of this group since the *märi* is where *yindi* and *yothu* come from. This is especially important in ceremonies. These groups all join together, with the *yothu* and *yindi* having the manager role on behalf of the *märi*.

We all have our own links as *yothu*, *yindi* and *märi* to many different tribes. My own links will be different to those of my children, my mother and my grandmothers, binding us and the tribes in this area all together in a complex way. This contrasts to our father's line where we are a single group. The *yothu*, *yindi* and *märi* relationships are important in linking us to others.

Although I have talked so far about *yothu*, *yindi* and *märi* in terms of the relationship between people, it is not necessary to think that these relationships are only between people. They could be between two places. For example, the Peter John and Cato rivers we see as mother and child. The land associated with the same clans as these rivers, that is, Ḏäṯiwuy and Wangurri, is also seen as *yothu yindi*. We also talk about these relationships between plants, areas of water, songs or our ancestral animals. We are all linked together. These relationships also hold between the land, songs, plants, animals and so on and, ourselves. We commonly make exclamations expressing these relationships when we see something in a particular relationship to us. For example, when I hear thunder I might say *Ya-a märiny waŋanan* 'Hey, grandmother's talking'. This is because thunder is the voice of the ancestral snake who is my *märi*.

I am a Ḏäṯiwuy woman. We have our own language, songs, lands, totems, paintings and dances. Through all these, people can identify me as a Ḏäṯiwuy person. By my language people will know my lands, songs, totems and so on.

There are two moieties (see page xvi above) in our Yolŋu world, which we call Yirritja and Dhuwa. Everything (including plants, land, animals, even directions, etc.) is either Yirritja or Dhuwa. It's a bit like Yin and Yang. So if I'm Dhuwa then my father is also Dhuwa and therefore so are my sisters and my brothers, whereas my mother is always the opposite moiety, which is of course Yirritja. If my mother is Yirritja then her father is also Yirritja and so are her brothers and her sisters. Their mother is Dhuwa. And so it is like this when you go back generation after generation forever, and from me to the generations to come.

Ḏäṯiwuy is just one of many tribes linked together in eastern Arnhem Land who are commonly referred to by outsiders as the Yolŋu (Aboriginal) people. Each tribe has its own lands, songs, totems, dances, paintings and language. Sometimes the sounds and words are similar but when you hear it spoken you immediately know which tribe the person belongs to.

Children automatically belong to the tribe of their father. People always marry someone from another tribe, and the opposite moiety.

In the past, children usually learnt both their mother's and their father's languages. It was most important that they learnt their father's language. This was especially important for the boys so they could carry on the language in the future. They should at least understand their mother's language because of the boy's future manager role for his *yindipulu*. Women had an important role in teaching children their mother's language, as well as teaching them the language of their father. It was normal for people to speak several languages.

Today things are different, although all of us still speak a Yolŋu language. In the last seventy years or so several missions were established in the eastern Arnhem Land area. Because many people from different groups came together, the children began using a single common language. So now not everyone is learning their father's language and this is a major worry for many of us.

Dätiwuy is a language I heard all through my childhood but didn't speak until I was in my middle twenties. I started speaking it because I was too old to talk in Dhuwaya, which is the children's language of this area. To begin with, I knew in my mind what to say, but I couldn't speak. When I finally did I made mistakes. My mother and father, uncles and aunties corrected me and taught me to speak properly. I'm still not an expert Dätiwuy speaker. I still make mistakes and learn new words every day.

When someone changes and speaks their own language other people notice. Some people are happy and correct you if you say something wrong, while others make it such a point of attention that it makes some people give up and turn back to Dhuwaya.

You have to get used to hearing yourself speaking your own language. It's hard work having to think about everything before you speak. This is also why some people give up.

Yirrkala, where I now live, is situated on the tip of north-eastern Arnhem Land, on the Gulf of Carpentaria in the Northern Territory. It is a well-established Aboriginal community with about 500 Balanda (non-Aboriginal) and Yolŋu (Aboriginal) people living in the community. Although it is Rirratjiŋu land, there are now about 15 different clans living here. Dätiwuy is just one of these clans. Dätiwuy speakers live back in our homeland, Rorruwuy, about three hours drive from Yirrkala. At Yirrkala we have a clinic, a school, a shop and an office which is run by the Yolŋu organisation called Dhanbul.

At Yirrkala our school is a bilingual one. In this school we teach both English and Yolŋu Matha (that is, Yolŋu languages). In the past, the children were being taught in English and Gumatj. But because Gumatj is just one of the languages and many of the children are not learning their own father's language at home, and their mothers are not encouraging them, we have now put in a program of teaching their own languages at school every Friday morning. On other days they are being taught in English as well as their common language Dhuwaya. All of the children only speak English as a second language.

These are the other clan languages that are spoken in and around Yirrkala today:

12. Dä<u>t</u>iwuy

Yirritja	Dhuwa
Gumatj	Gälpu
Dha<u>l</u>waŋu	Marrakulu
Munyuku	ŋaymil
Wangurri	Marraŋu
Maŋgalili	Rirratjiŋu
Ma<u>d</u>arrpa	Djambarrpuyŋu
Warramiri	Djapu

Spelling

These are the letters we use to write Dä<u>t</u>iwuy and the other Yolŋu languages:

a, ä, b, d, <u>d</u>, dh, dj, e, g, i, k, l, <u>l</u>, m, n, <u>n</u>, nh, ny, ŋ, o, p, r, rr, t, <u>t</u>, th, tj, u, w, y, ' (glottal stop)

Note that the ordering of the words in the wordlist follows the order of the letters as listed above.

For the reader's convenience, we have included in brackets the form of the word using a spelling system similar to that used for the other languages in this book.

DÄ<u>T</u>IWUY WORDLIST

WORDLIST CATEGORIES

1. Body parts and products
2. Kin relationships
3. Human classification
4. Language, mythology and ceremony
5. Human artefacts
6. Food, cooking and fire
7. Topography
8. Elements
9. Animals — general terms
10. Edible land animals
11. Inedible land animals
12. Aquatic life — general terms
13. Edible aquatic life
14. Inedible aquatic life
15. Plants — general terms
16. Billabong foods
17. Tuber foods
18. Nuts and vegetable foods
19. Fruits and sweets
20. Inedible plants
21. Physical qualities
22. Non-physical qualities
23. Motion
24. State
25. Vocalisation and thought
26. Bodily functions
27. Impact and violence
28. Holding and transfer
29. Location, direction and time
30. Interjections
31. Interrogatives
32. Demonstratives
33. Personal pronouns
34. Placenames

1. Body parts and products

barrwaṉ (*barrwarn*)	skin
biḏila (*birdila*)	liver
bindha (*bindha*)	rib
bulutju (*bulutju*)	beard
bunydji (*bunydji*)	bottom, bum
burumun' (*burumun'*)	cheeks
bun'kumu (*bun'kumu*)	knee
buthuru, mäkiri (*buthuru, maakiri*)	ear
ḏämbu (*rdaambu*)	forehead
ḏeny (*rdiiny*)	testicles
ḏoṯurrk (*rduurturrk*)	heart
dhala, dhaku (*dhala, dhaku*)	vagina
dhamunumun (*dhamunumun*)	chin
dharirr, biṉiny (*dharirr, birniny*)	fingernail
dhakal (*dhakal*)	cheek bone
dhulmu (*dhulmu*)	belly
dhungal, goŋ (*dhun.gal, guung*)	hand
dhurrwara, dhä (*dhurrwara, dhaa*)	mouth
djalkiri, ḻuku (*djalkiri, rluku*)	foot
djikarr (*djikarr*)	wart
gathin, mon (*gathin, muun*)	clitoris
galŋa (*galnga*)	body
gandarr-yol (*gandarr-yuul*)	fat (person)
gulaŋ (*gulang*)	blood
guḻa, dhuthu, män (*gurla, dhuthu, maan*)	faeces, shit
gupa (*gupa*)	nape, neck
gurak (*gurak*)	voicebox
gurrkurr (*gurrkurr*)	veins, capillaries, blood vessels
gurrka, nyalma, ḏulpurru, buruŋurr (*gurrka, nyalma, rdulpurru, burungurr*)	penis
ḻambarr (*rlambarr*)	shoulder
ḻikan (*rlikan*)	elbow
ḻirra (*rlirra*)	tooth
makarr (*makarr*)	thigh
maŋutji, mel (*mangutji, miil*)	eye
marwat, djamarriny (*marwat, djamarriny*)	hair
mayaŋ (*mayang*)	throat

melparrambarr (*miilparrambarr*) eyelashes
metha (*miitha*) chest
mi̲ngi (*mirngi*) eyebrow
mu̲lkurr, buku (*murlkurr, buku*) head
n̲epal̲ (*rniiparl*) knee
ŋamini (*ngamini*) breast
ŋaraka (*ngaraka*) bone
ŋän̲arr (*ngaarnarr*) tongue
ŋurru, gämurru (*ngurru, gaamurru*) nose
rerri (*riirri*) sickness
wakuy (*wakuy*) armpit
wambal (*wambal*) tail; lower leg below the knee
wan̲a (*warna*) arm
warŋgirr, bälkay (*warnggirr, baalkay*) urine, piss
wälk (*waalk*) placenta, afterbirth

2. Kin relationships

gäthu (*gaathu*) son or daughter (of a man or of a woman's brother)
gutha (*gutha*) your little sister or brother
mäl̲u, bäpa (*maarlu, baapa*) father, dad
märi (*maari*) grandmother, great-uncle (mum's mother and her brother)
momu (*muumu*) grandma (father's mother)
ŋathi (*ngathi*) grandpa (mum's father)
ŋän̲d̲i, ŋama (*ngaarnrdi, ngama*) mother, mum
waku (*waku*) son or daughter (of a woman, or of a man's sister)
yapa (*yapa*) sister

3. Human classification

dhalwaŋiny (*dhalwanginy*) female who can't have children
d̲arramu (*rdarramu*) man
djawul̲pa (*djawurlpa*) old man
djirrikay (*djirrikay*) master of ceremonies (calls out special names)
djuŋgaya (*djunggaya*) manager
gad̲aku (*gardaku*) young boy
gul̲unmirr, galŋa-yolŋumirr (*gurlunmirr, galnga-yuulngumirr*) pregnant
guŋman' (*gungman'*) female who has had children

gurrmul (*gurrmul*)	initiated adolescent boy
marrŋgitj (*marrnggitj*)	female and male traditional witchdoctors
miyalk, dhayka (*miyalk, dhayka*)	woman
ratha, yothu (*ratha, yuuthu*)	child, baby
wäwa (*waawa*)	brother
wirrkul (*wirrkul*)	female in her adolescence (not yet had a child)
yolŋu (*yuulngu*)	Aboriginal person
yothu, ratha (*yuuthu, ratha*)	child, baby

4. Language, mythology and ceremony

bäpurru (*baapurru*)	tribe, clan
buŋgul (*bunggul*)	ceremony, singing and dancing
buku-l̲up (*buku-rlup*)	cleansing ceremony
butju (*butju*)	feathers
dhapi (*dhapi*)	initiation ceremony for boys
dhäwu (*dhaawu*)	story, stories
girrikirri (*girrikirri*)	ceremony for both men and women, for the disciplining of the young boys and the ceremony of afterbirth for the young mothers
mad̲ayin (*mardayin*)	sacred objects (*Also means* beautiful)
matha (*matha*)	language of the speaker
milkarri (*milkarri*)	keening, tears
miny'tji (*miny'tji*)	paintings, art, designs
mul̲kurrwuy (*murlkurrwuy*)	headband made with feathers
nyäl̲' (*nyaarl'*)	untrue; you're joking (kidding)
rom (*ruum*)	law, custom, culture
waŋarr (*wangarr*)	animal totem
wäŋa (*waanga*)	house, land
wäyuk (*waayuk*)	armband made with feathers
yäku, ŋaykan̲a (*yaaku, ngaykarna*)	name

5. Human artefacts

bathi, nyäl̲ka (*bathi, nyaarlka*)	dillybag, stringbag, bag
bil̲ma (*birlma*)	clapsticks
bin̲gal (*birn.gal*)	short pointed sticks used by women to get shellfish or for cracking nits; small sharp kangaroo bone used for striking the head during mourning

burrkuwurrku (*burrkuwurrku*)	headband
duratj (*duratj*)	dress
ḏakul (*rdakul*)	axe
ḏikarr (*rdikarr*)	plane; dragonfly
ḏol, dharpa (*rduul, dharpa*)	wood carving
dhapatjuŋ (*dhapatjung*)	footwear (thongs, shoes, sandals, etc.)
djalwarra (*djalwarra*)	trousers, shorts
djät (*djaat*)	shirt
djimiṉdi (*djimirndi*)	three-pronged fish spear
djorra' (*djuurra'*)	books, papers, magazines
gara (*gara*)	spear
girri', muwayak (*girri', muwayak*)	clothes, bedding, towels, household things
ḻarrpan (*rlarrpan*)	special spear for Dhuwa people
ḻuŋiny (*rlunginy*)	tobacco pipe
marthaŋay (*marthangay*)	boat
marrwala (*marrwala*)	paddle
marryaŋ (*marryang*)	gun
murrŋiny (*murrnginy*)	shovel-nosed spear
ṉaku, lipalipa (*rnaku, lipalipa*)	canoe
ṉäku, ṉuwayak (*rnaaku, rnuwayak*)	bark painting (on bark canvas or board)
ŋarali' (*ngarali'*)	cigarette, tobacco
raki (*raki*)	string
wapitja (*wapitja*)	digging stick
wäŋa(*waanga*)	house, land
wurrwa (*wurrwa*)	armbands without feathers
yiḏaki (*yirdaki*)	didgeridoo, musical hollow wood
yiki (*yiki*)	knife, blade

6. Food, cooking and fire

balwur (*balwur*)	cooked, ready to be eaten
barrukala (*barrukala*)	food wrap made out of paper bark
dämba (*daamba*)	damper
ḏiku (*rdiku*)	not cooked, raw
djiḻka (*djirlka*)	leaves we use as herbs for cooking with meats like turtle, fish, etc.
gulaŋmirr (*gulangmirr*)	medium-rare, under-done or half-cooked
dhaŋutha (*dhangutha*)	fire, camp fire
ganu', ḻirrwi (*ganu', rlirrli*)	burning ashes

guḻayŋumirr (*gurlayngumirr*)	burning log, burning stick
gunḏirr (*gurnrdirr*)	ground oven (*Also means* anthill)
gurtha (*gurtha*)	fire
ḻirrwi (*rlirrwi*)	burning ashes
mapu (*mapu*)	egg
maṉmuŋa, ganguri (*marnmunga, gan.guri*)	yam
nharanhar (*nharanhar*)	burnt
ŋäṉarr-gurtha (*ngaarnarr-gurtha*)	flame, light, tongue of the fire
ŋatha (*ngatha*)	food
ŋurrŋgitj (*ngurrnggitj*)	camp, fireplace, ashes, shade
ramram' (*ramram'*)	crisp and burnt
wäyin, ŋanak, bawarraṉ' (*waayin, nganak, bawarrarn'*)	meat

See also the sections on edible animals, aquatic life and plants.

7. Topography

buku (*buku*)	hill, cliff
ḏamurruŋ-gapu (*rdamurrung-gapu*)	salt water, sea
ḏiltji (*rdiltji*)	inland
ḏorrum'-ḏurrum (*rduurrum'-rdurrum*)	open plain, woodland
gämurru (*gaamurru*)	point of land
gunḏirr (*gurnrdirr*)	anthills
gumurr (*gumurr*)	escarpment
gäwara, gäwa'-gawara (*gaawara, gaawa'-gawara*)	sandhills, mountains of sand, sand dunes
mani (*mani*)	creek, billabong
mani'-mani (*mani'-mani*)	creeks, streams
mathirra (*mathirra*)	cave
minydjirrminydjirr (*minydjirrminydjirr*)	stony area
mirrki (*mirrki*)	group of small trees (same height)
ṉinydjiya (*rninydjiya*)	mud plains, salt plain
wurrthal (*wurrthal*)	dense bush
raŋi (*rangi*)	beach

8. Elements

ban̲dja'-ban̲dja (*barndja'-barndja*)	branches
d̲ulpurru, makarr (*rdulpurru, makarr*)	root
dhol̲u (*dhuurlu*)	mud
dhukarr, gatjal̲ (*dhukarr, gatjarl*)	road
gamunuŋgu (*gamununggu*)	white clay; white
gangul, buthalak (*gan.gul, buthalak*)	yellow; yellow rock, yellow ochre
ganyu (*ganyu*)	star
gapu (*gapu*)	water
garminyarr (*garminyarr*)	earth, sand, soil
garramat, garrwar (*garramat, garrwar*)	sky
gun̲d̲a, bäthu (*gurnrda, baathu*)	stone
gun̲d̲irr (*gurnrdirr*)	anthills
gurrmur (*gurrmur*)	hot
maŋan (*mangan*)	cloud
mayaŋ' (*mayang'*)	big river
mulka' (*mulka'*)	warm, dry
mulmu (*mulmu*)	grass
munatha, garminyarr (*munatha, garminyarr*)	sand
munhawu, munhaku (*munhawu, munhaku*)	night
ŋal̲indi, wirrmu (*ngarlindi, wirrmu*)	moon
ŋawulul (*ngawulul*)	smoke
ŋulwitj (*ngulwitj*)	cold
ŋarkula (*ngarkula*)	water
riyala (*riyala*)	springs, streams, rivers
waltjan̲, mal̲wurrk (*waltjarn, marlwurrk*)	rain
walu (*walu*)	sun
waŋupini (*wangupini*)	clouds
wata (*wata*)	wind, breeze
wärrk (*waarrk*)	storm, cyclone
wulma (*wulma*)	thunder clouds

9. Animals — general terms

buṉulk (*burnulk*)	feather of any bird
wäyin (*waayin*)	land animals and reptiles (these can be classified as *lukanhamirr* (eaten) and *ḻukanhamiriw* (not eaten) or by their motions e.g. *buṯthunamirr* (flying animals e.g. birds and bats), *gaḻ'yunamirr* (crawling, slithering animals e.g. grubs, lizards, snakes and tortoises), *wapthunamirr* (hopping animals e.g. wallabies and kangaroos)
wuṉulŋ (*wurnulng*)	body hair of humans; animal fur

10. Edible land animals

biyay (*biyay*)	land goanna of any sort
dhambiḻiŋu, guŋaluŋ (*dhambirlingu, gungalung*)	blue-tongue lizard
dhum'thum (*dhum'thum*)	grey wallaby
djaḻarrpa (*djarlarrpa*)	red kangaroo
djanda (*djanda*)	water goanna
djaykuŋ (*djaykung*)	file snake
djirrmaŋa (*djirrmanga*)	echidna
gurrumaṯtji (*gurrumarttji*)	magpie geese
guwita (*guwita*)	witchetty grub
maḏalatj (*mardalatj*)	short-necked freshwater tortoise
maḻwiya (*marlwiya*)	emu
maṯtjurr (*marttjurr*)	flying fox, fruit bat
mayawa (*mayawa*)	frill-necked lizard
mewuŋ, gatabaŋa (*miiwung, gatabanga*)	buffalo
minhala (*minhala*)	long-necked freshwater tortoise
moku-milŋinymirr (*muuku-milnginymirr*)	water python
waṉ'kurra (*warn'kurra*)	bandicoot

11. Inedible land animals

bäpi, moḻŋu' (*baapi, muurlngu'*)	snake
bäru (*baaru*)	crocodile
berrkŋu (*biirrkngu*)	praying mantis
boḏuk (*buurduk*)	native cockroach
boṉba (*buurnba*)	butterfly

borrutj (*buurrutj*)	mosquitoes
buthuŋu (*buthungu*)	scorpion
buwat̲a (*buwarta*)	plain turkey
djuku (*djuku*)	nits, lice
d̲amala (*rdamala*)	sea-eagle
d̲apaliny (*rdapaliny*)	caterpillars
d̲etj (*rdiitj*)	grasshopper
d̲ilmurr (*rdilmurr*)	louse
garkman' (*garkman'*)	frog
garinyirrnyirr (*garinyirrnyirr*)	cicada
gälkal (*gaalkal*)	ants
gärr (*gaarr*)	spider
l̲indirritj (*rlindirritj*)	red-winged parrot
marurrumburr (*marurrumburr*)	cat
men̲d̲uŋ (*miirnrdung*)	snail
mil̲imil̲i (*mirlimirli*)	dragonflies; any hovering insects
mindjirri (*mindjirri*)	sandflies
munhaŋaniŋ' (*munhanganing'*)	gecko
nyiknyik (*nyiknyik*)	mice, rats
ŋat̲ili (*ngartili*)	black cockatoo
ŋät̲i (*ngaarti*)	soldier ants
wärraŋ (*waarrang*)	dingo
wuŋgan (*wunggan*)	dog
wurrul̲ul̲ (*wurrurlurl*)	fly

12. Aquatic life — general terms

binbin' (*binbin'*)	fish-scale (can also be the scale on reptiles)
guya, burirritj (*guya, burirritj*)	fish
maranydjalk(wapid̲i) (*maranydjalk(wapirdi)*)	name given to all stingrays, as well as baby sharks. The cooked meat is mixed with the raw liver and eaten
maypal, minaŋara (*maypal, minangara*)	name given to all types of seafood except fish, turtles and stingrays (e.g. shellfish and crabs)
miyapunu (*miyapunu*)	all deep-sea turtles

13. Edible aquatic life

dhalimbu (*dhalimbu*)	clam
dhalwaṯpu (*dhalwartpu*)	green turtle
dhuṉ'ku (*dhurn'ku*)	sea-snail found on the roots of mangroves (one of my favourites!)
dhän'pala (*dhaan'pala*)	big mussel that you dig up from the mud in mud plains near the mangroves; good to collect with kids as the shellfish are easy to find and the kids can play at the same time
djinydjalma (*djinydjalma*)	mud crab, the most popular food from the mangroves
djunuŋgayaŋu (*djunungaayangu*)	dugong, seacow
garriwa (*garriwa*)	flatback turtle
gayaya (*gayaya*)	a brown, dark black/purple shellfish that stands upright in the mud, about as long as the middle finger
gäŋalkmirr (*gaangalkmirr*)	stingray, brown-black in colour, one of the biggest
gaṉ'kurr (*garn'kurr*)	cone-shaped shellfish
gaḻkiyarr (*garlkiyarr*)	a shellfish, a bit like *munḏuka*, that sticks firmly to rocks and has long sharp spines, usually a black colour
girriwitji (*girriwitji*)	colourful little sea-snails found in rock pools
ḻatjin (*rlatjin*)	mangrove worms found in rotten mangrove trees and eaten raw; a delicacy for coastal people of the Top End (another of my own favourites!)
mäḏi (*maardi*)	crayfish
mäṉa (*maarna*)	shark
mekawu (*miikawu*)	an oyster collected on the open sea waterfront and not near the mangroves, the colour of the meat is whitish and milky and sweeter then the ones you would have at a restuarant
milka (*milka*)	a kind of mangrove worm which should be cooked briefly before it is eaten, it has a clear appearance and a milky juice

miriŋu (*miringu*) — another kind of mangrove worm that must be properly cooked, if you eat it raw or not boiled properly, you will cough for several hours. It is thinner than *latjin*, with a milky juice, and excretes a reddish colour while *latjin* excretes a brown colour

mitawara (*mitawara*) — brown *latjin* shellfish with a green and white 'cat's eye'

munḏuka (*murnrduka*) — a *latjin* shellfish, a bit like *gal̲kiyarr*, that sticks firmly to rocks, usually a greeny colour

nhamannhaman (*nhamannhaman*) — flat *latjin* shellfish that cluster in groups on mangrove roots

n̲irriwan (*rnirriwan*) — oyster found in the mangroves

ŋukaliya (*ngukaliya*) — 'long-bums', long shellfish found in the mangroves near the water's edge

ŋuykal (*nguykal*) — kingfish

wamurra (*wamurra*) — mussels that are dug up from around the roots of the mangrove growing along the water's edge

warrapal (*warrapal*) — small, sweet mussels found in the bed of river mouths

14. Inedible aquatic life

gaywarr (*gaywarr*) — any jellyfish, including the sea wasp (deadly jellyfish)

15. Plants — general terms

dharpa (*dharpa*) — trees and shrubs

man'tjarr (*man'tjarr*) — leaf, leaves

mulmu (*mulmu*) — grass

wurrki (*wurrki*) — flowers

16. Billabong foods

dhatam (*dhatam*) — waterlily flower shoots

ḏirrpu (*rdirrpu*) — a round bulb from a small waterlily plant which turns yellow when cooked

garku (*garku*) — a kind of fern, the roots of which are eaten

nyamnyam (*nyamnyam*) — root yam shaped like a peanut shell; when cooked it has to be pounded before being eaten: if eaten without pounding they say that you lose your voice

räkay (*raakay*) — waterlily roots, bulbs

wäkwak (*waakwak*) — waterlily flowers

17. Tuber foods

bin̲d̲iyalŋu (*birnrdiyalngu*) — round black-grey yam which has to be pounded before being eaten

butjuwutju (*butjuwutju*) — small yam shaped like a spinning top, which can be eaten raw or cooked

dhunguruk (*dhun.guruk*) — long black root; the leaves are long and fern-like

djitama (*djitama*) — round yam, like *man̲muŋa*; unless specially prepared it's very poisonous to eat

d̲uyŋa (*rduynga*) — long narrow yam which has long narrow leaves; found in the open woodland

mälŋany (*maalngany*) — long skinny tuber yam; the leaves are long and shiny like those of a young palm tree

man̲muŋa (*marnmunga*) — bush yam, like a potato

riny'tjaŋu (*riny'tjangu*) — round yam, eaten peeled after cooking in ashes or sometimes they are pounded and eaten

wanydjarrpu (*wanydjarrpu*) — long tuber yam like *yukuwa*, except when you peel the skin it leaves a red stain on your hands; this yam can be pounded and eaten after it's been cooked or eaten without pounding

yukuwa (*yukuwa*) — yam like *wanydjarrpu*; you peel the skin after it's been cooked but it can be eaten straight away

18. Nuts and vegetable foods

bal̲kpal̲k (*barlkparlk*) — round small black nuts, four or six in a pod which is bright red when the nuts are ready to be eaten

bulmurrk (*bulmurrk*) — the white vegetable-like stem inside the top of a particular palm tree

dharraŋgulk (*dharranggulk*) — the seeds found in a pod about the size of your hand. There are 20 or so seeds in a pod, the outside part of the seed is coated with tiny hairs which can irritate the eyes so care must be taken when unwrapping the seeds

d̲ingu (*rdin.gu*) — specially prepared nuts that are ground on smooth rocks to make a paste which is put in paperbark and cooked. These loaves are made for ceremonies and can be kept for long periods of time. The nuts must be soaked for several days before they can be made into a paste

ganyawu (*ganyawu*) — a nut like a cashew. Only the shrivelled, dried-up nuts can be used. These are cooked, but you must be careful not to sit in the smoke because it will wrinkle the skin. Special sticks (*bin̲gal*) are used to get the nuts out of the shell once they are cooked

lanhu (*lanhu*) — the inner white stem of a palm tree; it is softer than *bulmurrk*

lä̲luk (*rlaarluk*) — the pandanus fruit; we eat the little seeds inside it

munbi (*munbi*) — a little red fruit, although we think of it as a vegetable, found on long vines in the monsoon rainforest; it can be eaten raw or boiled

19. Fruits and sweets

bod̲aŋ' (*buurdang'*) — little round fruits in a bell-like case which turn yellow when ripe

borrpurr (*buurrpurr*) — little fruits that turn from yellow to red when they are ripe

bulunu (*bulunu*) — little white fruits that cluster together in bundles, usually found along the coast near the beach

burukpili (*burukpili*)	light clear pink fruits that also cluster together
burrumburrum (*burrumburrum*)	little clear white fruits found on very long vines, usually found along the coast near the beach
d̲angapa (*rdan.gapa*)	round fruit the size of a marble, it turns yellow when it is ripe
d̲apu (*rdapu*)	little round black fruits clustered together in 12 or more on long vines
d̲awu (*rdawu*)	little tiny figs
dhaŋgi (*dhanggi*)	green egg-shaped fruit. When you squeeze it the contents come out yellow just like a custard and that's what you eat. The bark of the tree can also be scraped and pounded to make a pulp; this is then carefully spread over the surface of the water to stun fish which float to the surface. We call this method of fishing *dhaŋgi wutthun*
d̲ilminyin (*rdilminyin*)	bright pink fruits usually found in the monsoon rainforest
djambaŋ (*djambang*)	brown bitter-tasting fruit in a fragile shell. It's not a native tree but was brought here by the Macassans from Sulawesi in Indonesia. We also use this as a cough medicine
djin̲'pu (*djirn'pu*)	a fig much bigger then the *d̲awu*
gäku (*gaaku*)	a small fig like *d̲awu*, but the fruit is white instead of black and the leaves of the tree are yellow instead of green
guku (*guku*)	wild honey found in tree trunks, under rocks, and inside anthills
gurrumu (*gurrumu*)	long orange fruits found in the monsoon rainforest
l̲arran̲i (*rlarrarni*)	wild apple, the colour is either red or pink on the outside but white on the inside
l̲ingarr (*rlin.garr*)	grape-like fruit; they are either black or purple and hang from vines just like grapes, they are green when not ripe

l̲irrl̲irrtjin (*rlirrrlirrtjin*)	little red fruit like cherries that grow in clusters in the monsoon rainforest
mapuḏumun (*mapurdumun*)	a billy goat plum like *ŋan̲'kapakarra*, but the plant of this fruit is a big tree
murrtjumun (*murrtjumun*)	little brown fruits larger then *mutamuta* and very sweet
muthi (*muthi*)	small black figs like *ḏawu*, but the leaves of this tree are like sand paper to touch
mutamuta (*mutamuta*)	like *murrtjumun*, these are little golden brown fruits when ripe; the stem of the plant is also used as a medicine for sores, especially boils
munydjutj (*munydjutj*)	green berries that fall to the ground when ripe; these berries taste like beer and are very refreshing to eat
ŋamal̲iya (*ngamarliya*)	fruits like *ḏapu*, but the taste is quite different to that of the *ḏapu* — it's bitter
ŋän̲'kapakarra (*ngaarn'kapakarra*)	billy goat plums; the plant is only a shrub that grows up to your knee if you're a grown person. They say that this fruit has the highest vitamin C in the world: only one of these fruits has the same amount of vitamin C as ten oranges
wa'wa (*wa'wa*)	small bitter fruits that are red when ripe, the leaves from the tree are used as a herb to cook with meats like turtle and fish
wälpalun (*waalpalun*)	black round fruits like *wun̲ḏan̲* which taste very sweet
wäwuru (*waawuru*)	round red fruits; if too many are eaten, your mouth feels dry, but otherwise it's a fruit that makes you want to eat forever, so make sure you have water with you when you eat it
wun̲ḏan̲ (*wurnrdarn*)	round black juicy fruit, like *wuŋapu* your tongue goes purple or black after eating this fruit.

wuŋapu (*wungapu*) — black or purple fruits which look like black olives; they are children's delight because after eating them, their tongues go purple and they love showing them off

20. Inedible plants

baḻwurr (*barlwurr*) — tree with red flowers; we use the bark to make dilly bags

djalkurrk (*djalkurrk*) — the bottom part of the different orchids that grows in the monsoon rainforest; these are also used as glue for bark painting

wärrkarr (*waarrkarr*) — these plants grows in the open woodland and marshes. They have beautiful white bell-like flowers and only come out between December and March

21. Physical qualities

barrpa' (*barrpa'*) — rotten (stinking rotten)

bäyŋu, dhäwul (*baayngu, dhaawul*) — nothing, none

bukmak (*bukmak*) — all

buruŋgulk (*burunggulk*) — rotten (about to disintegrate)

dharrwa, dhaŋaŋ (*dharrwa, dhangang*) — many

dhumbuḻ, gurriri (*dhumburl, gurriri*) — short

märrma' (*maarrma'*) — two

marrya (*marrya*) — hungry

miku, gulaŋ-gulaŋ (*miku, gulang-gulang*) — red

mel-waywa' (*miil-waywa'*) — a dress or other clothing that you can see through

mulka, banḏany (*mulka, barnrdany*) — dry

murrukay (*murrukay*) — big

ŋam'ŋam, dhaŋaŋ (*ngam'ngam, dhangang*) — full

waŋgany (*wanggany*) — one

watharr (*watharr*) — white

weyin (*wiiyin*) — long

yumurrku (*yumurrku*) — small pieces

yuluk, djurruk (*yuluk, djurruk*) — wet

yuṯa (*yurta*) — new

yutjuwaḻa, nyumukuṉiny (*yutjuwarla, nyumukurniny*) — small

22. Non-physical qualities

bawa'mirr (*bawa'mirr*)	mentally disturbed person
buku-duwat (*buku-rduwart*)	stubborn, single-minded about doing something that is wrong
dhä-bindharr (*dhaa-birndharr*)	someone who is always swearing
lirra-däl (*rlirra-rdaal*)	bully, always picking on others, scolding, being angry: *ŋarraku mari'mirriŋu lirra-däl* My granny is always scolding me (literally 'teeth-firm, strong')
manymak (*manymak*)	good
mel-mari (*miil-mari*)	troublemaker (literally 'eye-trouble')
mulkurr-dhumuk (*murlkurr-dhumuk*)	always forgetting things (literally 'head-thick')
ŋoy-däl (*nguuy-rdaal*)	brave (literally '(of the inner stomach area) strong, firm')
yätj (*yaatj*)	bad

23. Motion

barrwarryun (*barrwarryun*)	twist and turn (while sleeping, crying or laughing)
barraŋgayun (*barranggayun*)	distract by talk or a sound from a living thing
budapthun (*burdapthun*)	to cross over
butthun (*burtthun*)	to fly
dada'yun (*rdarda'yun*)	to perform the smoking ceremony (like a cleansing ceremony)
daŋgalkthun, galkirr (*rdanggalkthun, galkirr*)	to fall (descend quickly, unexpectedly)
dhaŋgam (*dhanggam*)	hanging
dhawalwuyaŋi (*dhawalwuyangi*)	to give birth
djakatthun (*djakartthun*)	to reach up to get something
galkin (*galkin*)	fell down
galyun (*garlyun*)	to crawl
guduyum, baduwaduyun (*gurduyum, barduwarduyun*)	to stop something from proceeding
gatjpuyun (*gatjpuyun*)	to wish for something
luplupthun, waythuyun (*rluprlupthun, waythuyun*)	to swim
mali-wirwiryun (*mali-wirwiryun*)	when someone or something you don't want or expect to be there is around you
maŋmaŋdhun (*mangmangdhun*)	to be impressed by someone or something

maŋutji-manapan (*mangutji-manapan*)	to look at someone and think it's someone else
maŋutji-ŋal'yun (*mangutji-ngal'yun*)	to stumble upon someone or something unexpectedly
marrtji, ŋirrimbum (*marrtji, ngirrimbum*)	to walk, go or come
marrtji lili (*marrtji lili*)	to come
marrtji bala (*marrtji bala*)	to go
marryun, giritjirr (*marryun, giritjirr*)	to dance
mayali-wilkthun (*mayali-wilkthun*)	to not do what someone expects you to do
märr-ŋal'yun (*maarr-ngal'yun*)	to worship or believe a person, persons, or things and objects
märr-yuwalkthirr (*maarr-yuwalkthirr*)	to believe and trust in something or someone
meŋiniyirr (*miinginiyirr*)	to twitch in your sleep
milthun (*milthun*)	to check on something once or lots of times
mu<u>l</u>kurr-djaw'yun (*murlkurr-djaw'yun*)	person or noise that's making you stop thinking
ŋa<u>n</u>baw'yun (*ngarnbaw'yun*)	to overflow
ŋirrimbum, marrtji (*ngirrimbum, marrtji*)	to go, move
marrŋga<u>t</u>thun (*marrnggartthun*)	to look about from a sitting position, moving only the upper body
ŋal'yun (*ngal'yun*)	to climb
ŋoy-djawarr'yun (*nguuy-djawarr'yun*)	to aggravate, to push someone to lose their temper
walmurum (*walmurum*)	to lift up the head to look for something, look up
wa<u>n</u><u>d</u>irr, <u>n</u>aŋ'thun (*warnrdirr, rnang'thun*)	to run
wa<u>t</u>thun (*wartthun*)	to look back over your shoulder
watjarryun (*watjarryun*)	to try and stop people from hurting each other
yalayalkthun (*yalayalkthun*)	to uncoil, unfold (blanket, rope, etc.) to the size you want
yupthun (*yupthun*)	to come down, descend steadily and slowly

24. State

buŋbuŋdhun (*bungbungdhun*)	to boil
<u>d</u>olpuyirr (*rduulpuyirr*)	to be full (after eating)

djingaryun, dhärra (*djingaryun, dhaarra*) — to stand, stand up
djitjun (*djitjun*) — to get smoke in your eyes
gorrmuryirr (*guurrmuryirr*) — to be hot
maḏakarritjthirr (*mardakarritjthirr*) — to be angry
mayaŋ-ḏapthun (*mayang-rdapthun*) — to have a dry throat
nhina, ḏäpthun (*nhina, rdaapthun*) — to sit, sit down
nyirrnyirryun (*nyirrnyirryun*) — to simmer
ŋandharkthirr (*ngandharkthirr*) — get thirsty
ŋorra yakurr, yukurra (*nguurra yakurr, yukurra*) — to sleep; asleep
ŋorra (*nguurra*) — to lie down
winya'yun (*winya'yun*) — to be lost

25. Vocalisation and thought

birrka'yun (*birrka'yun*) — to think
bukuway'yirr (*bukuway'yirr*) — to dream
ḏämbu-ŋänharamirr (*rdaambu-ngaanharamirr*) — let's put our heads together and talk
gukthun (*gukthun*) — to bark
lakaram (*lakaram*) — to tell
ḻikandhu-ŋurrkam (*rlikandhu-ngurrkam*) — to disagree, exclude
maŋutji-way'yun (*mangutji-way'yun*) — to tell someone to stop looking at you
mel-ḏiy'yun (*miil-rdiy'yun*) — to be jealous
mel-nherraṉ (*miil-nhiirrarn*) — to be jealous over something
mel-yurthirr, maŋutji-yurthirr (*miil-yurthirr, mangutji-yurthirr*) — to visualise a place, a person or a thing that is not actually present (could be in your mind or like a vision)
nyäyun, ŋäthi (*nyaayun, ngaathi*) — to cry
waŋa (*wanga*) — to speak
way'yun (*way'yun*) — to yell to attract someone's attention
yoram (*yuuram*) — to agree

26. Bodily functions

biḻkthun (*birlkthun*) — to have bowel movement
ḏirryun, djiwyun (*rdirryun, djiwyun*) — to fart
dhawal guyaŋirr (*dhawal guyangirr*) — to give birth
dhupthun (*dhupthun*) — to spit
gakthun (*gakthun*) — to vomit

gitgitthun (*gitgitthun*)	to laugh
maliyun (*maliyun*)	to buy
märr-ḏaw'yun (*maarr-rdaw'yun*)	to be satisfied
märr-ḏupthun, ŋayaŋu-ḏupthun (*maarr-rdupthun, ngayangu-rdupthun*)	to disregard the way someone has done something. (If you have done something and someone else comes and tries to change it, you might say *yaka ŋarrany märr-ḏupthurr* Don't disregard the way I have done it.)
märr-djawaryun (*maarr-djawaryun*)	to be/feel tired, bored, not inclined/able to do something (say you are weaving and kids are running around and you can't think straight you might say *märr-djawaryurr ŋarra* (*ŋarra* 'I') and stop until later)
märr-ŋaṉḏi'yun (*maarr-ngarnrdi'yun*)	to sulk
märr-ḻayyun (*maarr-rlayyun*)	to be/feel good, at ease (after some trouble, being ill or tired)
märr-witjun, ŋayaŋu-witjun (*maarr-witjun, ngayangu-witjun*)	waiting patiently for something that you are expecting
märr-yätjthirr (*maarr-yaatjthirr*)	to be upset (literally 'feelings-be bad')
mel-ḏälthirr, maŋutji-ḏälthirr (*miil-rdaalthirr, mangutji-rdaalthirr*)	to stare (literally 'eye-be firm, hard')
mel-winya'yun (*miil-winya'yun*)	to remain (with you). (If something is of value to you and you want to keep it, and someone asks for it, you might say *ŋarra mel-winya'yun ŋuriki* I want to keep that (literally 'eye-lose')
nhäma, wurrkwurrkthun (*nhaama, wurrkwurrkthun*)	to see
nyakthun (*nyakthun*)	to eat
ŋäthi, nyäyun (*ngaathi, nyaayun*)	to cry
ŋäma, buthuru-witjun (*ngaama, buthuru-witjun*)	to hear
rakunydhirr (*rakunydhirr*)	to die
rathalayun ŋurrtjiy (*rathalayun ngurrtjiy*)	to have a head cold, to have a headache caused by a runny nose
waŋgiyun, nyuŋayun (*wanggiyun, nyungayun*)	to smell something
warwuyun (*warwuyun*)	to be sad
waryun (*waryun*)	to urinate
wurkthun (*wurkthun*)	to drink

27. Impact and violence

bathan (*bathan*) — to burn, cook
bartjunmaram (*bartjunmaram*) — to hit; the hitting action follows through after the object is hit (like a slap)
dharpum (*dharpum*) — to spear
l̲awuman (*rlawuman*) — to bite
mar'yun (*mar'yun*) — to kill, strike
mitthun (*mitthun*) — to cut
yaw'yun (*yaw'yun*) — to dig
wutthun (*wutthun*) — to hit; the hitting action is directed at the thing being hit (like a punch)

28. Holding and transfer

dhä-manapan (*dhaa-manapan*) — to get people or animals to do something together, e.g. to match-make, incite people to fight
djud̲upthun (*djurdupthun*) — enter
gathan/gathul/gathar (*gathan/gathul/gathar*) — give/give!/gave
ganurr, gunha'yurr (*ganurr, gunha'yurr*) — leave it!
gurrunhan (*gurrunhan*) — put down
membum/membuŋal (*miimbum/miimbungal*) — forget/forgot
ŋawatthun (*ngawatthun*) — get
ŋurrkam/ŋurrkaŋal (*ngurrkam/ngurrkangal*) — throw/threw
warrkthun (*warrkthun*) — take off the fire

29. Location, direction and time

bala (*bala*) — movement away from you
buku-rangu (*buku-rangu*) — dark
bärra' (*baarra'*) — west (direction); west wind
barrku (*barrku*) — far
dharratharra (*dharratharra*) — season between May and July (cold and windy)
dhimurru, bulunu (*dhimurru, bulunu*) — east (direction); east wind
dhiyaŋun-wala (*dhiyangun-wala*) — now
djad̲aw'yun (*djardaw'yun*) — (of dawn) to break

djed̲an (*djiirdan*)	hours past midnight
dhulmuy munhay (*dhulmuy munhay*)	midnight
djinawa (*djinawa*)	inside
galki (*galki*)	near
god̲arr', boŋguŋ (*guurdarr', buunggung*)	tomorrow
god̲arr'mirr (*guurdarr'mirr*)	early in the morning
gurriri (*gurriri*)	soon
garramat, garrwar (*garramat, garrwar*)	up, above
l̲äy-wilyunar (*rlaay-wilyunar*)	afternoon
lili, räli (*lili, raali*)	movement towards you
l̲uŋgurrma, d̲irrmala (*rlunggurrma, rdirrmala*)	north (direction); north wind
mäd̲irriny, djalathaŋ (*maardirriny, djalathang*)	south (direction); south wind
mid̲awarr (*mirdawarr*)	tuber-growing season (March-April)
munhawun (*munhawun*)	evening
ŋoyŋur (*nguuyngur*)	beneath, underneath
rarranhdharr (*rarranhdharr*)	season between August and December (hot and dry)
walu (*walu*)	time, day, sun
warrarra wil̲aŋ'thunaynha (*warrarra wirlang'thunaynha*)	sunset
yawungu (*yawungu*)	yesterday

30. Interjections

bay' (*bay'*)	or what
d̲op (*rduup*)	throw it here!
d̲oy (*rduuy*)	go to sleep!
dhut (*dhut*)	sit down!
ga' (*ga'*)	give it here
git̲ (*girt*)	move over!
gul' (*gul'*)	let's go, come on
go (*guu*)	come here
goy (*guuy*)	you there?
ma' (*ma'*)	okay, all right, fine
mak (*mak*)	maybe
ŋay' (*ngay'*)	here take it
ŋini (*ngini*)	okay: *ŋarra marrtjin ŋini?* I'm going, okay?

ŋe (*ngii*)	(yes) agreement
ŋi'? (*ngi'?*)	is it?
way' (*way'*)	hey!
wap (*wap*)	jump!
yaka, bäyŋu (*yaka, baayngu*)	not, do not
yaka (*yaka*)	no
yaw (*yaw*)	oh, oh no
yitj! (*yitj!*)	annoyance (expresses annoyance)
yiw (*yiw*)	I don't know
yo (*yuu*)	yes

31. Interrogatives

nhä (*nhaa*)	what?
nhätha (*nhaatha*)	when?
wanhaka (*wanhaka*)	where?
wanhawal (*wanhawal*)	where to?
yol (*yuul*)	who?

32. Demonstratives

dhika (*dhika*)	here somewhere
dhuwal (*dhuwal*)	this (nearest), here, this one
dhuwali (*dhuwali*)	that (near, near the person being spoken to), there, that one near
ŋunha (*ngunha*)	there, that one there
ŋunhi (*ngunhi*)	that one (that we know about because we share the knowledge, or we have been talking about it already)
ŋuruk (*nguruk*)	for that one over there
ŋuriki (*nguriki*)	for that one we know about
dhiyak (*dhiyak*)	for this one
ŋuriŋi (*nguringi*)	by that one, at that time
dhiyaŋ (*dhiyang*)	by this one, at this time
dhuwalkay'yi (*dhuwalkay'yi*)	here it is

33. Personal pronouns

ŋarra (*ngarra*)	I
ŋarrak (*ngarrak*)	mine, for me
ŋilinyu (*ngilinyu*)	we two (not including the person that you are talking to)
ŋinyalaŋ (*nginyalang*)	ours (not including the person that you are talking to), for us two

ŋali (*ngali*) — we two (me and the person I am talking to)

ŋitjalaŋ (*ngitjalang*) — ours (belonging to me and the person I am talking to), for us two

ŋilimurr (*ngilimurr*) — we (many) (including the person you are talking to)

ŋilimurruŋ(*ngilimurrung*) — for us, ours (many) (including the person you are talking to)

ŋanapurr (*nganapurr*) — we (many) (not including the person you are talking to)

ŋanapurruŋ (*nganapurrung*) — for us, ours (many) (not including the person you are talking to)

nhe (*nhii*) — you (one person)

nhuŋu (*nhungu*) — yours, for you (one person)

nhuma (*nhuma*) — you (more than one)

ŋayi (*ngayi*) — he, she it

nhanŋu (*nhanngu*) — for him, her, it

ŋanya (*nganya*) — her, him, it

maṉḏa (*marnrda*) — they (two)

walal (*walal*) — they (many)

walalaŋ (*walalang*) — for them, theirs (many)

34. Placenames

Barrpira (*Barrpira*) — the closest island to Yirrkala, about half a mile off-shore, it's Yirritja land

Bawaka (*Bawaka*) — Yirritja land of the Gumatj clan. There are three Gumatj clans, one is Munuŋgiritj, one is Yunupiŋu and the other is Burarrwaŋa. The Munuŋgiritj own Bawaka

Bäniyala (*Baaniyala*) — Maḏarrpa land, this is the biggest homeland in the Laynha area. The people who live here are closely related to the people of Groote Eylandt

Biranybirany (*Biranybirany*) — Yirritja land owned by the Yunupiŋu Gumatj clan

Birritjimirr (*Birritjimirr*) — Yirritja land owned by the Yunupiŋu Gumatj just outside Nhulunbuy

Bukpukpuy (*Bukpukpuy*) — Dhuwa land owned by the Gälpu clan

Bukuḏal (*Bukurdal*) — Dhuwa homeland in the Laynha area owned by the Djapu clan

Butjumurru (*Butjumurru*)	Yirritja land of the Yunupiŋu Gumatj clan
Daliwuy (*Daliwuy*)	Yirritja land of the Lamamirr clan, Yunupiŋu Gumatj are the custodians
Dhambaliya (*Dhambaliya*)	Dhuwa island belonging to the Djambarrpuyŋu clan. There are small places on the island that belong to other clans, both Yirritja and Dhuwa, for instance Rirratjiŋu, a Dhuwa clan and Gumatj, a Yirritja clan
Dhälinybuy (*Dhaalinybuy*)	a Wangurri (Yirritja) homeland near a huge river
Dholtji (*Dhuultji*)	a Warramiri (Yirritja) homeland
Dhum'thumurru (*Dhum'thumurru*)	a small beach in the Yirrkala community
Dhumuḻumirr (*Dhumurlumirr*)	a Yirritja beach close to Yirrkala
Dhuraka (*Dhuraka*)	the point next from Dhumuḻumirr
Dhuruputjpi (*Dhuruputjpi*)	a Dhuwa homeland belonging to the Dhuḏi-Djapu clan
Djarrakpi (*Djarrakpi*)	a Yirritja homeland belonging to the Maŋgalili clan
Gaḏalathamirr (*Gardalathamirr*)	Dhuwa land belonging to the Gälpu clan
Galupa (*Galupa*)	a Yirritja place belonging to the Yunupiŋu Gumatj clan
Ganarri'mirr (*Ganarri'mirr*)	a Gumatj beach near Yirrkala
Garrthaḻaḻa (*Garrtharlarla*)	a Yirritja homeland belonging to the Yunupiŋu Gumatj
Gäluru (*Gaaluru*)	a Dhuwa place owned by four clans - Rirratjiŋu, Golumala, Marrakulu and Ḏäṯiwuy
Gäṉgaṉ (*Gaarn.garn*)	Yirritja country belonging to the Gumana Dhaḻwaŋu clan (there are two Dhaḻwaŋu groups)
Gärriri (*Gaarriri*)	Yirritja country belonging to the Gumatj clan
Guluruŋa (*Gulurunga*)	Dhuwa homeland belonging to the Rirratjiŋu clan on the Dhoḻu side (there are two Rirratjiŋu groups)
Gunyaŋara (*Gunyangara*)	Yirritja homeland belonging to Yunupiŋu Gumatj
Gurka'wuy (*Gurka'wuy*)	Dhuwa homeland belonging to the Marrakulu clan

Gurrumuru (*Gurrumuru*)	Yirritja homeland belonging to the Wunuŋmurra Dhaḻwaŋu (there are two Dhaḻwaŋu groups)
Gutjaŋan (*Gutjangan*)	homeland on Dhambaliya
Guwatjurumurruwuy (*Guwatjurumurruwuy*)	a river
Laynhapuy (*Laynhapuy*)	name for the peoples and country to the south-east of Yirrkala
Ḻombuy (*Rluumbuy*)	Dhuwa land near Nhulunbuy belonging to Rirratjiŋu clan
Maṯamaṯa (*Martamarta*)	Yirritja Warramiri homeland being looked after by the Burarrwaŋa Gumatj
Mayaŋ'mirr (*Mayang'mirr*)	Dhuwa land just near Nhulunbuy
Mänyumiwuy (*Maanyumiwuy*)	Yirritja land belonging to the Gumatj clan
Miritjaŋay (*Miritjangay*)	Yirritja land belonging to all three Gumatj groups
Muṉumbaḻwuy (*Murnumbarlwuy*)	Dhuwa land, a huge rainforest belonging to ŋaymil and Ḏäṯiwuy, near Yäŋunbi
Murrpanawuy (*Murrpanawuy*)	Yirritja islands off Dhambaliya
Nalilawuy (*Nalilawuy*)	Yirritja land just around from Mänyumiwuy
Nhulunbuy (*Nhulunbuy*)	Dhuwa land where the mining township is situated and which belongs to Rirratjiŋu
ŋaypinya (*Ngaypinya*)	Dhuwa land belonging to the Gälpu clan
Ṉowul (*Rnuuwul*)	Dhuwa place just near Yirrkala belonging to the Rirratjiŋu
Rathiyawuy (*Rathiyawuy*)	Dhuwa land belonging to the ŋaymil and Ḏäṯiwuy clans
Rorruwuy (*Ruurruwuy*)	Dhuwa homeland belonging to Ḏäṯiwuy and ŋaymil clans
Ruwakpuy (*Ruwakpuy*)	place on Dhambaliya
Waŋgarpanda (*Wanggarpanda*)	Yirritja beach belonging to the Yunupiŋu Gumatj
Warrimbiri (*Warrimbiri*)	Yirritja beach belonging to the Yunupiŋu Gumatj
Welama (*Wiilama*)	a rocky point at Yirrkala
Wirrwawuy (*Wirrwawuy*)	a place near Nhulunbuy belonging to the Gälpu clan
Wuḻwuḻwuy (*Wurlwurlwuy*)	a Dhuwa homeland in the Laynha area belonging to the Djapu clan

Dätiwuy

Yalaŋbara (*Yalangbara*)	Dhuwa place belonging to the Rirratjiŋu on the Gäwara side (there are two Rirratjiŋu groups)
Yamuna (*Yamuna*)	Dhuwa place past Ŋowul belonging to the Rirratjiŋu
Yäŋunbi (*Yaangunbi*)	Dhuwa homeland belonging to ŋaymil and Dätiwuy
Yirrkala (*Yirrkala*)	Dhuwa land belonging to the Rirratjiŋu clan. It is now the site of an established community. There are around 500 people from many different clans.
Yuduyudu (*Yurduyurdu*)	Dhuwa country belonging to the Djapu clan

Grammatical notes

Let me just show you a little about how important the endings of words are Dätiwuy. Consider *ŋirrimbuman ŋarrany yurru djunaman djämalilnha*:

ŋirrimbum-an	*ŋarra-ny*	*yurru*	*djunama-n*	*djäma-lil-nha.*
going-walking-now	me-myself	will	towards-now	work-to-now.

In English this means 'I am going to work now', since *ŋirrimbum* means 'walk', and *ŋirrimbuman* with an *-an* at the end means 'going now, at this minute'. But you can also jumble the words around from the middle to the front or from the back to the front, and it will aways mean the same thing. For example, *djämalilnha djunaman ŋarrany yurru ŋirrimbum* means the same thing, and the only thing different is that *ŋirrimbum* has no *-an* at the end.

Another example is:

be-ŋur	*ŋirrimbu-ŋal*	*ŋarra*	*djäma-ŋur.*
there-from	walk-past	I	work-from.

'I've come from work.'

When we say in English *John hit Mary* we all know that John had hit Mary. Why? Because *John* is before the verb and *Mary* is after the verb. In Dätiwuy and other Yolŋu languages we would say the same sentence this way: *John-dhu Mary-ny wutthurr.* The *-dhu* is telling you who did the action and the *-ny* is telling you who the action was done to. We could jumble the words around and it would mean the same. It doesn't matter which order the words go in, because we know who is doing what by the endings.

We classify living things differently to English. Some of the general terms are described in the wordlist above. We also use special words to talk about the food from different living things. When talking about kangaroo meat, turtle meat, goose meat, goanna meat and other animals eaten for meat, both white and red, we would say *linygun djukurrmirrnha* (*linygu-n djukurr-mirr-nha* 'already-now fat-having-now') or *linygun yaḻmangan* (*yaḻmanga-n* 'fatty-now') 'It is now fatty'. But when we are taking about edible shellfish we say *linygun ḏinipuwan* (*ḏinipuwa-n* 'firm and juicy-now') 'It is now firm and juicy'. When talking about yams and tuber food we would say *ḻinygun ḏikmantjan* (*ḏikmantja-n* 'firm and not tough or stringy-now') 'It is now firm and not tough or stringy'.

Yolŋu people of Yirrkala are lucky bush-tucker-wise. This is because the food that is collected from the sea (seafood) and the inland food are both eaten right throughout the year. Just what is eaten depends on what food is in season. Yolŋu people know when a particular food or fruit is in season by the blossoms of particular trees and shrubs that tell us that this food or fruit is now ready to be hunted and eaten. For example, when the *baḻwurr* tree flowers it tells us that the *maranydjalk* meat (stingrays and sharks) is now ready to be eaten.

13

Eastern Arrernte

JOHN HENDERSON and VERONICA DOBSON

Eastern Arrernte is part of the Arandic group of languages spoken in the region around Alice Springs. There is a relatively large number of speakers of Eastern Arrernte, probably around 1500 to 2000, and it is fairly healthy, in that children are growing up speaking it. Earlier spellings of the language name such as 'Aranda' and 'Arunta' are no longer used for Eastern Arrernte, but are sometimes still seen in English-language publications which rely on old sources.

Language identification is very important for Arrernte people, being strongly associated with family membership and ownership of land and dreamings. The Arandic area is large and there are many different family areas within it, all with their different varieties of Arrernte.

The term Eastern Arrernte is used in a number of ways, referring to different groupings of smaller local dialects. It is often (as in this volume) used to refer to a number of dialects of Arrernte belonging to an area which includes the communities at Ltyentye Apurte (Santa Teresa), Bonya, Alcoota and Harts Range. It does not include the very closely related language which belongs to the Alice Springs town area, which speakers nowadays identify separately as Central Arrernte, even though many speakers of Eastern Arrernte now also live in Alice Springs.

Nearly all Eastern Arrernte speakers are bilingual in English to some degree and the language is under considerable pressure from English. Older speakers are sometimes critical of the Arrernte spoken by younger people, who they believe are not learning their language properly, and it does seem that aspects of the older language may be being lost.

Family and Society

There is a rich terminology for family and social relationships which reflects the great importance Arrernte people place on these. Everyone you know is classified as a relation of some kind, even if they are not biologically related to you. Subsection terms, or 'skin' names as they are known locally, act as a kind of shorthand for family relationships and other aspects of social organisation, such as marriage rules (see page xvi above). Everyone has one of the eight skin names, and when you know someone's skin name you can work out what relation they are to you.

Now, there are three forms of all the pronouns that refer to more than one person, and the right one to use depends on how the people involved are related. Take for example the pronouns that are partly equivalent to English 'we' (except that they are only used of more than two people, rather than more than one as in English).

The first form, *anwantherre*, is used if the people being referred to are not all in the same one of the two main kinship groups. Very roughly speaking, these two groups are in part defined by marriage between families. For example, *anwantherre* is used for my brothers and sisters, me and our mother as a group, because the children are thought of as all belonging to the father's family, but the mother has married in from another family, and she is therefore not a member of the same kinship group.

The second form, *anwakerre*, is used if the people being referred to are all in the same kinship group, but are in different generation levels (see *nyurrpe* in the wordlist). So, for example, *anwakerre* can refer to my brothers and sisters, me and our father, who is in a different generation level.

The third form, *anwerne*, is used if the people being referred to are all in the same group, and are all in the same generation level, for example, my brothers and sisters and I. This last form is also used these days as a general term without regard to how the people involved are related, and there is some evidence that younger speakers are not acquiring this complex system of pronouns.

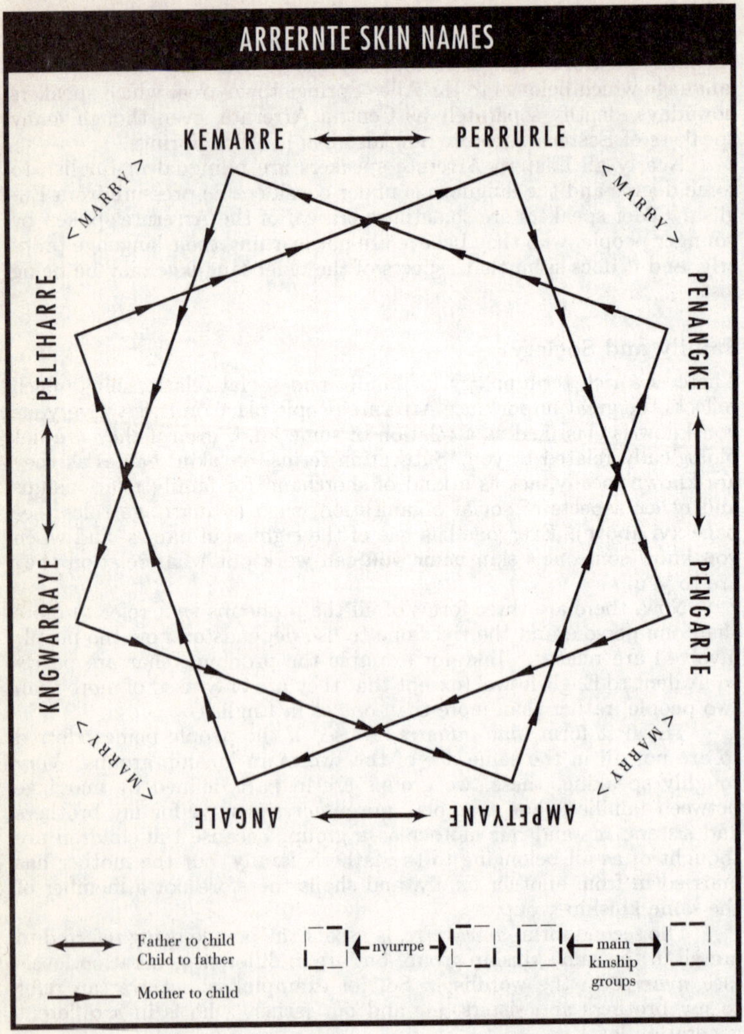

The state of the language

No-one can say whether this language will survive, or for how long, or whether it will be lost like so many other Australian languages, but for the moment it seems relatively healthy. In fact, it is now being used in more and more areas of activities where, until recently, English had been the only language.

There are bilingual education programs for Arrernte-speaking children at Yipirinya School (Alice Springs) and Ltyentye Apurte School (Santa Teresa). There are also language programs for Arrernte students in the Aboriginal Unit at the Our Lady of The Sacred Heart School, and in the Ntyarlke Unit at the Catholic High School, both in Alice Springs. Recently a project was run jointly by these schools and co-ordinated by the Institute for Aboriginal Development (IAD) in Alice Springs to further develop the Arrernte language curriculum, and a new project has begun which will develop an Arrernte pre-school curriculum.

Arrernte literacy courses for adults are run occasionally by the IAD in Alice Springs. There are also occasional one-day courses on spelling Arrernte for people who don't speak it. Short Arrernte language courses for adult learners are also run by the IAD, which also publishes language learning materials for individual use. Primary and secondary level Arrernte second-language courses for English-speaking children are provided by the IAD on request to a number of schools in Alice Springs.

Interpreting and translation services for Eastern Arrernte are available at the Aboriginal Interpreter Service at the IAD, and accredited Interpreter Training courses for Arrernte speakers are also provided. Arrernte interpreters are used occasionally in the hospital and courts, as well as in some meetings with government representatives.

There is a growing body of literature in Eastern Arrernte, much of it produced by the schools for primary school use. Summer Institute of Linguistics staff at Santa Teresa are undertaking translation of the Bible, and a number of other Arrernte language religious materials have been developed by the Catholic Church.

Eastern Arrernte dialects are used on CAAMA (Central Australian Aboriginal Media Association) Radio and occasionally on Imparja Television (an Aboriginal-run television station in the Northern Territory), and the Media Association at Santa Teresa also produces some Eastern Arrernte video material.

About the wordlist

The following wordlist has been prepared especially for this volume. The entries have been extracted from the fuller *Eastern and Central Arrernte to English Dictionary*, and this list gives only a portion of the number of words in the language, and for reasons of space, it does not represent all that is known about these words, although a few words have been selected for slightly more detailed treatment. Readers who would like more information on words are directed to the full dictionary, which also provides extensive examples to illustrate the use of the words.

13.1 Eastern Arrernte

Spelling and pronunciation

The sound systems of Arandic languages are complex and quite different from other Central Australian languages or English, and it has taken some time to develop appropriate spelling systems. The Eastern Arrernte orthography follows the Common Arandic system, which has been developed since the late 70s as the basis for orthographies for all Arandic languages. The following consonant and vowel symbols are used:

a, e, h, i, k, kng, l, lh, ly, m, n, ng, nh, ny, p, pm, r, rl, rn, rr, rt, rtn, t, th, thn, tn, tny, ty, u, w, y

A notable feature of the Arandic languages' sound systems is that pronunciation of the vowel written *e* is heavily influenced by surrounding sounds. For example, *e* following *w* may be pronounced as *oo* as in English 'cook', and *e* before *y* as *ee* as in 'feet'. When the surrounding sounds are ones which do not influence the *e* much, it is usually pronounced like the *e* in 'father' or 'pert', or even the *u* in 'butt'. The final *e* written on all words is often left off in ordinary speech, as is the initial *a* in some words.

EASTERN ARRERNTE WORDLIST

WORDLIST CATEGORIES

1. Body parts and products
2. Kin relationships
3. Human classification
4. Language, mythology and ceremony
5. Human artefacts
6. Food, cooking and fire
7. Topography
8. Elements
9. Mammals
10. Reptiles
11. Birds
12. Aquatic life
13. Insects
14. Plants
15. Physical qualities
16. Non-physical qualities
17. Motion
18. State
19. Vocalisation and thought
20. Bodily functions
21. Impact and violence
22. Holding and transfer
23. Location, direction and time
24. Interjections
25. Demonstratives and pronouns
26. Adverbs and particles
27. Placenames

1. Body parts and products

ahentye — throat (The throat is involved in expressions for thinking, wanting, and some other feelings, similar to the way that the heart is involved in expressions about certain emotions in English)

akwangenye	left hand (not used traditionally in directions)
akwarratye	right hand
alenye	tongue
alhe	1. nose 2. pointed part
alhwe	blood
alkngarlpe	hip
alkngarnte	eyebrow
alknge kwarte	eyeball
alknge	eye
alknge-arlpelhe	eyelash
alkngerurrke	ankle
alkngultye	tears
amake	elbow
ampere	knee
amulte	arm
antyeye	sweat, perspiration
arrakerte	mouth
arralte	beard, whiskers
arreltye	lungs
arrelyenge	cheek
artengkwelknge, atenkwelknge	cold; snot
artepe	back
arteperrke	kidney
artitye	teeth
atnerte	stomach
atnware	heel
atywe	calf
ayepe	umbilical cord
iltye	hand; fingers (Arrernte people shake hands to express their condolences to people who have lost a relative.)
ingke	1. foot, feet 2. footprints
inngerre	1. face, cheek 2. expression on someone's face
inwenge	chest
irlpe	ear
ite	throat
itelye	wart
lhenpe	armpit
lterre	shin bone

ngkerralye	rib
ngkwerne	1. bone 2. leg
pmulpere	windpipe
pulpule	thumb; big toe
tyepmware, tywepmare	fingernail; toenail
tyerrtye	1. body 2. person, people
ulte	side
ulyepere	thigh
untye	back of neck
urle	forehead
utyene	sore, wound
yenpe	skin

2. Kin relationships

akngeye	father; father's brothers
altyele	a woman's female cousin (not mother's sister's daughter or father's brother's daughter, who are thought of as sisters (*yaye* or *atyeye*). The children of female cousins are first-choice marriage partners.)
ampatye	niece, nephew (sister's child)
Ampetyane	one of the eight skin names
Angale	one of the eight skin names
angkwere	older sister
ankele	a male's male cousin (his father's sister's son or his mother's brother's son, but not his father's brother's sons or his mother's sister's sons. Traditionally, the relationship between male cousins is a fairly easy one, often involving friendship and joking.)
aperlangkwe	your father's mother, etc.
aperlatye	my/our father's mother, etc.
aperle	1. father's mother (and her brothers and sisters); grandmother, great-aunt, great-uncle 2. a woman's son's child; grandchild, grandson, granddaughter
aperlikwe	his/her/their father's mother, etc.

artweye	1. relations, family members, ancestors 2. owner (of land or other things)
atnyatye	mother's brother
atyewe	friend
atyeye	younger brother or sister
awenhe	father's sister
kake	older brother
Kemarre	one of the eight skin names
Kngwarraye	one of the eight skin names
kwertengerle	certain relatives of the *apmereke-artweye*, traditional owners of land and dreamings, particularly brothers-in-law and mother's brothers. These are sometimes referred to as 'managers' of the land, as opposed to 'owners'. A person is *apmereke-artweye* for the land and dreamings they inherit through their father's clan, and may be *kwertengerle* for the land and dreamings of the clans that their clan marries into, that is, their mother's clan or wife's clan. *Kwertengerle* have different responsibilities for the land and dreamings from those of the *apmereke-artweye* owners, including making sure that ceremonies and other duties (songs, dances, designs, etc.) are done properly.
mwere	1. man's mother-in-law (and her brothers and sisters) 2. woman's son-in-law (The relationship between a mother-in-law and her son-in-law is marked by great respect, which is shown in this case by avoiding direct contact with each other, for example, not speaking to each other or being too close to each other.)

nyurrpe — in the opposite generation group to someone (This includes people in the generation immediately before yours (e.g. mother, father, mother-in-law, father-in-law, uncle, aunt) and those in the generation immediately after yours (e.g. son, daughter, niece, nephew, son-in-law, daughter-in-law). Those relations who are two generations before (e.g. your grandparents) or two generations after (e.g. your grandchildren) are not *nyurrpe* to you. The division according to *nyurrpe* makes the two generation groups; in terms of skin names, one group consists of the people with the skin names Perrurle, Penangke, Angale and Kngwarraye, while the other group consists of Pengarte, Ampetyane, Peltharre and Kemarre people. A person in one group is *nyurrpe* to people in the other group. For example, an Angale person and a Peltharre person are *nyurrpe* to each other. The *nyurrpe* distinction is important in many aspects of Arrernte culture, including marriage rules: you are not allowed to marry anyone who is *nyurrpe* to you.)

Peltharre — one of the eight skin names

Penangke — one of the eight skin names

Pengarte — one of the eight skin names

Perrurle — one of the eight skin names

3. Human classification

akngerre-apate — older or senior person

alhampwe — a child who has lost one or both of their parents; orphan

ampe akweke — baby, small child

ampe — child (It is extremely offensive to refer to an initiated man as 'ampe'.)

ampwe	middle-aged
anewe	husband or wife, spouse, boyfriend, girlfriend
apekathe	part-Aboriginal (from English 'half-caste')
apmereke-artweye	traditional owners of an area of land, passed on to them from their father's side
arelhe	1. woman 2. person, especially Aboriginal
artwe	initiated man
awenke	teenage girl, young woman
aywe	middle-aged or older man
irrkwentye	policeman (literally 'grabber')
kwementyaye	a name used, out of respect, instead of someone's name when another person with that name, or a similar name, has passed away (It is also sometimes used about things as well as people. It is not used to refer to the actual person who has passed away — this person's name is not used at all.)
marle	girl, female
ngangkere	traditional healer, 'witchdoctor'
ngkarte	1. God 2. a priest
urreye	boy; male animal (It is extremely offensive to refer to an initiated man as *urreye*.)
utnenge	spirit or soul of a living person, their vitality (believed to be lost when a person is very sick)

4. Language, mythology and ceremony

aknganentye	1. the land and dreamings belonging to a person which are handed down through their father's side 2. the dreaming associated with a particular thing, e.g. rain dreaming 3. a distinctive birthmark, said to have been made by the dreaming it resembles: *alharrkentye aknganentyea* birthmark resembling lightning

13.5 Eastern Arrernte

altyerre — 1. the Dreaming, Dreamtime; the creation of the world and the things in it, and its eternal existence 2.(a) your mother's *aknganentye* dreaming, i.e. the dreaming she gets from her father's side 2.(b) the place where your mother's dreaming is from 3. particular dreaming stories, and things that are part of the story 4. a dream

angkentye — language, message, word

anthepe — women's dancing at the time of initiation ceremonies

arritnye, arrirtne — name

ayeye — story

urlpe — 1. red ochre 2. ochre (of any colour)

5. Human artefacts

akwintye, takwe — windbreak (traditionally crescent-shaped and made of branches)

alkwerte — shield

alye, ilye — boomerang

alyekwe, alyweke — stone knife

amirre — spear thrower, woomera

ankere — spinifex resin (used to stick parts of tools and weapons together)

atneme — digging stick

ilepe — stone axe

ilthe — humpy, shelter

interlpe — wooden skewer

irrketye — string made from human hair

irrtyarte — spear

kwetere — a type of stick used for fighting, a nulla-nulla

makite — gun (probably from English 'musket')

mantere — clothes; material

ngkweltye — 1. pieces or scraps of something 2. coins

urtne — wooden carrying dish, coolamon

warle — house, building

6. Food, cooking and fire

alepe — a piece of burning wood used as a torch, or a stick used to take a light from a fire; firestick, light (in traditional times, people carried a smouldering stick with them rather than have to start a fire from scratch at each camp)

alkngenthe — 1. flame 2. lamp, electric light 3. electricity

alpmanthe — hot sand and ashes under a fire which are used for cooking some foods in

antere — fat, grease, oil (Animal fat is a favourite food, and is also used in healing, mixing up paints and in other ways.)

aperrke — hot coals, charcoal

arturte — the small grinding stone you move backwards and forwards on the larger flat rock

athere — large flat stone used for grinding

iteme — 1. to cook 2. to light (a fire)

kere — 1. any type of animal, bird or reptile that you can eat the meat of 2. meat, flesh 3. general term for game animals which can go immediately before the word for a specific animal: *kere aherre* kangaroo 4. A general term for food from animals (mainly meat but, also fat, eggs and cheese: *kere antere* fat from an animal, *kere ulyepere* the thigh part of a cooked animal, *kere werrpe* the blood and juices from an animal 5. a victim, someone who is being picked on

merne — 1. food from plants and trees; fruit, vegetables, etc. (does not include honey-like foods (*ngkwarle*) or edible grubs (*tyape*) 2. general term for food from plants, which goes before a noun for a specific type of plant food: *merne alangkwe* bush banana

ngkwarle — 1. honey-like foods, juice 2. alcohol

ure — 1. fire 2. firewood 3. a general word for things associated with fire which goes before the word for a particular thing: *ure kwerte* smoke, *ure alepe* firestick, *ure aperrke* coals

7. Topography

ahelhe — 1. earth, sand, soil, dirt 2. flat ground 3. the ground (as opposed to sky, etc.) 4. country, land, area, region 5. the land and the things which grow on it; the countryside 6. the world, Earth 7. general word for earth, sand, etc., which goes before a noun for a specific type of earth, soil, etc.: *ahelhe lyerle* gravelly sand

akethe — 1. outside, in the open 2. clearing, plain 3. clear, open, uncovered, in view, exposed, bare, naked 4. clearly

apmere — 1.(a) country, land, region 1.(b) an area of land and the things on it (trees, etc.); countryside 2. home, house 3. place, location, site 4. general word for places and areas which goes before the word for a particular place: *Apmere Ltyentye Apurte* Santa Teresa, *Apmere Mparntwe* Alice Springs 5. goes before some words describing times: *apmere alakentyele* this time of the day

apwerte — 1. rock, stone, hill 2. money 3. stubborn

arnerre — rockhole, a place in hills where water collects

arnkarre — bank of creek, river

athirnte — smooth flat rock

aturle — plain

atwatye — gap, saddle in range

impatye — tracks

inteye — cave

lhere — creek

ngentye — a hole dug in a creekbed to get water

ntyange — permanent waterhole

urewe — water running in creeks, floodwater

8. Elements

alharrkentye — lightning

alkere — clear sky

angkulye — cloud

apwape, apwapwe — willy-willy, whirlwind

apweteke — hail

aretharre — west wind

arlewarrere — willy-willy, whirlwind

atnyentye — 1. moon 2. month

ilpenthe — steady rain

kwatye — 1. water 2. rain 3. general term for water and things consisting of it (e.g. ice, vapour, rain, rainclouds) which goes immediately before the word for a specific type: *kwatye ilweltye* frost, ice 4. general term for water in the form it is found in various places: *kwatye arnerre* rockhole, *kwatye angentye* soakage 3. weather related to rain: *kwatye alharrkentye* lightning, *kwatye pwere* forked lightning

ulye, ulyentye — shade

uterne — sun, summer

9. Mammals

The word kere *in an entry indicates that the animal is eaten by Arrernte people.*

aherre — red kangaroo (*kere*) (Traditionally, people speared kangaroos, or ran them down with hunting dogs, but rifles are usually used today. When the carcase is gutted, is it singed on top of the fire to remove the fur. It is then put in a fire pit and covered up to cook. It is cut up according to Arrernte law, into the two thighs, the two hips, the two sides of ribs, the stomach, the head, the tail, the two feet, the back and the lower back)

aherte — bandicoot (*kere*)
akngwelye artnwere — dingo
akngwelye — dog, dingo
antenhe — possum (*kere*)
antyipere — bat
arenge — euro (*kere*)
arrwe — rock wallaby (*kere*)
inape, inarlenge — anteater, porcupine (*kere*)
nanthe — horse

10. Reptiles

The word kere *in an entry indicates that the reptile is eaten by Arrernte people.*

alewatyerre, arlewatyerre — sand goanna, Gould's goanna, sand monitor (*kere*) (a popular source of food, hunted by women and children
ankerte — bearded dragon, carney (*kere*)
apmwe — any snake
arlantye, irlantye — bicycle lizard (It waves one of its front legs to bring rain.)
arntetherrke, antetherrke — carpet snake (*kere*)
atyunpe — perentie (*kere*)
kelyawe — dragon lizard (*Amphibolurus nuchalis*) (*kere*) (hunted and eaten by children)
ulhelke — blue-tongue lizard
unyerre — mountain devil, thorny devil

11. Birds

The word thipe *following an entry indicates that the bird is one of the class of fleshy, flying creatures (see entry for* thipe *below). The word* kere *indicates that it is eaten by Arrernte people.*

angepe — crow (*thipe*)
angkwene — Major Mitchell cockatoo, pink cockatoo (*kere thipe*)
apelkere — crested pigeon (*kere thipe*)
arleye — emu (*kere*)

arlpatye — ringneck parrot, Port Lincoln Parrot (*kere thipe*)
arrpwere — magpie (*thipe*)
artarre — tail feathers of emu
artewe — wild turkey, bustard (*kere thipe*)
artityerrityerre — Willie wagtail (*thipe*)
atetherre — budgerigar (*kere thipe*)
ilentye — galah (*kere thipe*) (The meat of the galah is sometimes eaten, but it is not a major source of food)
irrarnte — black cockatoo, red-tailed black cockatoo (*kere thipe*)
irretye — eaglehawk, wedge-tailed eagle (*thipe*)
irrkerlantye — a type of hawk, probably the brown falcon (*thipe*)
kwarte — egg
kwerrkwerrke — mopoke owl, southern boobook (*thipe*) (named for its call)
nturrerte — rock pigeon, plumed pigeon, spinifex pigeon (*kere thipe*)
thipe — 1. fleshy flying creatures, including bats and most birds, but not emus 2. a general word which goes before the name of a particular creature: *thipe irrarnte* black cockatoo

12. Aquatic life

antyetyerre, mpwaltye — frog
iltyarnme — yabby, and maybe crabs and other similar water creatures
irrpennge, irrpenge — any fish
pwepelye — tadpole

13. Insects and spiders

The word tyape *in an entry shows that this type of grub, caterpillar, etc., is eaten.*

ahernenge — a type of edible grub found in the roots of the river red gum, *apere* (*tyape*)
amenge, angeme — fly
ankerrutne — a type of edible grub found in the coolabah tree, *ankerre*

13.13 Eastern Arrernte

arnperrke	centipede
arntinye	wasp
arreme	lice
atnethakerte	scorpion
atnyematye	an edible grub found in the roots of the *atnyeme* witchetty bush, witchetty grub (*tyape*)
atyanke	bull ant
ayepe-arenye	a type of caterpillar found on the *ayepe* plant (*tyape*) (one of the major dreamings of the Alice Springs town area)
ingkwepeye	white ant nest
ingwenenge	a type of edible grub found in the trunk and branches of the river red gum (*tyape*)
inteltye	grasshopper, locust
interrke	white ant, termite
iwepe	1. itchy grub, processionary caterpillar (bag shelter moth larvae) (*Ochrogaster species*) 2. web
mweremwenke	blowfly
ntyarlke	'elephant grub' caterpillar (one of the important dreamings of the Alice Springs area)
pmware-pmware	beetle
tyape	1. edible grubs, mostly the larvae of various types of moths 2. a general word for edible grubs which goes before the name of a particular one: *tyape ahernenge* edible moth larva from the roots of river red gums, *tyape atnyematye* edible moth larva found in the roots of witchetty bushes
urltampe	1. native bee 2. wild honey, 'sugarbag'
utnerrengatye	edible caterpillar found on the *utnerrenge* bush (*tyape*)
yerrampe	honey ant (*Campanotus inflatus*) (These ants, which are found in underground nests, store sweet honey-like stuff in their inflated abdomens. This is a popular food.)

yerre — a general term for ants

14. Plants

The word arne *following an entry indicates that the plant is one of the class of woody plants and trees (see entry for* arne *below). The word* merne *indicates that part of the plant is eaten, and the word* ntange *indicates that the seeds of the plant are eaten.*

alangkwe — wild banana (The vine itself, *altyeye*, flowers, *urlkantyerrknge*, and roots, *atnetye*, are also eaten.) (*merne*)

anatye — bush potato plant, a type of yam (*merne*)

ankerre — coolabah tree (*arne*) (There is an edible grub, *ankerrutne*, that lives in coolabahs, and the bark of the coolabah is burnt for the ash to mix with native tobacco.)

annge — seed, fruit

apere — river gum tree, river red gum (*arne*)

arlatyeye — pencil yam (*merne*)

arne — 1. tree, bush, woody plant 2. a general word that can go before the word for a particular type of tree, bush, woody plant, or even grass: *arne apere* river red gum tree, *arne name* grass, *arne atnyeme* witchetty bush 3. stick, piece of wood 4. a general word that can go before the word for a piece of wood (or similar part of a plant) made into, or used as, a tool or weapon: *arne atneme* digging stick 5. a thing, things, something (not necessarily made out of wood) 6. someone's possessions, things

arne-artne — an area where there are a lot of trees, bushes, etc.; scrub, bush

arrkernke — bloodwood (*arne*)

arrkirlpangkwerle — a gall made on bloodwood trees by a type of wasp (The grub inside and the white lining can be eaten.)

13.14 Eastern Arrernte

arrutnenge	wild passionfruit (*merne*)
artetye	mulga (*arne*)
atherrke	grass, small green plants
atnyeme	witchetty bush (*arne*) (Ashes made from the bark can be used to mix with native tobacco for chewing.)
atwakeye	wild orange (*arne, merne*)
awele-awele	bush tomato
ayepe	tarvine plant
aywerte	spinifex grass (The waxy resin from a particular type of spinifex is used to stick things together when making tools and weapons.)
ilpeye	needlewood bush (*arne*)
inernte	bean tree (*arne*) (The wood is used to make utensils such as coolamons, wooden scoops, spear throwers (*amirre*) and, nowadays, carvings for sale. The bright red seeds of this tree are used to make strings of beads and other things for sale. The beads are traditionally made by threading the seeds onto string made from human hair (*ulirre*), although nowadays thread, wool or bought string is used.)
ingkwerlpe, ingkwelpe	pityuri, wild tobacco (The leaves are picked, dried in the sun, and ground up. This is then mixed with fine white ash made from the bark of bloodwood trees or witchetty bushes to make chewing tobacco.)
irrkepe	desert oak (*arne*)
ltyentye	beefwood (*arne*) (The sap which seeps through the bark is mixed with spinifex wax, *ankere*, and used to join the parts of weapons and tools.)
tunpere	a type of grass (A hook can be made from this grass to hook certain types of edible grubs from their holes.)

utnerrenge — emu bush (*arne*) (The leaves of this plant can be used to make a medicinal wash.)
uyenpere — spearwood (*arne*) (The long curled branches are straightened over a fire to make a type of spear.)
yalke — wild onion (*merne*) (The bulbs are dug up and eaten.)

15. Physical qualities

-areye	many
-arteke	like, similar to
-kenhe	belonging to, possessive marker (*'s*)
akarre	awake
akngerre	big, much, a lot
akweke	small, little
akwerrke	small; young of animals
alware, arlware	inflated
angayakwe, angayweke	hungry
antyenye	grey-haired
anyente	one, alone
apurrke	1. tired. 2. sick of something
apurte	heap, clump, ball of; together
arerte	1. deaf 2. mad, crazy
arlarte	(of trees, etc.) bushy
arlenye	dry
arletye	raw, green, uncooked
arlpentye	tall, long
arltwe	empty
arnterte, arntirte	bad, rotten
arrpe-anenhe	each, every
arrpenhe	1. other, another, different 2. a particular (one)
arrpenheme	some
arunthe	much, many
aternnge	dirty
atherre	two
atherrke-atherrke	green; yellow
athetheke	red
athnurte-athnurte	curled up
atnerte-atnerte	pregnant

atyete	soft
awethe	more; again
ingkirreke, ingkerreke	all; whole
intyerrke	dry, hard
iparrpe	fast, quickly
irrkerteye	bitter, sour
itethe	alive
karnte-karnte	round
lterrke	tight, strong, hard
lthangkwe	wet
metye	blunt; closed; corner
mpenge	ripe, cooked
mperlkere	white
mwantye	slow, careful
ngkethakwe	thirsty
ngkwerne-ngkwerne	bony
rante-rante	same, identical
rlkerte	sick
tharre	numb
ulpe	fine or smooth in consistency; powdery, soft; mashed up
ulthentye	heavy
urinpe	hot
urlpme	narrow, tight
urrpetye	three; a few
utyewe	skinny, thin

16. Non-physical qualities

ahe-akngerre	aggressive, angry, violent, 'cheeky', tough, mean, savage, vicious, dangerous, touchy
akaltye	knowing, knowledgeable
akurne	bad, wrong
akutne	not knowing something, ignorant of something
alhwarrpe	sad, depressed, sorry (particularly because of a loss or suffering, or in sympathy; often translated as just 'sorry', but doesn't really have the same sense of regretting something you've done — it is not used in apologies)

alkngwe	not aware of something, not paying attention
apure	shy, ashamed, embarrassed
arerte-arerte	silly
arnkelye	not talking to people because you're angry about something; sulking, in a sulk
arratye	1. true, correct, right 2. real 3.(a) actually, really, in fact 3.(b) indicates that something really happens after someone has been trying to do it or talking about doing it; actually, finally, really 3.(c) indicates that something happens even though you might expect that it wouldn't happen; despite (something), even though 4. really, very 5. right, proper, correct 6. straight (like a line) 7. right (side), especially the right arm
arrkene	fun, play, joking
atere	scared, frightened
atnewe-atnewe	relaxed, confident
atyepe-atyepe	lively, energetic
ingkerte	jealous
irrare	lonely, homesick
mwerre, mwarre	good
nterte	quiet

17. Motion

akngeme	to carry
akngetyeme	to bring
alheme	to go, walk
alkerele alheme	to fly (literally 'go along in the sky')
alpeme	to return, go back
aparlpe-irreme	to get lost
aperteme, aperreme	to stalk, sneak up on
apetyalpeme	to return, come back
apetyeme	to come
arnpenheme	to set off (walking)
arrateme	to exit, go out

atnarnpeme	to come down, jump down
aywepeme	to send someone away, let something go
irrpeme	1. to enter, go in 2. to put on (clothes)
itnyelhe-ileme, atnyelhe-ileme	to drop something (literally 'make it fall')
itnyeme, atnyeme	to fall
unteme	to run, hurry
untheme	1. to walk around, wander around 2. to look for something
urnteme	(of men) to dance
yerneme	to send

18. State

akangkeme	to be happy
ampeke-aneme	to be up against something and more or less vertical; standing supported by something, leaning, touching or resting against something, attached, clinging or sticking to something, resting on something
aneme	1. to sit 2. to live 3. to be (am, are, is, were, etc.)
apurrke-irreme	to get tired, sick of something
arrkene-irreme	to have fun, play
artepe-aneme	to bend over, be bent over
atertneme	to squat down
inteme	1. to lie, lie down 2.(a) to be (am, are, is, were, etc.) (where the shape and the position of something is thought to be more like lying down than standing up (*tneme*) or sitting (*aneme*)) 2.(b) there is . . . , there are . . . , there was . . . , etc. (where the shape and position of something is thought to be more like lying down) 2.(c) (a long thing) runs or goes (in some direction) (but is not actually moving); lies (that way) 3. to have a sleep, sleep 4. (euphemism) to sleep with someone 5. to be born

irreme	to become
mwernte-irreme	to refuse, be stubborn
ntyeme	to give off a smell
tneme	to stand

19. Vocalisation and thought

akaltye-irreme	to learn (literally 'to become knowledgeable')
akaltyele-antheme	to teach (literally 'to give knowledge')
akangkwirreme	to obey; to pay attention
akeme	to call someone something, refer to them as something
alkngwirreme	to forget
altyerre areme	to dream (compare *altyerre* 'the Dreaming')
alwarrerneme	to see something and decide to come back later to get it
alyelheme, ilyelheme	to sing (a song)
angkeme	to speak
antangkeme	to call someone over
apayuthneme	to ask
arlkeme	to shout
arntwerreme	(of an animal) to growl
arrpwerneme	to call out to someone
artneme	to cry
atere-irreme	to be scared
ileme	to say, tell someone something
ilteme	to swear at
ilyeme, alyeme	to sing (a person or thing) with magic
irrtyeme	to talk about going somewhere
itele-areme	to remember; to know; to decide; to think (literally 'to see with the throat')
itirreme	to think
tnakeme	to praise someone
uterneme	to order, force someone to do something

20. Bodily functions

aheye-angkeme	to breathe
ankwe-inteme	sleeping (literally 'lying down asleep')
antewe-irreme	to vomit
anteweke-antewe-irreme	to feel nauseated
antyweme	to drink
areme	to see, look at, watch
arralkeme	to yawn, open your mouth wide
arrkerneme	to try something, test it
atherreme	to laugh
aweme	1. to hear, listen to 2. to understand
ilweme	to die
kwerneme	to swallow
ntyerneme	to smell something
ntyerrknge itnyeme	to sneeze
pewileme	to blow on something
tnyelheme	to scratch yourself
ulheme	to urinate; to defecate
wangkeme	to swell up

21. Impact and violence

akakweme	to bite
akelheme	to cut yourself (When someone passes away, certain relatives may deliberately cut themselves in mourning.)
akeme	to cut
akiltye-ileme	to split something
altheme	to pluck
altyiweme	to tip out (liquid)
altywere-ileme	1. to open 2. to turn something on
anheme	to rain; to water something
anpeme	1. to come into contact with something; touch something, pat it, fiddle with something 2. to feel something 3. to rub or massage someone, especially in the way traditional healers do; lay on hands 4. to reach something
apekeme	to smash something

arteme	1. to build 2. to cover, bury
atantheme	to spear, poke; to sew; to write
ateme	to burst
atheme	to grind (seeds, etc.)
atweme	1. hit 2 kill
atwerreme	to fight (literally 'to hit each other')
atyerreme	1. to shoot 2. to cook in hot ashes and earth
ilyerneme, alyerneme	to squeeze
inkerreme	(of things) to make a noise by moving against each other, make rubbing, rustling, scratching, shuffling or, especially, rattling sounds
irlweme, ilyweme	to take something off or down
intelhe-ileme	to write, draw, paint
ltare-atweme	to knock
marteme	to shut, close, turn off
mpwareme	to make, do; to fix
nteweme	to dash against something
tnyeme	to dig
ultakeme	to break, chop
ultheme	to tread on, press down on (compare *ulthentye* 'heavy')
uthneme	to bite
weme	to throw something at something else and hit it

22. Holding and transfer

akalke-ileme, akalkelhe-ileme	to divide, share, sort out, separate
akngakeme	to pick out, choose; to cut out
akngarte-iweme	1. to turn over 2. to change into something 3. to translate
akwerneme	to put something in, insert
alengke-iwelheme	to hide yourself
alengke-iweme	to hide something
antheme	to give
antirrkweme, antwirrkeme	to catch, hold
aparlpe-ileme	to lose something
arrerneme	to put something down
arrernirtneme	to put back
atnyeneme	to keep, mind, protect

awakeme	to save, keep
impeme	to leave behind, leave alone
ineme	to take, get
irrkereme	to uncover; to sort through
iweme	to throw
ngkerneme	to set up, stand something up
rakeme	to grab
theleme	to pour, spill
tyarre-ineme	to pull
wanteme	to feed someone

23. Location, direction and time

-arenye	belonging to, from, associated with
-nge-ntyele, -ntyele	from, out of
-werne	to, towards
akertne	up, on top
akwete	still, yet
angwerre	1. afternoon, after the middle part of the day (rather than after exactly noon) until sunset, especially the earlier part of this time (mid-afternoon) 2. the end of the day, the start of the night
angwerre-angwerre	late afternoon, before sunset; 'evening' (In the English of many Aboriginal people, the word 'evening' refers to this time before sunset and not to the time from sunset to, say, bedtime.)
apmwerrke	1. yesterday 2. a few days ago, in the last few days, the other day
arlenge	a long way, distant
arlte	day
arrule	long ago
arrwekele	before, in front
arrwekelenye	1. first one(s), one(s) before 2. ancestors
ayerrere	north
ikngerre	east
ilengare	when?
ingwartentyele	all night

ingwe — night
ingweleme — morning
ingwenthe — tomorrow
intwarre — over there
kwene — down; low; inside
lyete — 1. now, just now; soon 2. today
lyetenye — today's, recent
mpepe — middle
urreke — 1.(a) later, in a while, in a minute, afterwards, after 1.(b) . . . and then (something else happens) 2. (do something) for a while, until later

24. Interjections

akunye — poor thing!
Alaye! — Look out!, Get out of the way!
Ayekaye! — Oh!
Kweye? — 1. an expression of surprise, such as 'Oh!', 'Gee!', 'I can't believe it!' 2. Used to ask for something to be confirmed or said again, as in 'Eh?', 'Isn't it?'
Me! — Here, take it!
Mpe! — Let's go!
Ngke! — 1. Give it here!; Give me a break!, Get out of it!
Werte? — What's up? (a common greeting to which a common reply is *Ware* nothing special
Yweke, yekwe — I don't know

25. Demonstratives and pronouns

alakenhe — like this, like that
angwenhe — who?
anwerne — we (more than two people)
atyenge — for me
ayenge — I, me (subject of intransitive verb or object of transitive verb)
ikwere — for him, her, it
ilerne — we two (subject)
itne — they (more than two)
iwenhe — what?

iwenheke	why?, what for?
iwenhenge	why?, because of what?, what from?
ngenhe	you (one person, object of transitive verb)
nhakwe	that, there (distant)
nhenhe	here, this
nhenhe	here, this
nthakenhe	how?
nthakentye	how many?
nthenhe	where?
nthenhe-werne	where to?
re	he, she, it (subject)
renhe	him, her, it (object of transitive verb)
the	I (subject of transitive verb)
unte	you (one person, subject)
yanhe	that, over there (not too distant)

26. Adverbs and particles

akwele	Generally, this shows that a speaker is not talking from their own knowledge, direct experience or authority, but is usually reporting what someone else has said, or appears to think. It is very common in traditional stories. It also occurs in descriptions of dreams and of what someone is thinking, which appear not to be thought of as direct experience 1. supposedly, supposed to be, so they say, reportedly, they reckon that ... 2.(a) used in describing what someone thinks, especially when this turns out to be wrong 2.(b) used in describing something in a dream 2.(c) pretending, acting as if something were true, making out that something is true, seem to think that ...

anamele	emphasises that the one doing the action is mostly or entirely responsible for the action; 'This is only happening because someone (or a particular doer) is doing this, it's not happening by itself or being done by others.'
ante	only
apeke	1. indicates that the speaker is not certain about the facts, or doesn't want to commit themself; maybe, might, perhaps, probably, 'I think (so)', 'I'm not sure if . . . ' 2. must (in the sense of 'judging from the evidence' not 'have to do something' 3. if 4. or
apele	In general, this shows that the speaker is sure that what they are saying is true or accurate, because they are speaking from their own knowledge, experience or authority. It is usually not easily translated into English; 'I know for a fact that . . . ', 'I know myself that . . . ', 'It's a fact that . . . ' 1. shows that the speaker wants to make a point of what's happened so that the listener will take special note of it, especially something that the listener probably wouldn't know already 2. when talking about something you are going to do, *apele* shows that you really intend to do it 3. shows that something really is the way it is being described, that a report of something is fairly accurate and complete 4. very commonly used in identifying something or explaining what a word means. It is usually common knowledge, or something that other people would also know.
irnterre, arnterre	intensely

kele — Generally, this signals a change of situation, event or topic. It often signals the end of something, or the start of something else 1.(a) finished, completed, already (happened) 1.(b) in the process of, now, already 1.(c) then 2. now, straight away (usually with orders or similar meanings 3.(a) indicates the end of a topic of conversation, or often the start of one, or even the end of the whole conversation; 'righto', 'OK', 'right, then' 3.(b) indicates that arrangements are finalised or agreement reached; 'OK', 'all right' 4. said to babies to pacify them

ularele — 1. (doing something) with something particular in mind; for a reason, deliberately, on purpose, knowingly, intending something, with a particular motive, for your own reasons 2. intending something which is not the obvious or direct result of what you are doing; pretending, making out to do something (but not actually doing it), tricking someone

uyarne, uye — unable to (do something), (do something) unsuccessfully, without any luck

ware — 1. only 2. nothing much, nothing special (reply to *Werte?*)

27. Placenames

Ltyentye Apurte — Santa Teresa (literally 'stand of beefwood trees')

Mparntwe — Alice Springs

Uyenpere Atwatye — Hidden Valley town camp on the eastern side of Alice Springs (literally 'spearwood gap')

Werlatye Atherre — women's sacred site in the Todd River (literally 'two breasts')

Grammatical notes

Eastern Arrernte has a number of interesting and unusual grammatical features. One of these is a way of showing on verbs that the doer of the verb moves somewhere during, before or after the action of the verb. For example, the following are some (but not all) of the possible forms of the verb *areme* (*ar* + *eme* 'see, look at, watch' + *present*):

arenheme	see while going past
arintyeme	see while coming in this direction
arirtneme	see while going back
arerle-alheme	see and then go
aretye-alheme	go and see
arerle-alpeme	see and then go/come back
aretye-alpeme	go/come back and see
arartne-alheme	quickly look and then go
arartne-alpeme	quickly look and then go/come back
aretye-akerleme	see while going down
aretye-antyeme	see while going up

These and other features of verbs mean that fairly complicated situations can sometimes be described with a single verb, as in the following particularly complex example where someone is describing what will happen if two children continue to hang from a weak branch and it breaks off:

re-atherre *art+elh+artne-akerl+irr+etyenhe*
he/she/it-two cover+themself+quickly-go down+two doing-this +future
'The two of them will fall down and be covered (by the branch that falls).'

Of course, Arrernte verbs are not always this complex, but they have the potential to be that way, a potential which allows great scope for creativity and verbal skill.

Another interesting feature of Arrernte grammar is that when more than one verb or clause is joined together, there is a system which can indicate whether the different actions are being done by the same doer or by different doers (see also page 142 in the chapter on Diyari). For example, compare the following:

The thipe areke arnele anem[ele].
I bird see-*past* tree-in sit-*present*-same doer
'I saw a bird (while I) was sitting in the tree.'

The thipe areke arnele an[erlenge].
I bird see-*past* tree-in sit-different doer
'I saw a bird (while someone other than me, most likely, in this context, the bird) was sitting in the tree.'

It is the ending on the second verb in each example which identifies who is doing the action. In the first example, the ending on the verb *aneme* 'sit' shows that the doer of this verb is the same doer of the main verb, *areme* 'see', in this case, *the* 'I'. In the second example, the ending on the verb for 'sit' shows that the doer of this action was not the doer of the main verb. It does not actually tell us who the doer of 'sit' was, but we can work out from the context that it was most probably the bird.

References

Further information can be found in the following books, which are available from the Publications Department of the Institute for Aboriginal Development (Box 2531, Alice Springs NT 0871):

Green, Jenny 1984, *A Learner's Guide to Eastern and Central Arrernte*, Institute for Aboriginal Development, Alice Springs

Henderson, John and Veronica Dobson (compilers) 1994, *Eastern and Central Arrernte to English Dictionary*, Institute for Aboriginal Development, Alice Springs

14

Murrinh-Patha

MICHAEL WALSH

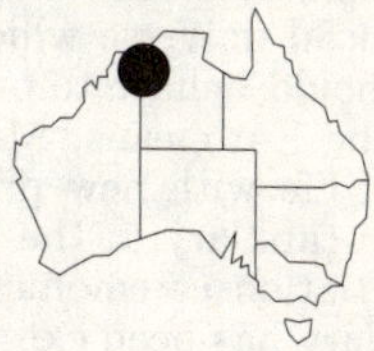

Murrinh-Patha is spoken by a majority of the population of Wadeye situated on the western coast of the Northern Territory. Wadeye (formerly known as Port Keats) has a population of around 1500, consisting of Murrinh-Patha, Marri-Ngarr, Marri-Djabin, Magati-Ge, Djamindjung and a number of other minority groups. A Roman Catholic mission, set up in 1935, brought together Aboriginal people from a range of backgrounds on what had been Murrinh-Patha land. Over time Murrinh-Patha came to be a common language (lingua franca) for the area so that Murrinh-Patha now has upwards of 1500 speakers if one includes those Aboriginal people who use it as a second language, and the Murrinh-Patha people who live at other settlements like Kununurra in the eastern Kimberley and Peppiminarti in the Daly River area. The traditional territory of the Murrinh-Patha takes in Wadeye and extends south to the Fitzmaurice River. The name of the language, Murrinh-Patha, literally means 'language-good'.

14. Murrinh-Patha

Bilingual education was introduced in 1976. This has given an added boost to Murrinh-Patha so that it seems that there may be some language shift to Murrinh-Patha at the expense of minority languages.

The Murrinh-Patha traditionally subsisted through hunting and gathering like many other Aboriginal groups. However, because of their coastal location they were able to harvest a wide variety of resources from the ocean and mangrove creeks including crabs, molluscs, turtle, dugong, mangrove worms and fish of many types.

The social organisation of the Murrinh-Patha is typical of Aboriginal groups and therefore quite different from the social organisation of Europeans. Each Murrinh-Patha belongs to one of two groups (called 'moieties'): *tiwungku* 'eaglehawk' or *karrthin* 'spotted/swamp harrier' (also referred to as 'chickenhawk'). Through membership of these moieties and a system of eight subsections, each Aboriginal person has a point of reference in the social universe which determines whom they can marry and how they should behave to other Aboriginal people.

Since the arrival of the Europeans, Murrinh-Patha people have merged traditional ways of life with new practices introduced by the Europeans. Some of the vocabulary in the following wordlist reflects traditional practices of initiation ceremonies, sorcery and traditional healing while some vocabulary has been extended to cover new objects or processes, for example: *birr* 'sew (with a sewing machine)' or 'spear (many objects)'; *ngkabing* 'lift eyelid' or 'turn over a page'; *rta* 'catch' or 'take a photo'.

Spelling

The letters used in writing Murrinh-Patha are the following:

a, b, d, dh, e, g, i, k, l, m, n, ng, nh, p, r, rd, rl, rn, rr, rt, t, th, u, w, y

MURRINH-PATHA WORDLIST

Much of this wordlist has been adapted and checked from Chester Street's English–Murrinh-Patha, Murrinh-Patha–English Dictionary.

WORDLIST CATEGORIES

Each noun is followed by its class in brackets. *See page 316 for a brief explanation of noun classes.*

1. Body parts and products

darripi *(ku)*	skin (animal)
darripi *(nanthi)*	skin (human)
dimu *(nanthi)*	tooth
kamarl *(nanthi)*	eye; face
karnkart; walmpu *(nanthi)*	testicles
kulpurru *(nanthi)*	hair (on body)
kumulung *(nanthi)*	blood
kurnthik *(nanthi)*	stomach; guts
lamala *(nanthi)*	shoulder
lawali *(nanthi)*	thigh
lumpu *(nanthi)*	buttocks
magulkul *(nanthi)*	heart
mange *(nanthi)*	finger; hand
mange ngala *(nanthi)*	thumb (literally 'finger big')
mange thingin *(nanthi)*	fingernail
marda *(nanthi)*	stomach (external), belly

mardayidi *(nanthi)*	chest
me *(nanthi)*	foot; toe
me ngardarda *(nanthi)*	ankle
me timelu *(nanthi)*	heel
mikmu *(nanthi)*	hip
mukmuk *(nanthi)*	brain
murnu *(nanthi)*	bone
net *(nanthi)*	boil
ngalarnarn *(nanthi)*	rib
ngapurlu *(nanthi)*	breast
ngerri *(nanthi)*	scar; cicatrice
ngi *(nanthi)*	penis
nginipunh *(nanthi)*	body
nginthirrin *(nanthi)*	sweat
ngukin *(mi)*	faeces
ngukin weyi *(nanthi)*	anus
ngurdengke *(nanthi)*	calf of leg
nimpithal *(nanthi)*	semen
nithi *(nanthi)*	arm
nithi kangkarl *(nanthi)*	arm, lower (literally 'arm above')
nithi pepe *(nanthi)*	arm, upper (literally 'arm below')
pangkin *(nanthi)*	back
parnta *(nanthi)*	groin
parnturtparn *(nanthi)*	lung
pelenangka *(ku/nanthi)*	fat
(pemarr) pulu *(nanthi)*	grey hair
pemarr *(nanthi)*	hair (on head)
pelpith *(nanthi)*	head
pelpith murnu *(nanthi)*	skull (literally 'head bone')
pingkarl *(nanthi)*	knee
punhu *(nanthi)*	liver
thamamay *(nanthi)*	beard
thamarl *(nanthi)*	neck
thamarl tungtung *(nanthi)*	throat
thamurru *(nanthi)*	cheek
tharrmu *(nanthi)*	lower leg; shin
thathpi *(nanthi)*	lip; mouth
thathpiwere *(nanthi)*	moustache
thathpi yuthpan *(nanthi)*	chin (literally 'mouth/lip straight')
the *(nanthi)*	ear
themen *(nanthi)*	tongue

thigath *(nanthi)*	urine
thiminkit *(nanthi)*	kidney
thimu *(nanthi)*	nose
thirrimeme *(nanthi)*	navel
thunmu *(nanthi)*	nape of neck
tumtum *(ku)*	egg
weyi *(ku)*	vagina
wulumu *(nanthi)*	forehead

2. Kin relationships

kaka *(kardu)*	mother's brother
kale *(kardu)*	mother; mother's sister
kangkurl *(kardu)*	father's father
kawu *(kardu)*	mother's mother
mangka *(kardu)*	father's mother
munak *(kardu)*	sister
nangkun *(kardu)*	husband
newuy *(kardu)*	daughter
ngathan *(kardu)*	brother
nginipunh *(murrinh)*	skin name
pipi *(kardu)*	father's sister
purrima *(kardu)*	wife; wife's sister
thamunh *(kardu)*	mother's father
thayikurta *(kardu)*	brother, deceased
wakal *(kardu)*	son
yile *(kardu)*	father; father's brother

3. Human classification

bamam *(kardu)*; ku	white man
birlmalu; ngarlarr *(kardu)*	policeman
dakarranh *(kardu)*	man with many wives
kanthirra *(kardu)*	namesake
karduma *(kardu)*	woman who has a husband (literally 'man-having')
kigay *(kardu)*	boy (teenage)
linku *(kardu)*	person marrying correctly
mardinhpuy *(kardu)*	girl (young, single)
mikmunurr *(kardu)*	widow(er)
muthingka *(kardu)*	old woman
ngamengka *(kardu)*	foreigner
nugarn *(kardu)*	man; male

palngun *(kardu)* — woman
palngun (bamam) *(ku)* — white woman
palngunma *(kardu)* — man who has a wife (literally 'woman-having')
pulangay *(kardu)* — friend
punh *(kardu)* — initiate; young man who has been through the *punh* ceremony
wadhi *(kardu)* — person marrying incorrectly
wakal *(kardu)* — child
wardam *(kardu)* — nobody, nonentity
warnangkal *(kardu)* — clever man, wise man, 'witchdoctor'
wemarda *(kardu)* — new-born baby, wrapped (originally in paperbark) (literally 'paperbark-container')

4. Language, mythology and ceremony

kangarlmawu *(kardu)* — God (literally 'above-dwelling')
karrath *(ku)* — devil
kitkit *(nanthi)* — clip-clop sound, as of horses' hoofs
kunmangkurr *(ku)* — rainbow serpent
kupek *(nanthi)* — splash sound in mud
mange *(murrinh)* — sign language
murrinh — language; name; word
ngakumarl *(ku)* — totem
ngarrithngarrith *(kardu/ku)* — spirit children
ngepan *(ku)* — spirit; ghost (of man)
ngerren *(murrinh)* — speech
ngugumingki *(da)* — totem site
thamarl *(nanthi)* — song
thurrpuk *(nanthi)* — splash sound in water
tul *(nanthi)* — tapping sound
yerrernti *(nanthi)* — sorcery

5. Human artefacts

da — camp
karlay *(nanthi)* — fishing net
kiningka *(nanthi)* — digging stick
kiniwu *(nanthi)* — dugout canoe
kum *(nanthi)* — bottle
kuragadha *(thu)* — boomerang
kuwarri *(nanthi)* — shield
larrwa *(nanthi)* — wooden pipe

lawalima *(nanthi)*	trousers (literally 'thigh-having')
lithpurr *(nanthi)*	axe
lithpurr malay *(nanthi)*	stone axe
mak *(nanthi)*	message stick
marluk *(nanthi)*	didjeridu
marrimarri *(nanthi)*	knife
menek *(thamul)*	ironwood spear
mirlmirlmirl *(nanthi)*	stick for popping pimples
mirnka *(nanthi)*	clapsticks
muthay *(nanthi)*	basket
nithima *(nanthi)*	shirt (literally 'arm-having')
paku *(thu)*	fighting club
pi *(nanthi)*	string; rope
puthputh *(nanthi)*	broom
tharntu *(nanthi)*	boat; coolamon
thelput *(nanthi)*	house
thening *(nanthi)*	female pubic covering
thunpith *(nanthi)*	spear thrower
waya *(thamul)*	fishing spear (literally 'wire')
yi *(nanthi)*	dillybag

6. Food, cooking and fire

dhepdhep *(mi)*	food (vegetable)
lawam *(mi)*	damper; flour
lelerr *(thungku)*	cooking coals
len *(nanthi)*	charcoal
len *(thungku)*	hot coals
ngen *(ku)*	meat
thay *(thungku)*	firewood
thitay *(ku)*	sugarbag; wild honey
thungku	fire
warnak *(nanthi)*	smoke
yulirn *(nanthi)*	ashes, grey

7. Topography

darrimurn *(da)*	beach
darrimurn *(nanthi)*	sand
darrinpirr *(da)*	plains country
kangathi *(da)*	country, mother's
mayern *(da)*	path, road, track
mulurn *(da)*	shade area

ngalburnu *(da)*	island
ngirru; ngirrwu *(nanthi)*	red clay
nguwurt *(nanthi)*	dust
palyirr *(da)*	hill; mountain
palyirr *(nanthi)*	rock; stone
pangkin *(da)*	ridge (literally 'back')
putek *(da)*	earth, ground, land
weyi *(da/nanthi)*	hole, large
weyi palyirr *(da)*	cave

8. Elements

kalakkalak *(nanthi)*	cloud
malarntath *(thu)*	lightning; thunder
marrurru *(nanthi)*	Milky Way
merrk *(nanthi)*	moon
ngunga *(nanthi)*	sun
pilinh *(nanthi)*	star
wirrirr *(nanthi)*	wind

9. Water

kanamkek/dimkek *(ku)*	rainbow (serpent)
kaputhkaputh *(kura)*	pool; well
ngipilinh *(kura)*	creek/river (fresh water)
ngurdaka *(kura)*	billabong
ngurntinh *(nanthi)*	wave(s) of the sea
manhpilyi *(kura)*	rain, cold, during dry season
thapak *(nanthi)*	dew; fog
tharr *(kura)*	water in log or stump (suitable for drinking)
therri *(kura)*	rain from ocean
thurrulk *(kura)*	beer (literally 'foam')
yelyel *(kura)*	rain

10. Mammals

baybaye *(ku)*	female antilopine kangaroo
kumpit *(ku)*	male antilopine kangaroo
lawarnka *(ku)*	wallaby
ngapapa *(ku)*	sugar glider
ngarriyeye *(ku)*	western native cat
nguluyguy *(ku)*	echidna
nini *(ku)*	buffalo

ninthi *(ku)*	Gould's fruit bat
nintu *(ku)*	horse
therlpung *(ku)*	common rock rat
thiniminh *(ku)*	small bat
were *(ku)*	dog
were pulangarr *(ku)*	dingo
yerl *(ku)*	ringtail possum
yirrthip *(ku)*	cat

11. Reptiles

kakalak *(ku)*	brown tree snake
kanarnturturt *(ku)*	crocodile (general term); gecko
kukpi; nhin *(ku)*	carpet snake
kunungkama *(ku)*	central sand monitor (literally 'small-hand')
kuydharr *(ku)*	taipan
nertpi *(ku)*	frill-necked lizard
ngi *(ku)*	death adder
ngirnu *(ku)*	long-neck (freshwater) turtle
ngunhpalin *(ku)*	black whip snake
ngupu *(ku)*	loggerhead turtle
nuth *(ku)*	water python
pangkuy *(ku)*	snake (general term) (literally 'long')
thaluwanh *(ku)*	copper-tailed skink
tharnkin; tharingkin *(ku)*	king brown snake
walumuma *(ku)*	blue-tongued lizard
wamparn *(ku)*	saltwater crocodile
wurdankangayiyip *(ku)*	western brown snake
yekpa *(ku)*	freshwater crocodile

12. Birds

kalampitpit *(ku)*	Australian magpie lark; peewee
kananganthan *(ku)*	emu
karrak *(ku)*	kookaburra
karrkurrk *(ku)*	tawny frogmouth
karrmi *(ku)*	straw-necked ibis
karrthin *(ku)*	spotted/swamp harrier (*Also* a moiety group)
kilikkilik *(ku)*	galah
kulerrkkurrk *(ku)*	brolga

kurlurnturtuk *(ku)* peaceful dove
kuywi *(ku)* pink cockatoo
larrplarrp *(nanthi)* shell grit
maminmanga *(ku)* black cormorant
mangul *(ku)* boobook owl
melkmelkthay *(ku)* royal/yellowbilled spoonbill
murntuykuy *(ku)* bustard
murrirr *(nanthi)* feather
murrirrbe *(ku)* bird (general term) (literally 'feather-arm')
pungpungti *(ku)* white ibis
tay *(ku)* egret
tek *(ku)* black cockatoo
thalagi *(ku)* crested hawk
thikin *(ku)* chicken
thilimpirrith *(ku)* Willie wagtail
thimerri *(ku)* jabiru
thinmel *(ku)* seagull
tiwungku *(ku)* wedge-tailed eagle (*Also* a moiety group)
tumtum *(ku)* egg
waluntak *(ku)* pelican
wak *(ku)* crow
werrk *(ku)* sulphur-crested cockatoo
wurdapan *(ku)* spotted nightjar

13. Aquatic life

balli *(ku)* mud crab
durket *(ku)* green frog
kerun *(ku)* shrimp
kunhpini *(ku)* yellow freshwater catfish
langkalangka *(ku)* pearl oyster shell
malawurru *(nanthi)* fin, spike of fish
mangkangunga *(ku)* octopus; squid
merrk *(ku)* pearly nautilus shell (literally 'moon')
neywuy/naywuy *(ku)* box jellyfish; sea wasp
ngurlmirl *(ku)* fish (general term)
nimpangart *(ku)* giant mitre shell
pangkithay *(ku)* swordfish (literally 'long-lip/mouth')
pilinh *(ku)* starfish (literally 'star')

tharnu *(ku)*	barramundi
therrngenen *(ku/nanthi)*	gills of fish
therri *(ku)*	abalone/triton shell
walmarr *(ku)*	hammerhead shark
warrgi *(ku)*	mangrove worm (type) (edible)
wemat *(nanthi)*	coral (live)
werntek *(nanthi)*	coral (dead)

14. Insects and Spiders

ba *(ku)*	march fly
dalmarnti *(ku)*	scorpion
kikmun *(ku)*	beeswax (used as a binding agent on spears and boomerangs)
lamunh wakal *(ku)*	large and edible green tree ant
manman *(ku)*	butterfly
mangurruwerr *(ku)*	spider (general term)
mayiyin *(ku)*	dragonfly
mimpi *(ku)*	head lice
murl *(ku)*	fly
ngalek; nhel *(ku)*	white mosquito
ngernte *(ku)*	tick
ngulli *(ku)*	centipede
ngurrmu *(ku)*	grub (general term)
pangkima *(ku)*	bee (literally 'long-finger/hand')
tharrmuba *(ku)*	wasp

15. Plants

dara *(nanthi)*	mangrove tree (type)
darripi *(nanthi)*	bark of tree (literally 'skin')
karruk *(mi)*	yam (type), round
kathan *(mi)*	waterlily (type), purple
kurrugurrukdarri *(nanthi)*	moss
marda *(nanthi)*	bamboo, large (used for spears)
menek *(nanthi)*	ironwood tree
mulurn *(nanthi)*	leaf
muth *(nanthi)*	tobacco plant (native)
ngulul *(mi/nanthi)*	flower (general term)
parnu *(nanthi)*	grass (general term)
tharnka *(mi)*	yam (type)
thawuy *(nanthi)*	chewing tobacco

thay *(nanthi)*	tree (general term); stick; twig; wood; splinter
thingkulng *(nanthi)*	mulga tree
wawa *(mi)*	yam (type)
we *(nanthi)*	paperbark (type)
yidingurr *(nanthi)*	tamarind tree

16. Physical qualities

bamam	white
batbat	right
batbat perrkenku	ambidextrous (literally 'right two')
birnu	alive
bukmantharr	red
burrburr	cold
dendurr	hot
dutmarnarri	crooked; bent
kamarrama	blind
kangkarl	above; aloft, on top
kunungangka/kunungingki	little, small
larrin	dead, dry (of leaves, grass etc.)
marra	new
mideyi	hungry
murntak	old
ngamere	few
ngatin	green (in colour); raw, uncooked
parnturtparn	light (in weight)
kupkup	soft
lewiye	tired
lurruth	strong, powerful
matharr	sick
mirrmirrmirrmam	thick (of blankets, etc.)
murruwurlngka	beautiful, good-looking
ngala	big
ngaliwe	short
pangkuy	tall; long
perrkenku	two
perrkenku numi	three (literally 'two one')
putput	pregnant
terert; wurnangat	many
thakunh	left
thawath	slow

thipmam	black, dark; dirty
thithimarnti	bitter
thungku	cooked; ripe (literally 'fire')
thutthutka	blunt (edge or point) (literally 'cut off-eye/face')
tumtum	dry
warda ngatha	all, everything
werlpen	flat
wunmuk	rotten
wuting	sharp-pointed
yitthit	heavy
yuthpan	straight

17. Non-physical qualities

murlak	cheeky; dangerous; nasty
patha	good
pelpith patha	balanced, sensible (literally 'head good')
pelpith wiye	foolish, stupid (literally 'head bad')
putputthe	stubborn (literally 'pregnant ear')
thathpirr	correct, true
walmamka	wild
wiye	bad, deteriorated, evil, inferior
yidiwe	ashamed; shy

18. Motion

bat	to fall; be born
kum	to swim
la	to climb up
lili	to walk
rdi	to enter, go in
ret	to begin, start
riwak	to follow
ruy	to arrive
tha	to chase
thurrk	(of the sun) to set (literally 'to dive')
winhadhath	to look for, seek
winhat	to run (away)
wurl	to return
wuteth	to move (intransitive)

19. State

bay	to be sated, be full
dim	to sit (down)
karrim	to stand
mardabay	to be disappointed with something, be disillusioned
mardamarda	to wait for
mardarlart	to be angry (literally 'belly-bite')
nham	to be afraid, fear
rlung	to be cold
yibim	to lie (down)
yel	to rain

20. Vocalisation and thought

bek	(of a dog or dingo) to howl
dharrpu	to ask
kampa	to laugh
karrk	to cry
kay	to call out
mam	to say
mardi	to marry (literally 'finger-put')
ngarakngarak	to whisper
ngeng	to speak, talk
ngkathan	to learn
rel	to chant a curse, to 'sing' a person
rnirn	to dream
winhingkayith	to instruct
yekum	to forget
yethith	to teach

21. Bodily functions

ath	to eat
be	to spit (out), vomit
gurduk	to drink
lele	to bite
minminka	to blink
ngkardu	to look; see
rdel	to yawn
thek	to defecate
warnkay	to have sexual intercourse
yepup	to hear; listen
yingap	to smell
yeyel	to urinate

22. Impact, production and violence

bang	to drill a hole, part way through
bat	to hit once (usually referring to a heavy blow, e.g. with a fighting stick)
bat	to throw at (with large spear or stone)
birr	to sew (with a sewing machine); spear (many objects)
dharl	to open
ku	to hit (with a missile)
kurrk	to dig a deep hole (*Also means* to sharpen a tool)
lerrkperrk	to crack
mel	to flatten out, by hand
ngkayeth	to hit lightly (e.g. with a cane or whip)
parl	to break
pek	to burn (intransitive)
purl	to pluck feathers (*Also means* to wash)
purrk	to wrap several round yams (only *mi karruk*) in paperbark and cook
puth	to sweep (with a broom)
rarath	to rustle leaves, dry grass, etc.
rde	to hit with something pointed or round (e.g. a short spear, fist, hammer, bullet, blunt end of an axe, etc.)
rdikurrk	to sharpen the edge of a tool (literally 'tooth-sharpen')
rdurt	to shake (e.g. a tree, for fruit to fall); shake awake; wake a person
rirda	to kick, push with foot
rirta	to pierce; puncture
rtal	to cut off
tha	to fight with spears
thi	to cook
thuk	to fight, by hand or with fighting sticks
warl	to spear
warnta	to split open

wath	to knock over
watha	to create, draw, fashion, make
wekarl	to roll it up
winhipak	to spill (transitive)
yerl	to draw, paint a design
yirr	to soak (intransitive and reflexive)

23. Holding and transfer

art	to get; take (only one item)
bath	to bring; take
birr	to bury
gat	to share food or goods that another has given you
kanthin	to bring; have; take
kut	to collect, gather (more than one item)
marta	to take from another
mut	to give
ngkabing	to turn over a page; lift eyelid
ngkale	to hang up
ngkat	to catch with a stick or tongue (as of a lizard)
pak	to put down (vertically)
pirt	to remove, take off
puth	to throw away (more than one item)
rdarrithuk	to conceal; hide oneself behind objects
rdi	to put into, insert
rirda	to push, with hand
rrurr	to pull
rta	to catch; take a photo
winhimardapak	to pour into
winhingurrunthat	to carry; to hold a baby on one's side
wirnturt	to lift up
wurr	to drag
wuy	to put small objects in a bag
yegarl	to drop
yit	to hold

24. Location, direction and time

dangatha	still; already
da panare; da pana ngangkare	everywhere
kangkarl	above; aloft, on top
kanhi	this; here
manta	close, near
marra	now
nakurl/nakurlnu	later
ngathparr	distant, far
nhinire	that time, at
pana	that; there (mid-distance)
pangu	that; there (long distance)
pelpith pepe	upside down (literally 'head down')
pepe	down; under
tiduk	behind; late

25. Interrogatives

kardu nangkal ngatha	whoever
na/nawa	hey? isn't it? (always expects a yes or no answer)
nangkal(yu)	who
ngarra	what; where; who

26. Interjections

awu; wurda	no
ba	excuse me; sorry; whoops
berengunh	all right, OK
ka	huh? what?
kama(ya)	maybe
kuguk mup	wait a minute (and) stay there
ma	give it to me!; ready?
mup	sit down; stay (used when one is leaving); stop
pirda	don't! stop it!
tharra	run!
ya	huh?; I don't know
yakay(ya)	golly! (surprise); hey!; ohhh (regret)
yu	yes

27. Pronouns

neki	we (you and me)
nganku	we (you and me, with you being my sibling)
ngankungime	we (excluding you; used for a small group of females or a small mixed group of males and females)
ngankungintha	we (me and one other person, excluding you; used for two females or a male and a female)
ngankunintha	we (me and him, excluding you; used for two males)
ngay	I; me; mine; my
nigunu	she; her(s)
nukunu	he; him; his

Grammatical notes

Two of the more interesting features of Murrinh-Patha grammar are the nouns which must be classified according to ten or so 'genders', and the verbs which package an amazing amount of information.

Each noun in Murrinh-Patha can be assigned to a noun class or 'gender'. This reflects the way that Murrinh-Patha people view the world. There is one noun class which groups together spears, one that refers to fresh water and things associated with fresh water, and another that refers to human beings:

thamul spears:

thamul nguni	short light spear
thamul menek	ironwood spear
thamul waya	fishing spear (literally 'fish wire')

kura fresh water and associated concepts, such as drinkable fluids, and different collective terms for fresh water:

kura thurrulk	beer (literally 'foam water')
kura ngipilinh	creek, river
kura yelyel	rain

kardu Aboriginal people and human classification (including human spirits):

kardu thipmam	black person (i.e. Aboriginal)
kardu pule	old man; husband; boss
kardu ngepan	spirit; soul of a living person
kardu warnangkal	clever man; witchdoctor
kardu kawu	mother's mother

Notice that the description of the *kardu*-class specifies Aboriginal people. If one is referring to a black person who is not Aboriginal, from Africa or the United States for example, then one can use a different class marker: *ku thipmam*. The *ku*-class includes non-Aboriginal people and all other animates and their products. From a Murrinh-Patha perspective one class groups together the birds and the bees and their products, eggs and honey, as well as snakes, wallabies and whitefellas! Some nouns in Murrinh-Patha may appear in a number of noun classes:

nanthi kamarl	eye/face
kura kamarl	water-hole
kardu kamarl	sweetheart
mi kamarl	seed

Body part terms are mostly assigned to the *nanthi*-class, which is quite heterogeneous. The *mi*-class includes fruits, flowers and vegetable food and products. The *da*-class refers to time and place: names for seasons, localities and features of the environment. In all there are about ten such noun classes and the wordlist above suggests how these classes work, but for further details see Walsh (forthcoming). The examples in the wordlist give some indication of the frequent use of body part metaphor in Murrinh-Patha (see also Walsh 1993). They also reveal a particular view of the world through the noun class markers used. From a Murrinh-Patha perspective, for example, 'rainbow' is not a thing or an 'it' (as English grammar treats it), but is alive and that is why it appears in the *ku*-class along with other animates (and their products).

In Murrinh-Patha, a single verb form can translate what amounts to a full sentence or even a paragraph in English. The single Murrinh-Patha word *nganhiwidhungnu* translates into English as 'I'm going to kiss you' or 'I will kiss you'. Whereas English spreads the intended meaning across four (or more) separate words, Murrinh-Patha links the separate pieces of meaning into one word:

nga-nhi-widhung-nu
I-you-kiss-will
'I will kiss you'

In English we can change the intended meaning by substituting one word for another and adding additional ones, but in Murrinh-Patha the intended change may be handled within a single word:

nga-nhi-ma-widhung-nu-ngani
I-you-hand-kiss-will-I do habitually
'I will keep on kissing your hand'

nga-nanku-ma-widhung-nu-ngani
I-you 2 siblings-hand-kiss-will-I do habitually
'I will keep on kissing the hands of you two siblings'

nga-nanku-ma-widhung-nu-ngintha-ngani
I-you 2-hand-kiss-will-2 non-siblings, at least one being female-I do habitually
'I will keep on kissing the hands of you two who are not siblings and one or both are female'

Three points need to be made about these few examples from Murrinh-Patha. Firstly, the information is packaged in Murrinh-Patha in quite a different way from English. Secondly, differences in grammar between languages create difficulties in translation. In the examples above it can be seen that Murrinh-Patha has three ways of expressing 'you-ness': *nhi* 'you singular'; *nanku* 'you two brothers/sisters (siblings)'; *nanku ngintha* 'you two who are not brothers or sisters and one or both are female' (and there are four other ways of expressing 'you-ness' in this language). Thirdly, the initial element in these verbal words, the auxiliary, varies according to the time reference of the action of the verb:

***ngam**nhimawidhung*	***ngani**nhimawidhung**tha***
'I kiss**ed** your hand'	'I **was** kiss**ing** your hand'

or, according to the action expressed by the verb:

***mam**nhimapurl*	***men**himapurl**tha***
'I wash**ed** your hand'	'I **was** wash**ing** your hand'
***pan**nhimabat*	***nguni**nhimabat**tha***
'I **struck** your hand'	'I **was** strik**ing** your hand'

Another difference between English and Murrinh-Patha is in the expression of bodily and emotional states. For many of these, Murrinh-Patha uses an impersonal verb construction which is reminiscent of English expressions like 'It behoves me. . . ' and 'It seems to me. . . '. These English expressions have an impersonal third person singular subject while the person affected appears grammatically as an object. Remembering that the subject appears first in a Murrinh-Patha verb, these examples show that the person affected by the bodily or emotional state appears in object position:

*mam**ngi**bay*	*mam**nhi**bay*
'**I** am full'	'**You** are full'
*bangam**ngi**mardalart*	*bangam**nhi**mardalart*
'**I** am angry'	'**You** are angry'
*pan**ngi**ngkawuy*	*pan**nhi**ngkawuy*
'**I** have blurred vision'	'**You** have blurred vision'

Such expressions are not easy to translate so as to reflect the grammar of Murrinh-Patha although the body part metaphor inherent in *bangamngimardalart* allows one to translate it as 'it bites my belly' reflecting the grammar which suggests an indefinite third person singular subject and the Murrinh-Patha view that the belly is the seat of the emotions. For further details see Walsh (1987).

Further reading

The most comprehensive recording of Murrinh-Patha has been carried out by the Summer Institute of Linguistics team, Chester and Lyn Street. They have produced numerous texts including translations from the Scriptures. Street (1987) includes a grammatical sketch, and there is also an on-line Murrinh-Patha vocabulary by Chester and Lyn Street (November 1989).

References

Stanner, W E H 1964, 'On Aboriginal Religion', *Oceania Monographs*, no. 11, Oceania Press, Sydney

Street, Chester 1983, *English–Murrinh-Patha, Murrinh-Patha–English Dictionary*, Wadeye Press, Wadeye (with the assistance of Gregory Panpawa Mollingin)

Street, Chester 1987, *An Introduction to the Language and Culture of the Murrinh-Patha*, Summer Institute of Linguistics, Darwin

Walsh, Michael 1987, 'The Impersonal Verb Construction in Australian Languages' in *Language Topics: Studies in honour of Michael Halliday*, eds Ross Steele and Terry Threadgold, John Benjamins, Amsterdam

Walsh, Michael 1993, 'Classifying the world in an Aboriginal language', in *Language and Culture in Aboriginal Australia*, eds Michael Walsh and Colin Yallop, Aboriginal Studies Press, Canberra

Walsh, Michael (forthcoming), 'Body parts in Murrinh-Patha: Incorporation, grammar and metaphor', in *The Grammar of Inalienability: a Typological Perspective on the Part-Whole Relation*, eds H Chappell and W McGregor, Mouton de Gruyter, Berlin

15

Meryam Mir

GAMALAI KEN PASSI and NICK PIPER

Meryam Mir is one of three languages spoken in the Torres Strait, that stretch of water which lies between Australia and Papua New Guinea. The other two languages are Kala Lagaw Ya, which is spoken on the western islands, and Torres Strait Creole, which is spoken throughout the Torres Strait as a kind of national language (see Chapter 17). Meryam was once spoken throughout the eastern islands of Erub, known in English as Darnley Island, Ugar, also called Stephen Island, and Mer or Murray Island. Nowadays, with more and more people speaking the creole, there are fewer people speaking Meryam – although some researchers (Wurm 1977, p. 328) have estimated that there would be around 700 speakers, which presumably includes all those people who have moved to mainland Australia and settled in places like Rockhampton, Mackay, Townsville, Cairns and Brisbane.

The Meryam people are ethnically Melanesian. They are a proud and independent people, who sometimes get called the 'Irish of the Torres Strait'! It is no surprise that they were the ones who decided to challenge the view that Australia was *terra nullius* ('land belonging to no-one') when it was settled by the British in 1788 and that they had 'native title' of Mer in that they were and continued to be the traditional owners of the land. Their case, known as the Mabo land claim because it was led by the late Mr Eddie Koiki Mabo, was won in 1992 and the judges recognised that they had a legal right to their land.

The Murray Islanders or *Mer le* are indeed fortunate to have such land, for their home is a tropical paradise with swaying palms surrounded by a deep-blue coral sea. Everything grows in its rich volcanic soil and the sea, reefs and weirs built by their ancestors always ensure there are plenty of fish. The story goes that a mythological ancestor, Gílam, travelled across to Mer from Mówa Island inside a wood-carved dugong in a desperate attempt to get away from his mother. When he reached Mer, he lay down on what became Gílam hill and flicked his left flipper which scattered food all over the eastern side of the island. He also let out a great big sneeze which blew two seeds into the water and created the two nearby islands of Dawar and Wayer.

All Meryam people, whether or not they are living on Mer, are linked together by a common ancestry, language and culture. This is not to say that there have not been influences from other peoples such as Western Torres Strait Islanders, Europeans and South Pacific Islanders, but there are ways of doing things that are uniquely Meryam. For example, the Meryam still have some of their own traditional dances and songs which are appropriately called *kabkar* 'true dance' and their language is unique in Australia for it is the only indigenous Australian language which is not an Aboriginal language. In fact, it is related to Papuan languages.

The name 'Meryam Mir' itself is drawn from the word *mir* which means 'word' or 'language', and *Meryam*, which is the name for one of the clans living on Mer. It can, however, also be used to refer to people from Mer. The name of the language is also written as Meryam, Meriam or Miriam.

About the wordlist

In some ways, the Meryam wordlist is a misrepresentation of the language situation, for people often use creole words when talking Meryam. To really understand the situation, you need to be aware that all Meryam speakers can and do talk creole, and they will sometimes use creole words quite unconsciously. The number of creole words used varies enormously from speaker to speaker. In some cases, people are fully aware of what they are doing and will switch from Meryam to creole and back again depending on what they are talking about and who they are talking to. For example, it is usual for islander or community business to be done in creole as many young people, in their twenties or younger, understand some Meryam but cannot speak it. However, in the family home, parents might talk to their children in creole but switch to Meryam if they want to discuss something private.

One of the interesting features of Meryam Mir is its idioms or sayings which are called *kokmir*, literally 'the joints of the language'. Some idioms refer to the weather, such as *ese gur wakay garkarem obay máyke aw wag* 'if the sea becomes a really deep green, there's a big wind close by'. Other sayings refer to people's physical appearance or their mood. For example, to say that someone is a spring chicken, you can say *mara sursur mena sorge epkedi* 'your nappy is still stuck on your back' or to say that someone is getting very stirred up about something, you might say *ma imut urker, uzer urker* 'you are punting anger, paddling anger'. When you want to say that something is delicious, you just point to your forehead and then to the back of your head saying *kari naski keko deketida* 'it enters me then peeks out again'.

Spelling and pronunciation

We have written Meryam Mir the way it sounds so that you can say the words for yourself. The sounds that are used in the language are the following:

a, b, d, e, g, i, k, l, m, n, o, p, r, s, t, u, w, y, z

Some of the sounds are said a bit differently to English, like the *r*, which in Meryam sounds more like the Scots *r*, although sometimes it is spoken just like the English *r*. The *i* is more or less like the 'ee' sound in English 'seed', the *a* is like the sound in 'far' and 'spa', and the *u* sounds a bit like the 'oo' in 'boot'.

A Meryam word with two syllables or more is usually said with the stress on the second syllable. When you are saying these words, try and make the second syllable sound harder and louder like you do in English when you say 'Narelle' rather than when you say 'Peter'. Sometimes in Meryam, however, the stress falls on the first syllable and in these cases, we have put an accent (´) on the first syllable. In some cases, it will mean something different depending on where the stress is. For example, *úni* means 'coconut juice' whereas *uní* is a 'box fish'.

MERYAM MIR WORDLIST

WORDLIST CATEGORIES	
1. Body parts and products	13. Plants
2. Kin relationships	14. Physical qualities
3. Human classification	15. Non-physical qualities
4. Language, mythology and ceremony	16. Motion
5. Human artefacts	17. State
6. Food, cooking and fire	18. Vocalisation and thought
7. Topography	19. Bodily functions
8. Elements	20. Impact and violence
9. Reptiles	21. Holding and transfer
10. Birds	22. Location, direction and time
11. Aquatic life	23. Interjections
12. Insects and spiders	24. Demonstratives and pronouns

1. Body parts and products

áwkey	thumb
bag	cheek
bub	chest, front of body
derged	fat
erkep	sight, gaze (*Also means* plant suckers)
gegur	skin; bark
gem	body
gilid	shoulder
ib	jaw, chin
idoni	brains
imus	beard
iraw	eyebrow
kem	stomach, abdomen, belly; pregnant (*Also means* company)
kenani	armpit
kerar	vein
kerim, kirim	head
kog	sexual desire or excitement
kokni	knee
komo mus, komus	pubic hair
kopor	navel
layp	ear

lid	bone (*Also means* plant stem)
mam	blood
med	flesh
megi	vomit
merod	calf
mit	lip
morop	forehead
mos	spittle; lungs
motop	bottom, buttocks
mus	hair
nano	breast
nerkep	heart (*Also means* favourite)
o	liver
op	face; front part of body (*Also means* in front of)
pagas	upper arm
pat	hip (*Also means* well, waterhole, creek, river)
pim	finger; toe
pit	nose
poni	eye
sor	back
tabo	neck
tag	arm, hand, lower arm
takok	elbow
tapot	fingernail, toenail, claw
te	mouth; opening
teter	leg or foot
téybur	guts or intestines
tirig	tooth
ut	sleep
wákey	thigh
wanta	penis
wáysu	vulva
wáysu neb	vagina
wer	egg; testicle (*Also means* star)

2. Kin relationships

ápu — mother; father's sister
arer — great-great-grandparents
ata — grandparent
bab — father; father's brother
berbet — sibling; father's sibling's child
kayed — grandparent
kéymer — younger sibling (*Also means* left, as opposed to right)
kimyar — husband; brother-in-law (*Also means* man)
koskir — wife; sister-in-law (*Also means* woman)
lugiz — ancestors
nap — grandchild
narbit — elder sibling (*Also means* right, as opposed to left)
náywet — son-in-law; brother-in-law; male cousin-in-law
negwam — cousin; mother's sibling's child; sister's child
nerbet — mother's sister; mother's brother's wife
néwbet — daughter-in-law; female cousin-in-law
newr — daughter; brother's daughter (*Also means* girl, young woman)
werem — son; brother's son (*Also means* boy, unmarried male)

3. Human classification

ad — god
agey — Aboriginal
águd — god
áwle — old or big man
bway — relative, countryman
gebarobi — Papua New Guinean
káymeg — mate, pal
kimyar — man (*Also means* husband; brother-in-law)
kole — white man; European
koskir — woman (*Also means* wife; sister-in-law)
lamar — ghost, spirit

le	person
makrem	unmarried man
newr	girl, young woman (*Also means* daughter; brother's daughter)
omaskir, omasker	children
sursur werem	baby
werem	boy, unmarried male (*Also means* son; brother's son)

4. Language, mythology and ceremony

ad	story
eswaw	thanks
gelar	law, rule
ginar	dance movement or steps
kab	dance
kodo	rhythm, tune, intonation, melody
mir	word, language
mirkok	idiom or meaning
ney	name
sasmir	noise made by talking, high-pitched chatter
si	thought (*Also means* goanna)
su	dancing skirt made out of green palm leaves
warup	traditional drum
wed	song

5. Human artefacts

bawr	spear
dári	headdress
dorge	work
epey	basket
karop	island flute
kep	arrow (*Also means* small reef)
koyr	stone knife
kusbáger	spear made from palm tree stem: *Pitaride tabara kusbager dikayrti, ge able sarup sorge iski* Pitar let go of his spear which pierced the castaway's back
mekik	fishhook and line: *ka naba mekikem* (literally 'I go fishing-to') I'm going fishing

meta	house
nar	boat (*Also means* car, truck)
nesur	skirt, cloth
papek	mat
sarik	shooting implement such as a gun
takar	platform for smoking objects
te	door (*Also means* mouth)
tulik	knife
uzer	paddle
wasnar	canoe
weris	fish trap used for scooping fish
zub	native tobacco; traditional smoking pipe; cigarette

6. Food, cooking and fire

amey	earth oven
bi	light, flame
dikasir	to cook
ditug	to put on the fire
ikayret	to burn or roast one or two things
irmad	stones that have been heated in the fire
kemur	smoke
lar	fish; meat
lewer	food
sabid	coconut scraped and milked into coconut milk: *sabidsabid kaba* bananas which have been cooked in coconut juice
tibi	ashes
ur	fire
wirwir	coals

7. Topography

aw, awak	hole
bakir	stone, rock (*Also means* money)
berder	mud
bidbid	light-blue sea around an island (lagoon colour)
déwday	mainland
gab	road, path

karem	ocean: *eypkárem* quite deep sea; *aw karemge* (literally 'big deep sea-in') into the deep blue sea
kawr	island
kep	small reef (*Also means* arrow)
kur	cave
lokot	scrub
nor	reef
Op Dewday	upper land, Papua New Guinea
Opnor	Barrier Reef (literally 'in front of-reef')
paser	hill, mountain
pat	well, waterhole, creek, river (*Also means* hip)
saw	jungle, rainforest
say	rock wall found near the edge of Mer where fish get trapped at low tide
sep	ground, earth, soil
ter	inner reef (the part of the reef that is connected to the island)
terkik	edge of reef
ubir	light-blue sea which lies a bit out from an island or cave under a flat rock or dead coral slab found mostly near the edges of reefs
we	sand

8. Elements

baz	cloud
bumer	rumble, thunder, bass sound made in music
gedub	garden
gerger	day
girgir	thunder
guni	seawater
irmer	rain
keper	pool, puddle, lagoon
ki	night
kotor	sky, heaven (*Also means* roof)
kub	storm (*Also means* crowd)
lim	sun
máyso	surf

meb	moon, month
meg	tide: *aw meg* high tide
meskep	low tide
mi	sky (*Also means* giant clams)
nedbi	dawn, daybreak; twilight
ni	(fresh)water, clear liquid
perper	lightning (*Also means* light in weight)
wag	wind
wer	star (*Also means* egg; testicle)

9. Reptiles and Mammals

kid	type of lizard (*Also means* rope made from coconut fibres)
mókepu	black snake (*Also means* cowrie shell)
pagey	sea snake
si	goanna (*Also means* thought)
tábo	snake

10. Birds

déwmer	Torres Strait pigeon
ebur	bird (general term)
kiriskiris	yellow-breasted sunbird
kor	grassbird
lub, welub	feather
mar	stormbird
pew	wing (*Also means* flipper; coconut leaf)
seprumrum	green-winged pigeon
serar	crested tern
waridub	eagle

11. Aquatic life

areg	barracouta
arti	octopus
as	helmet shell
asor	spider shell
at	smooth stingray
bawg	hawkbill turtle
bey	black marlin (*Also means* palm leaf)

bonaw	poisonous brain coral
bozar	small eel
dabor	mackerel
deger	dugong
galbol	whale
garom	coral cod
gas	large eel
gepi	fish scales
géygi	great trevally, turrum
geyn	oyster
goli	squid
gway	frog
irgar	rainbow mackerel
irir	wrasse
irwapawp	hammerhead shark
iwez	hermit crab
izir	bailer shell
keyar	crayfish, lobster
kirit	cone shell
kod	shark fin, dolphin fin
konay	back flippers
koyt	coral trout
kuk	periwinkle
kum	type of mullet
kurup	groper, rock cod (*Also means* freshness)
kuskus	blackfin shark, reef shark
lar	generic fish
maber	conch shell
málowap	tuna
máyu	golden trevally
melpal	eel
memsus	soft poisonous coral
mi	giant clams (*Also means* sky)
mókepu	cowrie shell (*Also means* black snake)
olay	back of turtle
nam	turtle (general term)
namkar	green turtle
papey	queenfish
paris	long tom

pew	flipper (*Also means* wing; coconut leaf)
pupwag	jellyfish
si	flying fish
tul	flipper on whale, dolphin or dugong
tup	sardine
uriz	flatback turtle
warib	type of garfish
weswes	coral
zab	garfish
zegnaypul	type of turtle
zogar	red mullet

12. Insects and spiders

ábob	blowfly
isi	centipede
izrum	ant
keroro, kiroro	locust
lag	mosquito
nab	wasp
narger	housefly
nem	louse
pim	grasshopper
pisoger	spider's web
seber	spider
soni	green ant

13. Plants

abal	pandanus
bam	turmeric
basor	coconut shell used as water container
bey	palm leaf (*Also means* black marlin)
éneyo	wongai tree and fruit
erkep	plant suckers (*Also means* sight, gaze)
gegur	bark
gerer	pandanus leaf used when weaving mats
giz	tree trunk (*Also means* family tree; end point)

kaba	banana (general term)
ketay	type of yam
kid	rope made from coconut fibres (*Also means* a type of lizard)
kokwam	hibiscus
kub	type of tree
kumala	sweet potato
kurup	freshness (*Also means* groper, rock cod)
lam	leaf
lewerkar	type of yam
lid	plant stem (*Also means* bone)
lu	tree, wood; any object
lumud	tree shade
lusik	blossom, flower
manyot	cassava
neru	sugar, sugarcane
new	something ripe (*Also means* blister)
omi	type of fig tree
pew	coconut leaf (*Also means* flipper; wing)
pot	stem on fruit
sip	roots of a tree or plant
sogi	grass
sorbi	wild plum
tam	branch
u	coconut or palm tree

14. Physical qualities

aregareg	edible
aw	big
bambam	yellow
barbar	crooked
bebeb	wet
beberbeber	heavy
buzi(g)buzi(g)	rotten, decayed
dobdob	fat
dudum	quickly
emeret	old
goligoli	black, dark
kebi	little, small

kela(r)kela(r)	strong, hard
kerkar	fresh, new; recent
lomlom	mouldy
mamam mamam	red
mitkar	many, a lot; full
neg	laughter
nerut	another, other, next, following
netat	one
neys	two
nyap	thirst
perper	light (in weight) (*Also means* lightning)
piripiri	long; tall
tebteb	alone
téwpay	short
werer	hunger; lust

15. Non-physical qualities

adud	bad
atkitatkit	jealous
debe	good, nice
gayr	every
gewm	fear: *ka géwmge náli* (literally 'I fear-in am') I'm scared
kemerkemerkemer	all
kepkep	few, several
okasosok	worry, sorrow
pardarpardar	clever, learned
paym	madness
peym	dream
serer	happiness
sirip	shame
umer	knowledge, ability
weku	anger
zogo	holy or sacred thing: *zogo le* priest, holy person

16. Motion

ábu	to come down, descend, fall
akarik	to climb, go up, land (from the sea)
ákomer	to return; go back
ays	to float (*Also means* to take several or many things)
bagor	to land, when coming from the sea (for many people or animals): *wa tabagor gurlam* you lot come up from the sea
bakes	to go to the same place habitually; stroll around: *e mekikem bakesli* she's gone off fishing
bakyamu, bakamu, baka	to go (for one or two people)
bakyaw, bakaw, baka	to go (for several people or many people)
barag	to dive close to the water surface (for several or many people)
baraygi	to dive close to the water surface (for one or two people)
bareb	to swim
barot	to enter (for several or many people)
baruk	to start off; feel; happen: *kara nyap barki* (literally 'my thirst feel') I feel thirsty
batar	to turn around (for several or many people)
batawrik	to turn around (for one or two people): *e batawrikda adem digmi Wáyer pitlam* he turned around (and) walked away from Wáyer point
baw	to enter (for one or two people)
bay	to become (for one or two things or people): *e wepigemeda, wéyakayda le obayda* she changed, became a person (again)
báyter	to sink (without anyone doing anything); dive deeply
ber	to become (for many people or things): *wi bapiger, baker lag oberare* they changed, became mosquitoes; *wi gayr legiz bakeri le ko berda* They all became people again

dáyu	to dig for non-vegetable food: *koskiride dáyuli siem* (literally 'woman-doer digging goanna-for') The woman is digging for goanna; *koskiride wersor dáyuli* (literally 'woman-doer shellfish digging') The woman is digging up shellfish
derawey	to go around: *wi baka deraweydaryey key Wayer peke* they went around that way, on the Wayer side
dig	to open several or many things
digem	to walk: *kay nagme pamasem* I'll walk to the shops
digraret	to start (something): *ka papek digrarti* I've started (making) a mat
dígwat	to fish for several or many fish (as in dragging to shore or hauling up several or many fish)
dígwatmu(r)	to fish for one or two fish (by pulling onto shore): *ka geka dabor dígwatmuda* I caught a mackerel there
diker	to shoot one or two things with an arrow (*Also means* to complain): *e bózer dikerda sariku* he speared a small eel with his arrow
dim	to close several or many things
dími	to close one or two things
díski	to open one or two things
ditimed	to start making a noise: *lamarira bumer i ditimdi* the ghost's sound travelled away (from him)
ditpur	to spout water (in the way that whales or dugongs do); (of a male) to piss; blow: *abi pesuru dámrikda, dámrikda, dámrikda, e espi ditpulu; abra espi penoko demgedi Dómge* they beat him with a dry palm leaf, they beat and beat him, he sprayed his piss; his piss is lying over there at Dom
eko	to stand up (for several or many people or things)

ekwey	to stand up or stop (for one or two people or things)
emri	to sit down or stay
ep	to float (for one or two people, things) (*Also means* to be carrying one or two things)
eper	to fly off (for birds)
etir	to get up, rise up, climb onto something (for many people)
etiri(k)	to wade through water in search of food: *kíkem meskep, wi obatirki larem* in the afternoon, low tide, they went walking through the water for food; *e etirida Wayerem* she set off towards Wayer for food; *etirik* dodge or duck
ew	to wade through water: *oba obeli able newr* they would go off, wading through the water, those girls
éwsmer	to come out (for one or two things or people)
éydi	to lie down
éyrsi	to get moored: *netat nar no kerkar éyrsida norge* the one boat just recently got moored on the reef; *mitkar nar no kerkar báyrsiri norge* many boats just recently got moored on the reef
igaweyr	(of birds) to circle around; scrape: *ege toli tabaperdarer, érerkem igawelare, pe tolira aw tonar ike náde le otaba máykem yabim...* then the sandpipers would fly off, circling with squawks, as is the habit of sandpipers when people come close to them
ik	to expel, squirt
ikase(redi)	is or are going along (for one or two people)
kab eri	to dance *wi kab barili Umarge* they're dancing at Umar; *ka kab narye* I'll be dancing
korider emri	to run

nakasir — are going along (for several or many people)

nar ereb — to row

og — to climb (up)

os — to come out (several or many things or people)

segur etug — to play

tabakyamu, taba, tabakamu — to come (for one or two people or things)

tabakyaw, taba — to come (for several or many people or things)

17. State

daw — is or are (staying) (for one, two or several people)

díkayr — to wait

dike(redi) — is or are (for one, two or several things that you are naming)

dikri — is stuck together (*Also means* to throw several or many things)

dikwey(redi) — is or are standing up (for one or two things); rise up (of sound); burning (of light): *able kérkerge, ese wa dásmerawem aw sager wámer, máyso mir i wáygarer Límoropge, Arpedge bumer wadikwey* nowadays, if you go (when) the south-east (wind) is blowing, the surf's noise can be heard at Límorop, the sound (of the surf) will be rising at Arped

dírsi(redi) — is or are moored (for one or two boats) *able nar dírsiredi norge* the boat's moored on the reef

egimur — is or are perched (for one, two, several animals)

emredi — are seated (for several or many people) *wa demre dáwa* stay seated (said to a few people); *wa namre dawa* stay seated (said to many people)

eskedi — is or are sticking up (for one or two or several things)

etkomaret — to dry *gergeride natkomareta* the sun dried them

ewe(redi)	is or are standing (for one, two, several things such as houses)
ig	to roast several or many things; undress: *ma mara wali igi* take off your clothes; *kebi maykmayk e emrida náde ge Warib urder tabara lar íglare* she sat closer to where the Warib (type of garfish) people were roasting their fish
ike(redi)	is or are (for one or two things)
ikwey(redi)	is or are standing (for people): *ma nakwey dáwa* stay standing; *wa dikwey dawam* you two stay standing; *wa dikwey, dikweydi darwem* you three stay standing; *wa ikwe, nakwe dáwa* you lot stay standing
imi(redi)	is or are seated (for one or two people) *ma nami dáwa* stay seated (said to one person); *wa dimi dáwam* stay seated (said to two people)
ípe(redi)	is or are lying (for one, two or several people)
namer (werteda)	are seated (for many people)
náysir (werteda)	are (for many things that are in a lying position)
nagri (werteda)	are (for many things that you are naming)
ner ezi	to pause, take a breather

18. Vocalisation and thought

(mir) agar	to speak, make noise (when it's a soft sound): *kara kem mir igali* my stomach is rumbling; *ter máyso mir igali* the surf is crashing; *waba mir ki dapigemeley, kebikebi wapum wapum obay; ableglam pa Erubge mir nagareda kebi wapum wapum* we'll change your language, it'll become slightly slower; and so that is why (they) speak

	slightly slower on Darnley Island; *ki laglag keriba mir adem dipigemertare, ki nole laglag dagalare mokakalam pe Mabyoge nagareda* we want to change our language, we don't like speaking like they speak on Mabyog Island
bar ditug	to correct or straighten
bérwer	to learn
dábger	to call out (to someone); name: *able kebi lar pe mimi dábgereda tup* that small fish which we call sardine
dámos	to ask someone: *ma abi dámsi* you asked him
detager	to tell (someone)
detawt	to say, tell (a story), talk to, talk about
dikepwar	to think
erer ekri	to cry out, yell, sing out
érwer	to teach
etaperet	to scold, growl (*Also means* to mix): *ka werem etaperti abi adud mirlam* I told the child off for his bad language; *ka mitkar le natapertare* I growled at them
etomer	to show one or two things: *kari able zyáwali natomer* show me the book; *karim able zyáwali tetomer* show the book to me
ítmer	to ask (someone)
kok dígwat	to tease: *wader mena sasmir demelare a yabi kok darawgwatlare* some were still chatting and teasing the two
mut igar	to growl, speak loudly and unpleasantly, make noise (when it's a hard sound): *e mut igali* he's growling
neg agar	to laugh
op dipit	to meet (someone)
peym éydi	to dream
segur etug	to play
umerkak	to not know
wed dikri	to sing

19. Bodily functions

asor	to hear, listen to
batay	to grow up
ekyam	to awaken
ereg	to eat meat
ero	to eat
espi tikyar	to urinate, take a piss
ezi	to breathe
i ezo	to cry
iri	to drink
iruser	to bite
lag	to smell; to taste; to desire
lag dasur	to smell
út eydi	to go to sleep

20. Impact and violence

dámrik	to beat, flog
digem	to squeeze (when making coconut milk): *ka u digemli* I'm squeezing the coconut
disirik	to light (a fire or lamp)
ditkir	to peel, scrape or skin: *ka kumala (gegur) ditkiri* I peeled the sweet potato
dezoger	to pierce right through body: *...korider temri, éwpamar ge ekwey able kusbáger ikalu abra kem dizogri, Géygi éwdi iki* ...she ran, jumped over him then she pierced his stomach with a spear (and) so Geygi spewed out
ekesmu	to split: *ni zor éwdi ekesmulu* thus the pumice stone with water split; *able nar éypuge ekesmuda* the boat split in half
erap	to break several or many things (*Also means* to buy several or many things)
erapey	to break one or two things (*Also means* to buy one or two things)
esak	to cut up
éwmi	to die; to ache: *kara teter éwmili* my foot's aching

ikris	to scratch or scrape (a coconut)
ipit	to hit; to kill
isim	to cut up several or many things or cut into many pieces
ismi	to cut in one or two movements (i.e. slice one piece or two pieces)

21. Holding and transfer

akay, ikay	to make (for one, two people or things): *e akayda kebile báyda* it's made itself little; *e akayda erar báyda* he changed into an erar fish; *kabayde abi ikayda ekesmuda* the banana tree has made it (the pipe) split
arot	to put inside several or many things
asesered	to take care of
aw	to put inside one or two things
ays	to take several or many things (*Also means* to float)
áyswer	to give several or many things; to bring up several or many children
ázig	to put several or many things inside something
ázirik	to put one or two things inside something; to lead the dance or dances: *mitkar taym, ka kab weyazigli* I often used to lead the dances; *ka kab azgi, azgi mena kara karopkarop kab ázirikta* I led many many dances until I led my native flute dance
batawered	to throw something
demay	to chase around: *(wi) bakir dikrilare, able lar daramaylare key éypem* they threw rocks, chasing those fish into the middle
desaw	to rub something on, paint
detar	to turn several or many things around: *ma able lu detarare* turn all those things around

detawerik, detawrik	to turn one or two things or people around
detkopar	to decorate
dewer	to build a shelter
dikayr	to leave something or someone
dikayret	to leave one or two things or people: *ka peka wabi dikayrti* I'm leaving you now
dikemur	to pull out one or two things: *bakyamulu, suni meta tidikemulu, suni meta tidikemulu, disiriklu* she went and pulled out a green ant's house, pulled out a green ant's house and lit it
dikew	to pull off or pull away: *ege éwdi kerbi daraysumdarda: wa kara lar dikayrtare, wa pe náluglam abra poni dipomdeda; ki éwdi tag dikewda* so he then told us off: leave my fish alone, why do you feel its eyes; so we thus pulled (our) hands away
dikri	to throw several or many things (*Also means* is stuck together)
dipigemer	to change or turn over one or two things (such as turtles) by one or two people; to change (for one or two people or things)
dipigemeret	to change or turn over one or two things by several or many people
dirsir	to prepare, fix, make
ekirik	to carry across one or both shoulders: *ege éwdi tabara basor kéwbu erep, ekirki, kéwbu bakyamulu* she thus picked up her coconut shells, loaded them onto her shoulders, then went off
emarik	to send one or two things or people
ep	to be carrying one or two things (*Also means* to float)
epayt	to pour several or many things
epaytered	to pour one or two things

epit	to hatch; blossom, bloom: *e umerkak wepit gergerge, e wepit kige* it can't hatch in the daytime, it hatches at night (talking about turtles)
erpey	to reach a point (for a time or state) (*Also means* to grab one or two things or people): . . . *mena 6 o'clock wáyrpey* . . . until 6 o'clock; *ese utide kari wanarpey, ma ge kari natirwa* if I fall asleep, then wake me up
etaker	to pick up several or many things
etaperet	to mix (*Also means* to scold, growl): *ka emetu able lu etaperti* I've mixed them together
etaruk	to pick up one or two things or people
etatko	to fill with liquid
etayu	to punt (a boat): *e uzer irbi, etaywi able wasnar Dawarem* he rowed it, punted the canoe to Dawar
etkor	to pick from a tree several or many flowers or leaves: *e baka able gerer detkori, e ikeri sepge idagi, ege baka digmi* he went (and) picked pandanus leaves , put them down on the ground and then went off walking
etopemer	to pick from a tree one or two flowers or leaves: *e tabakyamuda, kara lusik etopemeda* he came (and) plucked a flower off for me
ewer	to weave: *wi papek éwreda* they're weaving a mat
ídag	to put down several or many things
igared	to take one or two people or go and live with someone: *Dáwgiri, Wáyda a Pitari ekerdare, abi erpeydare a tabadoge igardidere Wayer pitem; gabge wi kikem Déwmerim*

	seksek tonar ikerdare a kéwbu ga abi ipitidare Dáwgiri, Wáyda and Pitari did things, they grabbed her and took her with them to Wayer point; along the way, they first did a bad thing to her and after they killed her
igur	to draw water
ikaw	to take and carry one or two things
ikedi	to put down one or two things
iker	to make (for several or many people or things): *wi gayr le giz bakeri le ko berda* the lot made themselves into people again
ikwar	to give one or two things or bring up one or two people
irit	to sow, plant
íser	to drag up onto shore (like a boat)
ispi	(of a man) to marry (*Also means* to hide)
íter	to sink: *e obakyamu Pomoy metaem, tarpor wáyter tankge niyem* he's gone to Pomoi's house to sink his water container in the tank for water; *ege éwdi tabara basor ítri* and then she thus sunk her coconut shell
iti	to take out several or many things
itkur	to take off coconut husk
etwak	to carve (out of wood) (*Also means* to make thinner): *e baka lu itwaker* he went off carving up trees. . . ; *baka itwaki, deger itwaki* 'he went off (and) carved a dugong
tikaw	to pick up and bring one or two things

22. Location, direction and time

abgerger	yesterday
apek	other side: *apeke* (literally *apek* other side + *ge* on) on the other side
arem	upwards, on top

éypu, eyp	midway, halfway: *éypu koki kérkerge* in the middle of the north-west wind time; *éypuge* halfway, midway
gako, ga	and then, and later, and so after, and also there, so, the one I'm talking about
gared	south
gared sager	south to south-east
ge	then, here, there, so, the one I'm talking about
idim	morning, tomorrow
ínoko	a long way away from this place
i, y	from now (onwards), from then (onwards), away from here, away from there: *e i ikase* there he goes (away from us); *able neys u i narayredi* there are two coconut trees growing (over) there
kérker	point in time or season
kew	downwards
kéwbu	after, last, behind
kéymer	left (as opposed to right) (*Also means* younger sibling)
kíkem	afternoon
kikem	first; before
koki	north-west; the north-west wind; the monsoon season
koki zyay	west
mop	end(point): *mop pe dike* this is the end (often used at the end of a story)
muris	far
múyge	inside, within (literally *muy* inside + *ge* on)
narbit	right (as opposed to left) (*Also means* elder sibling)
náyger	north-east to east; the north-east to east wind
op	the front of something (*Also means* face)
pako, pa	and now, and then (earlier today), and also here, and also there, and so, and also, and later, and after, and the one I'm talking about

páykay	tip
pe	now, here, there, so, the one I'm talking about
pek	side; a separate piece of an object: *wi népey mena Adud Nori erpeyley, able kebi nor irdi adge Dawarlam, koki peke, a ge, yaba wasnar báytri* they drifted until Adud Nor (Bad Reef), the small reef (which) lies on the outer side from Dawar, on the north-west side, and there, their canoe sank
sab	north to north-east; the north to north-east wind
sab koki	north to north-west; the north to north-west wind
ságer	south-east; the south-east wind
tumge	on top
urut	year
war	period of time
yako, ya, y	and later, and after, and from then onwards, and also away from here, and also away from there, and so after, and also after
yáma	not visible to you
zyay	south-west; the south-west wind

23. Interjections

agekar	true!?
aka	used at the beginning of a sentence to attract someone's attention: *aka, ma nalu náli?* hey, what are you?
akame, akasi	to express surprise
aw	y'know? (checking that the person you're talking to is following what you're saying)
baru	okay, all right
karim	probably, maybe, seems like
mayem	welcome!
nole akar	not have one, not be one: *abra koskir nagri?* has he got a wife? *nole akar* he hasn't got one

nole, ne	no, not
waw, wa	yes
way, wey	alas, poor one; dear one (*Also means* to show fear or jitters)

24. Demonstratives and pronouns

abi	him, her, it: *abidoge* at his/her place or with him/her/it; *abim* to/for him/her/it, *abiyalam* from him/her/it, *abitkem* with him/her/it, *abitkak* without him/her/it
able	this, that, this one, that one
ábra	his, her, its
e	he, she, it
ka(ka)	I
kababu	myself, by myself, on my own
kara	my or mine
kari	me, my: *karidoge* at my place or with me; *karim* to/for me; *kariyalam* from me; *karitkem* with me; *karitkak* without me
kerbi	us, our (but not you): *kerbidoge* at our place or with us, *kerbim* for us, *kerbiyalam* from us, *kerbitkem* with us, *kerbitkak* without us
keriba	our (but not including you); ours
ki(ki)	we (but not you)
ma(ma)	you (when talking to just one person)
mabu	yourself, by yourself, on your own: *mabu mabu* (literally yourself yourself) Help yourself (usually said at a feast to encourage people to help themselves to food)
mara	your (when it is just you and no-one else)
mari	you, your: *maridoge* at your place or with you, *marim* to/for you, *mariyalam* from you, *maritkem* with you, *maritkak* without you

merbi	us, our (including you): *merbidoge* at our place or with us, *merbim* for/to us, *merbiyalam* from us, *merbitkem* with us, *merbitkak* without us
meriba	our (including you); ours
mi(mi)	we (including you)
náde	where? when?
náket	how many?
náko	how?
néte	who? (with an intransitive verb)
netide	who? (with a transitive verb)
tababu	himself, herself, itself, themselves, on his own, on her own, on their own
tabara, tabra, taba, tara	his, her, himself, herself: *Lezide tabara imus itwi* Les shaved his own beard (as opposed to shaving someone else's beard)
wa	you (when talking to more than one person)
wába	your (when there is more than one of you); yours
wábi	us, our (including you): *wabidoge* at our place or with us, *wabim* for/to us, *wabiyalam* from us, *wabitkem* with us, *wabitkak* without us
wiyaba, yába	their; theirs
wiyabi, yábi	them, their: *yabidoge* at their place or with them, *yabim* to/for them, *yabiyalam* from them, *yabitkem* with them, *yabitkak* without them
wi, i	they (two, several or many)

Grammatical notes

Meryam is one of those languages that tends to stick things on at the beginning of a word (prefixes) or at the end of a word (suffixes) to give you information about how the people or things are involved in the action, or about when the action is happening and how many people or things are involved. It is called an agglutinating language because these bits of information are just stuck on the beginning or the end of a word. For example, to tell someone to go, you say *bakyamu* 'go!' but to tell someone to come, you just add *ta-* to the beginning of the word saying *tabakyamu* 'come!'. If you want to tell where the person has come from, you can just put *-lam* at the end of the placename and say *Sydneylam* or *Merlam.* On the other hand, if you want to tell where the person is going to, you can put *-em* at the end of the place name and say *Brisbaneem* or *Ugarem.*

In English, we know who is doing what to whom because of where the word appears in the sentence. If you think about English for a moment, you will see what we mean. If someone says to you *Bruce sent Narelle fishing*, it means something quite different to *Narelle sent Bruce fishing.* What makes the difference is the place where the words appear; that is, whether they are before or after the verb. In Meryam, however, words can appear more or less anywhere in the sentence, although the verb typically appears at the end of the sentence and the other words are ordered depending on what is being talked about. For example, if you want to say that Narelle sent Bruce fishing, you can say: *Brusi Narelide emarigda mekikem*, literally, 'Bruce Narelle send fishing-for', or you could say: *Narelide Brusi emarigda mekikem* or even *mekikem Brusi Narelide emarigda.* If you look closely at the example, you will see that the words have suffixes on them: *-ide* tells you who is doing the sending, *-i* tells you who is being sent and *-em* tells you what the person is being sent for.

One of the most interesting features of Meryam, and probably the hardest to learn for foreigners, is the number marking system. As well as having words like *netat* 'one', *neys* 'two', *kepkep* 'several' and *mitkar* 'many', verbs carry information about number. In some cases, there are completely different verbs depending on the number of people or things involved. For example, if you have given one or two things to someone, you would use the verb *ikwar* and say *ka mari able nam ikwari* 'I've given you this turtle' but if you have given the person several or lots of things, you would use the verb *áyswer* and say *ka mari able kemerkemer nam náysweri* 'I've given you all these turtles'. In some cases, the two verbs seem quite similar in form. For example, *etome(r)* is used for showing someone one or two things whereas *etomere(d)* is used for showing several or many things. In some cases, the verb will be more or less the same for all numbers, like in the case of *ipit* 'hit'. However, all verbs must have prefixes and/or suffixes added to give them number information. For example, with a verb like *ero* 'eat', the suffix *-i* shows one person has finished eating, *-iyey*, two people, *-idare*, several people and *-da*, many people. So, if you wanted to say that many people had eaten a turtle, you would say *able legize nam eroda* with *ero + da* to show it was many people. If you wanted to say that one person had eaten more than one thing, you would use the prefix *na-* with different endings. For example, if you had eaten a few mangoes, you could say *ka able wáywi narwidare* with *na+ero+idare* to show that you had eaten several. Other bits of information are added to the verbs such as when it happened and whether it was you, me or someone else involved.

In Meryam, there are two groups of verbs which differ from each other because of their special meaning and the particular prefixes and suffixes they take. The first group typically focuses on the endpoint or goal of the action whereas the other group usually refers to states or events which are just happening. To help you get a feel for this difference, think about actions like catching a fish as opposed to just fishing, going for a sailing trip as opposed to just sailing around, someone actually planting seeds as opposed to the seeds growing or someone about to sit down as opposed to someone who is already seated. The first example in each pair focuses on the endpoint or at least, you could imagine someone being interested in that endpoint whereas for the second example of each pair, the interest is more on what is happening. In Meryam, these two types of verbs belong to different groups. The first type, which could be labelled 'telic verbs', is listed by the form you use when telling someone to do the action: *u ikris* 'scrape a coconut'!, *dikayr* 'leave (it')!, *kab emar* 'dance'!, *tákomer* 'come back'!, *abi irmir* 'follow him'! For the other type, which might be called 'atelic verbs', the verbs have been listed in the forms used when they are happening at the time of speaking.

There is a special style of speaking used in Meryam when you feel sad for the person you are talking to or the person you are talking about. This special style is called *nasnas mir*, literally 'sad talk'. Often people will start talking this way by using the word 'wey,' which means something like 'poor one', 'dear one', or 'alas'. When they use this style, the beginning of verbs change; that is, the sounds *o*, *u* or *w* are used so that words like *dáli* 'is' become *dwáli* , *digem* 'walk' becomes *dogem* and words like *ero* 'eat' and *iri* 'drink or smoke,' both become *oro* . For example, in a story about a young boy called *Géygi* (literally, 'great trevally fish'), a man scoops him out of the water and eats him. Later, when his mother finds him by cutting open the man's stomach, she sends him into the sea to protect him and urges him to defend himself against those who might try to catch him. Then, having told him all this, she walks away and dives into the water. The storyteller says:

abra	*ama*	*detager*	*esemu-lu,*	*baraygi*	*aw*
3SG	mother-*absol.*	say-*past*	finish-*past*	dive-*past*	big

karem-ge;	*abra*	*ama*	*dogem,*	*baka*
deep sea-*loc.*;	3SG	mother-*absol.*	walk(sorry talk)-*past*	go

ke	*baraygi-lu*	*baka*	*Ne-ge*	*pa*	*dwa-li.*
way	dive-*past*	go	Ne-*loc.*	*pres.*	be(sorry talk)-*pres.*

'Having finished speaking, his mother dived into the deep sea; she walked away, that dear one, and dived in there and went to Ne where she now is.'

The storyteller uses the style to show how sad he feels for the mother and maybe to also show how sad the mother must feel at leaving her boy behind. The sorry style gives the speaker the chance to express sympathy for the person.

We hope that this brief introduction and the above wordlist will give you some understanding of Meryam. All that is left for us to say is: *no pe dike* 'That's all!'

References

Wurm, S (ed.) 1977, The Central and Western Areas of the Trans-New Guinea Phylum. The Trans-Fly (Sub-Phylum level) Stock, New Guinea Area Languages and Language Study, vol. 1, Papuan Languages and the New Guinea Linguistic Scene, *Pacific Linguistics* series C, no. 28, Pacific Linguistics, Canberra

16

Wik-Mungkan

BARBARA SAYERS

Wik-Mungkan is the main language spoken at Aurukun on the west coast of Cape York Peninsula. The people now living at Aurukun came together over a number of years from the mid-1920s to the early 1960s. They came from the inland from as far east as Coen and from the south almost as far as Pompuraaw (earlier known as Edward River). Most of these people spoke one of the Wik dialects; the remainder of the people came from the north and spoke unrelated languages.

Various Wik-speaking clans originally occupied most of the abovementioned region. The Wik groups in the immediate vicinity of the developing Aurukun community died out early, as did speakers of the northern group of languages. Aurukun became the gathering point for these dying groups. At the same time it attracted the more vigorous Wik-Mungkan-speaking people from inland along the Archer River. As these people settled at Aurukun their language became the main language of communication. Later arrivals also began to use Wik-Mungkan, possibly through use in the dormitories where the children stayed for education.

Since Wik-Mungkan was spoken by almost everybody, it became the language chosen for the bilingual program which began in the school in 1973. This program went through many stages and was finally dropped in 1988. Wik-Mungkan was re-introduced into the school program in 1994. In addition, the people who hold allegiance to other languages in the Wik group may be offered the opportunity to use their language in some form of modified program in the school system. This is particularly relevant for the Wik-Ngathan group, whose traditional land is along the coast and in the rich wetlands east of Cape Keerweer. These people, who were latecomers to Aurukun, have always been a numerical majority, but their language slipped from daily use by the young people who grew up at Aurukun. With the re-establishment of outstation schools, and changes in education policy, it is possible that these languages could see a revival.

Spelling and pronunciation

The spelling system presented below (and used in the following wordlist) follows the practical one used in the community. Final spelling decisions for the published dictionary from which this work is extracted, and for the published New Testament, were made by the people in the Aurukun Community. The sounds the letters represent in the Wik-Mungkan alphabet are as close to the English sounds for the same letters as possible.

The Wik-Mungkan alphabet consists of the following:

a, aa, ch, e, ee, i, ii, k, l, m, n, ng, nh, ny, o, oo, p, r, t, th, u, uu, w, y, ' (glottal stop)

Wik-Mungkan is unusual among Aboriginal languages in that it signals a distinction between verb tenses by means of a difference in stress, which is a combination of length, pitch and intensity. This distinction is marked on the stressed verb endings (suffixes) by means of a macron (flat accent mark) over the vowel. Another distinction of importance is between stressed and unstressed *ke'*. The stressed form is the negative form 'don't' preceding verbs, and the unstressed form is 'about to, begin to', which also occurs preceding verbs. Along with these distinctions is reliance on patterns of rhythm and stress to distinguish other features of the grammar.

A final non-contrastive vowel (written *a*) may optionally occur on any word, as may the suffix *-an*. These variant forms are part of the rhythm pattern which is basically a stressed-unstressed sequence. The unstressed vowel between certain sequences of consonants can be elided (left out), leaving clusters of consonants which do not otherwise occur. Readers prefer to have this elided vowel written *(a)*, since it assists in reading.

WIK-MUNGKAN WORDLIST

Selected and adapted from Dictionary and Source Book of the Wik-Mungkan Language, *Christine Kilham, Mabel Pamulkan, Jennifer Pootchemunka, and Topsy Wolmby*

WORDLIST CATEGORIES

1. Body parts and products
2. Kin relationships
3. Human classification
4. Language, mythology and ceremony
5. Human artefacts
6. Food, cooking and fire
7. Topography
8. Elements
9. Mammals
10. Reptiles
11. Birds
12. Aquatic life
13. Insects and spiders
14. Plants
15. Physical qualities
16. Non-physical qualities
17. Motion
18. State
19. Bodily functions
20. Impact and violence
21. Holding and transfer
22. Location, direction and time
23. Demonstratives and pronouns
24. Interrogatives
25. Interjections

1. Body parts and products

chaapara, wewm	blood
engka thaa'	rib area
irp	scars, tribal markings
kaa'uuyan	nostril
kaa', wuup	nose
kaanch	bone
kemp, yenkan	body; flesh
kompan, marp	scar
kongam	kidneys
koonh	teeth
kuchek, kootra, koyk	head
kuman, pemar, yeengan	thigh, leg
kun, kaka	faeces
kunch, wachamiint	penis
kuutan, ngoompang	umbilical cord; navel
kuuy, kuuy chaapar	vein
ma'kongk, ma'ochangan, ma'pungk	wrist
ma'mal	right hand
ma'piir, ma'ek	fingernail

ma'puk pi'an	thumb
ma'punth	arm
ma'thak	left-handed
ma'yuungk, ma'uliy	elbow
man	neck
man awal, man poonchal	voice
man ngaat, wukal ngaat	throat
mee'	eye
mun kaanch	tailbone
munth	rib
ngaap momp, pu'momp	uterus
ngangk	heart (centre of being)
ngangk, ngangk nyep	soul
ngul ngangk, uungk	forehead
nhok	groin
ocham, kump, cheelal	urine
paap, thuut, thuut nguw	breast, breast milk
pe'an	skin
pikpungk, nintan	back
pu', ngaap	vagina
pungk	knee
punt thuth	testicles
tha'puk	toe
thaa'	mouth
thaa'pench	beard
thangkar ip	semen
thip, iitun	stomach
um ik	chest
waanh, wongkanch	liver
wal	jaw, cheeks
yangan, angkalam	hair (on head)
yangk, yooman	lower leg
yeep, thip	belly
yi'pench	pubic hair
yuwan	armpit, underarm

2. Kin relationships

kaal	mother's younger brother
kaal-aamp	(prospective) father-in-law
kaath	mother (term of address)
kaath many, kaath ikampungan	mother's younger sister
kaath-kunch	mother (term of reference)
kemiyang	mother's daughter's child
kemwayyow	mother's mother
kuunch	siblings; father's brother's children; mother's sister's children
kuuth	man's child to younger sister's child; woman's child to younger brother's child
kuuth-muuy	marriageable relationship (cross cousins)
muk,	mother's elder brother
mukayng	father's or mother's younger sister's child
mukwayyow, kaath pi'an	mother's elder sister
muuy	man's child to older sister's child; woman's child to older brother's child
namp-piip	to any boy; takes totem ('big name') from father
namp-piny	to any girl; takes totem ('big name') from father's sister
ngalamp	share same totem ('big name')
ngeychiyang	father's daughter's child; mother's son's child
ngeychwayyow	father's mother
ngeychwuut	mother's father
nhengk, ngeyantang	father's child; father's older brother's child; mother's older brother's child
otham	father's older sister's child; mother's younger brother's child; mother's older sister's child
pam thum, pam muuy	husband (term of address)
pam-kunch	husband (term of reference)
piip	father (term of address)
piip many	father's younger brother
piip-kunch	father (term of reference)
piip-many	father's younger brother
piny	father's elder brother
piny, piny many	father's younger sister

piny, piny-wanchinth	father's elder sister
piny-kench	(prospective) mother-in-law
pinyayng	father's younger brother's child; mother's younger brother's child
puuliyang	father's son's child
puulwuut	father's father
thuwa	mother's child; mother's older sister's child
wanch thum	wife (term of address)
wanch-kunch	wife (term of reference)

3. Human classification

aymiy	bereaved mother of child
iimpanang, iithun	pregnant woman
kaa'ngeecham	firstborn
kaa'pach	white person
koman many	adolescent girl (mid-teen)
ngechwiy	man, before initiation
nooyan	doctor, traditional healer
pam	man
pam ma'wanchiyang	married man
pam ngotan	man, Aboriginal
pam pi'an	boss
pam pikiy	married woman
pam uchan	initiated man
puk	child
puk koman	girl, at puberty
puk ngechwiy many	boy, before puberty
puk wanch	girl
puk wuut	boy
puk, puk manya	baby, child
uchanam	initiation, first ceremony
wanch manth-thayan	woman, old (with authority)
wanch many	girl, baby girl
wanch ngotan	woman, Aboriginal
wanch, yangkapulan	woman
winchanam	initiation, second ceremony
wukal ongk, ma'thum ke'anang, angkalam	widow; widower
wuut	male
wuut kath	mature or old man

wuut mangk, wuut eempal	ancestor; very old man
wuut manth-thayan	elder of tribe
wuut, pam wuut	old man

4. Language, mythology and ceremony

aak koy	sacred place where initiations take place
aak ngench	sacred/taboo place due to a death there
aak puul	tribal country
apalech, puch, sara, wanam, winchanam	ceremony groups (major clans)
aw, aak puulway	totem place, sacred site, story place
awalang thee'	underarm perspiration, to rub on person, to protect from spirits on first encounter
chawaa! chawal! chawor!	curse you!
iinch, woolal	traditional dance to bring out young men after initition
kaa'kuchantan	ceremony to send spirit of deceased to resting place
kee'an, puungkan	dance
konchan	curse, to curse someone
kuutan	birth ceremony
ma'kuuy	murder by sorcery
ma'wop, ma'think, ma'mangk	sorcerer
mal ngep	tribe, clan, group
malp kee'an	any traditional dance/corroboree
man-monkan thenchan, mee'thenchan	deceive, betray, cheat
namp	name
ngeen-wiy	sacred objects (carved images)
ngench-thayan	sacred site
orangama	final death ceremony
pam ma'wop	sorcerer
pew nguchan kee'antan	mourning dance
pip morp	white ochre
puriy-puriy	sorcery
puthangk thee'	payback
thaapich	substitute name used after person with same or similar name has died
thum munth	cremation site
thuunth-thuunthan	angry/curse dance

waal-waal	substitute name for person who is away or dead
waykiyathan	to decorate oneself
wik	language
wik thayan	law; strong words
wu'	red ochre
yuwan poonchal	underarm perspiration

5. Human artefacts

thum pup, thum pupiy	firestick
almp	yam digging stick
kechan	wooden fighting or digging stick (general term)
kechan wuyngut	killing stick
kek achakum	small spear, used for sorcery
kek	spear (general term)
kempen	string bag (general term)
kuchek kuuy	headband
kuchek olk	headdress (made from white cockatoo feathers)
kuchek thankan	coil for carrying things on head
kuuy	string
kuuy makar	fishing line, gut
mangk kuuy	string belt
mant	kangaroo or wallaby jaw (with teeth) used as tool for spear making
muypak	bullroarer
nguchaman	resin, for woomeras, etc.
nhengk peempan	knife
pemar, pil	paddle for canoe
pengkar	stretcher for dead body
pu'an	shield
punth kuuy	man's string armband
puulway	totem
thayan kunttow	stone axe
thul, kunhan	woomera
winch	boomerang
wom	beeswax, used in making woomeras, firesticks, umbilical-cord-necklaces and ceremonial bands
yi'waath	traditional bush skirt
yuk kookal	string bag for carrying babies
yuk maak	message stick
yuk pil took (thaampanam)	walking stick

6. Food, cooking and fire

thum	fire
thum man winch wunpan	to set fire of crossed sticks
thum yoompan	firestick used to light another fire
thum nganth	firelight
may kiingkan	to cook food
pi'ang kaampan	to cook in antbed ground oven
penchan	to cook by boiling
may kiingkanam	cooked food
may enchan	raw food, ripe fruit
kurkang ngaakan	to cook in ashes
may	edible plant food (general or classifying term)
minh	edible animal food (general or classifying term)
minh nga'	edible fish (general or classifying term)
minh panch	edible birds (general or classifying term)

7. Topography

aak	ground, place; tradition, law
kikkiy	creek
kurk	dust
ngak kurk	muddy water
ngak paamp, uthuk,weenam	swamp
pintal	plain
pip	mud
thomp	beach
thunp	star
wo'uw, punth	river
yoyk	hill

8. Elements

aak kepamiy	moonlight
aak ngutang	night
kaa'ngench	westerly wind (literally 'whistle wind')
kaap	wet season (well-established)
karkan	hot
kayaman, aak kayaman	dry weather, dry season
kinch	sun, daytime

kinch chaaparang, yeep chaaparang	sunset
ku'mulam	tide coming in
kuchar, anar	really cold
kurk	dust
ngaa'am chintan (thant)	to become dark
ngaay	lightning
ngak ngunch	black rain clouds
ngak peeyan	thunder
ngak theth	dew
ngak ukan	rain
waampar	whirlwind
wuthuk, yuk pach	Milky Way
yuw	clouds

9. Mammals

kal	rat (general term)
kek wayang, kek uuyang	echidna
ku'ngekanam	dingo
ku'waak	domestic cat; native cat
ku', thoonth, iwal	dog
kulan, kaanchal	tree possum
minh kut, minh monk	bandicoot
minh kuympayng	big kangaroo
minh pangk, nhengk thutampak	wallaby
minh pukowanh, minh kanmul	cuscus
minh wuk, kaany-kaany minh mal, minh mukampang	flying fox varieties
wooyan	honey glider

10. Reptiles

koch	lizard
koch ngaa'	gecko
minh thech, nhengk yit	big goanna, with brown and yellow spots
minh wel	blue-tongue lizard
ooyngorpan	carpet snake
pikkuw, morrong	crocodile
ponchath, nhengk kaal'-we'ara,	frilled lizard
puparang	small goanna
that	green frog
thuuk	snake (general term)

thuuk thaypan	taipan
thuuk manch	death adder
thuuk mee'kulan, thuuk paay, thuuk meel	yellow tree snake

11. Birds

achamp	emu
chicharakang, chicherak	Willie wagtail
chokalang, lo'alang	scrubfowl
kaa'konkan	kingfisher (all except the laughing kookaburra, the blue-winged kookaburra and the azure kingfisher)
kang-kang	white-bodied sea-eagle
may-umpiy-maakan, may-kon-kooth-maakan	lotus bird or comb-crested jacana
minh (kaa') kayyuw	eastern curlew (large)
minh ko'an	pied or magpie goose
minh kor'	brolga
minh kuunth	Australian bush turkey
minh mont	jabiru
minh moot, minh man olathiy	Australian pelican
minh munkiyang	Torres Strait pigeon
minh muw	sulphur-crested cockatoo
minh ngoochiyang	bowerbird
minh nhomp, thepalang *(archaic term)*	wedge-tailed eagle
minh parp	black or fork-tailed, square-tailed or whistling kite
minh paypantang	black (straw-necked) ibis
minh thalampang, minh ngekthalampang	frogmouth
minh themp	duck (pacific black duck, but used as general term by children)
minh winy-winy	blue-faced honeyeater (locally called 'morning bird' or 'banana bird')
nguk	owls (all)
panch	bird (general term)
parp wuut	large hawk
tal-tal, kothampang	plover
thaa'pathalang	little pied and little black cormorant
tiin-tiin	peewee or mudlark
waath	crow

12. Aquatic life

kenh	freshwater crocodile
minh ka'anth	blue catfish
minh kalich	northern snub-nosed garfish
minh kek-kalan	freshwater stingray
minh kiikalkaath/minh keekalkeeth	sawfish (locally called 'swordfish')
minh kont	small freshwater prawns
minh kowan	barracuda
minh kuchan-kalan	large queenfish
minh kunmal, minh ochangan	round mudshell from mangroves
minh kurrow	salmon
minh kuuymungk	bream
minh miintim, minh punchiy	sea turtle
minh nungumpan, minh angkarathan	rock cod, includes estuary rock cod and gold spot cod
minh polam-wunth, minh ma'wunth	crayfish
minh punchiy, nhengk tung-tung	long-necked tortoise (locally called 'swamp turtle')
minh puuy	mud crab, mangrove crab
minh thathiy, minh miintin	seawater turtle
minh thungkan, minh nhaaliy	sand mullet
minh ur'-ur'	grunter, includes spotted javelin and small spotted javelin
minh waaram	dugong
minh walk	stingray
minh walkalan	big bonefish (milkfish)
minh war	oyster
minh wechan, minh wuungkam	barramundi, large juvenile up to small adult (locally known as 'nightfish')
minh weep-weenth	sleepy fish, includes bar-tailed flathead and red spotted flathead
otamat	porpoise
pikkuw	saltwater crocodile
remat	periwinkles
thapangumpan, thapumpan	shark (black whaler, graceful, hammerhead and tiger)
yaraman, yaraman ngakangan wookaman	seahorse
yulamul	large bluish jellyfish

13. Insects and spiders

iny	sandfly
konkoniyang	butterfly
ma'punth ongk	dragonfly
me'	mosquito
minh puuchamp	caterpillar (non-stinging, can be eaten)
moolan	ant
ngaat	spider
nyeeny	fly
panth-panth	maggot
pongkok	grasshopper
puuny	hornet; march fly
thal ma'puuy	scorpion
thal, thal ma'-uuy, thunch	centipede
thaw	native bee
thukkay	fleas, lice
wath	green ant

14. Plants

kangk	leaves, bush (general term)
may kooth	waterlily (general term)
pach, pach thupan	flower (general term)
wak	grass (general term)
wak wuupal	soft swamp grass (used to make baskets/bags called *kempan*)
wak yaath	long grass (used to make widows' mourning necklaces)
wayk	medicine tree root (used to dye pandanus)
yongk	ironwood (used in making spears and woomeras)
yuk chaangk	breadfruit tree
yuk kamp,	bloodwoodtree (used to make bush pipes)
yuk kich	tea-tree, paperbark (general term)
yuk kom	sandpaper fig (used as bush medicine)
yuk koonth	lawyer cane vine (split and used to sew ends of skin bark canoes)
yuk minchak	bloodwood (leaves add flavour in ground oven)

yuk nguchaman	gum tree (turpentine) (used to make dugout canoes)
yuk okanch	cottonwood tree (called 'spear handle tree') (used to make spears and firesticks)
yuk oonan	sandalwood
yuk ponth	messmate (used as timber, firewood, humpies, platform bunks and skinbark canoes)
yuk pooy	small tea-tree (used as medicine, leaves boiled with ashes used to relieve pain of catfish barb wounds)
yuk pukal	bamboo, large
yuk punthiy	banksia (locally called 'bottlebrush tree')
yuk thipan	gum tree (eucalyptus)
yuk upan	milky mangrove (called 'river poison tree') (used as poison on weapons)
yuk uungkath	kapok (wood used for making canoes and kapok in seed pods used for making pillows)
yuk wayk	medicine bush (root gives a yellow dye, turns red with addition of *yuk waath*)
yuk wenchapathan	cottontree, variety ('wool' used to stuff pillows)
yuk, yuunch	wood, tree, stick; general term for 'thing'

15. Physical qualities

thonam	one
kucham	two
ko'alam	three; few
thaa'wantanam	very many
ma'thonam	once
ma'kucham	twice
ma'yotam	lots of times
ngotan	black
pach	white; clean
wewm	red; blood
manya	small
pi'an	big

ongk	long
we'ara	wide
kath	rotten
karkan	hot
nyiingkanam	new
lokath, ngak lokath	brackish

16. Non-physical qualities

min	good
waya	bad
ma'kunch	clever
kon thaa'way	ignorant, having little understanding
ngangk min (wunan), ngangkam nyiin	happy
winyang mo'an	frightened
man um enyanam wunan	peaceful
maal	quiet, tame
kootra nyaa'ngul-nyaa'(iiyan/wunan)	ashamed
yangk (mo'an/peeyan)	greedy
ma'-kaa'-way	mean
ngangk kul wampan, man kul wampan	angry
kulliy	savage (dog)
kaa'-thayan	cheeky, bold
wal-thayan	serious, doesn't joke
mee'-wunan	jealous
ngench, ngench-thayan	forbidden, taboo, sacred
kul-min	obedient

17. Motion

iiyan, wenyan	to walk, go at ordinary speed
kamp wakan	to chase fast
kee'an	to fall
kee'an	to play
malp kee'an	to dance
mo'an	to run, go at fast speed (as a plane, boat, car etc.)
monkan wakan	to follow
ngoonchan, pek ngoonchan	to enter, go in
nyiinan	to sit
palam wampan	to return
pir kalan	to slip

tha'pemp weechan	to track
thang-thang iiyan	to limp
ukan	to descend
wampan	to come
weentan	to turn around

18. State

Most 'states of being' are made up of body-part words and a verb such as 'sit', 'stand', 'lie' or 'run'. Frequently used body parts include ngangk *'heart', 'centre of being',* ma' *'hand',* man *'throat' (mostly negative emotions) and* mee' *'eye'.*

kul karkan ikan	to be angry
kulliy weeman, man kul wampan	to become vicious
ma'mich wakan	to feel defeated in fight, or overcome with sickness, etc.
mee'chal ikan, kon enchiy nyiinan	to be alert
mee'ikan	to be amazed
ngangk akangam thanan	to feel guilty
ngangk enchan	to feel sad
ngangk maman	to feel compassion
ngangk mungkan	to be consumed with passion
ngangk peeyan	to feel strong emotion
ngangk thee'an	to put one's trust in
ngangkam nyiinan	to be glad, happy
nyiinan	to sit; to stop; to be
way-wayam iiyan	to behave angrily

19. Bodily functions

thathan	to see
mee'yenchang thathan	to stare
mee'wuthanaman	to close eyes; to pray
mee'yumpan	to wink
ngeeyana	to hear; to listen
lokang thu'an	to swallow whole or quickly
mungkana	to eat; to drink; to smoke
man apamp thee'an	to burp, belch
thip kur thawan	(of stomach) to rumble
nunk thawan	to cough
ocham thee'an	to urinate
kun nyiinan, kaka nyiinan	to defecate
kiimp enchan	to sweat

20. Impact and violence

ikathan	to split open, to chop
kaa'-wiinthan	to avenge wrong
kaampan	to bury
maakan	to crush, run over, tread on
manchathan	to crush, smash up, mash, flatten
mulathan; puparathan	to kill
ngoonchathan; thenchathan	to put inside; to hide
pungan	to shoot
tha'an	to push
thalokang umpan	to split in half
thanpan	to kick
thu'an	to stab
we'an	to dig up or out (plant food, dye, etc.)
winyathan	to scare, frighten

21. Holding and transfer

kaa'pathan, namp wichan	to tease, look for trouble
maman	to hold
kalan	to carry
chintan	to spear
piikan, thepan	to hit
awalang thee'an	to rub with underarm sweat
wunpan	to put
pachathan	to clean
kon aathan	to remind
winyathan	to frighten
thapathan; tha'athan	to detach, take off, peel fruit, scale fish, pluck feathers
ma'kee'wunpan	to be or feel protective of someone
ma'weechan	to blame or accuse
man aathan	to tease
ma'pithan	to suspect or distrust
aak ngeeyan	to obey; to believe
man ngeeyan	to disobey; to disbelieve
ngangk pathan	to hate someone
uthathan	to put out, extinguish
thaa'aathan	to teach

22. Location, direction and time

aakanak	up to there; up to that time
an	that, there
an-aniyangan	at the same time
anman, anpalan	from there, from then; for that reason
iikanank	up to here; up to this time
in	this, here
inman, in-inman	right here, right now; this same one
inpalan	from here, from this time; for this reason
kaap	year, wet season
kaaw	east
kan	right now (completed)
kan-ngul	already; about to
kep	month, moon
kungk	north
kuuw	west
nanan	that (mid-distance)
ngaa'thon-thon	another day
ngaa'tham	tomorrow
ngul	later on, and then
peetanan	yesterday
yiip	south

23. Demonstratives and pronouns

anan	that (remote)
anangan	those (remote)
inan	this (nearest)
inangan	these (nearest)
ngal	we (I and you, singular)
ngamp	we (I and you, plural)
ngan	we (I and other/others — not you)
ngatharam	mine
ngay	I
niiy	you (plural)
niiyantam	yours (plural)
nil	he/she/it
nint	you (singular)
nip	you (dual)

niparam	yours (dual)
nungantam	his/hers/its
nungkaram	yours (singular)
pul	they (dual)
pulantam	theirs(dual)
than	they (plural)
thanttam	theirs (plural)

24. Interrogatives

aak-ngeen	what time
ma'ngeen-ngeen	how many times
ngeen	what
ngeenak; wantak	what for
ngeenam	what from (nearest equivalent to 'why')
ngeenang	what with; what in
wantin	where (outside)
wantinak	towards what
wanting	where (inside)
wantinpal	from what, from where
wee'	who (singular subject)
wee'-wee'	who (plural subject)
wee'-wee'ang	who (ergative plural)
wee'-wee'antam	whose (plural)
wee'ang	who (ergative singular)
wee'antam	whose (singular)
wee'antang	with whom (singular)
wee'wee'antang	with whom (plural)

25. Interjections

aayang	hey you
appow	goodbye (general farewell)
apu'apiy	whoops, I made a mistake
chawaa; chawor; chawal	curse you
chey	go away (usually said to dogs)
e'e'; yaa	yes (in agreement)
ee'a	yes (affirmative response)
ke'a	don't, won't
paanthanow	goodbye ('camp well')
thup thul ey!	You are a good hunter!
ya'a	no (response or denial)
yakkay; yakkey, yakarey, yakakaathey	help! ouch!

Words and word groups

Words may occur singly or in groups of two or three as compound words. When words are compounded, the constituent words may have different (or extended) meanings to their meanings in isolation. Unless these compounds are read as a unit, the meaning of the individual words in that context may not make sense.

Compounds with rising pitch are not hyphenated, for example, *puk kaa'thonam* (literally 'child nose one'), 'only child', while compounds with falling pitch are hyphenated, for example, *aak-ngeeyan* (literally 'place hear') 'law-abiding (person or spirit)'. The latter example contrasts with the unhyphenated form *aak ngeeyan* (also literally 'place hear') 'to be born'.

Reduplicated forms are also hyphenated. In single-syllable words the whole word is reduplicated, as in *law-law* 'show-off, larrikin', and in longer words only the first syllable is reduplicated, as in *kach-kachar* 'rough surface'.

Terms for parts of the body may be used in both literal and extended ways. Many emotional states are expressed by the use of words for body parts and functions:

- Many negative expressions include the body part *man* 'throat', such as *man-ngeeyan* (literally 'throat(with)- hear') 'disbelieve/ disobey', and *man-aathan* (literally 'throat(with)- offer') 'tease'.
- The word *ngangk* 'centre of being (heart)' occurs in a wide variety of expressions such as *ngangk thayanathan* (literally 'heart-strong to make') 'to make someone brave', *ngangk-mungkan* (literally 'heart-eat') '(consumed with) passion', and *ngangk way wunan* (literally 'heart bad lies') 'mourn'.
- The word for 'ear' (*kon*) is used in expressions related to perception, alertness and memory such as *kon-aathan* (literally 'ear-offer') 'remind', *kon-ngath* (literally 'ear-shut') 'forget' and *kon-thayan* (literally 'ear-firm/hard') 'attentive'.

It is very difficult to separate expressions such as these into traditional categories such as noun, adjective, adverb and verb. There are a some simple descriptive words such as *pi'an* 'big', *manya* 'small', *ongk* 'long', *olmp* 'thin', *we'ar* 'wide', etc. There are also a few words which indicate how something is done, such as *itingam* 'slowly, carefully', *ya'angam* 'to no avail', *erkam* 'quickly'. However, by far the most descriptive or attributive expressions are compounds, largely made up of body parts and verbs.

Grammatical notes

The major word classes are nouns, pronouns, demonstratives and verbs. All of these can take endings which modify their meaning.

Nouns are basically singular. Dual (two) and plural (more than two) number are not shown on the nouns but by demonstratives and by endings on the verbs which match the subject of the sentence in person and number. Nouns have endings which show the possessive and other cases. Cases indicate things such as the doer of an action, the instrument with which something is done, the time, the location, and the source or cause of something. Demonstratives (for example, English 'this' and 'that') stand with nouns and have the same case endings in Wik-Mungkan. Pronouns (for example, English 'I', 'you' and 'they') stand instead of nouns and have case endings, but the case endings on pronouns work differently to those on nouns and demonstratives. Nouns and demonstratives have endings on the words which show who is the doer of an action while the noun or demonstrative showing who or what the action is done to has no ending. Pronouns work the opposite way. The pronoun standing for the doer has no ending, while the pronoun showing to whom or to what the action is done has an ending. In Wik-Mungkan, the actual endings for nouns and pronouns are the same. Thus a noun which is the actor takes the ending *-ang*, while it is a pronoun which is the recipient of an action that takes *-ang*.

More pronoun and demonstrative distinctions are made in Wik-Mungkan than in English. In the first person, for more than one individual ('we'), Wik-Mungkan makes a distinction as to whether the person spoken to is included in the 'we' or not. These forms are known as 'inclusive' when the person spoken to is included and 'exclusive' when the person spoken to is not included. The other distinction not made in English is the one called 'dual' which refers to two people.

Verbs in Wik-Mungkan agree in person and number with the subject. Also shown by the verb are tense/mood/aspect, which function as a single system. The terms 'accomplished', 'habitual/customary', 'projected' and 'hypothetical' are used in Wik-Mungkan to describe the different verb aspects. The term 'hypothetical' as used here has the restricted meaning of something unaccomplished, past or present. The Wik-Mungkan people do not normally put forward ideas only for the sake of discussion, but they readily use the hypothetical (unaccomplished) form when addressing a particular task or event. In the wordlist, the verb stem is followed by the suffix *-an*, indicating the habitual/customary aspect (previously present tense). This is the form the Wik-Mungkan speakers prefer to use when referring to verbs. The traditional infinitive form is used in the English gloss.

Temporal words indicate time, but in Wik-Mungkan these specifications are much less exact than in English. For example, *peetan* can mean 'yesterday', 'a few days ago' or 'last week'. Locatives indicate spatial orientation, such as *thinth* 'close', *pek* 'down' and *kaaw* 'east'. The four compass points are frequently used in Wik-Mungkan conversation in preference to left and right orientation as in English. For example, *his ear on the north side* and *take the piece of cake on the east side of the plate* are more likely than *his left ear* and *take the piece of cake on the right of the plate.*

There is no separate verb 'to be' in Wik-Mungkan. Instead, the verbs to 'sit', 'stand', 'run', and 'lie' are used. For example, the verb *mo'an* 'to run' is used in 'to be frightened' *winynyang mo'an*, which is literally 'frightened run', but which most probably does not involve any physical running. One of the ways of saying 'to be alert' involves the use of either *wunan* 'lie', *nyiinan* 'sit' or *iiyan* 'go', as in *kon-enchiy wunan, kon-enchiy nyiinan* or *kon-enchiy iiyan*, which literally mean 'ear- alert lie', 'ear-alert sit', or 'ear-alert go'.

Word order in sentences at first appears to be much freer than in English. This is largely due to the case marking system which indicates who did what to whom. There are however, some preferred orders, and shifts away from these orders indicate changes in such things as emphasis, theme and topic. In other words, such changes in word order are not related to the structure of the grammar but to broader issues, as indicated above. Clauses are usually short in spoken Wik-Mungkan, with only one or two references to people or things in each one. When there is need for more information, the verb is usually repeated with the added information, and often some of the old information is given as well.

References

Johnson, Steve 1988, From Kugu to Wik–Mungkanization at Aurukun, unpublished paper, University of New England, Armidale

Kilham, C A 1977, *Thematic Organization in Wik-Mungkan Discourse*, Pacific Linguistics, series B, no. 54, Canberra

Kilham C A 1974, 'Compound words and close knit phrases in Wik-Mungkan', *Papers in Australian Linguistics 7*, Pacific Linguistics, series A, no. 37, pp 45–73, Canberra

Kilham, C A 1987, 'Word Order in Wik-Mungkan', in *A World of Language: papers presented to Professor S.A. Wurm on his 65th birthday*, eds Donald C Laycock and Werner Winter, Pacific Linguistics, series C, no. 100, pp 361–368, Canberra

Kilham, C A, Mabel Pamulkan, Jennifer Pootchemunka, Topsy Wolmby 1986, *Dictionary and Source Book of the Wik-Mungkan Language*, Summer Institute of Linguistics, Darwin

Sayers, Barbara J 1976, *The Sentence in Wik-Mungkan: A Description of Propositional Relationships*, Pacific Linguistics, series B, no. 44, Canberra

Sayers, Barbara J 1982, 'Aboriginal Mathematical Concepts: A Cultural and Linguistic Explanation for Some of the Problems', *Work Papers of SIL-AAB*, series B, vol. 8, pp 183–200. Republished in *The Aboriginal Child at School*, 1983, vol. 11, no. 1, pp 3–18

Sayers, Barbara J 1990, A Matter of Choice: An Appropriate Exhortation from a Wik-Mungkan Perspective, unpublished manuscript

Sayers, Barbara J and Margaret S Bain (in press), 'A Pragmatic Analysis of a failed Cross-Cultural Communication', *Logical Connections*, workshop papers, consultancy seminar, Summer Institute of Linguistics, Dallas, 1989

17

Torres Strait Creole

ANNA SHNUKAL

Torres Strait Creole is spoken as a first or second language by over 18 000 Torres Strait Islanders living in the island communities and coastal cities and towns of Queensland, and by the Cape York Islander and Aboriginal people of Bamaga, Seisia, Umagico (Alau), Injinoo (Cowal Creek) and Mandingu (New Mapoon). It is the newest of the languages in this book, having been creolised from Pacific Pidgin English at the turn of this century by the Torres Strait Islander children of immigrant Pacific Islander, Malay and Filipino marine workers. (A pidgin is a simplified and restricted mixed language with no native speakers; a creole is a full language which is created when a group of children choose a pidgin as their primary language.) Its usefulness as a common language, or lingua franca, has led to its expansion at the expense of the two indigenous Torres Strait languages of the west and east, Kala Lagaw Ya and Meryam Mir, respectively.

Torres Strait Creole has several names: Broken

(from 'Broken English'), Pizin (from 'Pidgin English'), Big Thap ('Big Piece'), Blaikman ('Blackfellow') and Ailan Tok ('Island Talk'). Speakers who know English may 'shift' their creole towards English in formal situations and when speaking to Europeans. Because of its origin, it is not considered a 'proper' language like the two traditional languages and is negatively valued by many older Torres Strait people, who regard it (incorrectly) as a corrupt form of English. But it has become a marker of Torres Strait Islander identity for a majority of young people, almost all of whom are bilingual or trilingual in the creole, English and Kala Lagaw Ya.

The basis of Torres Strait Islander society has always been kinship and each person must observe rules of correct behaviour, including language use, towards relatives.

One important rule is 'name taboo', the avoidance of the name of any person related by marriage. Not to follow this rule is to behave 'shamefully' and cause offence, which can be remedied only by a gift *po kaba da sem* 'to cover the shame'. Not only must Islanders not *kole nem* 'say the name' of an in-law, but they must also avoid using a word which has the same sound. For example, if the name to be avoided is 'Lala', Lala's in-laws must not say the name of the hill on Darnley Island, 'Lalawa'. There are special expressions, *amagel* and *ateboi* in the eastern dialect, *akagel* and *atheboi* in the western dialect and *dadiboi*, used to address young people with taboo names. These mean 'girl with the same name as her grandmother', 'boy with the same name as his grandfather' and 'boy with the same name as his father', respectively.

Some young people use a secret language, called 'baikslaing', based on the creole, with every syllable reduplicated and beginning with 'k': *yu go deya?* 'Are you going there?' becomes *yuku goko dekeyaka?*

Islanders also have an elaborate sign language which may accompany or replace verbal language.

About Torres Strait Creole words

About 85 per cent of the vocabulary was borrowed from English, 14 per cent from the indigenous languages and 1 per cent from Japanese, Malay–Indonesian and Pacific languages. Typically, however, the borrowed words have changed their sounds and meanings. For example, *kese* from 'catch' means 'to catch, take, hold, grasp, learn informally, reach, seize, understand, embrace'. Moreover, English borrowings tend to reflect distinctions found in Islander languages rather than in English. Thus, *ankel* from 'uncle' refers only to father's brother, who was less important in traditional cultural and religious life than the mother's brother, called *awa*. *Oman* from 'woman' refers to a married woman and *gel* from 'girl' to an unmarried woman, irrespective of age; this is the same as the distinction between Meryam Mir *koskir* 'married woman' and *neur* 'unmarried woman'. Expressions like *bus said* 'left' from 'bush side' and *solwata said* 'right' from 'saltwater (that is, the ocean) side' reflect the Islanders' view of their natural and social worlds as composed of oppositions, most fundamentally that between sea and not-sea (land and air).

The unrelated indigenous languages influenced the development of the creole to such an extent that today we can speak of two major dialects, western and eastern, reflecting traditional language differences in vocabulary, pronunciation and grammar. Indigenous language words are most often used to name private body parts, illnesses, kin terms, objects and customs from traditional culture, flora, fauna and places. Often two or even three words have the same dictionary meaning, the choice being governed by a wish to produce a particular stylistic effect, to demonstrate traditional knowledge, to identify as a Western or Eastern Islander, or simply to speak appropriately as a younger or older person. For example, only an older Eastern Islander would normally use *beizam* from Meryam Mir, rather than *baidham* from Kala Lagaw Ya or *sak* from English, although all of these words mean 'shark'.

The vocabulary was also enriched by the creation of compound nouns, such as *kaikaispun* 'dessertspoon' from 'food spoon' and phrases using common adjectives like 'big' and 'small'. Some further examples are:

baby	*smol piknini*	blabbermouth	*big maut*
carbuncle	*big boil*	city	*big taun*
cyclone	*big win*	dawn	*smol delait*
flood	*big wata*	nap	*smol slip*
panting	*smol sotwin*	pebble	*smol ston*
shower	*smol ren*	snack	*smol kaikai*
sprinkle	*smolsmol ren*	storm	*big ren*
stroll	*smol wagbaut*	whisper	*smolsmol tok*

Torres Strait Creole, like the indigenous languages, makes a distinction between more general ('big') vocabulary and more specific ('small') vocabulary, the former being always borrowed from English, the latter from both English and the indigenous languages. For example, of the words associated with the life cycle and products of the coconut — food, water, fuel and medicine — the general word is *koknat* from 'coconut', whereas the more specific terms, such as *kupi* 'new coconut leaf', tend to come from the indigenous languages.

Spelling

Torres Strait Creole is predominantly a spoken language and its speakers, who are taught literacy in English, use modified English spelling when they write it down, for example *car-sa* rather than *kasa* 'for fun'. However, a linguist's orthography was developed for the creole in the 1980s using the following symbols:

a, ai, au, b, d, dh, e, ei, g, i, k, l, m, n, ng, o, oi, p, r, s, t, th, u, ui, w, y, z

For purposes of accuracy and convenience, this orthography has been used in the wordlist below.

TORRES STRAIT CREOLE WORDLIST

WORDLIST CATEGORIES

1. Body parts and products
2. Kin relationships
3. Human Classification
4. Language, mythology and ceremony
5. Human artefacts
6. Food, cooking and fire
7. Topography
8. Elements
9. Mammals
10. Reptiles
11. Birds
12. Aquatic life
13. Insects and spiders
14. Plants
15. Coconuts and coconut products
16. Physical qualities
17. Motion
18. State
19. Vocalisation and thought
20. Bodily functions
21. Impact and violence
22. Holding and transfer
23. Pronouns
24. Inhabited Torres Strait islands

Unless stated, the word is shared by both dialects. *(W)* = western dialect; *(E)* = eastern dialect

1. Body parts and products

adawaiwai	penis
ai	eye
an	lower arm, wrist, hand, fist; flipper
at	heart
awar *(W)*	fingertip, fingernail; claw
bag *(E)*	cheek
bag *(W)*	jaw, chin
bagur *(W)*	dry nose mucus
baik	back, spine
beli	stomach, abdomen; womb
blad	blood
bodi	body (*Also means* tree trunk)
bon	bone
brein	brain
bututui *(E)*	penis
byain	buttocks
dar *(E)*	dry nose mucus
din *(W)*	anus
dokap *(W)*	upper leg, thigh, lap

duldul *(W)*	penis
ed	head, scalp, skull
eya	head hair; fur
gar *(W)*	body (*Also means* tree trunk)
gas	intestines
giz *(E)*	body (*Also means* tree trunk)
kenani *(E)*	armpit
kikmir *(E)*	wet nose mucus
kiplid *(E)*	small of back, tail bone
kobar *(E)*	back of head, occiput, nape
komus *(E)*	body hair
kopor *(E)*	navel, belly button; umbilical cord
kothei *(W)*	back of head, occiput, nape
kubur *(E)*	anus
kuma	faeces
kup *(W)*	buttocks
kupai *(W)*	navel, belly button; umbilical cord
leg	lower leg, shin, ankle, foot
liba	liver
magadh *(W)*	body hair
mait *(E)*	stomach, abdomen; womb
maitha *(W)*	stomach, abdomen; womb
masa *(W)*	cheek
masel	back of upper arm; muscle
maut	mouth, lip; beak
merod *(E)*	calf
mimi *(W)*	urine
mit	flesh
morop *(E)*	forehead
motop *(E)*	buttocks
nek	neck
ngar *(W)*	lower leg, shin, ankle, foot
ngarang *(W)*	armpit
ngur *(W)*	nipple
nos	nose, tip; beak
nosol	nostril
nunu *(W)*	vagina
nursi *(W)*	wet nose mucus
paisu *(E)*	vagina
pes	face
pingga	finger

pipi	urine
poth *(W)*	forehead
skin	skin, pelt
solda	shoulder
spet	saliva, spit, spittle
string	tendon, sinew, vein
susu	breast
susupot *(E)*	nipple
swet	sweat, perspiration
talinga	ear
tang	tongue
tapot *(E)*	fingertip, fingernail; claw
tit	tooth
traik	sole of foot
trot	throat
ubal *(W)*	bladder
ubal madh *(W)*	calf
usi *(E)*	urine
waiwai	testicles
wake *(E)*	upper leg, thigh, lap
wiskit	facial hair, beard, moustache
zo	jaw, chin
zura	semen

2. Kin relationships

aka	grandmother
akari *(E)*	wife's sister's husband
ama	mother; aunt (mother's sister); mother-in-law
ankel	uncle (father's brother)
anti	aunt (father's sister)
ata *(E)*	grandparent
athei *(W)*	grandfather
awa, awade *(W)*	uncle (mother's brother)
bala, brada	brother
big bala, big brada	older brother
big sisi, big sista	older sister
boi	son; grandson; nephew; son-in-law
bradalo	brother-in-law
dadi	father; father's brother
gel	daughter; granddaughter; niece; daughter-in-law

ira	father-in-law; mother-in-law
kazenbrada	male relation; male cousin
kazensista	female relation; female cousin
mama	mother; aunt (mother's sister); mother-in-law
man	husband
napa *(E)*	grandchild
neitawet *(E)*	husband's brother's wife
ngyep *(W)*	grandchild
oman	wife
padalo	father-in-law
papa	father; father's brother
pop, popa *(E)*	grandparent
sisi, sista	sister
sistalo	sister-in-law
smol bala, smol brada	younger brother
smol sisi, smol sista	younger sister
tawi, tawiyan	brother-in-law

3. Human Classification

age *(E)*, agei *(W)*	Aborigine
ailanman	Torres Strait Islander
aka	old woman
ate *(E)*, athei *(W)*	old man
beibi	baby
boi	unmarried male
bos	expert, master
busman	uncivilised man; ignorant person
buspiknini	illegitimate child
gel	unmarried female
kantriman	countryman
kole	white person; master
lamar *(E)*	white man
maidman *(E)*	sorcerer
maret	married
markai *(W)*	white man
man	man; married man, husband
met	friend, companion
melanman	Aborigine
nasem	namesake
oleidi	old woman

olman	old man
oman	married woman, wife
piknini	child
puripuriman *(W)*	sorcerer
sarup	castaway
smol piknini	baby
waitman	white man
waitoman	white woman
widowoman	widow

4. Language, mythology and ceremony

augad	totem
bud	mourning
dogai	devil woman
kapkar *(E)*	traditional dance
lamar *(E)*	ghost, spirit
langgus	traditional language
maid *(E)*	sorcery
maidston *(E)*	sorcery stone
mar *(E)*, mari *(W)*	person's shadow
mari *(W)*	spirit
markai *(W)*	ghost
merkak *(E)*	songless dance
pleinem	nickname
puripuri *(W)*	sorcery
segur	island dance
sing	song
sweya	bad language
tok	utterance, speech

5. Human artefacts

anwok	handicraft, carving, needlework
augemwali *(E)*	Mother Hubbard dress (a full, loose dress)
basket	basket
bereg *(E)*	bough-shade, canopy
bid *(E)*, bidh *(W)*	necklace
bunara	bow and arrow
dari *(E)*, dhari *(W)*	feather headdress
dibidibi *(E)*	shell pendant
gabagab *(E)*	club

gor *(E)*	seed-pod rattle
kadik *(E)*	armguard, bracer
kaliko	lava-lava (loincloth); material, cloth
kamut *(E)*	cat's cradle
kenu	canoe
kolap *(E)*, kulap *(W)*	stone spinning top
komazer *(E)*	bamboo tongs
kosadres *(W)*	Mother Hubbard dress (a full, loose dress)
krosa	crochet work
kulap *(W)*	seed-pod rattle
longdres	Mother Hubbard dress (a full, loose dress)
lugup *(E)*	dancing gear
makar *(W)*	toy racing boat
makmak *(W)*	anklet
mara *(E)*, marap *(W)*	bamboo stick shaker
mat	mat
model kenu	toy racing boat
moder *(E)*	mat
mudhuruman *(W)*	weaving
naip	knife
net	fishing net
penikot	grass skirt
pens	stone fish trap (*Also means* fence)
pik	mattock
sai *(E)*	stone fish trap
serebsereb nar *(W)*	toy racing boat
siga	cigarette
spiya	spear
su *(E)*	grass skirt
tamyok	axe
tap *(E)*	weaving
tetermus *(E)*	anklet
uknaip	sickle
wagwag *(E)*	toy racing boat
wame *(W)*	cat's cradle
warup	island drum
zamyak *(W)*	dancing gear
zarzar *(W)*	bough-shade, canopy
zazi *(W)*	grass skirt

6. Food, cooking and fire

amai *(W)*, amei *(E)*	earth oven
asis	ashes
asise	to cook in ashes
biya	beer
buibui *(W)*	hot coals
dampa	damper
domboi	dumpling
gris	cooking fat or oil
isimur *(E)*	sweet potato dish
kaikai	food, meal, feast
kapmauri	earth oven
kuke	to cook, roast, fry
kuksang	cook
kuridh *(W)*	crust; burned food
mabumabu *(E)*	smorgasbord
mabus	mash, mince
madhu *(W)*, madu *(E)*	grater, scraper
masis	matches
mit	meat, flesh
mutki *(E)*	crust; burned food
nathan *(W)*	to smoke (seafood)
nini	boiled or poached in water
pakalolo	island porridge
papai *(W)*	root vegetable stew
payud	firewood
plawa	flour
pwakablad	pigblood (Pacific dish)
rais	rice
sakol	charcoal
sawa	bitter, sour, unsweetened
skon	fritter
skrase	to grate, scrape, shred
skreipa	grater, scraper
smase	to crumble, dissolve; grind, pound
smok	smoke
sokora *(W)*	shellfish preserve
sol	salt
sopsop *(E)*	root vegetable stew
streine	to brew, infuse
sugabaig	honey; honeycomb

swit	sweet; delicious, good-tasting
takar *(E)*	to smoke (seafood)
thuba *(W)*, tuba *(E)*	palm wine
ti	tea
zura	fish stew, fish soup

7. Topography

ailan	island, cay
aiwata	high tide
bus	bush
dini *(E)*	brackish
dodo *(E)*	running water
eiz	edge of reef
graun	earth, ground, soil
il	hill, mountain
kingtaid	king tide, spring tide
krik	tidal channel
lowata	low tide
mainguk *(W)*	brackish
maut blo krik	estuary
niptaid	neap tide
pasis	channel
pi *(E)*, pui *(W)*	dust
sanbaing	sandbank, sandbar
si	wave
sik	foam, froth
solwata	ocean, sea
spring	spring
ston	stone, rock
susu	sea spray
taid	tide, current
wata	water

8. Elements

bayu *(W)*	whirlwind
big win	cyclone
blaik	rain cloud
klaud	cloud
koki *(E)*, kuki *(W)*	north-west monsoon
mar *(E)*, mari *(W)*	person's shadow
mun	moon

naiger *(E)*, naigai *(W)*	north-east wind
nait	night
ren	rain
renpi	mist
sager	south-east wind
san	sun
skai	sky
sta	star
win	wind
zei *(W)*, zyai *(E)*	south-west wind

9. Mammals

bulmakau	cattle; cow
dhangal *(W)*	dugong
dog	dog
dugong	dugong
man paul	rooster
mukeis *(E)*	rat; mouse
nanigot	goat
oman paul	hen
pig	pig
pusiket	cat
pwaka	pig
rat	rat; mouse
saper *(E)*, sapur *(W)*	flying fox, fruit bat

10. Reptiles

algita	crocodile
biged	loggerhead turtle
gwana	goanna; lizard
kapasneik	carpet snake
platplat	flatback turtle
sis *(W)*	gecko
sneik	snake
totol	turtle
wanipol *(E)*	gecko
wipsneik	baby carpet snake; whip snake

11. Birds

baziguru *(W)*	quail
beuger *(E)*	booby
daumer *(E)*	Torres Strait pigeon
gawe *(E)*	spoonbill; pelican
ginau *(W)*	Torres Strait pigeon
kalu *(E)*	curlew
karbai *(W)*	white reef heron
kaubet *(E)*	black reef heron
kedakeda *(E)*	wagtail
kingpisa	kingfisher
kipro *(E)*, kipru *(W)*	seagull
kobebe *(E)*	curlew
kor *(E)*	quail
kunai *(W)*	black reef heron
kurukuru *(E)*	dove
kyau *(E)*	kingfisher
paret	parrot; rosella
pizin	non-marine creature; bird
sara *(W)*, serar *(E)*	crested tern
sigal	seagull
sir *(E)*	white reef heron
spunbel	spoonbill; pelican
waumer *(E)*, womer *(W)*	frigatebird; man-o'-war bird

12. Aquatic life

arti *(E)*	octopus
aryari *(E)*	Murray Island sardine
baidham *(W)*	shark
bayag *(W)*	long tom; needlefish
beizam *(E)*	shark
belimokan	pufferfish; toadfish
bidhai *(W)*	squid; small cuttlefish
bila	blue tusk fish
blainsak	blind shark
blupis	black-spot tusk fish
dabor *(E)*	mackerel
dhubui *(W)*	mackerel
erar *(E)*	golden-lined spinefoot
gaigai *(W)*	trevally; kingfish
gapu *(W)*	suckerfish; pilot fish

garom *(E)*	coral cod
geigi *(E)*	trevally; kingfish
githalai *(W)*	mud crab; mangrove crab
goskrab	ghost crab
ilpis	eel
kal *(W)*	blue parrot fish
kapapis	suckerfish; pilot fish
kar *(E)*	blue parrot fish
kayar *(W)*	crayfish
kibim *(W)*	black spinefoot; black trevally
kingpis	trevally; kingfish
kos *(E)*	bullhead sardine; hardyhead sardine
krab	mud crab; mangrove crab
kropis	crayfish
krosak	hammerhead shark
kurup *(W)*	estuary rock cod; honeycomb cod
maizab *(E)*	yellowtailed perch; bar-tailed grunter
matei *(E)*	golden trevally
nageg *(E)*	triggerfish
onpis	horn fish; unicorn-fish
pakor *(E)*	coral trout
papei *(E)*	queenfish
paris *(E)*	long tom; needlefish
parsa *(W)*	golden-lined spinefoot
pelet *(E)*	small coral cod
pewuk *(W)*	sweetlips
pis	marine creature; fish
pislama	trepang, sea cucumber, sea slug
pupwag *(E)*	jellyfish; medusa
puri *(W)*	reef shark; small sand shark
sabei *(E)*	horn fish; unicorn-fish
sadin	sardine; tiddler
sak	shark
simalet	mullet
snapa	snapper; grass sweetlips
skwid	squid; small cuttlefish
stonpis	stonefish
sugu *(W)*	octopus
taigasak	tiger shark

tekei *(E)*	estuary rock cod; honeycomb cod
teneb *(E)*	Moses perch; fingermark bream
thanik *(W)*	Moses perch; fingermark bream
thapis *(W)*	trepang; sea cucumber; sea slug
thukmul *(W)*	stingray
tingri	stingray
wanwan *(E)*	sea urchin
waitpis	Papuan trevally
withi *(W)*	coral trout
yalo waitpis	golden trevally
zaber *(W)*, zab *(E)*	garfish
zaram *(W)*	yellowtailed perch; bar-tailed grunter
zelipis	jellyfish; medusa
zogar *(E)*	mullet

13. Insects and spiders

abob *(E)*	blowfly
anis	ant
ausplai	housefly
auzi *(E)*	caterpillar
bataplai	butterfly
ger *(E)*	wasp; bee; horsefly
grasopa	grasshopper; locust
kemtan *(W)*	nit
kokros	cockroach
kurthur *(W)*	caterpillar
koyop *(E)*	dragonfly
kupas *(W)*	grasshopper; locust
kuyup *(W)*	dragonfly
laus	lice
maket	grub; maggot
maskita	mosquito
nab *(E)*	hornet
naisi *(E)*	centipede
pem *(E)*	grasshopper; locust
pisum *(E)*	grub; maggot
sag *(W)*	centipede
sentapid	centipede
skopyon	scorpion
spaida	spider
straik	cicada
sup *(W)*	nit
zori *(W)*	cicada

14. Plants

abal *(E)*	pandanus
bambu	bamboo
banana	banana
bisi	sago
bodi	tree trunk (*Also means* body)
boz *(E)*	lawyer vine
bunau *(E)*	bush potato
buruwa *(W)*	small pandanus
buwa *(W)*	white round yam
buzi *(W)*	lawyer vine
daub *(W)*	long wild yam
dhani *(W)*	island fig tree
enau *(E)*	island date; wongai
eror *(E)*	bellfruit
gagabe *(W)*	bellfruit
gaibu *(W)*	she-oak, casuarina
gar *(W)*	tree trunk (*Also means* body)
gidigidi sid	crab's eyes; gidee-gidee bean; rosary pea
giz *(E)*	tree trunk (*Also means* body)
iger *(E)*	tar tree; cashew tree
ipyus *(W)*	fine bamboo
itarkup *(W)*	cottontree; kapok tree
kaperkaper *(E)*	crab's eyes; gidee-gidee bean; rosary pea
katan tri	cottontree; kapok tree
kem tri	milk tree
ketai *(E)*	hairy yam
kithal *(W)*	pandanus
kob *(E)*	cottontree; kapok tree
kokwam *(E)*	hibiscus
kolap *(E)*	Queensland bean, matchbox bean
kukwam *(W)*	hibiscus
kulap *(W)*	Queensland bean, matchbox bean
kumala	sweet potato
kuthai *(W)*	hairy yam
loyakein	lawyer cane
manyota	cassava
meidu *(E)*	nipa palm
mekei *(W)*, meker *(E)*	island almond

melk tri	milk tree
oket	orchid
omei *(E)*	island fig tree
paiwa	sandalwood tree
pas *(E)*	basil
pater *(E)*	fine bamboo
plan	plant
roz	frangipani
sawur *(W)*	bush yam
sem tri *(E)*	yellow hibiscus tree; peace tree
sirisap tri	milk tree
sorbi *(E)*	island plum
sugaken	sugarcane
taro	taro
tereg *(E)*	lawyer cane
thakar *(W)*	basil
tri	tree
ubar *(W)*	island date; wongai
ubu *(W)*	tea-tree, eucalyptus, gum tree
urkar *(W)*	yellow hibiscus tree; peace tree
uzu *(W)*	island plum
wangai	island date; wongai
weskepu *(E)*	bush yam
wez	croton
yam	yam

15. Coconuts and coconut products

ageg *(E)*	overripe coconut (eighth growth stage)
basor *(E)*	coconut-shell water container
bei *(E)*	dry coconut leaf
bosokop	coconut fuel
buikuik *(W)*	coconut rubbish
drai koknat	dry coconut (seventh growth stage)
gad *(E)*	immature coconut (third growth stage)
gai *(W)*, gayu *(E)*	smooth-skinned coconut
giru *(E)*	sprouting coconut (second growth stage)
kero *(E)*	lower coconut leaf
koknat	coconut

koknat dampa	coconut milk damper
koknat melk	coconut cream
koknat oil	coconut oil
koknat tri	coconut palm
koknat wata	coconut milk
koknat zeli	coconut jelly
kopespes *(E)*	developing coconut (fourth growth stage)
kubar *(W)*	scraped coconut shell
kupi *(E)*	new coconut leaf
kyai *(E)*	shredded coconut
mes *(E)*	coconut husk and shell
musu *(W)*	coconut embryo (first growth stage)
musu koknat *(W)*	sprouting coconut (second growth stage)
muthi *(W)*	coconut husk and shell
pes *(E)*	ripe coconut (fifth growth stage)
pesur *(E)*	coconut stalk
piru *(E)*	coconut rubbish
pisur *(W)*	coconut stalk
sabi(sabi)	cooked in coconut milk
smol koknat	immature coconut (third growth stage)
su *(E)*, thu *(W)*	coconut spike
u *(E)*	mature coconut (sixth growth stage)
ulid *(E)*	scraped coconut shell
wai *(E)*	coconut embryo (first growth stage)
zyau *(E)*	coconut meat remaining after scraping

16. Physical qualities

ad	hard
angre	hungry
big	big, solid
blaik	black
long	long, tall
nyap	thirsty
plenti	many, several
smol	small, short

tri	three
tu	two
wait	white
wan	one

17. Motion

brok	to break
go	to go
kam	to come
kapsaiz	to overturn
klaimap	to climb up
lukraun	to search
pole	to follow
poldaun	to fall
ran	to run
rane	to chase
sidaun daun	to sit down
singdaun	to sink
sluraun	to turn around
stanap	to stand up
swim	to swim, bathe, shower
wagbaut	to walk

18. State

ledaun	to be lying
plot	to float
sidaun	to be sitting
stanap	to be standing
wet	to wait

19. Vocalisation and thought

akse	to ask
ala	to call out, shout
bes *(E)*	to lie; pretend
eso	to thank
geman	to lie; pretend
graule	to abuse, scold
gri	to agree
kareyan	to gossip
kese	to learn (informally); understand
kole	to address; announce; mention

lai	to make a mistake, be wrong
lane	to learn (formally); teach
lap	to laugh
maide *(E)*	to bewitch
maret	to marry
mudmir *(E)*	to gossip
okadikes *(E)*	to give marriage counsel
prait	to be afraid
puripuri *(W)*	to bewitch
sabe	to know
sem	to be ashamed
sing	to sing
singaut	to call out, shout
spik	to talk; tell
sweya	to swear, blaspheme, curse
tingbaut	to think, consider, imagine; remember
tok	to speak, say
wail	to be angry
wakaiwiyan *(W)*	to give marriage counsel
yan	to chat, tell (a story)

20. Bodily functions

baite	to bite
bar	to break wind
bon	to give birth; to be born
ded	to die
dring	to drink
gerap	to wake up; to get up
ikap	to hiccup
kaikai	to eat
kegar *(E)*	to have cramp
kop	to cough
kramap	to have cramp
kuma	to defecate
lap	to laugh; to smile
lesen	to hear; to listen
luk	to see; to look
makan	to eat
mimi *(W)*	to urinate
perol *(W)*, peror *(E)*	to have goose pimples
pipi	to urinate

slip	to sleep
sniz	to sneeze
sno	to snore
sowa	to hurt, ache
spakap	to get drunk
spet	to spit, cough up
spyu	to vomit
swele	to swallow
swet	to sweat, perspire
udup *(W)*	to hiccup
usi *(E)*	to urinate
zyam	to flinch, recoil

21. Impact and violence

bane	to burn
broke	to break
digine	to dig (up)
kike	to kick
kile	to kill
mekpase	to tie up
paite	to hit with hand
rabe	to rub
spere	to pierce
taimape	to tie up

22. Holding and transfer

aide	to hide
gibi	to give
kare	to carry
kese	to catch; to snatch, grab
libi	to leave
paine	to find
pekmape	to pick up
puse	to push
sake	to throw
teke	to take
teke kam	to fetch

23. Pronouns

ai	I
blo mi; blo yu	my, mine; your, yours, etc.
dempla	they (more than three), them (more than three) (definite)
demtu	they (two), them (two)
em	he, him, she, her, it
mi	me
mipla	we (more than three), us (more than three) (excluding you)
mitu	we (two), us (two) (excluding you)
ol	they (more than three) (indefinite)
yu	you
yumi	we (two), us (two) (including you)
yumpla	we (more than three), us (more than three) (including you)
yupla	you (more than three)
yutu	you (two)

24. Inhabited Torres Strait islands

Badu	Mulgrave Island
Boigu	Talbot Island
Dauan	Mount Cornwallis Island
Erub	Darnley Island
Keriri	Hammond Island
Mabuiag	Jervis Island
Masig	Yorke Island
Mer	Murray Island
Moa	Banks Island
Muralag	Prince of Wales Island
Nurupai	Horn Island
Purma	Coconut Island
Saibai	Saibai Island
Ugar	Stephens Island
Waiben	Thursday Island
Waraber	Sue Island
Yam	Turtle-Backed Island

17. Torres Strait Creole

Grammatical notes

Torres Strait Creole, like other creoles but unlike most Aboriginal languages, has few suffixes. The same word may be a noun or a verb: for example, *kaikai* means both 'food' and 'to eat'. Of the sixteen suffixes, most attach to verbs but three attach to pronouns, which have different forms depending on whether one (singular), two (dual), or more than two people or things (plural) are referred to, and whether the hearer is included or excluded.

Dual or plural number in pronouns is shown by the use of the suffixes *-tu* and *-pla*, respectively. Most transitive verbs of English origin take the suffix *-e* (probably from 'him'). Nouns are not suffixed: case relationships (for example, location, possession and instrumentality) and definiteness or indefiniteness, are shown by separate words, as are verb tense (present, past and future) and aspect (such as 'already completed'), as demonstrated by the following sentences:

Ai	*luk*	*wan*	*gel*	*i*	*kam*
I	see	*singular-indefinite*	girl	*predicate marker*	come

'I can see a girl approaching.'

Mitu	*Bakoi*	*bin*	*wagbaut*	*lo*	*sanbis*
I-*dual-exclusive*	Bakoi	*past*	walk	*location*	shore

'Bakoi and I walked along the shore.'

Dem	*piknini*	*go*	*luk*	*ama*	*blo*	*dempla*
plural-definite	child	*future*	visit	mother	*possessive*	they

'The children will visit their mother.'

Em	*pinis*	*skras*	*-e*	*koknat*	*lo*	*madu*
She	*completive*	scrape	*-transitive*	coconut	*instrumental*	scraper

'She has already scraped out the coconut with a scraper.'

The order of words in basic clauses is similar to English, with the subject first, then the verb, then the object. When the subject is a noun, rather than a pronoun, the verb is usually preceded by the predicate marker *i* (probably from 'he').

Pupwag	*i*	*bait*	*-e*	*mi*
jellyfish	*predicate marker*	sting	*-transitive*	me

'The jellyfish stung me.'

Unlike English, however, not all clauses have subjects or verbs, although clauses without subjects or verbs must take the predicate marker. Examples of the three main clause types are given in the three following sentences: subjectless clauses which express states; verbless clauses which express relations; and 'full' clauses which express events.

Subjectless:

I	*ren*	*nau*
predicate marker	rain	now

'It's raining.'

Verbless:

Mislam	*i*	*mo*	*big*	*lo*	*Pele*
Mislam	*predicate marker*	*comparative*	old	*locative*	Pele

'Mislam is older than Pele.'

Full:

Em	*bin*	*pain*	*-e*	*da*	*sing*
He	*past*	find	*-transitive*	*singular-definite*	song

'He composed the song.'

To talk about things moving, you need to use special particles, *go* (from 'go') or *kam* (from 'come'), to show whether it is moving away from you or towards you.

Em	*bin*	*ran*	*go*	*sanbis*
She	*past*	run	*movement-away-from-speaker*	shore

'She ran to the shore.'

Pase	*siga*	*kam*	*diswei!*
Pass	cigarettes	*movement-towards-speaker*	here

'Pass the cigarettes over here.'

When someone or something is at rest, you need to use *ya* (from 'here') or *de* (from 'there) before the verb to show whether it is close to you or at a distance.

Gemai	*ya*	*slip*
Gemai	*location-close-to-speaker*	sleep

'Gemai is sleeping.'

Trakta	*de*	*kam*
Tractor	*location-distant-from-speaker*	come

'The tractor is coming.'

A grammatical description and dictionary of Torres Strait Creole is contained in Shnukal (1988a).

References

Crowley, T and B Rigsby 1979, 'Cape York Creole' in *Languages and their status*, ed. T Shopen, pp 153–207, Winthrop Press

Dutton, T 1970, 'Informal English in the Torres Straits' in *English transported: essays on Australasian English*, ed. W Ramson, pp 137–160, Australian National University Press, Canberra.

Ray, S 1907, 'The Jargon English of Torres Straits' in *Reports of the Cambridge Anthropological Expedition to Torres Straits*, vol. 3, pp 251–254, Cambridge University Press

Shnukal, A 1983, 'Torres Strait Creole: the growth of a new Torres Strait language', *Aboriginal History*, vol. 7, no. 2, pp 173–185

Shnukal, A 1985, 'The spread of Torres Strait Creole to the central islands of Torres Strait' *Aboriginal History*, vol. 9, no. 2, pp 220–234

17. Torres Strait Creole

Shnukal, A 1988a, *Broken: an introduction to the creole language of Torres Strait*, Pacific Linguistics C-107, Pacific Linguistics, Canberra

Shnukal, A 1988b, 'Australian Aboriginal and Torres Strait Islander pidgins and creoles' in *Bicentennial Encyclopedia of the Australian People*, ed. J Jupp, pp 153–159, Angus & Robertson

Shnukal, A 1991, 'Torres Strait Creole' in *Language in Australia*, ed. S Romaine, pp 180–194, Cambridge University Press

Shnukal, A 1992, 'Meriam Mir lexicon in Torres Strait Creole' in *The language game: papers in memory of Donald C. Laycock*, eds T Dutton, M Ross & D Tryon, pp 385–403, Pacific Linguistics C-110, Pacific Linguistics, Canberra

Contributors

Rob Amery	Aboriginal indigenous languages framework, Senior Secondary Assessment Board of South Australia
Peter Austin	Linguistics Department, La Trobe University
Alan Dench	Centre for Linguistics, University of Western Australia
Veronica Dobson	Institute for Aboriginal Dvevelopment
Tamsin Donaldson	Australian Institute of Aboriginal and Torres Strait Islander Studies
Merrkiyawuy Ganambarr	Laynhapuy Education Resource Centre, Yirrkala
John Henderson	Centre for Linguistics, University of Western Australia
Luise Hercus	Linguistics Department, Australian National University
Dianne Hosking	Australian Institute of Aboriginal and Torres Strait Islander Studies
William McGregor	Linguistics Department, Melbourne University
Sally McNicol	Aboriginal and Torres Strait Islander Commission
Ken Gamalai Passi	Murray Island
Nick Piper	Linguistics Department, Melbourne University
Barbara Sayers	Summer Institute of Linguistics, Aurukun
Margaret Sharpe	Department of Aboriginal and Multicutural Studies, University of New England
Anna Shnukal	Australian Studies Centre, University of Queensland
Jane Simpson	Linguistics Department, University of Sydney
Sue Smythe	Wangka Maya, the Pilbara Aboriginal Language Centre
Nick Thieberger	Australian Institute of Aboriginal and Torres Strait Islander Studies
Jakelin Troy	Aboriginal and Torres Strait Islander Commission
Michael Walsh	Linguistics Department, University of Sydney

LANGUAGE INDEX

Each entry consists of a Language word in bold followed by equivalent terms in English. The language is given in abbreviated form in brackets, followed by a chapter number and a second, smaller number which indicates the category section where the word can be found. These numbers can be found throughout the main part of the book at the top corner of each page.

It should be noted that words in the index are not always exact translations. Quite often there is no simple English equivalent expression, especially in areas such as kinship. The reader should check the reference at the language chapter to be certain of a particular meaning.

Note also that the spellings used for Dät̲iwuy in the Index have been standardised to match the spelling systems of the other languages.

Abbreviations

Arr	Eastern Arrernte
Bun	Bundjalung
Dat	Dät̲iwuy
Diy	Diyari
Goo	Gooniyandi
Kau	Kaurna
Mer	Meryam Mir
Mur	Murrinh-Patha
Ngi	Ngiyampaa
Nyu	Nyungar
Paa	Paakantyi
Syd	Sydney
Tor	Torres Strait Creole
Wem	Wembawemba
Wik	Wik-Mungkan
Wir	Wiradjuri
Yin	Yindjibarndi

ENGLISH INDEX

Each entry consists of an English word in bold followed by equivalent terms from one or more of the languages. The language is given in abbreviated form in brackets, followed by a chapter number and a second, smaller number which indicates the category section where the word can be found. These numbers can be found throughout the main part of the book at the top corner of each page.

It should be noted that words in the index are not always exact translations. Quite often there is no simple English equivalent expression, especially in areas such as kinship. The reader should check the reference at the language chapter to be certain of a particular meaning.

Note also that the spellings used for D̲äṯiwuy in the Index have been standardised to match the spelling systems of the other languages.

Abbreviations

Arr	Eastern Arrernte
Bun	Bundjalung
Dat	D̲äṯiwuy
Diy	Diyari
Goo	Gooniyandi
Kau	Kaurna
Mer	Meryam Mir
Mur	Murrinh-Patha
Ngi	Ngiyampaa
Nyu	Nyungar
Paa	Paakantyi
Syd	Sydney
Tor	Torres Strait Creole
Wem	Wembawemba
Wik	Wik-Mungkan
Wir	Wiradjuri
Yin	Yindjibarndi